LIBRARIES, HISTORY, DIPLOMACY, AND THE PERFORMING ARTS

Essays in Honor of
Carleton Sprague Smith

Carleton Sprague Smith

LIBRARIES, HISTORY, DIPLOMACY, AND THE PERFORMING ARTS

Essays in Honor of Carleton Sprague Smith

Edited by

Israel J. Katz

Associate Editors

Malena Kuss and Richard J. Wolfe

Editorial Board

Angel Alcalá

Sidney Beck

Howard Boatwright

Jean Bowen (NYPL)

Richard De Genarro (NYPL)

Wiley L. Housewright

Kenneth Maxwell

Richard Newman (NYPL)

Charles Wagley

Karna Wilgus

FESTSCHRIFT SERIES No. 9

PENDRAGON PRESS, STUYVESANT, NY
IN COOPERATION WITH THE NEW YORK PUBLIC LIBRARY

The publication of this volume was made
possible through the generosity of
ELIZABETH PETERFREUND
of the Hastings Foundation

The Festschrift Series

No. 1 *A Musical Offering: Essays in honor of Martin Bernstein* edited by E. Clinkscale and C. Brook (1977) ISBN 0-918728-03-7

No. 2 *Aspects of Medieval and Renaissance Music: A birthday offering to Gustave Reese* edited by Jan LaRue (Pendragon Edition 1978) ISBN 0-918728-07-X

No. 3 *Music East and West: Essays in honor of Walter Kaufmann* edited by Thomas Noblitt (1981) ISBN 0-918728-15-0 Out of print.

No. 4 *Essays on the Music of J. S. Bach and Other Divers Subjects: A tribute to Gerhard Herz* edited by Robert L. Weaver (Univ. of Louisville, 1982) Out of print.

No. 5 *Music in the Classic Period: Essays in honor of Barry S. Brook* edited by Allan A. Atlas (1985) ISBN 0-918728-37-1

No. 6 *Five Centuries of Choral Music: Essays in honor of Howard Swan* edited by Gordon Paine (1989) ISBN 0-918728-84-3

No. 7 *Explorations in Music, the Arts, and Ideas: Essays in honor of Leonard B. Meyer* edited by Eugene Narmour and Ruth A. Solie (1989) ISBN 0-918728-94-0

No. 8 *Modern Music Librarianship: Essays in honor of Ruth Watanabe* edited by Alfred Mann (1989) ISBN 0-918728-93-2

Library of Congress Cataloging-in-Publication Data

Libraries, history, diplomacy, and the performing arts: essays in honor of Carleton Sprague Smith / edited by Israel J. Katz.

p. cm.

ISBN 0-945193-13-0

1. Smith, Carleton Sprague, 1905– . 2. Music—History and criticism. 3. Performing arts libraries. 4. Music librarianship. 5. Diplomacy. I. Katz, Israel J. II. Smith, Carleton Sprague, 1905– .

ML55.S673 1991

780—dc20

91-20069
CIP
MN

Copyright 1991 Pendragon Press

CONTENTS

HISTORY

APPENDICES:

Israel J. Katz

INTRODUCTION

No title more befitting than that which this homage volume bears can justly describe the humanistic and political spheres to which Carleton Sprague Smith devoted his life. For Carleton, these spheres were inter-dependent, perhaps even inseparable. It was unthinkable to view the humanities, particularly the musical arts, apart from a multi-cultural perspective. Likewise, it was unthinkable to remove from the political the humanistic cultural foundations upon which it drew. Although Carleton never entered the political arena, he has earned, among those familiar with his life and achievements, the status of an elder statesman.

A scant knowledge of his family history, his remarkable parents, and childhood can be found in a beautifully-sketched essay which he contributed to a book of collected memories in tribute to his mother. His description of his formative years—nurtured in an environment surrounded by love and respect, exemplified by good manners, em-phasizing life preparedness, and, above all, providing intellectual stimulation—was essentially an environment that he carried into his professional life, which spanned more than half a century. Not only did he impart it to others; it became the very hallmark of his dealings with others.

Israel J. Katz, a former Guggenheim Fellow, is presently a Research Associate with the University of California at Davis. He taught at McGill and Columbia Univer-sities and the City University of New York. He specializes in the music of the Mediterranean region, with an emphasis on Spain and the Judeo-Spanish Romancero.

Early on Carleton came to appreciate the classics in poetry, literature, and music. He was captivated by the dramatic readings that were commonly heard within his family circle, and he displayed a keen interest in languages, which he studied with greater thoroughness than most of his colleagues. At the age of twelve, having expressed a desire to play the flute, his parents enrolled him at the Institute of Musical Arts. There he studied with a student of the eminent flutist Georges Barrère and began a serious study of music. From this point on, music occupied a great part of his schooling.

In 1922, upon leaving the Hackley School for Boys, in Tarrytown, New York, he spent a year in Paris, studying French at the École Yersin, while advancing his flute technique under the guidance of Louis Fleury. Entering Harvard University the following year, he took advantage of its music and music history offerings, continuing his private flute lessons with Georges Laurent, premiere flutist of the Boston Symphony Orchestra, and singing with the Harvard Glee Club. Throughout his Harvard years, he participated in such choral masterpieces as Bach's *B minor Mass*, Beethoven's *Ninth Symphony*, and Brahms' *Requiem Mass* under such eminent conductors as Pierre Monteux, Serge Koussevitzky, and Archibald Davison. He also performed the flute *obbligato* in Bach's *Jesu, meine Freunde,* as well as solo parts in Bach's *B minor Suite* and fifth *Brandenburg Concerto* with the Eighteenth-Century Musical Ensemble. Playing with such talented musicians as Bruce Simonds, Mariana Lowell, and George Brown was an inspiration to him.[1]

During his graduate year at Harvard (1927–28), he also served as music critic for the *Boston Transcript.* Among the many concerts he attended, the most cherished of his recollections was that given by Belá Bartók, at which Carleton turned the pages. It was the composer's first trip to the United States.[2] For the Harvard Tercentenary of 1936,

---

[1]The enthusiasm generated by Carleton's playing was described by Catherine Drinker Bowen in her book *Friends and Fiddlers* (Boston, 1935), pp. 184–85. Gilbert Chase in his *America's Music*, Second edition (New York, 1966; p. 344) wrote that "it has been my privilege to hear [Sidney] Lanier's *Wind-song* admirably played by that modern "gentleman amateur" of American musicians, Carleton Sprague Smith, and the piece is certainly worthy of being included in the permanent repertoire of American music."

[2]The concert tour, lasting from late December to mid-February, was sponsored by Pro-Musica, Inc. Among Carleton's other cherished recollections was his performance of chamber music at Princeton with the great scientist, Albert Einstein, who played second violin and who remarked, after a reading of Bach's *B-minor Suite,* "this is one of the fields in which one can go no further." Carleton and his wife Elisabeth were also involved with the Trapp Family Singers, upon their arrival at Ellis Island in October of 1939.

Carleton selected, together with Mrs. Elizabeth Sprague Coolidge, samplings of music associated with the University from the seventeenth to the twentieth century. In the same year, for the opening of the Fogg Art Museum, he was in charge of providing appropriate music.

By his sophomore year, he found himself concentrating more on history and literature. The latter interest was rekindled by the stimulating courses in sixteenth- and seventeenth-century literature given by Irving Babbitt and André Morize. Carleton also took part in the French plays offered by the Cercle Français.

Although Carleton was "plus français que les français," his interest in the Iberian Peninsula took the upper hand after earning his M. A. in 1928. His advisor at Harvard was Charles Homer Haskins, who gave a course on bibliography, and the Hispanists with whom he studied were Roger Bigelow Merriman, Clarence Henry Haring, Samuel Eliot Morison, and Chandler R. Post. The John Barnard Associates, a club which attracted him to books, furthered his interest in bibliographical research. He spent most of his Junior year in Spain, where, in Madrid, he became involved with the Centro de Estudios Históricos, founded by Ramón Menéndez Pidal, whose lectures he attended, as well as those of Américo Castro, Tomás Navarro Tomás, Dámaso Alonso, and Antonio Ballesteros y Beretta.

Following a suggestion of Charles Homer Haskins, that he study Spain and the Casa de Austria from Middle Europe—which most Americans approached from a New World point of view—he enrolled at the University of Vienna in 1928. There his teachers included Alfred Francis Pribram and Heinrich von Srbik. Working on Austro-Spanish relations entailed research not only in Vienna, but also in Prague, and Spain. During his sojourns in Spain, he became familiar with the leading libraries, particularly the Archivo General del Reino, at Simancas, and the Archivo de las Indias, in Seville. One of the side products was a bibliography on Spanish philosophy that still remains unpublished. His dissertation, presented at the University of Vienna, was entitled *Ein Vetternzwist im Hause Habsburg*. It is a study of seventeenth-century Austrian and Spanish Habsburg rivalries.

The year 1931 marked the beginning of his professional career, for upon his return to the United States, Carleton was appointed as an instructor in the History Department at Columbia University and gave lectures at the Casa de Españas. At the same time he was chosen as the new Chief of the Music Division of the New York Public Library. It is from this point in time that many of the essays presented herein cover, with greater detail, his magnificent career.

Carleton, a man of vision and untiring energy, has left a legacy of achievements that continues to be fully appreciated. It was he who founded the Music Library Association, which now flourishes as an organization with several thousand members. As Chief of the Music Division of the New York Public Library, he initiated the Music-Americana and Dance Sections, the latter being the best in the world today. From his early days, Carleton was exposed to the dance, and not only did this include Serge Diaghilev, Anna Pavlova, and Mikhail Mordkin, but also Isadora Duncan, Martha Graham, Ted Shawn, Ruth St. Denis, and other remarkable choreographers of modern dance in the twentieth century. He derived great satisfaction from the appointment of Curt Sachs as a consultant at the library, and thanks to Sachs, what was a collection became a whole division. Sachs was a great teacher and a giant among musicologists. His studies in the field of primitive music were thought provoking and his major cultural contributions to the performing arts were his *History of the Dance* and *The Commonwealth of Art*.

During his long tenure as Chief of the Music Division, Carleton continued to seek support for a Library-Museum of the Performing Arts which would integrate music, drama, dance, and recorded sound archives. Later, as administrative head of both the Brazilian Institute at New York University and The Spanish Institute, in successive periods, he furthered Luso-Brazilian and Hispanic studies and activities in this country, exhibiting the positive values of international cultural relations.

Carleton wrote on a variety of topics [see Appendix III], wherein his historical skills, critical acumen, and careful use of language converged. His knowledge of early American music increased in proportion to the continued growth of the Americana section. Source material was at his finger tips and his contributions to the subject are well worth reading. His writings on Latin American music are based on first-hand experiences as are those devoted to music librarianship. Through his efforts, he advanced the cause of American musicology and at the same time drew performers into that other world, where otherwise unaccessible musical documents would have never been seen or heard.

Finally, it is mostly as a teacher that many people think of him. His enthusiasm has encouraged students and colleagues to work the whole spectrum of research, thereby expanding their vision and understanding of the world. This homage volume, dedicated to our dear and beloved friend, is but a token of appreciation for his selfless contributions which have enriched not only our professional lives, but which have provided us with a greater understanding of ourselves in the broadest cultural sense.[3]

[3]On October 21st, 1985, some ten-and-a-half weeks after his eightieth birthday, the Trustees of The New York Public Library commemorated the event by organizing a gala reception in his honor at the Vincent Astor Gallery of the Performing Arts Research library at Lincoln Center. A movement was already underway to prepare a *Festschrift* for the occasion, but difficulties in coordination proved otherwise and many circumstances intervened, causing unavoidable delays. Still the editors wish to express their apologies to all who participated, and to thank them for their patience.

I wish to express my deepest gratitude to Malena Kuss and Richard J. Wolfe for their help and advice in planning and coordinating this homage volume. For resolving particular problems confronting endeavors of this kind, I relied upon the good offices of our Editorial Board (Angel Alcalá, Sydney Beck, Howard Boatwright, Jean Bowen, Richard De Genarro, Wiley H. Housewright, Kenneth Maxwell, Richard Newman, Charles Wagley, and Karna Wilgus), comprising Carleton's closest associates and friends. Both Karna Wilgus and Richard J. Wolfe were kind enough to lend their critical editorial skills to the entire manuscript before it was sent to the printer. Translations of the Portuguese articles (Marcos Carneiro de Mendonça, Luiz Azevedo Corrêa de Azevedo, Gilberto Freyre, and Américo Jacobina Lacombe) were made by Kenneth Maxwell and Ligia Pavo of the Camões Institute, Columbia University), Manuel da Costa Fontes (Kent State University), David P. Appleby (Eastern Illinois University), Ana Peres, Ricardo Alvarenga, and Jordan Young (Brazil Institute, Pace University), and Jean Longland (Hispanic Society of America). Barbara Heliodora (Rio de Janeiro), daughter of the late Marcos Carneiro de Mendonça, assisted in clarifying matters pertaining to her father's article. William Shank (Graduate Center, CUNY) and George Thompson (New York University) were most helpful in solving the numerous bibliographical problems, as were Zilia Osorio de Castro (Universidade Nova de Lisboa) and Virginio Montezzo Neto (São Paulo, Brazil) with the Portuguese citations. I would also like to acknowledge the assistance of Donald McCormick (Rodgers and Hammerstein Archives of Recorded Sound, NYPL), Madeleine Nichols (Dance Division, NYPL), and Mercedes Orbón (former librarian of the Spanish Institute). Our special thanks go to Mrs. Elizabeth Peterfreund, who most graciously subvented this publication as a personal tribute to her long friendship with Carleton. It has been a particular pleasure to work closely with Nanette Maxim, Associate Editor at Pendragon, whose editorial assistance proved invaluable throughout the various phases of this publication. Finally, mention must be made of two most loyal colleagues, Samuel G. Armistead and Barry J. Luby, who could be counted upon for sound advice when needed, and, of course, all this would have been impossible without the moral support of Marcia, my dear wife, who stood patiently by.

Barry S. Brook

CARLETON SPRAGUE SMITH:
MAN OF THE MUSICOLOGICAL WORLD
(An Affectionate Reminiscence)

Carleton Sprague Smith is a man of many worlds, as this volume demonstrates. I will speak here specifically of his role in the world of American musicology during the 1930s, and recount an unforgettable incident that occurred some thirty years later, an incident of which Carleton was the hero, endearing himself to all those present.

The "world" in question was centered around three closely related organizations: the pioneering New York Musicological Society, established in 1930 and dissolved in 1934; the American Musicological Society founded immediately thereafter; and the Greater New York Chapter of the AMS, created in 1935.

The archives reveal that Carleton, who has been a catalyst and a prime mover in so many fields, was involved with the short-lived New York Musicological Society and presented one of the final papers before the group in 1934. He also became a member of the first Executive Board of the AMS along with such other giants of our profession as Otto Kinkeldey, Charles Seeger, Oliver Strunk, Gustave Reese, Paul Henry Lang, Jean Beck, and Archibald Davison. In 1935 he was one of the first members of the Greater New York Chapter of the AMS, then its only chapter, great or small.

Barry S. Brook, CUNY Distinguished Professor of Music Emeritus, is Director of the Center for Music Research and Documentation, Executive Editor of RILM Abstracts, *and Director of the Research Center for Musical Iconography.*

Those were heady times for American musicology, which, with a learned society of its own, was at last beginning to take itself seriously as a discipline. Recognition from the academic world, however, was slow in coming. In 1930, Otto Kinkeldey, at Cornell, became the sole Professor of Musicology in the country and he was asked to serve simultaneously as University Librarian (1930–46). It was not until the 1940s that Paul Henry Lang (Columbia) and Gustave Reese (NYU) achieved professorial status. So inhospitable was academia to the musicological rubric that at first both Carleton Sprague Smith and Oliver Strunk were appointed to positions in the history departments at Columbia and Princeton, respectively.

In the first decade of the New York Chapter's existence, the roster of speakers at its meetings was wide-ranging, containing many surprises. In addition to most of the above-mentioned AMS board members, one could hear ethnomusicologists like George Herzog, Helen H. Roberts, Jaap Kunst, and Curt Sachs; theorists like Joseph Schillinger, Joseph Yasser, and Ernst Lévy; composers like Arnold Schoenberg, Colin McPhee, Béla Bartók, Ernst Krenek, Roger Sessions, Henry Cowell, and Paul Hindemith; performers like Rudolf Kolisch, Ralph Kirkpatrick, Noah Greenberg, and Leopold Stokowski (Edgard Varèse took an active part in that discussion); also, of course, numerous "historical" musicologists, many who were already major figures in the field, such as Willi Apel, Hugo Leichtentritt, Edward J. Dent, Leo Schrade, Manfred F. Bukofzer, Edward E. Lowinsky, Alfred Einstein, Arthur Mendel, and "Lieutenant" William S. Newman.

The topics they dealt with could hardly have been more varied, nor "musicology" defined more broadly, for example: "Do Animals have Music?" (Herzog); "Historical and Systematic Orientations in Musicology" (Seeger); "The Mode in Byzantine Music" (Strunk); "A Neglected Branch of Musicology: the Dance" (Sachs); "Melody and Theme" (Schoenberg); "Remarks on the Methods of Transcribing and Grouping Folk Melodies" (Bartók); "The Origins of Romantic Opera" (Dent); "An Unknown Chansonnier of the Fifteenth Century" (Bukofzer); "The Psychological Interpretation of Schopenhauer's Theory of Music" (Carroll C. Pratt); "W.A. Mozart, *fils* " (Karl Geiringer); "Spoken Drama and Music Drama: A Comparison" (Lang); "Music in Carácas during the Colonial Period (1770–1811)" (Juan Bautista Plaza); "Petrucci's Odhecaton" (Helen Hewitt); "Daniel D. Emmett, the composer of *Dixie*" (Hans Nathan); "The Relation of the Performing Artist to the Critic and Scholar," with "The Future of Electronic Music," and

"Has the Symphonic Orchestra Reached the Limit of its Development?" (Stokowski). A number of the talks were illustrated by performing groups ranging from an accompanied violin to "a small chorus and orchestra." Several dealt with musical iconography, and, as the minutes indicate, "many beautiful slides of works of art that contained musicians and instruments" were shown.

Carleton played a central role in the early development of the AMS Greater New York Chapter. He was elected its second chairman, for 1937 and 1938, and addressed the members on three occasions:

April 18, 1939: *Music of the Ainsworth Psalter and Bay Psalm Book*

> Musical illustrations were supplied by members of the Columbia University Chapel Choir, conducted by Lowell P. Beveridge. The talk was illustrated by the projection of film copies of first editions of and illustrations from sixteenth- and seventeenth- century psalters.

April 1, 1950: *Women Composers Before 1800*

> With musical illustrations by Winifred Cecil and Genevieve Johnson, with Fernando Valenti at the harpsichord.

Feb. 22, 1955: *Benedictions Mensae (Grace Before and After Meat)*

> A group of six, led by Prof. Howard Boatwright, illustrated the talk with performances. One of the many interesting points was the musical knives, *i.e.*, knives with engraved parts for polyphonic settings of grace.

As chief of the Music Division of the New York Public Library (1931–59), Carleton was the unofficial host to the Chapter which began to meet regularly at the 42nd Street Library in November of 1946 (and continued to do so for almost two decades). It should be added that he was elected President of the Music Library Association (1937–39) and of the American Musicogical Society (1939–40). While president of the AMS, he chaired the committee that, in 1969, organized the first International Musicological Congress held in the United States. During these same years, in addition to his activities as scholar, author, editor, and extraordinarily innovative librarian, Carleton also found time to pursue a distinguished career as a professional flutist, demonstrating his skill both in public concerts and on recordings.

Now for the background of the "incident" referred to in the first paragraph of this offering. It happened on December 10, 1965 at about 8:40 PM. The occasion was the Thirtieth Anniversary Festivities of the Greater New York Chapter of the American Musicological Society "celebrated with appropriate fanfare and mathematical inexactitude a full thirty-one years after the chapter's founding."[1]

The event, which included cocktails, dinner, speeches, and music, took place at the Harvard Club of New York. It was formal in dress, gala in spirit, and a triumph both gastronomically and enologically. Well over two hundred people crowded the main dining hall, many coming from distant parts of the country. As chairman of the Greater New York Chapter at the time, I was in charge of the entire fandango; I had the able assistance of a five-person dinner committee chaired by Richard F. French, then president of the New York Pro Musica board, and of Carleton Sprague Smith, who was appointed the official Toastmaster. Everyone there knew Carleton. The NYPL's music division, which he had headed for almost three decades and helped to make great, was a second home to most of us.

The "incident"—which I will describe very soon—occurred during the after-dinner speech period, which in turn was followed by a concert in the adjacent Harvard Hall, a sumptuous high-ceilinged, oak-paneled room with unsurpassed acoustics. It was a vocal and instrumental "Concert of Florentine Medieval and Renaissance Music" given by the New York Pro Musica directed by Noah Greenberg. (This was one of the last concerts Noah ever conducted and, most of those present agreed, one of his greatest. He died suddenly a month later.)

The obligatory nostalgia-and-thank-you-speech-making period between dinner and concert included the presentation of a special citation to Philip S. Miller, Carleton's successor as head of the New York Public Library's Music Division, the delivery of a humorous chronicle of the early history of the American Musicological Society by our principal speaker, William S. Mitchell (then its president),[2] and the introduction of our Guests of Honor—three great scholars who had had

---

[1] Quoted from the Introduction to *American Musicological Society Greater New York Chapter; A Programmatic History 1935–1965.* Ed. by Barry S. Brook (New York, 1965). iv, 32 pp. This pamphlet presents the thirty-one year history of the Chapter in terms of its papers, programs, and symposia. Brief annotations, extracted from the scrupulously kept minutes of each meeting, are included.

[2] William Mitchell's speech, "A Hitherto Unknown—or—a Recently Discovered. . ." was published as the Introduction to *Musicology and the Computer; Three Symposia.* Ed. by Barry S. Brook (New York: CUNY Press, 1970), pp. 1–8.

so much to do with the establishment of musicology in the United States: Gustave Reese, Paul Henry Lang, and Otto Kinkeldey. Each was introduced, toasted, and invited to say a few words (in three minutes or less).

Reese and Lang spoke beautifully for about *four* minutes each and were duly toasted and roundly applauded. There was a hitch, however, when Kinkeldey's turn came.

It should be mentioned, parenthetically, that although less well-known today than his fellow Guests of Honor (both a generation younger than he), Kinkeldey was revered by all who knew him. Born in 1878 in New York, he received his Bachelor's degree from the College of the City of New York and his Masters at New York University. He studied with Edward MacDowell at Columbia University, and left for Berlin in 1902 to study music, literature, and philosophy. He obtained his doctorate there in 1909 with his path-finding *Orgel und Klavier in der Musik des 16. Jarhhundert*. He embarked on a promising career as musicologist and organist at Breslau University, where he attained the honorary title of Professor in 1912. With the outbreak of World War I in 1914, he returned to New York to head the Music Division of the New York Public Library. He was the first president of both the Music Library Association and the American Musicological Society, and author of many seminal and prophetic articles. His teaching career at Cornell and at half a dozen other universities throughout the country ended with his retirement in 1958 to his home in Orange, New Jersey. When this dinner took place he was a frail 87-year old.

Carleton Sprague Smith and Otto Kinkeldey shared the distinction of being the only persons ever elected to the presidencies of both the MLA and the AMS. In the opening article of the December 1948 issue of *Notes* dedicated to "Otto Kinkeldey in honor of his seventieth birthday," Carleton wrote a splendid, superbly documented chronicle of Kinkeldey's extraordinary career until then, emphasizing his work in music librarianship. Donald Jay Grout, in his entry on Kinkeldey in *The New Grove* sums up his influence on music scholarship as follows: "[He] was the founder of American musicology. It was owing to him more than to any other individual that musicology, after a long struggle for recognition as a serious discipline, became an accepted subject in the curriculum of American universities; and it was chiefly to him that subsequent American music scholars, many of the first generation directly, and all of them indirectly, owed (and often acknowledged) their livelihood."

When first invited to participate in this thirtieth-anniversary celebration, Kinkeldey demurred on the grounds of advanced age and sundry infirmities. It was only when the husband of musicologist Elaine Brody, David Silverberg, who had known Dr. Kinkeldey at Cornell, offered to send a limousine to pick him up and return him home, that he most graciously accepted.

When it was time for him to speak, he reminisced wittily for about a minute, then he stopped, suddenly, at a total loss for words. After several seconds of terrible silence he said: "That's what happens when you get to my age. You forget what it was you wanted to say."

Once again, silence.

No one breathed.

No one moved. . . except perhaps to exchange embarrassed glances. After what seemed like an eternity, Carleton Sprague Smith stepped up to the podium and said, "Dr. Kinkeldey, you have forgotten more than anyone of us will ever know!" The spell was broken; the audience rose to its feet, cheering wildly. We could all proceed happily with the Anniversary festivities.

Carleton's sensitivity, quick-wittedness, and talent for *le mot juste*—attributes that have characterized his entire career—had saved the day. No one but he could have done it as well.

Gilberto Freyre

CARLETON SPRAGUE SMITH

A tribute to Carleton Sprague Smith could not fail to include an enthusiastic contribution from Brazil—a meaningful expression of solidarity.

I know of no other United States citizen, who, in our times, has better understood Brazil, lovingly comprehending it through his many qualities: erudition, discrimination, perceptiveness, and a high artistic feeling, in addition to strict intellectual integrity.

Brazil was lucky to have been discovered by Carleton, who, as a young man, identified with the country and revealed its idiosyncrasies to a large English-speaking public. As a skilled writer on literary and general subjects, Carleton would broach complex topics in their inter-disciplinary relationships and thus appeal to a vast audience.

Above all, he had talent, sensitivity, and the artist's good taste. There was nothing—but nothing— technocratic, bureaucratic, or official in Carleton's way of dealing with Brazilian matters. He was totally free of such conditioning.

It was impossible to imagine him serving a cause to which he was not devoted. He was a romantic, with a romanticism preserved by a youthful spirit that was never replaced by more conservative attitudes.

This, however, did not prevent him from being an intuitive researcher. Without his acute perception, certain opinions might never have become known to Brazilians, such as the fascinating one held by the great William James about the intelligence of the Brazilian negro.

Gilberto Freyre (1900 – 1988) was a leading Brazilian sociologist. Author of many works on Brazilian history and culture, he was, in 1949, a Brazilian delegate to the General Assembly of the United Nations.

Who could be greater than William James as a psychologist of literary merit? In his view, the negro of the United States, his intelligence distorted by poor living conditions, was one type; and the negro of Brazil, whose blood ran in the veins of so many outstanding Brazilians, was quite another.

This revelation was one of Carleton Sprague Smith's contributions to the intimate knowledge of Brazil by Brazilians, and it places him among those foreigners of high stature who identified with Brazil to such an extent that they became Brazilian.

Yet Carleton did not take the easy path of the inveterate apologist. His intellectual integrity never permitted him to go to extremes. He was—and is—a scholar, a wise and learned man conscious of his responsibility. He is also an artist, aware that the artistic sense requires no less balance, wide perspective, and all-encompassing approach than the scientific.

He has always been one of the outstanding social scientists of his period in the United States, but not in the narrow, limited or exaggerated scientific approach that has made a caricature of the typical Ph.D. His artistic sensitivity, his scholastic qualities, and the sense of humor which has never failed him have delivered him from such danger. His sense of humor, in fact, contributed to the charm, easy literary style, and fascinating quality of his prose in dealing with complex matters. He handled such subjects with skilled professionalism, without resorting to the pedantry of those who cannot smile while dealing with serious topics.

Carleton Sprague Smith is an outstanding figure. His writings are classics that will always be read and reread. He will always be remembered for the qualities of his personality combined with a superior intellect.

Sir Yehudi Menuhin

TRIBUTE TO CARLETON SPRAGUE SMITH

Carleton Sprague Smith is that most rare phenomenon—today, as the twentieth century reels to its dizzy end—an American renaissance man, or in view of the growth and variety of the arts up to and including the French Revolution, a Baroque figure.

It was Carleton, indeed, as a musician and a musicologist, who uncovered interesting pieces, which we played with pleasure and delight in his New York home. As a diplomat, administrator, writer, and conversationalist, he is a man in whom knowledge, wisdom, compassion, and aesthetics are as naturally integrated as the very limbs of his body. But for me, it is as a free and kindred spirit that I treasure him above all.

I first met Carleton and his lovely wife Elisabeth in Rio de Janeiro during the Second World War and found them truly inseparable—as enchanting together as only a fusion of beauty and love (which for me is the definition of art) can render a human union.

Erudite and fluent in Portuguese, Carleton was the American who gave the United States special insight into the heart and mind of Brazil. Few before or since have better revealed the essence of their respective cultures, their expression in the vibrating patterns of art and society, as he did during those extraordinary years. It was he who introduced me

---

Sir Yehudi Menuhin, one of the foremost violin virtuosos of the twentieth century, has also earned wide acclaim as conductor and author. He founded Live Music Now and the International Menuhin Music Academy in Gstaad, Switzerland, and has promoted cultural exchange programs to further the careers of talented young musicians, and has played an important role in UNESCO.

to Candido Portinari, who painted my portrait, following a final concert in Rio, a portrait whose unfinished ears bear testimony to my having to rush off to catch a 5:00 a.m. plane.

Many of the professional responsibilities he undertook were imbued with a sense of high purpose and direction. In the same way as another man whom I loved and respected—my teacher Georges Enesco—Carleton is possessed of an invincible courtesy. I can only compare his life with an extended beautiful musical score.

Carleton embodies and enshrines ideals of human thought and conduct from past generations of Americans, among whom the freedom of the spirit was not to be confused with the freedom of the market.

I remember an incident which occurred at the Gstaad Festival in the summer of 1964. I invited Carleton to play with our group and to choose a Spanish program. One of the pieces was Luigi Boccherini's sextet for flute, strings, and harpsichord. Boccherini, of course, was an Italian, but had spent the major part of his creative years in Spain. This particular piece, instead of a cadenza for flute, as one might expect, contained an unusually difficult one for two cellos. One of the performers, the distinguished Catalan Gaspar Cassado, was fully prepared, the other shall remain nameless. At the rehearsal in the morning of the concert at the Church of St. Peter, at which Carleton's playing was impeccable, I suggested a little concentrated practice in the adjoining room and one of the cellists left the room. Two hours later he announced to me that he was ill and had retired to a hospital. This indeed affected the entire program. Carleton, however, provided a cover-up—the stunning virtuoso *Fandango* by Antonio Soler for harpsichord. The performer, a Colombian, knew the score well, but he would not perform it in a church. After much consternation, someone recommended Carl Philipp Emmanuel Bach's *Variationes über Die Folie d'Espagne*, which was brilliantly played. The audience was thrilled, Carleton's face was a study, and we both chuckled.

How often Diana and I spent deeply rewarding evenings with Carleton and Elisabeth and their friends that were always stimulating. The subjects discussed varied from music to education, from the historical to the political. I want to believe that such special friends as Carleton and Elisabeth, who mark the subject of my modest tribute, will set an example for future generations.

Nicolas Slonimsky

A SALUTE TO CARLETON SPRAGUE SMITH

Carleton Sprague Smith is a music scholar of patrician splendor. He is renowned a prime librarian of things musical, conversant with all things musical. I have met Carleton in various situations and under changing moons. Some fifty years ago I was a fellow passenger on the boat bound from New York for Rio de Janeiro. I remember him a splendidly attired gentleman, in the combination of an American dress suit and a colorful Latin American Jacket. He was remarkably handsome.

A few years later I met Carleton in the marble halls of The New York Public Library building on the corner of Fifth Avenue and 42nd Street, where a pair of lions guard the entrance. Our encounter was a gathering of multilingual delegates to a musicological convention. I recall him, so pluralistic in his linguistic ability, speaking with utter fluency in what I believed, listening at the distance, to be the Spanish language. No, it was not Spanish; it was Portuguese. But Carleton, I soon learned, was fluent in French as well. Most guests, however, were German-speaking individuals. Sure enough, he also addressed them in fluent German. It was the Austrian dialect that he spoke, as I learned shortly afterwards, for he had taken a Ph.D. in history at the University of Vienna. I was completely engulfed in his literary and musical brilliance and multiple tongues; all I had that he didn't have was my native Russian.

Nicolas Slonimsky, a Guggenheim Fellow and presently Regent's Lecturer at the Univ. of California at Los Angeles, enjoyed a distinguished career as a pianist, composer, conductor, teacher of music theory, and author. As the creative and meticulous editor of Baker's Biographical Dictionary of Musicians, *beginning with the fifth (1958), he has just completed the eighth.*

Switching to English, Carleton spoke of his exploration of flute music of the eighteenth century and his intention to publish a collection of American flute music of that period. He also had something to do with a demonstration of flutes at an otherwise lackluster session of the American Musicological Society. The lecturer tried to demonstrate a gigantic bass flute, but he could never get the sound through that megalolithic tube. I do not recall whether Carleton came to his rescue, but I do recall his playing a flute sonata on another occasion, and he certainly could give a proper pastoral inflection.

During Carleton's tenure as Chief of the Music Division of the New York Public Library, from 1931 until 1959, he added to the regular Division a novel section which he called Musical Americana. He realized that music librarians were concerned mainly with printed editions of music classics, but he always felt that performers were as important as music scholars and editors. Through his initiative and guidance, the library issued such important works as Hans T. David's *Music of the Moravians in America* (1954), Sydney Beck's *The First Book of Consort Lessons Collected by Thomas Morley 1599 and 1611* (1959), and Richard J. Wolfe's *Secular Music in America, 1801–1825: A Bibliography* (1964), for which he wrote enlightening introductions in the latter publications. As early as 1932, he formed the prototype of a library-museum of the performing arts at The New York Public Library, which offered not only live music but theatrical performances, dance, film, and audio-visual equipment and program. This idea was realized as the core of his ambitious plan when, in 1965, the Music Division moved to its new location in the Lincoln Center for the Performing Arts.

Music and diplomacy seldom mix. Perhaps the most famous statesman who was also a celebrated musician was the pianist Paderewski. There is a story about his being the representative of the newly-independent Polish state and meeting Clemenceau at the Versailles Conference. The latter wanted to know why Paderewski changed his career as a virtuoso to that of a diplomat. "What a fall down!" the famous Frenchman is supposed to have exclaimed.

In 1936, he served as the United States delegate at the International Congress on Music Education in Prague and the International Musicological Congress at Barcelona. He also represented the International American Societies of Art and Music at conferences in Copenhagen, Berlin, and Paris. Between performances on the flute and working closely with European and Latin American scholars, Smith also acted a cultural ambassador. He held rather important positions as a representative of the United States at various conferences, but no diplomat would have stuck to playing the flute as he did. He spent the war years in Brazil as a United States Foreign Service Officer and lectured in the Brazilian version of the Portuguese language all across the Amazon basin. In 1960, he accompanied Adlai Stevenson and Nelson Rockefeller as advisor and interpreter on a three-month tour of Latin America. The following year, he was appointed by President Kennedy as a member of the Advisory Commission of the National Cultural Center, known today as the John F. Kennedy Center for the Performing Arts. From 1963 to 1966, he was a panel member of the United States Department of State in the Office of Cultural Presentations. In more exotic lands, he was Discussion Leader at the Asian-American Symposium on "Cultural Affairs and International Understanding in Kuala Lumpur, the Federation of Malaya, and, still later, at a conference in remote and mysterious Uganda.

With all of these extraordinary international activities, Carleton never travelled without his revered flute. He gave performances with music groups both here and abroad. Famous composers dedicated flute works to him. Moreover, his many achievements were recognized through honorary degrees and awards.

I would like to complete this tribute by acknowledging my personal debt to Carleton. He encouraged me to explore the musical wealth of Latin America, resulting in the publication of a book on the subject. While the book was criticized as a tourist's account of an international traveller, it was the first compendium on the music of the twenty Latin American republics and, as such, it received Carleton's approval. Somehow, I always see him smiling in all my remembrances of him; it was a smile that was invariably encouraging.

LIBRARIES

Sydney Beck

CARLETON SPRAGUE SMITH AND THE SHAPING OF A GREAT MUSIC LIBRARY

Harbinger of a Center for the Performing Arts (Recollections of a Staff Member)

Dr. Carleton Sprague Smith was appointed Chief of the Music Division in the Reference Department of The New York Public Library (NYPL) on 15 January 1931. My first contact with him occurred later that year by way of an introduction from Dorothy Lawton, who was head of the Music Library at the 58th Street Branch. The recommendation was the outcome of one of my many visits to the Music Library, following the rehearsals of the American Orchestral Society's training orchestra which were held tri-weekly in the Liederkranz Building adjoining the branch library. The Music Library's relatively modest holdings, housed in a small back room on the main floor, boasted a growing collection of phonograph records and a fairly large number of orchestral scores that were purchased with funds generously provided by a committee of music lovers, headed by the Countess Mercati, a board member of the New York Philharmonic-Symphony Society. I was a regular reader and borrower, and one of my fondest memories of Miss Lawton is the warm welcome with which she greeted all visitors to her enclave, especially young people, in whom she often took a personal interest. To those who would listen she divulged her ambitious plans for the future, the latest

---

Sydney Beck was the first Curator of the Toscanini Memorial Archive and Head of the Music Division's Rare Book and Manuscript Collections at the NYPL. From 1968 to 1976, he was Director of Libraries at the New England Conservatory of Music in Boston.

and most enthusiastic of which was to further the cause of American music both here and abroad. (She was still glowing from her extraordinary success of the previous summer in Paris, where she established a substantial music section in the American Library, devoted primarily to this purpose.) It was during one of our occasional chats that I confided my desperate need to find temporary part-time employment in order to continue my studies. After repeated inquiries about my progress, she suggested that I see the new music Chief at the 42nd Street Library, and provided me with a helpful note to him.

I shall never forget my first encounter with CSS—as he was later frequently addressed. He was much younger than I had expected, not at all professorial, nor as awesome as I had imagined a man in his position would be. Previous visits to the Music Division of the Central Library had left lingering impressions of the cloistered, scholarly atmosphere of its reading room, presided over by the forbidding, white-bearded Mr. Edward Silsky, one-time Chief. CSS and I plunged almost immediately into a discussion of Baroque performance practices—at that time a rare subject—during which he produced a manuscript copy of a Scarlatti cantata which lacked the figured bass realization for a planned performance. Could I do it for him? If so, it would be a one-time personal assignment to help me out, there being no opening on his Staff at the moment. I returned two weeks later with score in hand. Presumably the results were to his satisfaction, for shortly thereafter he created a special project so that I could "do this sort of thing" on a regular basis, working several hours a week at the library.

After a brief period my place on the staff was "legitimized" and my duties extended when I was offered the opportunity of filling a part-time vacancy as a reference librarian. "The special project" consisted of the scoring, from original parts, of selected items from a vast store of unpublished works from earlier centuries, to make them more accessible for study and performance. Under CSS's guidance, the copying was soon expanded to transcribing from tablature, transposing, reconstructing missing parts, realizing the figured bass parts, and eventually editing scores and parts for concert use. Though the bulk of the source material was part of the library's rich collection, certain rare items were occasionally borrowed from the Library of Congress, The British Museum, Christ Church Library at Oxford, and other institutions, as well as from a few private collections.

By 1935, a list of sixty works—some in sets of six or twelve—was published in an annotated thematic *Catalogue of Music Available in Black Line Print*,[1] prepared by Dr. Harold Spivacke, shortly before he became Chief of the Music Division of the Library of Congress. Most of this scoring and publishing activity was undertaken with the assistance of twelve music copyists, provided by the Federal Music Project of the Works Progress Administration, and the engagement of Dr. Hans T. David, an eminent displaced German scholar, to assist in the supervision and editorial work.[2] The publications project ultimately encompassed five general categories under the series titles of: 1) English Instrumental Music of the 16th and 17th Centuries from Manuscripts in the NYPL; 2) Psalmody in 17th-Century America from the Psalters used in Colonial America with the original tunes in harmonizations current at the time: *The Ainsworth Psalter*, *The Bay Psalm Book* and the *Dathenius Psalter* (edited by Carleton Sprague Smith); 3) Music of the Moravians in America from the Archives of the Moravian Church at Bethlehem, Pennsylvania (edited by Hans T. David); 4) Early Symphonies and Concertos; and 5) Chamber Music and Choral Works.

It was not long before I came to realize that the publishing of rare music—certainly a unique service for a public library—was only a small

---

[1] Black Line Print was a practical method of reproduction allowing for single copies to be made and sold at moderate prices. Earlier duplication had been made by a gelatin process (hectograph), which proved unsatisfactory and led to a series of experiments conducted by CSS, with the cooperation of a blueprint company. The so-called Black Line Print process—now known as Ozalid—using originals written in black ink on transparent "master" sheets, was adopted for the project and has since been widely used by composers whose works were not yet printed.

[2] During a period of seven years, approximately 20,000 pages of unpublished material were copied on "master" sheets. Since performance was one of the prime objectives, a more practical catalogue was issued in 1941, offering carefully edited scores and parts of fifty works chosen for their artistic value as well as historic interest. After the War some of them were reproduced in limited editions by photolithography and distributed by Music Press and later C. F. Peters, acting as agents for the library. Among the more ambitious endeavors were the reconstruction of Thomas Morley's *First Booke of Consort Lessons*, 1599 and 1611, which included a critical study of the broken consort of Elizabethan times, and the facsimile edition of the *Parthenia-In-Violata*, a unicum in the library's collection. Through the years the Black Line Prints had found their way to most of the major music libraries, performance organizations, and individuals throughout the world. Performances based on many of the library's publications have been recorded commercially, as well as for the division's record collection. At this writing, announcement has been received of the plan by Garland Publishing, Inc. to reissue 250 of the Black Line Print scores.

part of a larger plan germinating in the mind of a vital and ambitious Chief. Inspired by a concept of Oscar Sonneck, the distinguished scholar heading the Music Division of the Library of Congress who advocated "museums of music"[3] following the pattern long established by the Gesellschaft der Musikfreunde in Vienna, and more recently the Musik-Historisches Museum in Cologne, CSS drew up a report early in 1932, outlining a grandiose scheme of his own by which New York City's music libraries would offer the broadest possible service to the community, while at the same time provide for the special needs of scholars.

The occasion for the report ostensibly was to draw attention to the continuing frustration of working in the poorly ventilated quarters of the Music Division (Rooms 324–326)—a condition dictated by the exigencies of an architect's design in the planning of a monumental structure—and the even more serious problem of the acute lack of space alloted to the growing music collections of both the Reference and Circulation Departments. The scheme ultimately would provide the solution for a situation fast becoming desperate.[4] It involved the creation of a "Music Library and Museum for the City of New York, equal if not superior to any of the world's music centers, where the neglected branches of music could be concentrated and centralized." The "neglected branches," identified as "aids in the scientific study of music" were: 1) an instrumental collection—for studying the history, construction and acoustical properties involved, as well as for performance; 2) an iconography department—for pictorial insights into the history and practice of music; and 3) a phonograph archive—for listening as well as

---

[3]In characterizing the music library of his day as containing the composer's "thoughts. . . practically buried alive, encapsuled in books of mute hieroglyphics," Sonneck insisted that some day we must have "museums of music, where in sundry feasible ways the public appeal of works of musical art will be made to endure, in effect similar to the permanent and ever-direct appeal of paintings, sculptures, etc., in museums of Fine Arts" (1917:242).

[4]CSS had the good fortune of assuming his post at a time when Harry Miller Lydenberg became Director. A more sympathetic and cooperative administrator can hardly be imagined. Lydenberg welcomed and supported all initiatives and original ideas that might enhance or widen the library's services and bring attention to its resources. He was particularly interested in highlighting the wealth of the performing arts materials, and gave the new Chief of the Music Division every opportunity to develop them. "Without such an ally at the top," wrote CSS, in a recent letter to the author, "the outcome would have been very different."

research.[5] To these would be added the existing resources of the two music libraries, with space for exhibitions and for a small concert hall so that the library-museum's rarities become known and attract people (and gifts); in short, it would make the library "a living organism." It was prophetic for the time—and essentially an imaginative blueprint for the future shaping of the Music Division.

The inclusion of iconography among the three pillars of CSS's master plan was apparently prompted by his contact with Joseph Muller, with whom he had become acquainted sometime earlier. Muller was the proud possessor of the largest and most valuable collection of musical iconography in the country. According to his own account, collecting music and pictures of musicians was an all-absorbing youthful pursuit during his student days at the Brussels Conservatory, where he studied violin with the great Eugène Ysaÿe. "I early left [Rodolphe] Kreutzer and [Pierre] Rode *études* for salt water voyaging," he wrote, "and for more than thirty years have had unusual opportunities for travelling the world over. In the course of these wanderings I gathered thousands of musicians' portraits, musical mementoes, title pages and autographs when they were within reach of my purse-strings." His meeting with CSS in later years was providential, for it led to some interesting developments.

Joseph Muller was one of the first wholehearted supporters of the library-museum plan, even to the point of offering his entire collection for the purpose. Understandably, he hoped to be a participant so that the "Iconography Department could become the finest and most complete in existence." Muller's offer received the enthusiastic support of the library authorities, and in 1934 he was invited to join the staff to help build the Iconography Section. But more important for the future course of the Music Division, he was shortly thereafter made Curator

---

[5]The "aids" are more fully explained in an unpublished paper entitled, "Fugitive Material, the Music Library's Problem," in which he wrote: "A music library is a great deal more than a place to store books and music. It is a living archive, or a depository of numerous sorts of fugitive materials, which must be kept active. . . the Chief of the Music Division of the New York Public Library believes that there are five types of fugitive material which are bound up with music libraries." He added to them material on the dance and musical Americana "the chief interest [in the latter] being historical rather than musical. . .Ideally speaking, music libraries should attract such materials and should be centers for the community interest in music."

of the newly created Americana Section, established to satisfy the current interest in the history of American music. It appeared that Muller's collecting instincts extended into the field of American musical imprints and music publishers wherein he had acquired a special interest and expertise.[6] His appointment thus became an opportunity, both for him and for the library, to continue this pursuit, working with a fairly good collection, already in hand, and with a sympathetic and knowledge-able chief. Together they collaborated on a number of bibliographical tools to provide the public with useful information on early American musical life, and devised an ambitious acquisitions program which laid the groundwork for a valuable scholarly resource.[7]

The proposal for a library and museum (entitled *A Worthy Music Center for New York*) also stressed the urgency of taking practical steps to implement the plan, "steps which if taken now will mean a great saving for future generations"—a recommendation which was given serious consideration by the Library administration. As a preliminary move in this direction, Dr. Smith was sent abroad, in 1932, to study the leading European libraries and museums, where he discussed his ideas with such renowned scholars as: Guido Adler, Karl Geiringer, and Rudolf von Ficker in Austria; Wilhelm Altmann, Oskar von Millar, and Wilhelm Krabbe in Germany; and Henri Prunières, Jacques Gabriel

[6]Muller had built a great following among serious American collectors and dealers over a long period of years. His publications include: *The Star-Spangled Banner: Words and Music Issued between 1814–1864*, an annotated bibliographical list of the different versions, and many facsimiles (New York: G. A. Baker and Company, 1935).

[7]CSS's interest in all aspects of American music, with particular emphasis on its early history, was reflected in the continued growth of the Americana collection, now perhaps the most extensive in the country. He was also one of the first to give courses on the subject of "Music in American Civilization" at Stanford University (1938) and intermit-tently at New York University, and elsewhere thereafter. While his personal researches centered around the ballads and psalmody of Colonial America, he encouraged and supported many worthy projects in the field, such as: Virginia Larkin Redway's *Music Directory of Early New York City* [a file of musicians, music publishers, and musical instrument makers. . . from 1786 through 1835] (New York: NYPL, 1941); Hans T. David's study, *Music of the Moravians in America. From the Archives of the Moravian Church at Bethlehem, Pennsylvania* (New York: NYPL, 1954; printed earlier under the Federal Music Project [New York: NYPL, 1938]) and Richard J. Wolfe's monumental, *Secular Music in America, 1801–1825: A Bibliography* (New York: NYPL, 1964), the publication of which CSS considered "an important event in our cultural history." (Joseph Muller's curatorship was followed by that of John Tasker Howard, John Edmunds, Karl Kroger, and Richard Jackson.)

Prod'homme, André Schaeffner, and André Pirro in France—all of whom took a great interest in the plan and made many constructive suggestions. In the same year, Walter H. Kilham Jr., an architect friend with whom CSS had some preliminary discussions, also made a first-hand study of European museums in order to further the project. In August of 1933, Dr. Smith and Mr. Kilham, accompanied by Mr. Harry M. Lydenberg, the Director, inspected the old Juilliard School of Music on East 52nd Street as a possible site for a museum. This did not prove feasible. A subsequent offer of the private mansions of the Warburg and Blumenthal families was considered, but given up as impractical. Meetings were also held with the Directors of the Fogg Museum in Cambridge, Massachusetts and The Museum of the City of New York to benefit from their experiences in matters of construction and costs of operation and maintenance.

Nothing further was done to solve the building problem until 1935, when plans for the establishment of the Music Library-Museum were revived. It was then to be included in the blueprints for the International Building at Rockefeller Center and as a possible extension of the library's main building on 42nd Street. In May and June of the same year the matter cropped up again in the planning of the proposed Museum of Modern Art on West 53rd Street, this time with the idea of sharing space with the graphic arts. Some months later a combination of another kind, far more in keeping with CSS's original scheme, was considered under a tentative agreement and announced publicly in the *New York Times* of 15 January 1936. The Music Departments of the Metropolitan Museum of Art and the NYPL were to be consolidated as an independent unit, wherein the magnificent Crosby-Brown Collection of Ancient Instruments would be housed together with the library's extensive holdings in music, books, manuscripts, recordings, etc.

The plan met with a warm response on the part of officials from both institutions, and, according to a press interview with Herbert E. Winlock, Director of the Museum, it was readily endorsed by the Brown heirs, since it would make possible a wider and more practical use of the instruments "now confined to be viewed, and then only occasionally, behind glass." It was understood that as many of the instruments as were possible would be effectively restored and heard in concerts, demonstrations, and other educational activities.[8] Various schemes were considered to realize this, yet each was dependent upon finding a suitable building. There was some hope it might come about through Mayor Fiorello La Guardia's proposal of a municipal art center, a constituent of which was to be a music museum.

While the search for a proper home remained elusive, plans were under way to develop the so-called "neglected branches" by building on the available resources of the Music Division. The establishment of an exhaustive archive of recorded music was one of the major long-term projects. A gift of 500 records from the Columbia Phonograph Company in July, 1937, together with other gifts and a fairly large number of discs on hand (including some rare items from the nineteenth century) provided a promising start. It was to be known as the Thomas Alva Edison Phonograph Archive and was to include the Edison Collection from the museum at Orange, New Jersey, which comprised a complete set of the current production of the Victor and Columbia Phonograph Companies. It also contained duplicates from the Folksong Archive of the Library of Congress and pressings of the primitive music recorded for the American Museum of Natural History, as well as copies from its Anthropological Collection. Plans also included the production of original recordings of performance of early music on period instruments (hopefully supervised by Dr. Curt Sachs, long experienced in historical recordings), as well as of important new music. The organization and development of this section of the Music Division was placed in the hands of Philip Miller, the most knowledgeable person on the staff, and a nationally recognized authority in the field. However, a project of such magnitude was a dubious challenge without adequate work space and operating funds. Furthermore, listening facilities were then out of the question, even if staff were available to service them. The immediate problem was the proper care and storage of an ever-growing accumulation of recorded sound materials, largely unprocessed—a vital concern which had caused some embarrassment over the years with regard to

---

[8]The Museum's agreement led to Dr. Smith's recommendation of Lotta Van Buren as a likely Curator. She had long been associated with early musical instruments, both as a performer and craftsman. Specialists in the restoration of early instruments were then exceedingly rare; those who entered the field generally did so as an avocation.

A few offers of private collections had to be deferred until housing and administration questions were resolved even at the risk of losing some of these treasures.

their preservation and ultimate use. (An excellent account of subsequent efforts to solve these basic problems is given in David Hall's essay, pp. 43–66.) It was not until after the War that Mr. Miller was able to begin offering the public interim access to the collection through a series of informal concerts of recorded music in the Library's Lecture Room.

Concerts of any kind in the central building were hardly conceivable before 1935. The rule of silence was inviolate. The first musical sounds tentatively allowed to penetrate the prevailing quiet were in the nature of an experiment. This was brought about when the idea of initiating a program of "readings from the shelves" was proposed as a means of reviving "forgotten" musical gems worthy of consideration for the publication project. CSS was most interested and readily obtained permission for a trial run. A suitable location in the central building had to be found where regular rehearsals might be held and which would least disturb the readers. After exploring the many cavernous passages beneath the building—constructed over what was once the Croton Distributing Reservoir—and other remote areas, we came upon a well-ventilated and heated extension to the cafeteria, a frame structure on the ground floor, jutting out to an inner court in the vicinity of the 40th Street delivery entrance.

We were permitted to carry out our plan with the understanding that the first complaints would put an end to the enterprise. A small chamber orchestra assembled on Friday evenings, leaving the building from the guarded rear entrance long after closing hours. The orchestra included many of the finest professional musicians in town who came regularly, considering it a privilege to explore with us the uncharted by-ways of music history. A prime incentive was the adventure of discovering desirable additions to their repertoires. "Beck's Cafeteria Boys"—as the group came to be known—received only compliments for the "sweet strains" that occasionally reached the reading room which opened out on the court.[9] Our first "public appearance" was an informal concert, in 1936, for the staff only.

[9]Occasional daytime rehearsals were later held on the tenth floor of the library's warehouse on West 25th Street. The orchestra then included a number of recently arrived European refugees. Dr. Curt Sachs was often in attendance, seeking likely material for a continuation of his *Anthologie Sonore* recording series, begun in Paris before the war.

Music proved to be a welcome intrusion in the hallowed atmosphere of a busy research library. The success of the experiment obviously called for a bolder move. Why couldn't a series of public concerts be given, offering programs of an appropriate nature along the lines of those sponsored by the Elizabeth Sprague Coolidge Foundation at the Library of Congress? Foreseeing another fruitful avenue of development to further demonstrate the library's role as "living museum," CSS promptly took action. The search for a proper "concert hall" was undertaken with the full cooperation of the director. The various art galleries and the main exhibition hall were investigated as the only possibilities. Most promising was the Lenox Gallery, large enough to seat two or three hundred. It was an excellent choice, aesthetically and acoustically, and so conveniently located that it could easily be controlled by the guards. Plans for its use were allowed to proceed, again on a trial basis.

Contact was made immediately with the Library of Congress, and Mrs. Coolidge generously offered the NYPL several free chamber music concerts of the kind so successfully given in Washington. The first program took place on 6 January 1937, with the newly organized Coolidge String Quartet initiating the series. It included, in its first half, modern premieres of works transcribed and scored by the library's publication project, two of which comprised the first string quartets ever composed by French musicians. Later performances, throughout the year, were given by the Kolisch, Pro Arte, Gordon, and Roth String Quartets to the delight of an ever-growing audience of discriminating music lovers. New works by celebrated European and American composers—some commissioned by and dedicated to Mrs. Coolidge—were featured. Public concerts thus exhibited every promise of becoming an integral part of the activities of the Music Division.

For the following two years the concerts were neglected, because the chief became extremely involved in furthering plans for the consummation of the library-museum. Three institutions were now actively interested in pooling their resources, New York University having joined the Metropolitan Museum of Art in support of the library's project. The educational advantages to the university, both for advanced study and for the enlightenment of the general public, was considerable in view of the many possibilities they offered for an expanded lecture program. Furthermore, the university had already established connections with the Music Division; three of its graduate faculty, Drs. Curt Sachs, Hans T. David, and Carleton Sprague Smith, were on the library staff, and by special arrangement, graduate courses—those relating to the overall music-museum scheme—were given in the central building. New York University students were also allowed stack privileges—in a designated area—while the university was in the process of building its own music collection.

In a ten-page memorandum prepared for the Joint Committee of Board Members, Dr. Smith provided a general background of the project since its inception, outlined the pertinent collections, and pointed out the enormous potential for new and unique services by consolidating them under one roof. "New York has the opportunity to lead the way," he wrote, "in the creation of a wholly new type of music center which will transform our great collections of musical books and instruments into vital, living things." The underlying purpose of establishing such a center in New York was to make it a focal point for coordinated musical activities, which eventually would become a dynamic force of national significance. He listed the immediate steps to be taken to assure further progress in pursuit of these goals. The question of housing was paramount. Accordingly, the first order of business concerned the "thorough investigation" of the sizeable legacy willed to the NYPL by Ezekiel A. Donnell that was apparently earmarked for the construction of a special branch, which "if practicable" might serve as an excellent solution to this problem. It offered attractive possibilities for sharing administrative and maintenance costs. The Donnell Branch, however, was destined for other purposes.

Under the circumstances the committee confined its deliberations to general policy and procedures, and deferred matters of administration and long-term financing until decisions could be reached on the degree of independence the library-museum was to have and where it was eventually to be located. Meanwhile generous assurances of support had been received from the Carnegie and Rockefeller Foundations, and an anonymous donor had given $10,000 "to promote the amalgamation of the collections and forward the joint aims of the three cooperating institutions." An offer of financial assistance had also come from the Trustees of the Metropolitan Museum of Art, who had promised to contribute $10,000 a year for a period of five years. The committee was further encouraged by numerous endorsements from prominent musicians and leaders in closely related fields, many of whom took an active interest in the project.[10] Yet with the gathering of war clouds and the difficult economic situation, it was clear that it was not a propitious time for solving the complexities of the major issues. Planning for the library-museum was once again postponed.

Notwithstanding the temporary setback, the concept of the center continued to motivate CSS. In addition to the already established Americana section, the recorded music program, the publications project, and the introduction of public concerts, he had encouraged the founding, in 1936, of the Toscanini Microfilm Archive of holographs of the great composers—short-lived for lack of funds, but successfully revived as the Toscanini Memorial Archives in the 1960's—and now sought to augment and develop the Dance Collection. Attention had already been drawn to this somewhat neglected aspect of the division's holdings with the purchase, in 1937, of the Walter B. Graham Collection, a major portion of which was devoted to the dance. Duplicate volumes were sent to the Music Library on 58th Street, where a fair amount of material on the subject had been brought together by the indefatigable Dorothy Lawton—including some rarities, especially those pertaining to the earlier attempts in establishing a dance notation, and an exhaustive bibliography which was in progress there with the help of WPA workers, covering a whole spectrum of dance and related fields, culled from various libraries in the New York area.

In view of this, CSS welcomed the opportunity to discuss the possibilities of expanding the library's dance holdings as well as the special nature of the materials needed, with Rolf de Maré, founder and president of the Archives Internationales de la Dance (Paris), who had come to this country for the purpose of gathering authentic folk dance material, as well as aiding in the establishment of an American Archive

---

[10]Among the endorsers were: Richard Aldrich, Harold Bauer, Chalmers Clifton, Walter Damrosch, Otto Kinkeldey, David Mannes, Douglas Moore, Olga Samaroff, Leopold Stokowski, and Thomas Whitney Surette. Among those who actively participated in discussions were: Reginald Allen, Mrs. Henry Breckinridge, Eric T. Clarke, Lauder Greenway, Arthur Houghton, Jack Kapp, David M. Keiser, Walter H. Kilham, Lincoln Kirstein, Goodard Lieberson, Nelson A. Rockefeller, John D. Rockefeller III, Davidson Taylor, and Emanuel Winternitz.

of the Dance similar to his own. Apparently he was prepared to cooperate both materially and financially, an offer which attracted the keen interest of Malvina Hoffman and Ann Morgan, who together with Louise Branch, were busy organizing films and pictures for the International Exhibition of the Dance.[11] Nothing came of it at the time, but the contact did serve to point out the urgent need for a national archive, as an important part of a performing arts center.

Public concerts in the Lenox Gallery were resumed in 1939, and thereafter pursued energetically. They began with three programs of Renaissance music given by Lehman Engel's Madrigal Singers, sponsored jointly with the Works Progress Administration. These were followed by a concert of rare eighteenth-century music by a chamber orchestra made up largely of the old "cafeteria group," with assisting artists, under my direction—an informal affair presented, again, solely for members of the staff and their friends. Featuring three major works for orchestra, published for the first time in a modern edition by the library, the program also included two pieces of chamber music, one of which displayed a fine viola da gamba from the collection of "several old instruments recently acquired by the Music Division." This was a trio by Rameau in which CSS was the flutist; Fritz Magg, the gambist; and Yella Pessl, the harpsichordist, all recognized exponents of the early music *avant garde*. On September twelfth there was a reception and concert for the distinguished scholars attending the International Musicological Congress that was held for first time in the United States. Part of the June staff program was repeated, with the addition of choral music by American Moravian composers, published by the Music Division from manuscripts housed in the Moravian Church Archives at

---

[11]Rolf de Maré (1937:[32]) echoed CSS's plea for the creation of a library-museum of the Performing Arts: "What a deep joy one has in seeing how dance-conscious is the United States. The immense resources of this country,. . . the spirit of peace in mind and body, are the natural elements towards new forms of dance, and with the united efforts of your libraries, of your museums, of your universities, and your private collections, it should be possible to create in New York a center wherein everything connected with dance and music may be [found] under one roof." The occasion for the article, from which his words were excerpted, was the first great International Exhibition of the Dance, held in New York, 29 November 1937 through 2 January 1938, entitled "Dance International 1900–1937." More than forty nations participated in a varied program of dance recitals, motion pictures, lectures, broadcasts, costumes, paintings, sculpture, books, and other materials related to the dance.

Bethlehem, Pennsylvania. This part, of course, was of especial interest to the distinguished audience.

A disappointing interlude in concert activities, threatening their continuation, came with the announcement that the trustees had decided to assign the Lenox Gallery area to the newly acquired Berg Collection, a fabulous gift of rarities in English and American literature. This brought an end to its use for public gatherings. The last concerts held there were for sessions of the Composers' Forum Laboratory,[12] and a third performance of the Library Chamber Orchestra, once again for staff and friends. The program this time (January, 1940) included seldom heard works of Handel, Mozart, and Berlioz, and the first modern hearing or an eighteenth-century symphony by Gaetano Brunetti, another library publication scored from manuscripts borrowed from the Library of Congress.

The enthusiastic response to the library's free concerts made it evident that they could not be abruptly halted for want of a place to hold them. In all the sprawling magnificence of the central building, the only possibility for carrying on such events appeared to be the modest oak-panelled Lecture Room 213, adjacent to the Adminstration Offices at the far end of the second-floor corridor. Its shallow "stage" and limited seating capacity (175) meant that future programs would have to be confined to informal recitals of soloists and small chamber groups. Having the advantages of a more suitable location—well removed from the reading rooms and offering direct access to the grand stairways leading to the main entrance on Fifth Avenue—Room 213 proved to be a workable solution. (Programs requiring larger forces, or of wider audience appeal, were on occasion held elsewhere, generally in cooperation with other institutions.)

---

[12]The Composers' Forum was part of the Education Program of the Federal Music Project, a most constructive innovation, established in 1935 by its capable director, Ashley Pettis. It enabled American creative musicians to gain a hearing before a sympathetic audience, while the latter had the opportunity to question the composer about his work. As might be expected, many interesting and amusing situations arose, often making the composer and audience a bit uncomfortable. The fortnightly sessions at the library or at the Juilliard School were a popular success. In one season 180 works by twenty-seven mature and thirty-nine student composers were performed. Most of the scores became part of the library's growing collection of contemporary American music.

In the following years, over 150 successful concerts were given in Room 213, making the most of these circumstances. They were devoted as much to new music by European and American (both North and South) composers as to seldom heard works of the Renaissance and Baroque, performed as often as possible on period instruments.[13] A special series was introduced in the 50's, called "Regional Concerts," covering the creative activities of younger musicians in many of the smaller countries of the world—a pattern adopted by the League of Composers, featuring lesser known Americans, in its contribution to the series. The regular library-sponsored concerts were interrupted during the war years by the weekly "Victory Concerts" for servicemen, organized jointly with the Juilliard School of Music and the Metropolitan Museum of Art (all repeated in the auditorium of the Juilliard School).

By advancing the cause of music of earlier centuries, CSS not only enriched the musical life of the community—incidentally setting an example for libraries and museums throughout the country—but he also provided yeoman's service to the growing field of musicology. The scientific study of music had already gained a sufficient foothold in the university curriculum a decade or so before, to justify the founding of the American Musicological Society in 1934. CSS was active in bringing this about, becoming a member of its first executive board and later its president in 1939. Three years earlier he had been a prime mover, along with nine key figures in the profession, in the founding of the Music Library Association, organized to improve service, and recognizing the library's role as the indisputable handmaiden for the advancement of

---

[13]Opportunities for hearing such presentations of "early music" were relatively rare then. The restricted space of Room 213 became a real problem at times, particularly when a concert of historical interest was announced and the public unexpectedly responded in record numbers. A most embarrassing instance was the appearance in January of 1942 of Ralph Kirkpatrick in a Bach lecture-recital on the clavichord and harpsichord, which brought a near riot when more than two hundred people had to be turned away. The influence and ramifications of these "pioneer" efforts in creating an audience for a "living history of music" (beginning in the late 30's, both through publications and performance) were all the more significant when one considers the incredible developments in the last three or four decades of the revival of this music and the impact on concert life today. The roster of specialist-performers appearing in the library's early music concerts reads like a Who's Who in the revival movement at the time; in addition to those already mentioned, there were: Suzanne Bloch, Margaret Dodd, Lonny Epstein, Eva Heinitz, Charles Hobbs, Ruth Kisch-Arndt, Alfred Mann, Arthur Mendel, David Randolph, Fritz Rikko, Janos Scholz, Carleton Sprague Smith, Edith Weiss-Mann, Blanche Winogron, Ernst Victor Wolff, and others.

musicology. As Music Division Chief and university professor, he took every opportunity to find recruits for musicological careers.[14] On the occasion of the International Congress of Musicology (September, 1939), Dr. Smith played host to the many eminent scholars who had come from Europe and became stranded here at the outbreak of the war. Several among them were later helped to find permanent teaching posts in American universities, through his direct intervention and recommendation—a situation which ultimately left an indelible imprint on musical scholarship and music librarianship in this country.

For the further enlightenment of the general public, CSS initiated a series of fourteen bi-monthly free lectures by Dr. Curt Sachs, covering a wide range of subjects in the history and practice of music and the dance, "demonstrated by recordings, scores and unusual books from the library's collections." So popular had these talks become, that a similar series was offered annually throughout Dr. Sachs' tenure. A complementary program of exhibitions on a regular basis was not possible at the time, since the available facilities limited each division to an occasional show of timely interest, and more extensive displays or those of major import (which were held in the main lobby at the Fifth Avenue entrance or in the large exhibition hall, later reduced to office space) required special planning. Coordination was maintained by an official committee, there being no formal exhibitions department. However, the relocation of the Music Division in 1942 to more spacious quarters on the 42nd Street level allowed for the construction of modest though

[14]During the depression years he engaged three promising young candidates to fill a single full-time opening on his staff in order to encourage them to continue their graduate studies in music. The incumbents were Margaret Wing, Catherine Keyes, and Henry Leland Clarke, all of whom became successful scholars. He later arranged for Margaret Wing to teach at Sarah Lawrence College, and Catherine Keyes to take a post in the art library at Columbia University. (Ms. Keyes turned to librarianship, which she served with great distinction as Head of the 58th Street Music Library and one-time Acting Chief of the Music Division.) Henry Leland Clarke remained as reference assistant for four years, after which he entered a long teaching career as musicologist and composer. On principle, CSS refused to be bogged down by the narrowing requirements of a Library-School degree, preferring rather to have specialists in the subject field. The Music Division Staff subsequently included one or more eminent scholars trained abroad. Notable among them were Dr. Curt Sachs, engaged as Consultant (1937–52), Dr. Hans T. David, an assistant editor of music publications (1937–49), and Dr. Joseph Braunstein, as paleographer and Beethoven specialist (1950–57).

attractive exhibit cases in its entrance corridor, giving it a measure of independence in carrying out a full program.

Lectures and concerts correlated with exhibitions became a pattern, and as often happened, one or another of these activities resulted in the enhancement of the division's collections, through gifts of valuable material it would not otherwise have acquired.[15] During the years 1942 to 1959, eighty-nine exhibitions were mounted in the Music Division cases,[16] most of them organized by this writer, although the program was initially assigned to Dr. Sachs. A joint staff effort, they covered a broad spectrum of subjects, the majority within the scope of individual specialties: Americana, dance, rare books and manuscripts, instruments, recordings, opera, etc. All exhibits were designed to attract the casual viewer as well as the informed musician and scholar.

During this period, the Dance Section was especially active—in the occasional use of building-wide facilities—in planning elaborate exhibitions and receptions for international dance companies and leading dance personalities. The first visit to New York of the Paris Opera Ballet (Fall, 1948) was thus honored by several displays and a specially arranged concert of music in the time of Louis XIV. Another such occasion centered around a series of six lectures on the subject of "Dance and its Allied Arts," inaugurated with the cooperation of Walter Terry, dance critic of *The New York Herald-Tribune*. The speakers, in addition to Mr. Terry, were Ruth Page, American choreographer, and

[15]Notable examples of this were two exhibitions: "Ten Celebrated European-American Composers," autographs, manuscripts of their works created while residing in the United States; and "Pathfinders in American Music." Both of these brought permanent deposits of all the manuscripts exhibited, including those of Martinu, Rathaus, Toch, Varèse, Ruggles, Ives, etc. Two concert series: the "Regional Concerts" highlighting the work of the younger composers in Austria, Belgium, Brazil, Canada, Denmark, Finland, Greece, Holland, Hungary, Israel, Norway, Rumania, Sweden, Switzerland, and Yugoslavia (yielding substantial gifts of their published music through the cooperation of national agencies—a fine gesture toward improving international understanding); and "The Composer's Forum Laboratory Concerts" (making regular deposits of works performed in the Library's Americana Collection, from the time of its inception in 1935 through the period of its reactivation in 1947).

[16]In previous years, music was represented in several major shows occupying the Exhibition Hall, as well as a number of others held elsewhere in the building. It also figured prominently in the library's "Exhibition of One Hundred Treasures" celebrating its one-hundredth anniversary, and in the five-year "Notable Acquisitions," shows. Perhaps the most outstanding exhibition in the history of the division was the display of 450 rare items acquired in the Berlin auction of the famous Wolffheim Collection shortly before CSS's appointment.

Norman Lloyd, composer. The highlight of the following year was the reception for the Sadler's Wells Ballet Company, again with elaborate exhibits, and seen by several thousand people. These events succeeded admirably in drawing attention to the long-felt need for establishing a dance research center in New York.

Traditionally the art of the dance had been treated by librarians as a subject most closely allied to music and was therefore always conceived as part of the music collection. It was not until the Music Division moved, in 1942, that the idea of creating a separate section, devoted solely to the literature and iconography of the dance, was first made possible. The welcome change offered an opportunity to restudy the entire shelving situation since the music collection was now brought together in one area for the first time. Books on the dance were pulled from their customary locations in the stacks, and, together with all related materials, were placed temporarily in the rear office. By 1944, two staff members were given part-time assignments to deal with the complex task of sorting, filing and processing the many different items in the collection, and developing a variety of auxiliary files as necessary research aids.

Like many of the larger music libraries of the world, the NYPL already possessed a respectable collection of books on the art and history of dancing (an estimated 5,000 volumes in the central building alone), much of which was scattered and poorly catalogued, making their access difficult, even for the most experienced researchers. A full-time librarian with curatorial skills and an enthusiasm for the subject was needed to draw the material together and to begin building a true archival collection. Fortunately for the library, and for the world of the dance at large, such a person appeared in 1947. Genevieve Oswald accepted the challenge, and by 1948 assumed full responsibility. With incredible energy and imagination, and with the constant assistance and encouragement of the chief, together with a number of foundation grants, and important people in the field, she took hold of the monumental task. In due course she was able to attract substantial gifts of great historical value from illustrious dance personalities and private collectors, and to process and catalogue them, along with complementary material of many kinds. All this was accomplished while engaging in special projects, such as promoting an international exchange of copies of rare photos, and exploring every possible means of recording dance history in performance, as well as maintaining up-to-date coverage of the contemporary scene.

One of CSS's hopes from the beginning was that one day the Dance Archives would be in a position to document as completely as possible modern dance in America. This had come close to being achieved, even as early as 1952, by the acquisition in rapid succession of the personal collections of Ted Shawn and Ruth St. Denis (1950), Charles Weidman and Doris Humphrey (1951) and Hanya Holm and Mary Wigman (1952). Together with the fabulous Cia Fuonaroli Collection presented by Walter Toscanini in memory of this wife (1955), rich in historical, theoretical, and technical documentation, these collections had placed the Division in the foremost position among dance libraries in the United States. CSS could hardly have conceived of such progress when he assigned Miss Oswald to the dance project in 1947, much less that she would ultimately build an archive of world importance and bring it to the status of an independent Division in the relatively short span of seventeen years.

What could not be done sooner for the dance, by the end of 1945, had already been accomplished for the Theatre Collection when it finally attained division status after functioning for years as a subsection of the main reading room. Its extraordinary development, particularly in the documentation of the American Theatre, was largely the work of one man, the eminent critic and scholar, George Freedley. Common interests with the Music Division and overlapping of materials (in musical comedy, opera, theatrical dance, incidental music to the drama, etc.) drew the two department heads together in frequent conferences and decisions. CSS subsequently played a leading role in persuading the authorities to place the theatrical arts on the same level as that of music in the hierarchy of research collections in the NYPL.[17]

In the midst of these notable developments for the performing arts collections, the Administration was wrestling with the gravest financial

---

[17]So spectacular was the growth of the Theatre Collection in the following decade that two awards were presented to Mr. Freedley by theatrical groups in recognition of its "exceptional and outstanding service" and "unusual contribution to the American Stage." In the same year (1956), Miss Oswald received the Capezio Award for her work as curator, which was undoubtedly inspired by Freedley's dedicated leadership.

crisis in the history of the century- old institution. The private support
of its foundation funds was being eroded by fifteen years of depression,
war, and inflation, resulting in a progressive deterioration of some of its
collections and services, just when these resources should have been
expanding. Funds were sorely needed to counter the higher costs of
materials and the disgracefully low staff salaries. While preparing for an
annual gift campaign to be initiated among corporation users of the
library,[18] division chiefs were asked to reexamine their budgets and
estimate immediate needs. In his report to the trustees, CSS used this
opportunity to make a strong personal plea on behalf of the grossly
underpaid music librarians and the need to recognize them as
"specialists" (conceded by the American Library Association)—a battle
he ultimately won when position classifications and pay plans introduced by the new Director were drawn up and approved. About the
same time he also managed to obtain support for an urgent remodelling
of the Music Division's reading room after some alarming losses, to
insure the protection of rare materials and to make possible a properly
controlled study area for their use. A glass-panelled "reserve" alcove
was constructed and constant supervision instituted—a move long over-
due. By assigning a senior staff member to take responsibility for the
administration, care, and growth of the rare book, manuscript, and other
special collections, another vital subsection of the Music Division was
brought into being.[19]

More frustration came in the early 1950's, this time in the name of
progress. It was the institution of the so-called "jet" cataloguing proce-

---

[18]A more vigorous, full-fledged fund raising effort was later adopted that was directed
to the general public. This was realized in time to coincide with the library's 100th
Anniversary. The annual fund drives were placed in the hands of an executive officer,
one of several new positions created by the recently appointed Director, Ralph Beals,
for the sake of a more efficient, library-wide administrative structure.

[19]The enormous task of reorganizing and recataloguing these precious resources was
completed only after the move to Lincoln Center (in 1965), when lavish space and
modern air-conditioned facilities were provided. The area set aside for this purpose,
which also included the Americana Section, is known as "Special Collections." The
move provided the opportunity to house the rich collection of letters and manuscript
scores of the great composers formerly held in the Manuscript Division, and to process
the Muller Iconography Collection. Since 1944, microfilm reproductions of rare
materials in other libraries had been acquired to fill gaps in Music Division holdings and
have become a major resource with the establishment of The Toscanini Memorial
Archives at Lincoln Center. A special room filled with numerous reading machines now
makes up for the lack of such facilities at 42nd Street.

dures, devised after a survey by an outside agency to relieve the crippling backlog of new acquisitions. Simplification was the key toward hastening the process. Unfortunately, it resulted in destroying the very features of the Music Division Catalogue which made it a unique research tool in the field.[20] Ironically, the special nature of music was recognized by the surveyors who found it "unpractical to study its problems intensively" (as had the American Library Association when it relinquished the established cataloguing code in favor of the one drafted by the Music Library Association.) To make matters worse, the Preparations Division chose to ignore the highly trained and experienced music cataloguers (including the distinguished and scholarly Inger Christensen, nationally known as one of the innovators of the Code) by placing them under non-specialist supervision, to the obvious detriment of the quality of the work produced. Even priorities were left to the decision of the General Catalogue Section. What had been desperately needed was the employment of additional qualified music cataloguers—only two were on the staff—an ever recurring recommendation of the Chief of the Music Division over the years. (CSS was supported in the 30's and 40's by Mr. Lydenberg, who was committed unconditionally to accurate and informative cataloguing, and would have frowned upon the "jet" production introduced in later years, certainly in the case of music.)

A happy set of circumstances in 1955 presented more than a glimmer of hope that the dream of establishing a music-library museum might yet be realized. The antiquated structure long occupied by the Metropolitan Opera Company on West 39th Street had been demolished, and Carnegie Hall, where the New York Philharmonic Orchestra performed for almost a century was about to meet the same fate. The trustees of each of these venerable institutions, having become

---

[20]The Music Division Catalogue, painstakingly built over a period of twenty-five years, was second to none. The inclusion of useful bibliographical information, often difficult to obtain otherwise, as well as the wealth of analytical notes, made it a boon to both laymen and to the serious researcher. Its scope was considerably extended by the inclusion of cards for books having sections on music and located elsewhere in the central library, and, for a brief period, musical *incipits* were added at the behest of the Chief, who was a firm believer in such aids. Numerous specialized auxiliary files were developed and maintained, even if only sporadically in times of stress or reduced staff. One of Inger Christensen's greatest contributions to the profession was the extensive publisher's plate file she developed which provided a valuable means for dating musical materials of the eighteenth and nineteenth centuries.

involved in urgent planning for permanent homes, happened to consult
with the same architect, Wallace K. Harrison, and it was he who suggested the idea of a common site which could be made part of a
performing arts center. When the possibility arose of purchasing land
in a slum area at Lincoln Square which was marked for urban renewal,
an approach was made to John D. Rockefeller III, Chairman of the
Rockefeller Foundation, for his reaction and support. A series of conferences resulted and an Exploratory Committee for a Music Arts
Center, headed by Mr. Rockefeller, was formed to investigate the
potentialities of such a partnership. CSS, a member of the Board of both
the Metropolitan Opera and the New York Philharmonic, closely followed the developments, and before long was able to inform the library
authorities of a tentative, though positive interest in his library-museum
project as part of the future planning.

In June of 1956, the Lincoln Center for the Performing Arts Inc.
was officially announced as a membership organization. To fulfill its
mission in advancing the performing arts, education was an essential
consideration. The most appropriate constituents in this area were the
Juilliard School of Music, which had just added a drama department to
its music and dance programs, and the NYPL with its fine circulating
facility, world-famous research collections, and rapidly developing unique resources in both theatre and dance, making it equally attractive to
the supporters of the center. The chief functions of the proposed
library-museum, as initially envisioned by them, were to receive the
anticipated throngs of visitors during the daytime hours, i.e., "to serve
as a focal point for guided tours of the center," the museum activities
"to interpret and illuminate the entire range of the performing arts."
Apparently the research aspects were considered secondary.

In the following year, the library trustees appointed a committee
of distinguished citizens of varied points of view to consider the need
for a specialized library-museum,[21] and CSS was asked to prepare a
preliminary report for the committee, giving his ideas derived from years

[21]The committee was made up of the following: Gilbert W. Chapman, Chairman ,
President of the Library; Frederick H. Burkhardt, President of the American Council
of Learned Societies; C. Scott Fletcher, President of the Fund for Adult Education;
Donald Oenslager, Scene Designer; and Howard Taubman, Music Critic of *The New
York Times*. Davidson Taylor, then the new Director of the Arts Center Program at
Columbia University, served as Consultant.

of planning, and including the more recent results of his intensive consultations with library and museum specialists, educators, and authorities in the performing arts. A nineteen-page preliminary report, submitted in December of 1957, was meant as a guide for the *ad hoc* committee or "summary of your thinking." It described in some detail the objectives and scope of "the various elements which could make up a well-rounded and serviceable whole." After receiving a favorable report, the library board, on 10 June 1959, approved "in principle" its entry into the center as a constituent member, provided that financial arrangements "be obtained outside the library's present resources."

Having established the mold for the Music Division's future, CSS felt the moment had arrived for him to leave his library post, which he had held for twenty-eight years, and focus his energies on his Latin-American interests.[22] Nelson Rockefeller, with whom he had been associated earlier in the performing arts section of an inter-American affairs exchange program, urged him to take on the directorship of the newly founded Brazilian Institute at New York University. The timing of the decision to resign may also have been prompted by dissatisfaction with certain ill-advised actions taken by top administration following the trustees' tentative acceptance of the Lincoln Center constituency. Be that as it may, his invaluable services were lost to the institution just when they were most needed.

It was not until the Spring of l961 that the Library authorities gave their final approval to the transfer of the music, dance, and theatre collections to Lincoln Center as part of a performing arts complex. The years of setbacks in the implementation of the library-museum concept

---

[22]Dr. Smith's wartime service as Cultural Relations Officer in Brazil for the State Department, his lecture tours in South America, and university courses on Latin-American Civilization are representative of these interests. In music, his efforts toward a closer cooperation between North and South America began in the late '30's, when he delivered a report in Washington to a State Department Committee on library aspects of the problem (9 October 1939). The next year representatives of the Pan-American Union came to New York to consult with him about material to acquire for a better understanding of LatinAmerican music in this country. The library's collection (including folk music, printed works of serious composers, and several hundred items in manuscript) still continues to grow. It should also be mentioned that, at this time, he was also quite active in establishing contact with the leading musical scholars and composers, many of whom were later frequent visitors to this country. A special effort was made to secure funds to enable him to invite "ten musicologists or composers interested in research from the Southern continent" to attend the International Musicological Congress held in New York in September of 1939.

undoubtedly contributed to an atmosphere of over-caution on their part. To compound matters, strong protests came from important members of the scholarly community (through an official petition from the American Musicological Society), appalled at the prospect of being deprived of ready access to material in related subject fields, a feature which had earned the NYPL a unique place among the great libraries of the world. Furthermore, grave doubts were expressed about the research potential in a center primarily orientated toward performance. Deliberations were carried on for many months before the overriding physical advantages—the promise of lavish space and modern facilities, including air-conditioned stacks—and the opportunity for better working conditions, as well as new and improved services ultimately prevailed. The Library and Museum of the Performing Arts opened its doors in November of 1965.

Despite his no longer being a party to the proceedings, CSS has maintained a lively interest in the development and activities of the center, though some of them have fallen short of his ideal. He views, with understandably paternal pride, his thriving brainchildren in the Performing Arts Library: the newly created Division of the Dance, the impressive facilities of the Rogers and Hammerstein Archives of Recorded Sound (which has since also attained division status), the ever-expanding Americana section, sharing space in the Special Collections area with the Rare Books and Manuscripts, and Iconography, and the flourishing Toscanini Memorial Archives of the great composers' holographs, the latest addition to the research resources designed to encourage scholarship among performers. The ultimate realization of the latter was a matter of vital interest to him; he was a member of the original committee of five, organized in 1961, to consider its reactivation after a lull of twenty-five years, later lending his name as a founder and member of the official working committee. More recently he conducted one of the series of lecture-demonstrations. These occasional forays into the old influence pattern, and his constant readiness to offer advice and guidance to younger colleagues, serve to endear him among those fortunate enough to have this contact.

After many years of separation from the library profession, the Music Library Association saw fit in 1984 to honor him with the following citation:

> In recognition of his distinguished services the Music Library Association awards this citation to Carleton Sprague Smith, flutist, scholar, librarian, administrator, and friend to all who care for music. His imagination has inspired the achievements of three generations, and his vision of the performing arts has been realized in the structure of librarianship and scholarship today.

The following year a reception was held in the Vincent Astor Gallery at Lincoln Center, where the library staff, administration officials, colleagues, and many friends and scholars gathered to pay tribute to CSS on his eightieth birthday. The audience was reminded of the role he played through the years in furthering the concept of a library-museum of the performing arts, reflected in the manner in which he shaped the Music Division, and its relation to the sister arts of dance, theatre, and recorded sound.

REFERENCES CITED

Maré, Rolf de
    1937   "New Directions in the European Ballet," *Dance International 1900 – 1937* (Rockefeller Center, New York, Nov. 29, 1937 to Jan. 2, 1938). Souvenir program (New York: n. p.), 31–32.

Sonneck, Oscar
    1917   "Music in Our Libraries," *The Art World*, 2(3):242–44 (New York).

David Hall

THE RODGERS AND HAMMERSTEIN ARCHIVES OF RECORDED SOUND, THE NEW YORK PUBLIC LIBRARY AT LINCOLN CENTER

A Personal View of its Evolution and Essence (1965–1985)

PREFACE

That the Rodgers and Hammerstein Archives of Recorded Sound (RHARS) came into being and became eventually one of the world's great repositories and research services in its field was due in a very significant measure to the encouragement of Carleton Sprague Smith during his tenure as Chief of The New York Public Library's (NYPL) Music Division (1931–43; 1946–59). After World War II, Dr. Smith was fortunate to have as his Assistant Chief, Philip L. Miller, a major authority on the history, literature, and materials of recorded sound, to whom he delegated the task of acquiring—for the Library—recordings and printed materials that were to become the basis of the RHARS which opened for public service at Lincoln Center in November of 1965. (In 1959, Mr. Miller succeeded Dr. Smith as Chief of the Library's Music Division.)

Dr. Smith's efforts on behalf of establishing a sound archive at the NYPL were focused on stimulating interest among recording and broadcasting executives, as well as other arts institutions that had potential for playing a cooperative role. After the RHARS became a

---

David Hall was Head, then Curator of the RHARS from 1967 to 1983. He is presently classical recordings consultant to the National Academy of Recording Arts and Sciences and contributing editor to Stereo Review.

fact of life at the Performing Arts Division's new quarters at Lincoln Center, Dr. Smith continued his active interest; and after this writer became Head of the RHARS, in 1967 (having been previously a classical recordings producer and magazine editor), Dr. Smith was a frequent visitor and user of the facilities, as well as a provocative and highly constructive gadfly for a then novice in the art of research library administration. A major result was Dr. Smith's enlistment of the interest of philanthropist Francis Goelet in the fortunes of the RHARS. Goelet, together with the Rodgers and Hammerstein families and the late George Lauder Greenway, became one of the chief and continuing benefactors of the archives.

What follows is an updating and revision of articles written by the undersigned in 1974 and 1977.[1] Most of the first-hand material stems from the author's tenure as Head, and subsequently as Curator of the RHARS from February of 1967 until late June of 1983, as well as Consultant until late May of 1985. Special thanks are due the present Curator of the RHARS, Donald McCormick, for allowing me un-restricted access to internal files and annual reports. The views expressed here are the author's own and do not necessarily reflect those of the NYPL or its administration.

CRITERIA AND PRE-HISTORY

In the 1977 *Billboard* article, cited in note 1, this writer set forth in question-cum-commentary format what he deemed to be basic standards differentiating a sound recordings archive from a record collection or a sound recordings repository:

1. Is the collection comprehensive—in terms either of broad coverage for the whole field of recordings, or in terms of intensive and deep coverage of a special area: jazz, classical, country, spoken, vertical-cut records, radio daytime serials, etc.?

2. Is there catalog access to the collection? Without a catalog providing minimum basic access by way of performer, com-

---

[1]See "The Rodgers and Hammerstein Archives of Recorded Sound," *Journal of the Association for Recorded Sound Collections*, 6(2) (1974): 17–31 and "Storing Solid Gold for the Future," in the special sound recordings centennial issue of the recording industry trade publication, *Billboard* (May 12, 1977), 108–9, 115.

posers, title, geographical region, label-number—either singly and/or in combination, the largest and most carefully assembled collection is of use only to its original owner.

3. Is the collection and its catalog open to the public? "Public" in this instance means those qualified by interest and/or experience to make fruitful use of the collection and its catalog. Public use in this context would indicate that the collection holdings are available for properly controlled on-premises listening.[2]

4. Are there facilities for assuring preservation of the collection holdings, in terms of both temperature-humidity controlled storage and in terms of transfer of unique and fragile. . . recordings to on-premises public service tapes?

5. Does the collection maintain a comprehensive reference library of books, discographies, periodicals, company catalogs, sleeve/album notes, etc.?

6. Does the collection issue or sponsor publications that contribute to the sum total of knowledge in the field? Does it collaborate with other archives and/or private collectors in the pooling of knowledge and techniques in the area of archival sound recordings collecting and service?

The road traversed by the RHARS toward meeting these standards has been an arduous one for its staff and for the NYPL administration. While lack of know-how has occasionally resulted in crisis or outright failure, the major roadblocks along the way have been those suffered in common by most library-archival institutions—money and effectively deployed manpower.

June 1937 marks the date when the Music Division of the NYPL began to acquire and catalog recorded sound materials and to include by extension, under this rubric, record manufacturers' catalogs and related periodical and printed materials, much of which had already been part of the division's holdings. The stimulus for this came as the

---

[2]The conclusion of no. 3, as published in 1977, inconclusively touched on the knotty and delicate subject of acceding to user requests for single-copy audio duplications from collection holdings. Today, it would appear reasonable and realistic that a sound recordings archive should be able to provide such service insofar as it does not infringe on copyright, or legally constituted proprietary right, or constitute unfair commercial competition.

result of a gift of 500 78 rpm phonograph discs from Columbia Records instigated by the Music Division Chief, Carleton Sprague Smith. Philip L. Miller, most knowledgeable among the Music Division staff on the matter of sound recordings and a well-established reviewer of vocal discs in his own right, was invited to take on the organizational and cataloging work with an eye toward a future establishment of a sound recordings archive. Shortly thereafter, Mr. Miller prepared a memorandum-prospectus: *Proposed Phonograph Archive–New York City* which encompassed the record collection proper, listening facilities, record manufacturer's catalogs and related materials, a recording studio, and a phonograph collection. An eleven-hour, six-days-a-week public service schedule was indicated.

Philip Miller's memorandum of January 11, 1938 suggested the use of help from the Works Progress Administration and from a Carnegie Corporation Grant to develop and catalog sound recordings holdings. The WPA proposal was subsequently implemented and the Music Division also became recipient of the special Carnegie Collection of 78 rpm phonograph recordings, its card catalog, and associated playback equipment.

The following year brought into the picture the first of several major benefactors, in the person of George Lauder Greenway, then associated with the Metropolitan Museum of Art, who eventually became Board Chairman of the Metropolitan Opera. The first of Mr. Greenway's benefactions was seemingly modest—but in view of future developments, of special significance—for he enabled the library to purchase from a private collector a dozen of the unique wax cylinder recordings that Met Librarian, Lionel S. Mapleson, had taken from 1901–03 actual stage performances during the pre-Caruso "Golden Age." Heretofore, it had been believed that the extant cylinders, some 120 in all, had come into the custodianship of William H. Seltsam of Bridgeport, Connecticut, whose International Record Collectors' Club had been instrumental in making available on its label historical vocal discs that had become unobtainable over the years following the advent of electrical recording in 1925. The entire saga of how the library, through Mr. Greenway's good offices, gained access to all of the known surviving Mapleson cylinders, and how it succeeded by the end of 1985 in issuing an integral LP album edition of their contents is recounted in full detail by this writer and others in the album monograph and in three issues of *Recorded Sound*.[3]

In 1941, with World War II ravaging Europe and Pearl Harbor only months away, a revised sound archive proposal submitted to Davidson Taylor of the CBS radio network elicited, on August 4, a courteous but non-committal reply. United States entry into the war following the December 7th attack on Pearl Harbor, and Philip Miller's entry into military service, put an abrupt halt to further efforts along this line until 1947. In that year Dr. Smith had returned to his post as Music Division Chief following a three year stint in Brazil for the United States Foreign Service in the field of inter-American cultural exchange.

As part of a renewed and more intensive effort to get the sound recordings archive project off the ground, a committee was established which included officials from the "Big 3" United States record companies—RCA-Victor, Columbia, and Decca. An immediate result was the agreement among the three firms to contribute current classical music product to the library's collection.

As far back as 1932, Dr. Smith had conceived the idea of a "Library-Museum" of the Performing Arts incorporating music, theatre, dance, and sound recordings, as well as related film materials. This thinking was reflected to a degree in the May 1935 proposal that the Museum of Modern Art might become involved. Now, in 1947, the thought was to house the proposed sound archive in the Andrew Carnegie Mansion at 91st Street and Fifth Avenue, along with the early instrument collection from the Metropolitan Museum of Art. Also involved in these discussions was the Juilliard School of Music and its innovative composer-president, William Schuman. This writer, too, became seriously involved, to the extent of being invited to prepare a detailed prospectus—a document that subsequently gained wide circulation via the United States Commission for UNESCO. Regrettably, no solid agreement was reached among the interested institutions. Nor

[3]See "The Mapleson Cylinder Project: A Preliminary Report," *Journal of the Association for Recorded Sound Collections*, 13(3) (1981): 5–12; "A Provisional Mapleson Cylinder Chronology," *Op. cit.*: 13–20; and "A Mapleson Afterword: Further Notes on the Mapleson Cylinder Project," *Ibid.* 14(1) (1982): 5–10. See also "The Mapleson Cylinder Project," *Recorded Sound*, No. 82 (July 1982): 35–39; "The Mapleson Cylinder Project: Repertoire, Peformers and Recording Dates," *Ibid.*, No. 83 (January 1983): 21–55; and "The Mapleson Cylinder Project: A Mapleson Cylinder Notebook," *Ibid.*, No. 86 (July 1984): 5–28.

did any positive results come of the approaches made during 1951–53, first to the Reichold Foundation and then to David Kapp at Decca Records, with the suggestion that the proposed archive be a memorial to his late brother and company founder, Jack Kapp. Even so, the library's sound recordings holdings continued to grow, so that in the 1957 summer issue of the *Bulletin* of the newly established British Institute of Recorded Sound, Philip Miller was able to report, in an article on sound archival activity at the NYPL, that the record collection then numbered some 30,000 items.

BREAKTHROUGH AND BIRTH OF THE RODGERS AND HAMMERSTEIN ARCHIVES OF RECORDED SOUND

By 1962, Dr. Smith had been succeeded as Music Division Chief by Philip Miller; but his 1932 dream of a Library-Museum of the Performing Arts, which he had set forth in full detail in December of 1957 (*The Lincoln Center Library-Museum of the Performing Arts–A Preliminary Report*) was now well on the way to realization, for the NYPL had now made firm the decision to incorporate its Performing Arts Divisions—Dance (which Dr. Smith had originated initially as part of the Music Division in 1947), Music, and Theatre—into the Lincoln Center for the Performing Arts complex, for which ground had been broken by President Dwight D. Eisenhower on May 14, 1959.

After the NYPL Board Chairman Gilbert Chapman had conducted his friend, composer Richard Rodgers, through the makeshift basement storage facilities for the sound recordings collection, Rodgers agreed to contribute through the Rodgers and Hammerstein Foundation $150,000 toward the establishment of a sound archive to be incorporated into the library's new performing arts facilities at Lincoln Center as part of the Music Division, thus fulfilling twenty-five years of unremitting effort on the part of Division Chief, Philip Miller.

Jean Bowen, one of the most forceful and imaginative of the Music Division's staff members, was named Head and was charged with organizing and cataloging the collection's sound recordings and printed materials, recruiting staff, and having public service audition and research facilities ready for the Fall 1965 opening. By this time the sound recordings collection had grown to more than 100,000 items—most having been contributed by private donors, with the balance being represented by recording industry gifts of current product, which for the past dozen or more years had been appearing in micro-groove long-play and 7-inch 45 rpm formats.

PREPARATION: "THE RODGERS AND HAMMERSTEIN PROJECT"

Jean Bowen and her staff of four were faced initially with moving the more than 100,000 78 rpm, LP, and 45 rpm discs, along with several hundred cylinder recordings, including the unique Maplesons, from the basement of the 42nd Street Central Building to the Library Annex on the far West Side at 43rd Street. Following a basic sort-search-weed operation, crucial decisions had to be made regarding what was to be included in the public card catalog. For some 36,000 78 rpm discs. there already existed a card catalog, compiled by a variety of hands and in a variety of styles over a twenty-five year period under Philip Miller's direction. Even so, there remained a sizable backlog of uncataloged and unsearched 78 rpm material that would have to wait a good twenty years before a serious effort could be made to provide minimum basic public access.

In terms of providing immediate public access per repertoire item in the collection, there was no alternative but to concentrate cataloging effort on the 29,000 LP's and on the relatively small quantity of 45's. Besides these and the aforementioned cylinder recordings, uncataloged holdings to be moved to Lincoln Center included several thousand 16-inch radio transcription discs, as well as 12- and 16-inch instantaneous "acetate" discs stemming from broadcast or field documentary sources, as well as the beginnings of an audio tape collection. Also to be included in the official public catalog were all printed materials pertaining to sound recordings heretofore stored in the Music Division stacks. In addition to the standard book literature on the subject, there were virtually complete runs of every English language record periodical on recorded sound and substantial holdings of material in French and German—the latter including the *Phonographische Zeitschrift*, the industry periodical dating from the turn of the century. Finally, and most importantly, there were extensive holdings of record manufacturers' catalogs and supplemental flyers from all over the world, dating from the earliest Edison and Bettini cylinders to that time. For relevant printed material held by other divisions—Dance, Music, Theatre, and Science and Technology—catalog cross-index entries were provided.

While the Rodgers and Hammerstein Project staff was providing the groundwork for the full cataloging of micro-groove discs and printed material that eventually was to emerge from the Preparation Services at the Central Building, there was the physical plant to be attended to at Lincoln Center. This phase of the operation included not only all the special shelving and office equipment, but more especially the audio playback and control equipment, the design, construction, and installation of which was contracted to the firm of Bolt, Baranek & Newman.

The reading areas for the Dance, Music, and Theatre Divisions were spread over the entire top floor of the library's new Lincoln Center building at 111 Amsterdam Avenue, together with executive offices for Division Chiefs and for the Group Chief of the Performing Arts Research Center, Thor E. Wood. The listening-reading area for the RHARS was cleverly sandwiched on the north side of the floor between the Dance and Theatre areas, with the public card catalog ranged along the north wall and shelves for current printed material and the reference desk placed just adjacent to the entrance way. Directly opposite the public reference desk were placed, running south to north, two double rows of ten carrels each equipped for headphone listening. Of the total of twenty carrels, only ten were provided with control units. However, four of these had auxiliary headphone receptacles, thus making it possible for two users to hear the same program material. For group listening, there was a special loudspeaker-equipped audition room with its own control unit. A sizable reading table completed the major furnishings of the listening-reading area. There was also "backstage" office space, as well as a workroom behind the public reference desk.

The listening carrel stereophonic control units were a unique and innovative feature for the middle 1960's; in addition to controls for adjusting volume, treble-bass balance, stereo separation and balance, each unit was provided with a set of controls for use with tape playback—*start*, *stop*, *reverse*, and *fast-forward*. Finally, each unit had a set of command buttons —chiefly for use with disc audition—enabling the user to let the playback operator know 1) when he was ready to listen, and 2) if there was playback trouble, such as a mis-tracking disc or faulty audio reception.

When actual audio equipment installation was begun at RHARS, the initial plan was to have the disc and tape playback equipment on the top floor, easily accessible to the carrel listening stations. But with the sound recordings shelved five floors below, the impracticability of this arrangement quickly became evident, and, at great expense, wiring and conduits had to be installed, allowing all playback equipment to be placed in the basement, in the area adjacent to the sound recordings collection.

As finally installed, the playback equipment included six three-speed disc turntables with weight-adjustable tone-arms and interchangeable styli, thus enabling accommodation of both micro-groove (LP and 45 rpm) and coarse-groove (78 rpm) records. There also were four professional Ampex tape machines, which, between them, could handle playback speeds of 3.75 ips, 7.5 ips, and 15 ips in any currently standard track configuration. Audio and servo-patch bays made it possible to change playback channels from one carrel to another, as necessary. Playback monitoring on the part of the operator was carried out via headphones, but this was soon supplanted by a loudspeaker system and push-button bay that could tap any channel at will.

PUBLIC SERVICE AT RHARS—THE FIRST YEARS

The brand new building that housed the NYPL at Lincoln Center and which opened its doors to the public on November 30, 1965 contained not only the Performing Arts Divisions of the Research Libraries and the newly inaugurated RHARS, but also the corresponding circulating library (Branch Libraries) facilities, including a superb open-shelf record library and do-it-yourself on-premises playback equipment. A children's library, two handsome exhibition galleries, and an elegant small auditorium completed the areas open to the public. The basement area, in addition to the RHARS sound recordings and playback equipment, boasted a superbly equipped work shop and photo processing laboratory for exhibition projects.

For all the sparkling new appearance of things, the process of developing truly efficient and relatively error-free servicing of audition requests submitted by RHARS users to the public reference desk was an extraordinarily long and arduous one. It was not until the end of 1980 that verbal communication by internal phone to the playback operators became supplanted by closed circuit television that could display the request slips as written by the user. This eventually was replaced by computer print-out key- boarded from the public reference desk. Meanwhile phonetic ambiguities, such as confusing "A" for "8" when transmitting record numbers, not to speak of problems inherent in pronouncing titles in many languages other than English made for frequent service delays. Nor need we dwell on the problems of dealing with the varied styles, legible and otherwise, of user penmanship.

Servicing printed materials from the closed-stack collections was a fairly straightforward affair, save that in the early days of the RHARS, these were at the other end of the floor adjacent to the Music Division stacks, thus requiring the use of not-always-available page service. This was solved over the years by moving all printed materials into the RHARS office areas, which for a variety of reasons did not become possible until the mid-1970's.

As with most major research libraries, particularly those accessible to the general public, letter and telephone reference services were provided from the start. However, the lack of adequate secretarial help, through the early 1980's, made for difficulties in promptly servicing letter inquiries. Local area inquiries, were handled by phone whenever possible; the telephone reference service, as it developed over the years, became a point of pride with the R & H staff.

During the first years, the RHARS attempted to maintain public service on a basic six-day 12 noon to 6:00 P. M. schedule. In September 1984, this schedule was later arranged to match that of the other Performing Arts Divisions, including night hours to 8:00 P.M. on Mondays and Thursdays.

As with other major research libraries accessible to the general public, there has always existed the problem of restricting accessibility to a public qualified in terms of professional/scholarly interest and need—an acute situation when dealing with users involved in the performing arts. At times it was almost impossible to distinguish between the would-be user, whose interests and qualifications were "professional," and one, whose primary interest in occupying the limited carrel space and playback schedule was purely for personal pleasure. It was hoped that the existence, on the main floor and mezzanine of the Lincoln Center building, of an open-stack record lending library of some

20,000 LP's, plus on-floor listening facilities, would ease the demands on RHARS from unqualified users; but since many record requests were not available in the record lending library, there was need for a somewhat restrictive policy. Early attempts by the Performing Arts Divisions to maintain an admission card system did not take long to break down; and it was left to the individual public reference desk librarian to handle all requests for use on case-by-case basis.

Until the RHARS achieved status as an independent Performing Arts Division as of January 1, 1980, basic full-time staffing during the greater part of the preceding decade-and-a-half remained at five— three librarians, including the Head, a Library Technical Assistant qualified to man the public reference desk, and a Supervising Audio Technician, eventually raised to the level of Sound Engineer. All were qualified to operate the disc and tape playback equipment, and only the Supervising Audio Technician was exempt from handling librarian and public reference desk assignments. Part-time help, nominally pages, were eventually trained to operate the playback equipment and to handle user audition requests.

Given this staffing arrangement, public services at RHARS could be handled by as few as three on a 12:00 noon to 6:00 P.M. schedule, as well as on Saturdays—usually the busiest day of the week.

While the public service schedule followed that format, staff hours on either a 9:00 to 5:00, or 10:00 to 6:00 individual schedule allowed for the performance of basic housekeeping and administrative chores, plus a modicum of cataloging and accessioning, essential sorting and searching of the disc collection, playback equipment maintenance, and a modest amount of transfer to service tapes of disc material deemed too fragile or too rare for regular playback use.

COLLECTION DEVELOPMENT—FIRST PHASE

Not until the 1980's did the RHARS begin to have regular new acquisitions funding for current sound recordings. Primary sources for additions to the collection comprised private gifts-in-kind and record company donations of current product, in that order. Over the years, monetary gifts and foundation grants played an increasingly significant role. Of singular importance in the former category were early contributions from George Lauder Greenway, and subsequently, a continuing series of generous annual donations from Francis Goelet by way of the Rhode Island Corporation Fund.

As initially shelved at Lincoln Center, the sound recordings collection stood at an estimated 132,175 items. News that the NYPL's record collection was about to become a public service facility at the RHARS provided a major stimulus for large additions donated by New York radio stations, including WQXR and WCBS, which were all too glad to dispose of their holdings of 78 rpm discs. Exceptional, however, was the collection of some 20,000 78 and 45 rpm discs of popular and jazz repertoire from Station WNEW which included, by way of bonus, an elaborate card catalog—one section was comprised entirely of title entries, the other of performers. Despite the fact that the performer entries had to be rigorously weeded to account for the WNEW items that were never sent to Lincoln Center, the end result was incorporated as a separate element of the RHARS public card catalog. In view of their unique value as a reference tool for those interested in documenting American popular music recordings of the 1920 to 1960 era, the title entry trays were left untouched.

A gift from the Calder Foundation made possible the notable acquisition of the remarkable collection of historical piano recordings from the Estate of Jan Holcman.

The development of holdings in the area of non-commercial sound recordings—on instantaneous "acetate" discs, but preferably on tape—was an area of acquisition actively pursued by the RHARS. These included chiefly recordings of broadcast opera repertoire not available in commercial formats, as well as theatre, spoken word, and documentary field recordings.

Even so, the collection, as it existed when the present writer came to RHARS as Head in early 1967, had vast lacunae in many areas, including even electrically-recorded classical fare on 78's, not to mention original cast LP's of Broadway musicals, film soundtrack LP's, historic violin discs, and sizable areas among rarer historic pre-LP labels (in the United States, at least), such as Fonotipia, Gramophone and Typewriter, Zonophone, and Pathé.

While such firms as Columbia, RCA, Mercury, Philips, Deutsche Grammophon, MGM, CRI, and Louisville had been unstintingly generous in providing current releases, many others remained to be added to the corporate donor roster. This writer's previous experience of twenty-five years in and around the recording industry helped remedy this situation to a significant extent; and in a number of instances his efforts resulted in acquisition, not only of current product, but of all available back-catalog material as well: Atlantic, Elektra/Nonesuch, and Folkways come most immediately to mind in this category.

Even so, collection development at RHARS was something of a hit or miss affair. No major gift offerings (1,000 or more items) from private collectors were turned down in the early days, and, as a result, one might wind up with a batch of 78's in wretched condition, mostly surplus duplicates when searched against present holdings, or they might be duplicates that would represent an up-grading over items presently on the shelf, or perhaps there might be a veritable gold mine, figuratively speaking, in the form of Broadway original cast LP's or really rare and valuable historic vocal discs. George Lauder Greenway's 1967 donation of 10,000 discs in the latter category, painstakingly assembled over many years, stands as a prime example in point.

Broadcast tapes acquired from private collectors, such as Barbara Stone, or as donated from the International Music Fund of the Serge Koussevitzky Music Foundation, could be both a boon and a curse. The Stone tapes embodied many unusual operatic broadcasts from the 1950's and 1960's, while the Koussevitzky Foundation tapes offered unusual contemporary music repertoire for which recording grants had been bestowed. However, over the years, it turned out that some of the tape stock was of less than prime quality, with resultant breakage and physical deformation in playback. A continuing problem for many years with donations in reel format was the tendency, on the part of some donors, to have done their taping in speeds and track configurations difficult or impossible to service for RHARS listeners without first re-recording them to a standard format, which was very time-consuming, especially when several hundred items might be involved. The process usually was reserved for truly rare or unique finds, such as the CBS Omnibus TV voice track of *The Green Pastures*.

The biggest single tape acquisition at RHARS came in 1978, when the Brooklyn Public Library turned over 8,000 tapes from the sound archive of New York's Municipal Radio Station, WNYC, with 10,000 instantaneous "acetate" discs following five years later.

While much of the sound recordings acquisition program at RHARS was seemingly hit or miss, major efforts were indeed expended on building up holdings in special subject areas. The Benedict Stambler Memorial Collection of Recorded Jewish Music, the A. F. R. Lawrence Collection of spoken word and documentary recordings, the Maloney Collection of Broadway show and motion picture sound track LP's (the latter two purchased through contributions from Francis Goelet), are just a few outstanding instances of successful efforts along this line. Another prime gift was the Railroad Hour broadcasts of operetta and musical comedy given by Jerome Lawrence and Robert E. Lee.

By the late 1970's the last thing that was needed at RHARS was more gift collections of miscellaneous 78 rpm discs. Monophonic LP's also were becoming a bit much in terms of the proportion of surplus duplicates to welcome new additions. The collection had virtually quadrupled in size, approaching the half-million mark, and by this time had exceeded the nominal capacity of available shelving in the basement of the Lincoln Center building. The whole business had been further complicated, in 1970, with the decision by the Arturo Toscanini family to place on deposit at the Lincoln Center building the entire contents of the Toscanini Riverdale Archives, including all tapes and discs of the Maestro's performances. This collection, now titled "The Toscanini Legacy," was officially acquired by the archives only in 1987.

THE BATTLE FOR BIBLIOGRAPHIC CONTROL

Not only was there no funding available for systematic collection development in the early days of the RHARS, there was nothing available for the cataloging of sound recordings. The funds for this purpose, from the original Rodgers and Hammerstein grant, had been substantially exhausted by the time the Archives opened in late 1965. It was fine to have the existing collection of LP's and the classical music 45's set up in the public card catalog in apple-pie order. The "Miller" card catalog of mostly classical 78's offered a modest bibliographic handle for a decent portion of that part of the collection as then constituted. The WNEW performer card catalog gave public access to a very decent collection of "oldies," popular 78's, and more recent 45's. There was the beginning of a tape collection catalog. But what to do about a collection growth rate that over the following decade would average 20,000 items yearly.

Though the bulk of the RHARS sound recordings collection comprised 78 rpm discs, by far the majority of user requests were for the LP's, with current releases being in as much or more in demand than older items or those deleted from the Schwann catalog.

Sending discs to the cataloging staff at the 42nd Street Central Building was quite out of the question for a variety of reasons, practical as well as fiscal. There was no choice but for the RHARS staff, however minimal, to develop and implement its own bibliographic control procedures.

The public catalog of LP's and classical 45's was a classmarked affair that also had, in addition to a shelflist in classmark order, a full set of cards arranged by record label and serial number. The "Miller" catalog of 78's was likewise classmarked and shelflisted, but lacked a set of alphanumeric cards by label and serial number, a situation that was to give rise to major problems in later years. The WNEW catalog of popular music 78's and 45's used the radio station classmarking system, which was left unchanged in the public catalog. The card catalog of tapes was, for the most part, a composer main-entry affair, with each item assigned an accession number for shelving purposes.

It was decided at the outset of the RHARS public service operations that the classmarked LP catalog could not be continued inasmuch as staffing limitations precluded such full cataloging as had been accomplished under the Rodgers and Hammerstein grant. The "Miller" and WNEW catalogs likewise remained static. The tape catalog, however, continued to expand on the composer main-entry basis, since it never had been subjected to the rigorous procedures applied to the LP/classical 45 discs. To put the matter briefly, it was decided that all new acquisition discs would be shelved in alphanumeric order by label and serial number. As had been the case previously, tapes would continue to appear in the public catalog with composer main-entry and assigned accession number.

It was apparent that the already existing backlog of new acquisition 78's, together with the thousands of additional discs coming in each year would be impossible for the existing staff to cope with. As a result, it was decided that such minimal basic cataloging as could be done would be

restricted to new acquisition LP's and the more important tapes. Even
so, not many years passed before the growth rate of new acquisition LP's
far surpassed this limited cataloging production capacity of the staff, so
that cataloging priority was given to materials received directly from
record manufactures as against those culled from collections received
from private donors. Very rarely, if ever, were such gift collections
accompanied by any kind of catalog or finding list, a notable exception
being the Benedict Stambler Memorial Collection of Recorded Jewish
Music, where the inventory was so arranged as to permit separate
shelving and preparation of a finding list with separate accession numbering.

In the absence of public catalog carding, some control of the
collection was achieved thorough the sizable body of published discographies and catalogs in the respective areas of LP's, 78's, and 45's.
Complete holdings of the *Schwann Long Playing Record and Tape
Guide*, the *Gramophone Classical Catalogue*, and substantially complete runs of the major European LP catalog publications such as
Bielefelder, *Diapason*, etc., as well as the Kurtz Myers MLA compendia,
were indispensable aids for checking holdings on the new acquisition
record shelves as requested by RHARS users. This held true to a wholly
comparable extent for 78's where the *World Encyclopedia of Recorded
Music*, the compendia on pre-electrical recordings by Julian Morton
Moses and Roberto Bauer, plus comparable publications in the areas
of jazz, blues, and spoken word, were essential finding tools. Over the
years, the RHARS staff resorted to comprehensive marginal annotation
of second copies of the major book-format discographies, so that direct
shelf check in response to a user request or telephone inquiry could
become the exception rather than the rule. Indeed, such improvisation
became a regular order of affairs at RHARS, extending to such matters
as using stacked milk bottle crates for shelving tape or polystyrene wine
racks for the storage of Edison Amberol cylinders.

BREAKING THE LOG JAM—THE ADVENT OF THE RIGLER AND DEUTSCH RECORD INDEX AND THE BEGINNINGS OF AUTOMATION

By 1971 sound recordings holdings at RHARS were estimated at
just over 300,000, with fully one-third of the total lacking any public
catalog access. The decision made a year later to adopt the Library of

Congress cataloging procedures made it possible for the RHARS staff to resume making additions to the public card catalog of the new acquisition LP's, by drawing on the LC's very sizable body of printed catalog cards for interfiling; however, this was a mere finger in the dike relative to the public catalog access backlog as a whole.

The year 1974 marked a major turning point for the RHARS. The professional librarian staff achieved a definitive stability by way of a triumvirate composed of Donald McCormick, Gary Gabriel Gisondi, and the present writer. The combined determination, derring-do, and imagination represented in this team paved the way for major breakthroughs over the following decade in areas of public catalog access, public service, and innovative audio technology. The growth rate of the Archives' sound recordings holdings versus problems of user access became compounded with acquisition by the RHARS of the holdings of the then defunct Institute of Sound that had been housed at Carnegie Hall. Some 10,000 LP's, 21,000 78's, and 2,000 tapes were involved, much of which consisted of Broadway shows and film sound track repertoire, plus large quantities of opera.

While a modicum of public access could be maintained for the LP's, the ever-growing 78 rpm disc holdings, including a backlog and duplicates in the six figures bracket, not only was creating a near-insoluble storage problem, but a steadily growing user interest in historical recordings from the pre-electric era made imperative a concentrated attempt to bring the 78 rpm holdings at the RHARS under some measure of bibliographical control. It was clear that none of the major institutional sound archives with collections of broad general scope could command, from their parent establishments, the funding and manpower necessary to catalog their 78's. (The archives in this group were those at the Library of Congress, NYPL, and Stanford, Syracuse, and Yale Universities.) Perhaps the cutting of this particular Gordian Knot could be achieved by developing a shared cataloging scheme. The initial germ of the idea came by word of mouth that Yale Historical Sound Recordings had fully cataloged its 78 rpm disc holdings—which turned out not to be the case. Resulting from a meeting at the RHARS of representatives of the five archives, the concept was explored, including the idea of funding from the National Endowment for the Humanities (NEH). It was realized that a request for such funding for a multi-institutional project would have to go through an established third party in which each archive held membership. Luckily, the Association for Recorded Sound Collections (ARSC),the organization of sound archivists and private collectors, was about to hold its ninth annual conference at Montreal jointly with the International Association of Sound Archives (IASA). In Montreal the cooperation of ARSC became assured and the five archives, plus, for a time, that of the University of Toronto, constituted themselves as a consortium, Associated Audio Archives (AAA), dedicated to implementing the shared cataloging concept.

The grant proposal submitted by ARSC to the NEH indicated as its ultimate goal the development of a national union catalog of institutionally held sound recordings, beginning with the commercially issued 78 rpm holdings of the participating AAA archives. The specific funding request was for a planning study to determine whether and how such an objective might be achieved. The NEH grant application was successful, and over the following eighteen-month period, representatives of the participating AAA sound archives not only developed a close collaborative relationship, but emerged from their series of meetings with a wholly innovative methodology involving the use of microfilm photography and data processing technology. Preparing a catalog by manual methods, including spot auditioning of discs, was found to be totally out of the question in point of financing and time considerations, given the combined holdings of almost a million discs to be dealt with. The end result was a recommendation that a high-speed microfilming operation be undertaken that would yield legible high-resolution photographs of the record labels, as well as of matrix number figures on the inner margins. This information would then be read off from the film frames by clerical personnel and input into a computer data base. This data base could then be processed into a microfilm index, which, in its final collation, would offer for each 78 rpm record side, label and serial number, matrix/take number, composer, title, performer, and *siglum* of holding institution.

To develop an innovative methodology is one thing, but to find the technological means for its implementation was, in this instance, a formidable task. The Syracuse University representative came up with a firm in that city, Mi-Kal Countymatics, which had been involved in the microfilming of deteriorating legal documents, and its president, Ed Hayes, took up the challenge of developing a workable and reliable microfilming-data processing procedure.

Meanwhile out of the planning study meetings came a number of noteworthy by-products, the most important of which were *Rules for Archival Cataloging of Sound Recordings*, published by ARSC in 1980, and a survey undertaken by the Library of Congress AAA representative, Gerald D. Gibson, of pre-LP era record manufacturers' catalogs.

A pilot project funded by the West Coast Hewlett Foundation enabled testing of the basic microfilm-cum-data processing method, which was judged sufficiently feasible to warrant application to the NEH for assistance in funding the 78 rpm project. The possibility of including LP's and 45's was also considered, but the final challenge grant approved by the NEH in 1979, based on combined public and private sector contributions of $1,000,000, restricted the project to 78 rpm discs. By this time it was understood that the resulting computer microform output would not be a union catalog of the AAA's holdings, as understood in library parlance, but rather a rough and ready working index with the six access points as noted above. It was realized that refining the index to the point where it would constitute a catalog meeting Anglo-American Cataloging Rules standards would constitute a future project requiring additional manpower and funding.

Meanwhile the index and microfilm photographs of the discs themselves would open up whole new vistas for discographic and sound archival researchers. Because the film could be ordered in whole or in part by other individuals and institutions, this meant that research could be carried out without necessitating a personal visit to the archives represented in the index. The existence of record label photographs in microfilm format would provide opportunity for research into record label typology on a scale heretofore impossible.

A casual visit to the RHARS by Lloyd E. Rigler, President of the Ledler Foundation in Burbank, California, resulted in an initial expression of interest, and within the year his decision to undertake private sector funding of the project. The index, which came to final publication by ARSC in microform in 1983, bore the name of Mr. Rigler and his late partner as the *Rigler and Deutsch Record Index*, complete sets of which were distributed initially to the charter AAA sound archives, save for the University of Toronto which had dropped out because of financial stringencies.

The nearly ten years of effort attendant to developing the *Rigler and Deutsch Record Index* brought in its train the most intensive efforts at the RHARS to achieve bibliographic control over its sound recordings holdings, both by manual methods and by exploring developing computer technology. Here the eventual aim was not only to have the RHARS sound recordings fully incorporated into the main catalog of the NYPL Research Libraries (which after going through an interim "dictionary catalog" format to replace the old card catalog, would be converted into a local "on-line" data base), but also to gain incorporation into the fast developing nationwide RLIN catalog network of major research libraries. This work was, of course, concentrated on prospective LP and tape holdings and has involved extensive financing by way of public and private sector grants to the Performing Arts Research Center (PARC) as the combined Performing Arts Divisions of the NYPL are now collectively styled.

With regard to the retrospective catalog of LP and tape holdings, the separate card catalogs, as of 1981, were amalgamated and published in a fifteen-volume dictionary format by G. K. Hall Co., under the direction of Donald McCormick.

Following the 1983 completion of the *Rigler and Deutsch Record Index* project, the AAA sound archives through ARSC submitted to NEH a proposal for a similar indexing of LP and 45 rpm holdings of the combined archives, and an approved challenge grant resulted. However, despite wide national and international publicizing of and interest in the microfilm-cum-data processing procedure, no private sector funding had come forth as of the close of the Fall 1985 challenge grant deadline.

SOUND RECORDING RESTORATION, PRESERVATION, AND SPECIAL PROJECTS

While the Lincoln Center facilities, into which the NYPL Performing Arts Division moved in 1965, were fully air- conditioned and offered a measure of temperature-humidity control, it cannot be said, in all honesty, that they offered for the holdings of the RHARS the degree of absolute control that matched the standards set forth in the classic

Pickett and Lemcoe study, *Preservation and Storage of Sound Recordings* (Library of Congress, 1959). The expression, "good as any and better than most" applies, in terms of comparable sound archives facilities, up to the 1980's. Financial limitations have precluded any large-scale use either of humidity-proof record sleeves or, until recently, acid free sleeves. Use of ultra-sonic record cleansing devices employing freon was not feasible for financial and safety reasons. It was not until the Keith Monks record cleaning apparatus became available, in the 1980's, that the RHARS had on hand an inexpensive, effective, and efficient method for both cleaning incoming discs from private gift collections and for keeping those of its own holdings free from dust and grime. Other than this, physical preservation, for the most part, took the form of careful monitoring of daily playback conditions, including painstaking equipment maintenance and avoidance of excessive playback of individual discs. When overuse, wear or damage occurred, transfer to service tape was standard procedure, or replacement by a duplicate in good condition. At least twice between 1965 and 1985, extensive modification or substantial replacement of public service playback equipment was undertaken with the objective of bringing the facilities up to "state of the art" in terms of reliability, ease of handling, and minimum record or tape wear. The most dramatic change occurred in 1979 with the arrival of Tom Owen in the newly created position of Sound Engineer. He had been involved in commercial sound recording work, was *au courant* with the latest and best in audio and video equipment, and was reasonably conversant with computer technology— the latter proving to be a major asset as he and Gary Gisondi worked as a team to develop automation technology at RHARS.

Not only did Owen tackle the job of putting the public service facilities into shape, he also took on the task of up-dating the sound restoration laboratory. A grant from the Avalon Foundation had enabled RHARS, in its first years, to set up a sound restoration laboratory, under supervising audio technician Sam Sanders, which was top of the line, by the standards of the middle 1960's. But by 1979, when Sanders left the audio engineering post, audio technology had made quantum leaps.[4] A first step had been made toward improved sound restoration work at RHARS with the acquisition of a Packburn Transient Noise Suppressor to eliminate, electronically, clicks and pops from old source material without compromising the musical result. But Owen was determined not to settle for a piecemeal approach and, within two years, the sound restoration facilities at RHARS were second-to-none. As with the original sound recording laboratory, the development of up-dated laboratory and public service audio facilities at RHARS was carried out with the help of major grants from the Rodgers and Hammerstein Foundations and from agreement by Francis Goelet to allow use of his Rhode Island Corporation Fund contributions to assist in sound restoration work and necessary associated facilities—most notably the phonocylinder apparatus subsequently used to produce the LP discs from the 1900–03 recordings of Metropolitan Opera performances recorded by the Met Librarian, Lionel S. Mapleson.

By 1983, among the major decisions made at RHARS was the institution of on-premises video servicing to its users, chiefly of music material (by this time, the Dance Collection and Billy Rose Theatre Collection had likewise instituted this service in their special areas). Another major decision was to phase out, prospectively, service tapes in reel format and to utilize cassettes instead. From here on, reel format would be used for long-term preservation until such time as future technology would provide a more stable medium for that purpose.

The services of the RHARS facilities were by no means restricted to its on-premises listeners. With proper written clearances from copyright and proprietary rights owners, single-copy tape duplications could be supplied to individuals requesting them, as well as to radio and television broadcasters. More significant, however, was the assistance rendered to record companies such as RCA, Columbia, Deutsche Grammophon, and others in supplying high-quality tape masters for use in their LP reissue programs of historical recordings. In most instances, the companies themselves no longer had masters or even usable copies of their original discs, so that RHARS as well as other institutional sound archives became the source of last resort.

---

[4]Anthony Griffith at EMI in England had demonstrated, both in the LP's made under his supervision and by way of a paper delivered at the ARSC conference in Washington, D. C., what really could be done in terms of quality transfer to LP format of 78 rpm original source material.

Shortly after Tom Owen's arrival on the RHARS scene, the sound restoration laboratory undertook the production of master tapes for the series of annual LP albums issued by the Metropolitan Opera Guild in limited editions to donors of $125 or more and featuring historic Met Opera broadcast performances. Among them were a 1939 *Rosenkavalier* with Lotte Lehmann, a 1941 *Tristan und Isolde* with Lauritz Melchior and Kirsten Flagstad, and a 1937 *Carmen* with Rosa Ponselle. Most of the source material came from the RHARS holdings of 16-inch "acetate" discs of the original broadcasts.

Dario Soria, veteran executive in charge of operatic recordings for his own Cetra-Soria label, for Angel, and for RCA, was in charge of the Metropolitan Opera Guild program, and it was not long before a far more ambitious scheme began to germinate—the assembling at RHARS of a complete archive of all the Met broadcasts, insofar as the source material was locatable and usable. Midway in the late planning stages, Mr. Soria died suddenly while working on the master tapes of the 1940 *Un Ballo in Maschera* with Jussi Bjoerling and Zinka Milanov, but his widow, Dorlé Jarmel Soria, saw to it that the project came to fruition and was funded. Not only did this require additional personnel, especially trained to deal with the material and associated audio equipment, it also required setting up a second sound restoration studio at RHARS.

By the time RHARS had gained full division status within the NYPL, not only was the Met archive project in the advance planning stage, but the decision had been made to attempt an integral transfer to master tape of all the Mapleson cylinders at RHARS, 118 at that time, and to prepare a research tape for on-premises listening, arranged in rational program order. The final objective was to issue the whole series in LP format with the fullest possible documentation as to casting, provenance, and the like. This project had been mulled over and explored since 1967, but it was not until 1980 that it was judged feasible to undertake from a technological standpoint. After intensive research, definitive taping was begun in early 1981 and completed in June. The LP disc issue, eventually produced by the Archives and distributed through the Metropolitan Opera Guild, became available in the Fall of 1985, with complete documentation as a six-disc LP album.

RHARS AFTER TWENTY YEARS

Since becoming a division in its own right in 1980, the RHARS has continually expanded its programs in the areas of public service and sound restoration work. The main thrust of its efforts, however, has been twofold: 1) to increase access in the most efficient possible manner to both its audio and printed material holdings; and 2) to accomplish this, not only by way of providing up-dated catalog access to readily-serviced materials, but to make full use of the sound restoration facilities and to make available for audition the vast quantities of audio materials not presently serviceable via direct disc playback.

The substantial start that has been made in this direction, during the first half of the 1980's, was due in large measure to increased staffing and financial backing from both the public and the private sector. What had become something of an Augean Stables situation in terms of audio material to be sorted, searched, and weeded, has been brought under a decent measure of control. But it has become clear that storage and working space, not only in RHARS, but also in other Performing Arts Divisions at Lincoln Center, have become insufficient to meet the demands of the public and to fulfill the obligations imposed on those undertaking custodianship and public servicing of valuable and often unique performing arts materials. Plans are afoot for an expansion of the NYPL at Lincoln Center. If and when this takes place, then perhaps it will be possible for RHARS to tackle a very sizable quantity of unfinished business, such as sorting and transferring to tape some thousands of instantaneous recordings in disc and tape format, completing a phonocylinder-to-tape transfer program, and getting its collection of record manufacturers' catalogs into definitive order and fully cataloged.

Over the longer term looms the larger task, to be undertaken in collaboration with other general and specialized institutional sound archives, namely, the creation of a true union catalog of audio holdings, and the eventual electronic transference of these holdings—as technology becomes available—to formats that are more stable, more compact, and more readily accessible than the discs and tapes which presently consume so much archival space.

Alec Hyatt King

THE CHICHELE PLOWDENS AND THE BRITISH MUSEUM

Footnotes to a Musical Bequest

The only published account of this matter was given half a century ago by Edward Speyer, a famous patron of music, who, during his long life (1839–1934), had enjoyed a vast acquaintance among composers, per-formers, and many other artistic people. What he wrote runs as follows:

> My friendship with William Barclay Squire (1855–1927) dates many years back. He was one of the most genial, sympathetic and warm-hearted of men. He spent the greater part of his life in the British Museum as Keeper of the Department of Printed Books. His chief interest lay in the study of music in its bibliographical and historical aspects, and in this field, by rare devotion and industry, he made himself widely known and esteemed, not only in this country, but perhaps even more on the Continent, particularly in Germany and France. Although over-burdened with work, he was ever ready to satisfy the frequent demands made upon his rich store of erudition. He often spoke to me about a wonderful treasure of musical autographs in the possession of an old spinster lady, Miss Harriet Chichele Plowden. It consisted of Mozart's ten great String Quartets, one of Beethoven's Violin Sonatas, and a few other items. All these had originally belonged to [Johann] Stumpf [*sic!*], the well-known London harp-maker and friend of Beethoven, and after his death, in

---

Alec Hyatt King was Superintendant of the Music Room (1944–72) and Music Librarian (1972–76) of the British Library. He is the author of books on Handel, Mozart, music printing, and musical bibliography.

1842, were sold by public auction in London at about £2 to £4 apiece, and thus acquired by Miss Plowden's father. In our own time the news of this old lady's treasure had spread in musical circles, and many efforts were made to induce her to part with them. Barclay Squire, whose one aim in life was to benefit the British Museum, contrived to baffle the machinations of all other pretenders to the prize, and induced her to bequeath it to the Museum. After her death Squire triumphantly told me the news. I was so impressed by it that I was moved to address a letter to *The Times* on August 15th, 1907, showing that the value of the autographs was not less than £6,000, praising this act of generosity and holding it up as an example to others. To my utter astonishment and dismay, this letter gave rise to an action against the British Museum by Miss Plowden's heirs. My relief was great when the court pronounced in favour of the Museum. When talking the matter over afterwards, Barclay Squire remarked, with a sardonic smile: "Never rush into print too soon!" (1937:208–9).[1]

This makes fascinating reading, not least because of the description of Squire and because his comment seems to be a unique instance of one of his remarks being recorded in print. But Speyer's recollections, published some thirty years after the occasion, are defective, and since what he wrote is neither accurate nor complete,[2] the true sequence of events deserves to be set out and glossed in some detail.

The ill-considered letter which Speyer wrote to *The Times* gives a fair enumeration of the purchases made at the Stumpff sale by Harriet Plowden's father, Charles Hood Chichele Plowden (1796–1866), but it omitted one fact which subsequently became of cardinal importance— namely that at the latter's death the autographs passed not to her but to her brother Charles Chichele Plowden (1825–1878),[3] who remained unmarried and was the sole survivor of five sons, the other four having

---

[1]The ten Mozart quartets (K387, 421, 428, 458, 464, 465, 499, 575, 589, and 590) are now Additional MSS 37763–37765, and the Beethoven violin sonata, op. 30, no. 1 in G major, is Additional MSS 37767.

[2]Squire, who retired in 1920, was not "Keeper of Printed Books" (*i.e.*, head of the department), but had risen in his last years of service to be one of three Assistant Keepers, the then title of the grade immediately below that of Keeper. Stumpff's name has two 'ff's not one, and his collection was sold in 1847, not 1842.

[3]Augustus Hughes-Hughes (1909:419) was the first to state, erroneously, that Charles Chichele Plowden bequeathed the manuscripts to his daughter. Many other writers, including myself (1984:42), have repeated this.

died in infancy or youth.[4] Only at Charles's decease did the autographs pass to Harriet (1830–1907). Moreover, the legal action presumably consequent upon Speyer's letter, was not brought against the British Museum, but originated among members of the Plowden family. Reference to *The Times* law reports shows what a curious action it was.

The whole affair began with a brief note printed in this newspaper on 10 August 1907:

> Miss Harriet Chichele Plowden, of Albion Villas, Folkestone, who died on June 26, aged 76, left estate of gross value of £21,296. She left the original MSS of Beethoven's First Sonata for violin and piano and Mozart's Ten Quartettes to the British Museum.

The bequest was contested in the Chancery Division of the High Court of Justice on 31 July 1908, and was reported in *The Times* on 1 August. The case was heard by Mr. Justice Swinfen Eady, and was headed: "A summons on the construction of the Will of Charles Chichele Plowden. In re Plowden deceased: Plowden v Plowden." Mr. Gatey appeared for the Trustees of Mr. Plowden's Will; Mr. C. W. Turner for Miss Plowden's executor, representing the interests of the British Museum.

Charles Chichele Plowden had left most of his estate to his sister Harriet, and the salient clause in his will read thus: "Such of my books as my sister may desire to retain, and also all my furniture, pictures, musical instruments and other articles of domestic use and enjoyment." Summing up, his Lordship said that Miss Plowden had bequeathed the manuscripts to the British Museum, but her powers to dispose of them as her brother's moiety depended on whether they could be considered as included in the bequest to her as "books" or otherwise, and if as books, whether she had expressed a wish to retain them. Pointing out that she had included the manuscripts in her inventory of 1889, the judge held that, even if not "books," the manuscripts could be included among "articles of domestic use and enjoyment" and in his opinion the manuscripts were books within the meaning of the bequest.[5] It might be added that even if the manuscripts were worth the £6,000 estimated by

---

[4]This and all other dates and facts about the Plowden family given here are taken from Walter F. C. Chicheley Plowden (1914). The family name is variously spelt 'Chicheley' or 'Chichele.' One branch emigrated to Maryland in the United States in 1684 (*op. cit.*:99ff).

[5]Harriet Plowden's intended bequest is further attested by a note in her hand on a label affixed to the old front cover of the manuscripts, which reads: "To be given to the British Museum. H.C.P."

Speyer—and this was surely far higher than the probate valuation—there was still over £15,000 for Miss Plowden's heirs.[6]

The identity of those who, as Speyer alleged, sought earlier to persuade Harriet Plowden to part with the autographs cannot now be discovered. But while she clearly remained protective all her life, she could be generous to an enquirer if he were genuine,[7] even though his world were totally different from her own. One such was William Warde Fowler, whose name is probably little known today, even to those who take a degree in "classical studies." Yet in his time he enjoyed a very wide reputation, and his brief acquaintance with Harriet Plowden affords a pleasing glimpse into late Victorian civilities. Born in 1847, Fowler was educated at Marlborough College, and entered New College, Oxford, as a commoner, moving to Lincoln College as a scholar during his first year. One of Fowler's tutors, Henry Nettleship, fostered his musical interests as well as his classical education. In 1872 Fowler was elected a Fellow of Lincoln College, where in 1881 he became Sub-Rector, and held that office until 1906. As a Latinist, Fowler was world-famous: his best known book, *The City State of the Greeks and Romans* (London, 1893) is one of the most attractive and lucid expositions of the subject ever written. It was last reprinted in 1966. Fowler was also a distinguished naturalist and ornithologist, and from his eleventh year onwards totally devoted to Mozart.[8]

Fowler's study of Mozart (1910), which he issued privately under his initials, is delightfully modest, and gives a beautifully written account of the way in which tentative study could lead to gradual revelation and rich understanding. He was a passionate searcher after the truth, and was anxious to establish the proper order of the movements in Mozart's great string quartet in A major. He suspected—rightly, as it transpired—

---

[6]There may be a veiled reference to this affair in Plowden (1914:165–66), where he refers, rather confusedly, to the bequest of these autographs, and adds: "They now possess great value."

[7]The autographs of the Mozart quartets may have been made available for study to the editors of *Wolfgang Amadeus Mozarts Werke. Kritisch durchgesehene Gesamtausgabe* (Leipzig: Breitkopf und Härtel, 1877–1905). The *Revisionsberichte* to Series 14 (1888) states wrongly that they were in possession of "Mr Plowden," this being presumably taken from the 1862 edition of Köchel's *Chronologish-thematisches Verzeichnis sämtlicher Tonwerke Wolfgang Amadé Mozarts* (Leipzig: Breitkopf und Härtel). The second edition of 1905 has "Mrs [sic!] Plowden, London."

[8]An excellent biography of Fowler by Raymond Huntington Coon (1934), then Associate Professor of Latin, Indiana University, does full justice to his many-sided character and powerful influence.

that they had been disturbed in most mid- nineteenth century editions, and was therefore anxious to consult the autograph:

> With the help of Professor Case, the late Mr. Taphouse and lastly of Sir George Grove, who most kindly took much trouble for me, I found that the MSS of all the ten quartets were in the possession of a Miss Plowden of Chislehurst.[9] To this lady I wrote at once, asking her to put on paper for me the order of the movements in all the ten quartets, as it stands on the MSS (Fowler 1910:20).

Miss Plowden duly sent the required information, and must have kept in touch with Fowler, for there was a gratifying sequel:

> But Miss Plowden was not content with doing me this kindness; she came to stay at Oxford not long afterwards, and brought her treasures with her for me to examine. They included not only Mozart's ten quartets, but the MS. of Beethoven's first sonata for piano and violin in D Major [in fact in G Major]. I spent two hours going over these manuscripts, not without an 'invigilator' indeed (so we call at Oxford the authority who presides at an examination) to see that I did not steal or maltreat them; but this showed that the owner fully recognised her responsibility, and I accepted the situation joyfully (Fowler 1910:21–22).

What a charming picture of a vanished world, where an old lady could safely travel quite a long way by train, with Mozart autographs in her bag![10]

As a final "footnote," something should be said about the Plowdens, one of the oldest families in England. "The family of Plowden," wrote their remembrancer (Plowden 1914:15), "has been settled at Plowden in the parish of Lydbury North, Salop, beyond record, but the pedigree goes back no further than Roger de Plowden the Crusader who was at the siege of Acre in 1191. . . Longvill Castle was in the possession of the Plowdens from 904." Today, the family still lives at Plowden Hall, near North Lydbury in Shropshire. It was early in the

---

[9]Chislehurst is a small, pleasantly wooded town in Kent, some ten miles southeast of London.

[10]The date of Harriet Plowden's journey cannot be fixed precisely, but it must be after 1889, when Case was elected to his Professorship, and before 1900, when Grove died. *Pike's Folkestone, Hythe and Sandgate Directory* first records her residence at 2 Albion Villas, Folkestone, in the 1895/6 issue, which suggests that she had moved there by 1894. As Miss Plowden's removal would have lengthened her journey to Oxford by some sixty miles, it seems likely that she made it in the early 1890s.

eighteenth century that they intermarried with the ancient family of Chichele, from whose second recorded generation came Henry Chichele, the Archbishop of Canterbury who found All Souls' College, Oxford in 1437.

The Chichele Plowdens were early active in the East Indian Company, and in later generations many of them served in the Indian Army and in the India Board of Control, later the India Office, in London. Among the latter were both Charles Hood Chichele Plowden and his son Charles Chichele Plowden.[11] Charles Hood, who lived at 152 York Street, Portman Square, was a Fellow both of the Royal Geographical Society and of the Society of Antiquaries, but was never at a university. His son Charles, however, graduated at Christ Church, Oxford in 1848. As his will shows, he had some musical instruments.

But of his father's musical interests there is no evidence at all;[12] his will does not mention manuscripts or instruments. One can therefore but speculate why he bought the autographs from Stumpff's collection. Did he, perhaps, know him?[13] For sixty years, however, spanning two generations, whatever their degree of musicality, the scions of this house cherished their musical autographs, and so ensured that they would remain safe for posterity.

REFERENCES CITED

Coon, Raymond Huntington
    1934   *William Warde Fowler, An Oxford Humanist.* Oxford: Black-
                well.

[11]Some of Charles C. Plowden's work in the Indian Office was concerned with the complex health problems of the British Army in India and of the civilian population. His numerous letters (British Library, Additional MS 45782, July 1868 to October 1870) to Florence Nightingale, the government adviser, reveal a thoughtful mind and a remarkable grasp of detail and principles.

[12]No earlier Plowdens seem to have been musicians, though several married musical wives. One such was Francis Peter Plowden (1749–1829), who married Dorothea Phillips in 1779. She composed *Virginia. A comic opera,* which was produced at Drury Lane, and was published in vocal score by Clementi & Co. in 1802. She is named on the title page as "Mrs Frances [*sic*!] Plowden." Copies are in the British Library (signed "D. Plowden") and in two other libraries (RISM A/1/7 P 4960, where her Christian name is correctly given). See also Plowden (1914:17).

[13]Johann Stumpff's manuscript journal, which is mentioned by Victor Schoelcher (1857:395, n. 1), cannot unfortunately be traced.

Fowler, William Warde

1910   *Stray Notes on Mozart and his Music.*Edinburgh: Printed
              Privately.

Hughes-Hughes, Augustus

1909   *Catalogue of Manuscript Music in the British Museum* .Vol. III.
              London: Trustees of the British Museum.

King, Alec Hyatt

1984   *A Mozart Legacy: Aspects of the British Library Collection.*
              Seattle: University of Washington Press.

Plowden, Walter F. C.

1914   *Records of the Chicheley Plowdens, A.D. 1590 – 1913.* London:
              Heath, Cranton & Ousely. Printed for Private Circulation.

Schoelcher, Victor

1857   *The Life of Handel.* London: Trübner & Co.

Speyer, Edward.

1937   *My Life and Friends.* With a Foreword by H. C. Colles.
              London: Cobden-Sanderson.

Francis Mason

CARLETON SPRAGUE SMITH AND THE DANCE COLLECTION OF THE NEW YORK PUBLIC LIBRARY

All the world knows, or ought to know, that Carleton Sprague Smith is responsible for initiating the finest collection of materials on dance in the world, the Dance Collection of The New York Public Library (NYPL). Only Carleton, as head of the Music Division of the Library, recognized the need in the 1940's for an independent dance collection. Rather than hoard it for his own division, where it had begun to flourish with magnificence, he gave it over to a sprightly magpie on his staff, Genevieve Oswald, who was not only a balletomane but a complete dance fanatic. She was also a musician and knew all about the floor dance appears on. The result of this independence for dance magnetized the NYPL as the American locus for dance materials: books, manuscripts, photographs, prints, drawings, and later films and tapes.

Carleton saw at once that New York was about to become the dance capital of the world. All the great talent of native American dancers was capped by the genius of dancers who had come here from round the world. While American dance audiences might continue to think for decades that only dance talent from abroad, like so-called Russian ballet, was pre-eminent, Carleton knew that the dance professionals had their eyes on Balanchine, Martha Graham and her followers,

---

Francis Mason, former chariman of the Committee for the Dance Collection, is editor of Ballet Review *and author of* I Remember Balanchine.

and the creativity in dance set in motion by the generosity and push of Lincoln Kirstein.

Kirstein, who had given his superb dance holdings to the Museum of Modern Art in the 1930's, asked that they be transferred to the NYPL. Other knowing donors were quick to follow, the dancers saw the light and the Dance Collection grew by leaps and bounds. It took off into outer space when Jerome Robbins assigned a portion of his royalties for *Fiddler on the Roof* to a project for filming or taping dance performances.

The Dance Collection's holdings are now unrivalled anywhere. For reconstructing dances and ballets, for knowing what they looked like with sets and costumes and what contemporaries thought about them in words and pictures, this is the pre-eminent authority. Genevieve Oswald accomplished it and Madeleine Nichols now continues to add to the awesome achievement Carleton began; and while the capitals of old Europe, where ballet started, groan with envy, the NYPL's Collection shows the way to the future of the art by its commitment to the present and past.

The moral of this story: curators who are artists, like Carleton Sprague Smith, realize with uncommon perspicacity that curators with other gifts for arts, who may appear to be on the fringe, are really the best bets for the future. It is a pleasure to try to put into words the historic achievement of this extraordinary man. Not only the Lincoln Center for the Performing Arts, but the incorporation, within the Center, of dance as a vital element at the NYPL's Research Center, came about because of Carleton's vision and energetic leadership.

Genevieve Oswald

ONE APPROACH TO THE DEVELOPMENT OF A DANCE ARCHIVE

The Dance Collection in the Library and Museum of the Performing Arts (The New York Public Library at Lincoln Center)[1]

In discussing the rich field of material concerning the dance that needs to be collected before it is lost to posterity, one must address the challenges that the future will hold for those who undertake this task, and examine some of the problems that must be solved. They include such difficult considerations as definition of styles, terminology, and techniques of research, to name just a few; all aimed at considering, in depth, the task at hand.

Perhaps it is appropriate to consider, first and foremost, where all this material will be housed, its storage or care, as well as the proper archival techniques that will insure its utilization as a living collection

---

[1]In offering this essay in honor of Dr. Carleton Sprague Smith, the author is keenly aware that this great archive and her work in it were made possible only because of his idea of a library for the three performing arts (music, theatre, and dance), which he proposed as early as 1932. His awareness of the need for documentation for dance, and his willingness to nurture this effort in its early phases, are responsible for the archive's existence today. The joy and excitement of working with Carleton Sprague Smith will nourish the author all the days of her life.

Genevieve Oswald was Curator of the Dance Collection at the NYPL from 1948 to 1988. She was largely responsible for developing the collection into a multi-media archive of more than two million items and for creating a computer-produced catalog published in twenty-three volumes.

rather than one comprising dead or ancient artifacts. The views, which follow, reflect a background of many years of documenting the ephemeral art of the dance—an art and an activity which in its elusiveness shares so many of the problems that are confronted in the collection of oral histories or folktales, and the recording of untranscribed music and ritual—in other words, the search for that essential, rich culture which is part of our lives, that exists but is unrecorded.

Dance is not an new art. Curt Sachs, the eminent musicologist, anthropologist, and art historian, wrote that:

> dance is the mother of the arts [and that] music and poetry exist in time; painting and architecture in space, but [that] dance lives at once in time and space. [In the dance] the creator and the thing created, the artist and the work are still one and the same thing [and the elements of dance] rhythmical patterns of movement,. . . the vivid representation of the world seen and imagined—these things man creates in his own body in the dance, before he uses substance and stone and word to give expression to his inner experiences (1937:3).

The fact that dance lives in time and space leads to the consequence that dance is quickly lost as time passes, as soon as the curtain falls or the performance ends. The challenge of documenting this elusive art fascinates all of us who have tried to record today's dancing as it is performed. All of us who have confronted the problem have asked: What are the archives of the performance of the past, even of yesterday? And more importantly, how can we create the documents we need to transmit performances of the dance today?

Can we find an approach that will satisfy so many needs? That of a national archive? That of the international scholarly community, which serves the cultures of more than one society *even* as it aims to serve each of them as they develop? Those of individual artists within each culture, whether they are professional or unskilled dancers? And finally, what about the needs of those who "appreciate," *i.e.*, the general public which seeks information, arranged in such a way that it will be useful perhaps in a broader yet meaningful way?

One realizes immediately how unlikely it is that peoples and institutions of the world can have the *same* goals as to *what* they want. But we can at least discuss and discover the techniques and methods that do exist, in order to satisfy those aims, avoid some of those experiments that have proven fruitless, and allow each institution to concentrate on what it does best for the common good.

Technically, an archive is created for the convenience of retrieving sought for materials. That, in a sense, is its basic function. However, experience has shown that records, or archives of records, including verbal and iconographic material, cannot help but extend the range and depth of contemporary understanding and practice. The emergence of new archives can only offer greater nourishment and benefit to any tradition, whether it be folksong, music, or dance. It is also a fact that the growth of an archive has a direct impact on a community and a country's sense of self or their personal self-esteem. It is a force which guards its heritage, while at the same time providing educational materials on traditions of the past and customs of the present for its members.

Taken in this context, the creation of such archives throughout the world, wherever they may be established, should be regarded as a bold step forward—as a gesture which expresses how deeply communities care about their traditions, giving them an historical dimension as they preserve them in a meaningful way as an enrichment for future generations. As documenters of dance, we have learned that even with a community's renewed interest in a style of the recent past, we often cannot recover what has been lost. Even the absence of interest among one or two generations can terminate the existence not only of a dance, but, occasionally, a form or a style.

Documentation includes seeking answers to such basic questions as "what, when, where we shall collect, as well as by whom and for whom." Moreover, this material must be assembled with as much detail as possible and must be readily accessible to its users. Let us return to the dance to see what the problems have been.

Today we can notate, but the records of the past are meager and imperfect, and the archivist has to search far and wide for them. Graphic artists recorded movements, or poses, of dances and of dance scenes. Critics wrote about them, so did historians, biographers, social historians, and anthropologists, who often described them in tantalizingly vague generalities. In recent times, dancers and other people in the professional dance theatre saved clippings, scrapbooks, letters, and those who had much to say wrote books. Buried among the working collections of the past of the great national libraries and theatres are materials, not necessarily cataloged under the subject of dance, that are yet to be discovered. Much precious information is buried in travel books, diaries, cultural histories, and other sources. Any competent librarian can imagine what sorts of books to collect, but the challenge of documentation for dance lies beyond books and the obvious kinds of photographs and prints.

From a historical point of view, as we have learned, the art of dance has limitations in that it possesses no easy means of recording itself. Dance has no equivalent of the musical score or the written text. Although several forms of dance notation are available, they are not easy to learn nor to read, and are not as commonly used as we wish them to be. Dancers must have prodigious kinesthetic memories; the true literature of the dance has, in the past, been transmitted by kinesthetic rote. One could compare the feat of remembering thirty works of an average professional dance company's repertoire to that of a musician remembering thirty pieces from his orchestra's repertoire. Jerome Robbins, a distinguished American choreographer, concerned with this problem, wrote: "How marvelous that museums can hang, side by side, the currently considered masterpieces of past and present" (1963).

Perhaps the easiest way to outline what can be done to preserve dance is to describe some of the aspects of the archive recently developed at the Dance Collection in the Performing Arts Research Center of The New York Public Library at Lincoln Center, which is my principal experience. The Dance Collection's archive has not tried to develop a universal conceptual framework of what dance is or should be, but rather has attempted to illuminate each kind or style of dance, each one presenting a new set of problems, taking into consideration the groups, organizations, or societies that have devised these various styles.

From the beginning the Dance Collection has had to innovate and to expand the usual concepts of collecting. It has attempted to assemble a reference collection which will transmit not only the history of the art, but the choreography itself in tangible form. (By choreography, I mean the actual steps and sequence of steps.) Where reference documents on the dance did not exist, it has had to create them, most notably in the form of motion picture film, as well as video, and audio tapes. With that aim in mind, it could hardly limit its acquisitions to books and pamphlets. The subject has rightfully determined the nature of material collected— oral history tapes, motion-picture films, videotapes, music scores, photographs, prints, librettos, letters, manuscripts of all kinds, notation scores, clipping files, and original decor and costume designs. Some ninety-seven percent of its acquisitions are non-book in nature. Of necessity, it has assembled a variety of forms of material that mesh together in a curious way to create a picture of the dancer, his art, traditions, works, and techniques.

An innovation in the Dance Collection, but not found within the systems of most national or large libraries, is that the forms of material mentioned above are housed in one place, to be utilized interchangeably. In most archives, photographs, drawings, and prints are each located in separate, specialized rooms; motion picture films and videotapes are found in one section; books are in another; programs, clippings and loose material in still another, and the user must proceed from unit to unit without having the possibility of using these items together in one place.

In the Dance Collection reading room, one finds a row of videotape and motion-picture viewing machines on one wall; five large tables—each twenty-two feet in length with fifty-eight chairs—for use of flat box material, books, and so on; audio listening machines for listening to oral tapes, as well as a computer-produced book catalog which lists the Collection's holdings. All materials are available to readers who are given service by a professional staff forty-six hours a week. The material sought for is brought to the reading room by an attendant, and can be used only in this room, as no material is permitted to be taken home or to be used outside the Dance Collection's reading room. The reader, however, is able to use as many types of different material together as his or her needs require. They can turn from viewing a film to reading about the film or the culture it represents, the technique of the dances seen, the style of the dance and its meaning in its own culture, or its derivation. They can also examine the roots of a particular style that has spanned many cultures, or even civilizations. The aim is to surmount technological barriers and furnish sources, so that the professional scholar or student can use them freely, searching one and then another with the variety of information needed right at hand.

Again, dance does not lend itself easily to the printed page. Books represent only about three percent of the Dance Collection. While it is essential to emphasize the importance of non-book material, the subject is not without an accumulation of several centuries of important printed documents. Even though it does not have an adequate encyclopedia, it has a literature of its own. It is a highly developed art in almost every area where it is found, with articulated traditions and a long history of technical manuals, codified techniques, and a history of great choreographers, performers, and reformers.

Most of the known book literature, including rarities, are represented by some 36,000 books and librettos from the seventeenth
through the twentieth century.

Among our earliest records of dance, over 6,000 wood-cuts and
engravings, some dating from the fifteenth century, recreate our earliest
scenes of dance. At the end of the Romantic era (mid-nineteenth
century), photography was invented and 260,000 photographic prints
and negatives provide us with a record up to the advent of motion
picture film.

Filling out the story, bringing it to life in a human way are letters,
manuscripts, and diaries, and 4,000 oral tape interviews which supplement the printed material and furnish us with fresh and informative
insights into performance history. To tap the large body of performers
who have not written about their theories or experiences, we initiated
an extensive project of recording interviews with dancers, choreographers, musicians, and scenic designers on audio tape, encouraging
them to reminisce or tell us of their experiences as fully and as candidly
as possible. To protect those who have been interviewed, neither the
oral tapes nor the transcriptions made from them are loaned, duplicated, or used in any printed sources without their permission.

With all this—books, photographs, audio tapes, drawings—we are
still talking about externals, as far as dance is concerned. No matter how
much one reads or how much one pours over drawings, photographs,
or newspaper clippings, the action of dance is still necessary.

With the development of our film and videotape archive, the
possibilities of transmitting dance, movement by movement, or step by
step, if you wish, become a reality. A random sampling of the variety of
the footage acquired, which numbers about four million feet, might
include: dances of South Africa; children's dances around the world; a
short film of the great Isadora Duncan; animal mating dances; the
modern dance of avant-garde groups in New York (among them such
artists as Don Redlich, Yvonne Rainer, and Twyla Tharp); historical
American social dances, including the "Cakewalk;" ballroom dance
competitions held in Europe; the Classical Khmer Ballet; a computer
ballet; as well as thousands of titles of films of theatrical dances and
traditional and folk dance throughout the world.

Because those who are actively making dance, whether it be
traditional or folk in a small village, or in a theater with an organized
company on a city stage, performers usually care little about recording
themselves. As a result, we have had then to film and videotape them

to capture their dances as they are being performed today. We have carried out an active program of live recording of dance works in the current professional repertoire, as well as traditional and folk dance around the world. Of the 5,000 titles of film in our catalog, we have produced about 770 films—working as far from the United States as Indonesia and India. Filming the dances of professional companies in our country requires agreements with the unions, and all countries require an agreement with the artists or at least their written permission.

Filming or videotaping is the most economical way of preserving a sequence of movements. It does not have the accuracy of notation, but it is more accessible as an historical record. Experience has taught us that a photograph or an article will stir the imagination. A segment of film or videotape does not halt the movement, but rather enables us to recreate the same few minutes of time, so as to relive again the movement. If holding fast to cultural conventions is a force that deters imaginative change or exploration, film and videotape can aid the performer to think in new ways by exhibiting contrasting artistic styles enabling him or her to acquire a reorientation of the body that will encourage new departures from those that tradition mandates. With the meeting of the art and the equipment necessary to grasp it, its variety can become easily available for the first time in history.

Since much of this material is rare or unique, the Dance Collection has had to find a way to share it. It has tried to do so by publishing a ten-volume *Dictionary Catalog of the Dance Collection*, which lists its holdings and unifies all material, regardless of medium or form under the author, subject, and title in one alphabet. This bibliography of 675,000 entries, published by G. K. Hall, is updated annually by supplements and is purchased by libraries throughout the world. The Catalog's ten original volumes took fifteen years to prepare. We had to create a new list of some 8,500 subject headings that would cover the subject of dance, under which films, articles, photographs and books could be listed, as there was no list developed for this purpose. It was also necessary to study the types of material collected and to note size, condition, and subject matter, and to devise a letter-code system so that they could be marked, filed, and stored for ready accessibility to the thousands of users who study them annually.

The preservation of materials acquired is always a problem, particularly in an archive such as this. Each type of material presents a new difficulty—we have all the problems of deterioration to solve, from brittle pages and mold to the shrinking and curling of motion picture film. Materials come to us in every possible state. But conservation and preservation is an enormous topic, one to be addressed at another time.

When archival collections such as this begin to proliferate, we can begin to ask the great questions: How does dance fit into society, and where does society fit into dance? How does having the experience of one dance technique or style influence one's perception and performance of another? What part does dance have in human development? Is it as crucial as so many ethnologists and historians have told us? In a sophisticated society, what is the role of dance as communication? Has, or, how has it been used as a means of political manipulation?

At the very least, we now have learned that these new archives open vistas, offering new conceptualizations of man's contribution to culture. They offer, as well, a deeper understanding of man's role in the development of his culture at a time when humanity needs it most in this rapidly changing technological society.

REFERENCES CITED

Robbins, Jerome
    1963   "Recording of Dance." *The New York Times* (Nov. 24).

Sachs, Curt
    1937   *World History of the Dance.* Translated by Bessie Schönberg. New York: W. W. Norton.

Robert M. Stevenson

LATIN AMERICAN MUSIC BIBLIOGRAPHY

Immediately after their publication in 1945 and 1962, both Gilbert Chase's *A Guide to Latin American Music* (Washington, D.C.: Library of Congress, Music Division) and its enlarged successor, *A Guide to the Music of Latin America* (Washington, D. C.: Pan American Union and the Library of Congress), took rank as indispensable tools for any researcher working in the Latin American music area. Both were organized after a pattern that was to become familiar in all subsequent bibliographies: General, followed by nations routed in alphabetic sequence. Each national section—whether Argentina, Bolivia, Brazil, or any of the rest—began with an epitome of the nation's musical history and an evaluation of the landmarks in its musical bibliography. Next, Chase provided an annotated listing (alphabetically by author) of relevant books, articles, and (in some instances) music publications. On the other hand, unpublished materials such as theses and dissertations escaped Chase's dragnet—which in the 1945 book ran to 2,688 items and in the 1962 edition, to an added 1,072 entries.

In the expectation that either he or his eminent pupil Gerard Béhague would bring out an updated third edition, other music bibliographers' attempts have usually withered on the vine. Only Guy A. Marco and Sharon Paugh Ferris dared go beyond Chase in their *Information on Music: A Handbook of Reference Sources in European languages*, vol. 2: *The Americas* (Littleton, Colorado: Libraries Unlimited, 1977; 296

Robert Stevenson, one of the most versatile men of the arts, is a foremost musicologist, musician, Hispanist, archivist, and bibliographer. He has taught at UCLA since 1949.

pp., indexes). Superseding Chase, this vademecum earned enthusiastic reviews (in *Notes of the Music Library Association*, June 1978, p. 881; *The Musical Times* [London], April 1979, p. 310; and *Inter-American Music Review* [Los Angeles], Fall 1980, pp. 113–14).

In Malena Kuss's landmark survey, "Current State of Bibliographic Research in Latin American Music," *Fontes Artis Musicae*, 31/4 (October–December, 1984), 206–28, she annotated item 134 in her Appendix III with this confirming judgment of the *Information on Music. . . The Americas* volume: "An excellent contribution toward bibliographic control of materials on Latin American and Caribbean music and the most comprehensive since Chase's *Guide* (1962)."

In her three appendices, Kuss lists 149 titles—most of them annotated. She devotes the first to "Dictionaries, encyclopedias, and literature about lexicographical coverage of Latin America" (56 items); the second to "Bibliographies and reference sources for Latin America, Studies that include music" (43 items); the third to "Bibliographies of music literature (written and oral traditions)" (50 items). Although she does occasionally quote Marco's annotations, Kuss is herself uniquely qualified to pass value judgments of her own on everything that she lists. A front-ranking world class scholar, she brings to bibliography both a sophistication and comprehension of the problems unique to Latin America that, joined with superior musicianship, place her on a pedestal.

She precedes the 149–item bibliography with a discussion of various problems not well understood by aliens to Latin American music research. For one matter, the only Spanish-language dictionary that up to now has made any attempt to scrutinize the whole of Latin America was published as long ago as 1947. Otto Mayer-Serra (1904–1968), the Hitler-epoch emigrant from Spain who compiled the two-volume *Música y músicos de Latinoamérica* (México: Editorial Atlante, S.A., 1947) did produce a handsome set, replete with photographs and some color illustrations; he did include national anthems in easily legible music script, and he nicely balanced entries on art music with alphabetized information on dances. But he was victimized by an almost complete lack of any reliable scholarly literature on the historic music of Latin American nations. Nor did he deal in any effective way with even the contemporary music adored by the urban masses. The single individual country music lexicon that up to now has paid urban "mesomusic" its due is the two-volume *Enciclopédia da música brasileira. Erudita, folclórica, popular* (São Paulo: Art Editôra, 1977;

1,190 pp.). But innovative and forward-looking as is this Brazilian music encyclopedia, so far as recent commercial music goes, it constantly betrays the researcher into Brazilian historic music by altering the spelling of even such a composer's name as Heitor Villa-Lobos or a scholar's as Luiz Heitor Corrêa de Azevedo.

Among other challenges, Kuss also comprehends the vastly difficult problems posed by the wide dispersal of music and music information in sources extremely difficult of access, many of them not catalogued under either M, ML, or MT numbers at the Library of Congress or elsewhere. What she does not dwell on, but what she well understands, is the economic plight throughout Latin America that forbids any concerted effort to bring its historic music treasures into monumental publications or to divulge its music patrimony in worthy recorded performances.

II

Turning for the moment from encyclopedias to musical travelogues and general histories: first in the field with an English-language compendious nation-by-nation survey was Nicolas Slonimsky (1894–). His 374–page *Music of Latin America* (New York: Thomas Y. Crowell, 1945) immediately stimulated a Spanish translation, *La música de América Latina* (Buenos Aires: El Ateneo, 1947; 430 pp.). Immensely popular in its own time and later, this genial book was reprinted at New York by Da Capo in 1972, with a foreword by the author and an appendix of death dates since 1945.

True, when he went searching for scores, Latin America was, as he put it and as Kuss reminds us (her page 215), still *terra incognita*. But Slonimsky's 30-page "Dictionary of Latin American musicians, songs and dances, and musical instruments," followed by a 47-page index of composers, works, and subjects, makes it even now a coveted source of information for the layman. Moreover, Slonimsky's wit captivates even the most casual reader.

Not valued like Slonimsky's book as a repository of witticisms, Gerard Béhague's *Music in Latin America: an introduction* (Englewood Cliffs, N.J.: Prentice-Hall, 1979; 379 pp.) contrasts still further with Slonimsky's by placing events in the whole of Latin America within a chronological continuum. As one result, events in such smaller nations as Honduras, El Salvador, and the like, often fall "between the cracks." In compensation, Béhague's treatment of contemporary composers (to 1979) reveals insights and critical ability rarely found among analysts of

Latin American music. His uniqueness in this respect earned for him
the editorship of all Latin American entries in the twenty-volume *New
Grove Dictionary of Music and Musicians* (London: Macmillan, 1980).
The Spanish translation [by Miguel Castillo Didier] of Béhague's Prentice-Hall text, *La música en Latinoamérica: una introducción* (Caracas:
Monte Ávila, 1983; 502 pp.), presently circulates as overall the best
treatment of Latin American music in that tongue—thus rivalling the
reputation of its English-language original.

Leaving histories of music in individual nations for later discussion
and reverting to dictionaries: although the Latin American entries in
The New Grove that were solicited and brilliantly edited by area
specialist Béhague now show no promise of being compiled into one
single easy-to-use volume, general editor Stanley Sadie rightly foresaw
that the 250 biographies of Latin American composers and performers,
seventy entries dealing with Latin American dances and other local
forms (such as *bambuco, bossa nova, cueca, milonga, sanjuanito,* and
tango), and the city and country articles (ranging from Mexico City to
Buenos Aires and Guatemala to Chile), would outdistance everything
in the lexicographical line hitherto available.

Both Sadie and Béhague are to be thanked for *The New Grove's*
Latin American superiority. But as Kuss only too rightly observed (her
page 210): "With two exceptions, the unprecedented coverage of Latin
America in *The New Grove* escaped the attention of some of the most
perceptive reviewers, including an entire issue of *The Musical Quarterly.*" The only exceptions in this critical silence—if we leave out of
account "Latinoamérica en el nuevo *Grove,*" *Revista Musical Chilena,*
30/134 (April–September, 1976), 69–74—were the reviews in *Notes,*
38/1 (September, 1981), 55–59, and in *Inter-American Music Review,* 3/2
(Spring/Summer, 1981), 159–207. To these two may be added a remark
on "Latin American Music in *The New Grove Dictionary of Music and
Musicians,*" in *Latin American Music Review* (University of Texas), 2/1
(Spring/Summer, 1981), 168. Béhague there rightly echoed Sadie when
he called it "the most comprehensive and up-to-date coverage of Latin
American music and musicians" to be encountered in any language.

Only the immense cost of the twenty volumes continues placing
the information in them beyond the price range of all but the most
privileged Latin American libraries and institutions.

Further to restrict access, it must again be acknowledged that the
likelihood of the Latin American material being now gathered a decade

later into one minimally expensive, convenient handbook remains extremely remote. Kuss's hope for a *LatinoAmeriGrove* (her page 207) that would replace Otto Mayer-Serra's still useful *Música y músicos de Latinoamérica* and the uneven but also useful bio-bibliographical coverage of composers in the [Organization of American States] *Composers of the Americas* series (1955–) seems all the less likely to be realized at the end of the 1980's than in 1984. For one good reason, the Spanish Ministry of Culture presently projects a multivolume *Diccionario de la música española e hispanoamericana*, the first tome to appear in 1992—the Columbus Quincentennial Year.

III

If the Latin Americanist must continue waiting for the sunrise of truly effective Spanish-Language dictionary until then, at least there continues being published with sections in both languages the "fundamental tool for bibliographic control of publications on Latin America in the humanities and social sciences" (Kuss's item 88).

This prime series bringing Latin American music bibliography under control on a year-by-year basis has been, from its inception in 1935, the *Handbook of Latin American Studies [HLAS]* that in 1988 reached Volume 48. Items 22 and 23 in the first volume hailed Francisco Curt Lange's *Boletín latinoamericano de música*, as "an important journal which every library interested in Latin American culture should order." Irma Goebel Labastille contributed the section "The Music of Mexico and Central America" to the 1936 *HLAS*, pp. 469–72. *HLAS* 3 (1938), 528–46, contained among "other special articles and notes" Lange's "Los estudios musicales en la América Latina publicados últimamente"—an essay that at the end listed alphabetically by author the articles published in the first three thick volumes of his *Boletín*. Ralph S. Boggs's section on Folklore in *HLAS* 4 (1939), 159–65, gave item numbers for the first time to articles published in Lange's *Boletín* (1852–53, 1857–58, 1860, 1862, 1865–69, 1870, and 1873–74).

HLAS 5 (1940), 403–17, inaugurated a section specifically entitled "Music." Contributed by William Berrien, items 4309–400 were now divided alphabetically by nations, smaller nations being grouped under The Antilles and Central America. (Berrien, however, annotated music and records separately—a practice not thereafter continued.) Gilbert Chase took over the section on Music in *HLAS* 6 through 8, Charles Seeger those in *HLAS* 9 through 16, Richard A. Waterman those in *HLAS* 17 (1954) through 20 (1958), Bruno Nettl those in 21 through

25. Beginning with *HLAS* 26 (1964), the music sections appeared in even-numbered volumes. Gilbert Chase provided the sections in volumes 26, 28, and 30; Gerard Béhague those in volumes 32 (1970), 34 (1972), and 36 (1974); Robert Stevenson those in 38 (1976) through 50 (1990), even-numbered years. In total, Seeger therefore contributed the music sections in eight volumes, Chase and Stevenson in six and seven, Nettl in five, Waterman in four, Béhague in three, and Berrien in one.

Since the items, whether books, monographs, articles, or music, always had to be current publications, older literature entered the *HLAS* scheme only when classic works were reprinted. Fortunately, the exponential publication of facsimiles and reprints did bring back into circulation after World War II many of the consecrated classics of both North and South American historiography. This was true, for instance, of the first booklength histories of music in the United States (by Frédéric Louis Ritter) and in South America (by Ramón de la Plaza), both of which had initially appeared in the same year, 1883. Their facsimile reprints emphasized sharply how the authors had differed in evaluating their nations' musical patrimonies. Ritter, a snobbish immigrant from Alsace-Lorraine who misrepresented his own age by a decade, sniffed at everything indigenous. On the other hand, Plaza's *Ensayos sobre el arte en Venezuela* (Caracas: Imprenta al Vapor "La Opinión Nacional," 261 pages [facsimile reprint, Imprenta Nacional, 1977]) placed music at the pinnacle of Venezuela's artistic accomplishments, and lauded without reserve musical forefathers.

Himself a scion of an old Venezuelan family that included a Caracas *alcalde* ('mayor') in its tree as early as 1716, Plaza at thirty years of age emigrated to New York (1861–1863), where he studied "artes y comercio." Six years after returning home he married into a family of even greater wealth. The reprinting at Caracas in 1977 of his *Ensayos*, with an introduction specifying the few errors in the 1883 *editio princeps*, solidified Plaza's prestige as a careful historian and resulted in a warm review published in *Notes of the Music Library Association*, 35/3 (March, 1978). Concentrating on art music, Plaza also broke ground not trod by Ritter with an appendix of engraved music by excellent composers. Juan Manuel Olivares (1760–1797), eldest of Venezuela's mulatto pleiad, took equal stance with a genius of purely European descent, José Ángel Lamas (1775–1814), in Plaza's scheme. Not neglecting the anonymous, he also included a fandango in his musical appendix. What was not be proved unique about his *Ensayos* in Latin America was its funding. In company with many music history publications to follow, it was published to celebrate an important national anniversary.

So influential was Plaza's pioneer history, that authors as recent as Andrés Sas (1900–1967) began their research into South American colonial music believing that Venezuela boasted the earliest important school of composers. Instead, Peru and what are now Bolivia and Colombia attracted renowned creators and performers to the ranks of their cathedral musicians more than two centuries before Olivares, the first Venezuelan whose compositions survive. The documentary record of achievements by Gutierre Fernández Hidalgo (*ca.* 1553–1620), maestro successively at Bogotá, Quito, Cuzco, and La Plata (= Sucre); Estacio de la Serna, organist and maestro at Lima 1595–1604; Pedro Bermúdez, director at Cuzco, [Antigua] Guatemala, and Puebla (where he died *ca.* 1606); and even more profusely by Hernando Franco, maestro in Guatemala *ca.* 1560–1575 and at Mexico City 1575–1585; Gaspar Fernandes, organist-maestro in Guatemala and at Puebla (where he died in 1629); not to go further with a list of other paramount seventeenth-century masters at Puebla and Mexico City; assures their dates of service. Moreover, their surviving compositions testify to their admirable creative abilities.

In 1878 José Sáenz Poggio published at Guatemala City an *Historia de la música guatamalteca desde la monarquía española, hasta fines del año de 1877* (Imprenta de la Aurora: reprinted in *Anales de la Sociedad de Geografía e Historia de Guatemala*, 22/1 [March–June, 1947], 6–54) that preceded even Ramón de la Plaza's *Ensayos*. However, Sáenz Poggio wrote chiefly to enshrine the memory of his grandfather, Vicente Sáenz (1756–1841), and his grandfather's associates. Not until 1934 was a truly scientific history of music in any Mesoamerican country published when medically trained Dr. Gabriel Saldívar [y Silva] (1909–1980) aided by his wife-to-be Elisa Osorio de Bolio brought out their epoch-making *Historia de la música en México (épocas precortesiana y colonial)* (México: Editorial "Cultura," 324 pp.; facsimile reprint, México: Biblioteca Enciclopédica del Estado de México, 1981, xxiii, vii, 324 pp.).

Other now standard histories of music in Latin American nations that skirt developments after 1820, 1901, or 1950 emphasize an ever-present problem in Latin American musicography. The only histories of music in their nations with which reigning Latin American composers are pleased are those narrated by themselves. An example of such a history that comes immediately to mind is the 270-page *La música en el*

Perú (Lima: Patronato Popular ProMúsica Clásica, 1985) by six composers born at Lima in 1918, 1927, 1931, 1951, 1953, and 1964—Enrique Iturriaga, Enrique Pinilla, César Bolaños, José Quezada Macchiavello, Raúl Romero, and Juan Carlos Estenssoro. In Chile, the preeminent Domingo Santa Cruz Wilson spent his retirement years writing a history of events since 1900 "to set the record straight." Unlike Europe, the musicians who hold political posts in Latin America are almost invariably themselves composers. Their chief goals whether in Peru, Chile, or elsewhere, are necessarily the propagation of their own works, usually at the expense of their predecessors, and always at the expense of competing contemporaries.

IV

Reviews of books are occasionally mentioned in the *HLAS* annotations. However, the *Hispanic American Periodicals Index*, edited at the University of California, Los Angeles, by Barbara G. Valk since its inception in 1970, initiated in the 1981 volume a "Book Review Index" section. Particularly important can be rated such a section so far as authorities of such stature as Carleton Sprague Smith are concerned. As an example of articles by him, *HLAS* 7:5515–517 and 5567 indexed:

> "Music Libraries in South America," *Notes of the Music Library Association* [Chicago], 1st series, no. 11 (1941), 19–31.

> "Musicology as a Means of Intercultural Understanding," *Proceedings of the Music Teachers National Association* [Pittsburgh], 35th series (1941), pp. 54–57.

> "What not to Expect of South America," *Musical America*, Vol. 61, no. 3 (February 10, 1941), pp. 217–220.

> "The composers of Chile," *Modern Music*, Vol. 19, no. 1 (November–December, 1941), 26–31. [Enrique Soro, Humberto Allende, Domingo Santa Cruz, Próspero Bisquertt, Carlos Isamitt, Jorge Urrutia, Alfonso Leng, Acario Cotapos, Alfonso Letelier, and René Amengual.]

HLAS 15:2847, 18:3008, and 48:7036 indexed three further articles:

> "Relações musicais entre o Brasil e os Estados Unidos de Norte América," *Boletín Latino-Americano de Música*, año 4, [Parte I] (1946), 141–148.

"Contemporary music in Chile," in *Conference on Latin-American Fine Arts, June 14–17, 1951. Proceedings.* Austin, Texas, University of Texas, Institute of Latin American Studies (Latin American Studies, 13 [1952]), pp. 115–123.

"Alberto Ginastera's *Duo for flute and oboe*," *Latin American Music Review*, 6:1 (Spring–Summer, 1985), 85–93.

The *Index to Latin American Periodical Literature, 1929–1960*, compiled in the Columbus Memorial Library of the Pan American Union (Boston: G.K. Hall & Co., 1962), VII, added "The Song Makers," *Survey Grafic*, 30/3 (March 1941), 179–183, and "Villa-Lobos, músico rebelde," *Américas* (OEA), 2 (11), (November 1950), 14–16, 43, 47, to Smith's budget of Latin American music articles. *The Music Index*, 1960, page 680, lists "Heitor Villa-Lobos (1887–1959)," published in both English and Spanish editions of *Inter-American Music Bulletin*, January 1960.

Additional contributions by Smith that were not recorded elsewhere include:

Musical Tour through South America, June–October, 1940 Manuscript. New York: The New York Public Library, 1940. xxxiv, 290 [33] pp.

"The Music of Latin America," *Progressive Education*, 18/6 (New York, October, 1941), 307–9.

"Music Publicatins in Brazil," *Notes of the Music Library Association*, 4/4 (September 1947), 425–30.

"Brazil's Big Four (Heitor Villa-Lobos, Camargo Guarnieri, Oscar Lorenzo Fernández, and Francisco Mignone)," *The Musical Digest*, 29 (New York, November 1947), 22–25.

"Brazil in Songs," *Brazil*, 23/3 (New York, March, 1949), 3–6, 17–18.

"Song of Brazil," *Américas*, 2/10 (Washington, D.C., October, 1950), 14–16, 43–44.

Yet it is Smith's reviews extending from *Journal of Research in Music*, 11/1 (Spring, 1963), 83–85, to *Latin American Music Review*, 6/2 (Fall–Winter, 1985), 266–80, that often carry information nowhere else available. His review of Vasco Mariz's *História da música no Brasil*, 2nd

ed. (Rio de Janeiro: Civilização Brasileira, 1983; 352 pp., 53 illus.) has
the added great virtue of epitomizing a history much more useful than
the one book on the subject in English. Smith correctly says at the end,
"any English translation of Vasco Mariz's [book] should be seriously
considered."

Gerard Béhague, Gilbert Chase, Malena Kuss, Carleton Sprague
Smith, and Robert Stevenson are but five representative authors whose
reviews in *Ethnomusicology*, *Journal of the American Musicological
Society*, *Latin American Music Review*, *Music and Letters*, *Musical
Quarterly*, *Notes*, and a few other English-language publications can be
tracked down through the *Music Index*. But for reviews in the *Hispanic
American Historical Review*, in anthropological, folklore, and geography
journals, the researcher still needs to follow the Biblical injunction:
"Seek and ye shall find."

APPENDIX

What titles should enter a minimal shelf-list of books and
monographs pertaining to the music of each mainland Latin American
nation speaking Spanish and one speaking Portuguese can be lengthily
argued. The ABC nations do obviously boast more extensive bibliographies than do Bolivia, Ecuador, and Paraguay, for instance. The
following items sample those not mentioned in preceding paragrahs.
Book and magazine acquisitions at UCLA are controlled by area bibliographers, not by teaching faculty. Moreover, what remains on shelf,
rather than being sent to storage, remains the prerogative of librarians,
not area specialists. *Inter-American Music Review*, edited by Robert
Stevenson, 4/1 (Fall 1981), pp. 1–112, contains "Caribbean Music History: A Selective Annotated Bibliography with Musical Supplement"
that, in addition to Antilles, covers Surinam and Guyana.

Argentina

Caamaño, Roberto. *La historia del Teatro Colón 1908–1968*. Buenos Aires:
   Editorial Cimenta, 1969. 3 vols. 493, 615, 503 pp.

Gesualdo, Vicente. *Historia de la música en la Argentina*. Buenos Aires:
   Editorial Beta, 1961. 2 vols., 593, pp. *HLAS* 25:5211

   An abbreviated revision with same title (Buenos Aires: Libros de
   Hispanoamérica, 1978. 2 vols. 107, 124 pp.) (*HLAS* 44:7016) contains
   valuable new data, such as (1) the fact that Bartolomé Massa (1721–

1796) produced his own opera *Las Variedades de Proteo* in Buenos Aires between November 4–21, 1760, and (2) the dates and places of birth and death of Blas Parera, composer of the Argentinian national anthem (Murcia, Spain 1776; Mataró near Barcelona, January 7, 1840).

_____. *La música en la Argentina*. Buenos Aires: Editorial Stella, 1988. See *Inter-American Music Review*, 9/2 (Spring–Summer, 1988), 24, note 20.

This lavishly illustrated text brings Argentinian music history up to the present. Because of the wider public for which it is designed, documentation has had to be severely retrenched.

Bolivia

Auza León, Atiliano. *Historia de la música boliviana*. Sucre, Bolivia: Tupac Katari, 1982. 212 pp. Bibliography.

_____. *Simbiosis cultural de la música boliviana*. La Paz: Producciones CIMA, 1989. 151 pp.

García Muñoz, Carmen and Waldemar Axel Roldán. *Un archivo musical americano*. Buenos Aires: Editorial Universitaria Buenos Aires, 1972. 166 pp.

Roldán, Waldemar Axel. *Catálogo de manuscritos de música colonial de la Biblioteca Nacional de Bolivia*. Lima: Proyecto Regional del Patrimonio Cultural y Desarrollo, [1987].

Brazil

Appleby, David P. *Heitor-Villa Lobos: A Bio-bibliography*. Westport, CT: Greenwood Press, 1988. 358 pp.

Béhague, Gerard. *The Beginnings of Musical Nationalism in Brazil*. Detroit: Information Coordinators [1971]. 43 pp. music. *HLAS* 34:5023.

Revised portion of the distinguished author's Tulane University Ph.D. dissertation. Composers treated include Brasílio Itiberé da Cunha, Alexandre Levy, and Alberto Nepomuceno, "all active between about 1870 and 1920."

Corrêa de Azevedo, Luis Heitor. *Bibliografía musical brasileira (1820–1950)*. Rio de Janeiro: Instituto Nacional do Livro, 1952. 254 pp. *HLAS* 18:2993.

_____. *150 [Cento e cincoenta] anos de música no Brasil (1800–1950)*. Rio de Janeiro: Instituto Nacional do Livro, 1952. 254 pp. *HLAS* 18:2993.

Côrte Real, António T. *Subsídios para a história da música no Rio Grande do Sul*. 2nd ed., rev. and aug. Porto Alegre: Editora Movimento, 1984. 351 pp. Bibliography.

França, Eurico Nogueira. *Música do Brasil: fatos, figuras e obras*. Rio de Janeiro: Ministério da Educação e Cultura, Instituto Nacional do Livro, 1957. 141 pp. *HLAS* 21:4721.

      Preceded by França's *A música no Brasil*, 1953. 69 pp. (*HLAS* 20: 4707).

Lange, Francisco Curt. *Historia da música na Capitania Geral das Minas Gerais*. Belo Horizonte: Conselho Estadual de Cultura de Minas Gerais, 1983. Vol. 8: Vila do Príncipe do Serro do Frio e Arraial do Tejuco. 470 pp.

      For attention to vols. 1 and 2 of this proposed twelve-volume series, see *HLAS* 41:7055 and 44:7028.

Mariz, Vasco. *História da música no Brasil*. 2nd. ed. rev. and aug. Rio de Janeiro: Civilização Brasileira, 1983. 352 pp. Includes bibliographies and index.

Mello, Guilherme Theodoro Pereira. *A música no Brasil: desde os tempos coloniais até o primeiro decênio da República*. 2nd ed. Rio de Janeiro: Imprensa Nacional, 1947. 362 pp.

Mohana, João. *A grande música do Maranhão*. Rio de Janeiro: AGIR, 1974. 135 pp. *HLAS* 38:9068.

      The half-century from 1875 to 1925 was a golden age of Maranhão music. Of 169 composers catalogued by the author, at least a dozen deserve encyclopedia coverage.

Salles, Vicente. *Música e músicos do Pará*. Belém: Conselho Estadual de Cultura, 1970. (Coleção Cultura Paraense)

_____. *A música e o tempo no Grão-Para*. Belém: Conselho Estadual de Cultura, 1980. 426 pp.

Vasconcelos, Ary. *Panorama da música popular brasileira na belle époque"* Rio de Janeiro: Liv. Sant'Anna, 1977. 454 pp. Bibliographies and discographies.

Chile

Claro [Claro-Valdés], Samuel, and Jorge Urrutia Blondel. *Historia de la música en Chile*. Santiago de Chile: Editorial Orbe, [1973]. 192 pp. Bibliography, music, plates. *HLAS* 88:9096.

Claro-Valdés, Samuel. *Oyendo a Chile*. Santiago: Editorial Andrés Bello, 1979. 139 pp. Bibliography, index, 52 musical fragments in cassettes, accompanied by a fifteen-page booklet listing durations, performers, and other recording details. *HLAS* 42:7100.

_____, Juan Pablo González Rodríguez, and others. *Iconografía musical chilena*. Santiago: Universidad Católica de Chile, 1988 [1989]. 2 vols. 626, 570 pp.

Pereira Salas, Eugenio. *Historia de la música en Chile, 1850–1900*. Santiago: Universidad de Chile, 1957. 379 pp.

_____. *Los orígenes del arte musical en Chile*. Santiago: Imprenta Universitaria, 1941. 373 pp.

Colombia

Bermúdez, Egberto, ed. *Antología de música religiosa, siglos XVI–XVIII, Archivo Capitular, Catedral de Bogotá*. Bogotá: Presidencia de la República de Colombia, 1988. 79 pp.

Escobar, Luis Antonio. *La música en Cartagena de Indias*. Bogotá: Intergráficas, 1983. 120 pp. Bibliography. [Homenaje de la Compañia Central de Seguros a Cartagena de Indias en el 450 aniversario de su fundación.]

Perdomo Escobar, José Ignacio. *Historia de la música en Colombia*. 3rd ed. Bogotá: Editorial ABC, 1963. 422 pp. Bibliography, facsimiles, music (Biblioteca de historia nacional, 103). *HLAS* 28:3083.

   Earlier versions of Perdomo Escobar's history of Colombian music are noticed in *HLAS* 4:1870 and 11:3825. His monumental 219-page *El archivo musical de la Catedral de Bogotá* (1976) and handsomely produced 107-page *La ópera en Colombia* (1979) are noticed in *HLAS* 40:9093 and 44:7071.

Stevenson, Robert. *Colonial Music in Colombia*. Washington, D.C.: Academy of American Franciscan History, 1962. 16 pp. [Repr. from *The Americas*, 19/2 (October, 1962).]

_____. *La música colonial en Colombia*. Traducción de Andrés Pardo Tovar. Cali, Colombia: Instituto Popular de Cultura, Departamento de Investigaciones folclóricas, 1964. 62 pp.

   Contains translation of preceding and El archivo musical de Bogota, pp. [29]–60. Includes bibliographies.

Ecuador

Jaramillo Ruiz, Rogelio. *Loja, cuna de artistas: monografía sobre la música de la provincia de Loja*. Quito: Banco Central del Ecuador, 1983. 470 pp. Bibliography, music. *HLAS* 48:7128.

Stevenson, Robert. *Music in Quito: Four Centuries*. [Repr. from *Hispanic American Historical Review*, 43/2 (May, 1963), 247–66; updated and augmented version, "Quito Cathedral: Four Centuries," *Inter-American Music Review*, 3/1 (Fall, 1980), 19–38 (with bibliography).

Guatemala

Lehnoff, Dieter. *Espada y pentagrama. La música polifónica en la Guatemala del siglo XVI*. Guatemala: Universidad Rafael Landivar, 1986. 154 pp.

Mexico

Estrada, Julio, general editor. *La música de México*. Mexico City: Universidad Nacional Autónoma, Instituto de Investigaciones Estéticas, 1984–1986. 6 vols. 1108 pp. [Reviewed in *Latin American Music Review*, 8/2 (1987), 269–92.

Parker, Robert L. *Carlos Chávez, Mexico's Modern-Day Orpheus*. Boston: Twayne, 1983. 166 pp.

Stevenson, Robert. *Mexico City Cathedral Music, 1600–1750*. Washington, D.C.: Academy of American Franciscan History, 1964. 25 pp. Expanded and complemented by "Mexico City Cathedral Music, 1600–1675" in *Inter-American Music Review*, 1/2 (1979), 131–78 and 9/1 (1987), 75–114.

_____. *Music in Mexico: A Historical Survey*. New York: Thomas Y. Crowell, 1952. 300 pp.

Paraguay

Boettner, Juan Max. *Música y músicos del Paraguay*. Asunción: Autores paraguayos, [1956]. 294 pp. Bibliography, Index. *HLAS* 21:4738.

Riera, Federico. *Recuerdos musicales del Paraguay*. Buenos Aires: Editorial Perrot, [1959]. 53 pp.

Peru

Stevenson, Robert. *The Music of Peru: Aboriginal and Viceroyal Epochs*. Washington, D.C.: Pan American Union, [1960]. 331 pp. Index, musical supplement [pp. 225–320].

Torrejón y Velasco, Tomás de. *La púrpura de la rosa,* ed. Robert Stevenson. Lima: Instituto Nacional de Cultura; Biblioteca Nacional, 1976.

Uruguay

Ayesterán, Lauro. *La música en el Uruguay.* Montevideo: Servicio Oficial de Difusión Radio Eléctrica, 1953. Biblioteca Nacional, 1976. 818 pp. [Part 1: La música primitiva; Part 2: La música culta hasta 1860.] *HLAS* 19:5646.

_____. *La música indígena en el Uruguay.* Montevideo: Impresora Uruguaya, 1949, 40 pp. [*Separata* from *Revista de la Facultad de Humanidades y Ciencias,* 3/4.] *HLAS* 2825.

Salgado, Susana. *Breve historia de la música culta en el Uruguay.* Montevideo: *AEMUS,* Biblioteca del Poder Legislativo, 1971. 350 pp. [Catálogos de obras, pp. 205–327.] *HLAS* 36:4609.

Venezuela

Calcaño, José Antonio. *La ciudad y su música: crónica musical de Caracas.* Presentación Walter Guido; Bibliografia Rafael Angel Rivas. Caracas: Monte Avila, 1985. 515 pp.

Plaza, Juan Bautista. *Música colonial venezolana.* Caracas: Ministerio de Educación, Dirección de Cultura y Bellas Artes, 1958. 34 pp.

Ramón y Rivera, Luis Felipe. *La música colonial profana.* Caracas: Instituto Nacional de Cultura y Bellas Artes, 1966. 20 pp.

_____. *El joropo: baile nacional de Venezuela.* Segunda edición. Caracas: Ernesto Armitaño, 1987. 152 pp.

Ramón y Rivera has published more than a dozen valuable works dealing with aspects of Venezuelan traditional music. His wife, Isabel Aretz, counts among the most prolific authors of fundamental studies concerning Argentinian, Venezuelan, and other Latin American folk and traditional musics.

Stevenson, Robert. "Musical Life in Caracas Cathedral to 1836," *Inter-American Music Review,* 1/1 (Fall, 1978), 29–71 (with bibliography); Spanish version, "La música en la Catedral de Caracas hasta 1836," *Revista Musical Chilena,* 33/145 (January–March, 1979), 48–64.

Ruth Watanabe

SOME PERSONAL OBSERVATIONS ON THE TRAINING OF MUSIC LIBRARIANS (BY WAY OF REMINISCENCES)[1]

Upon reading Carol June Bradley's excellent article (1986) on our earliest librarian-forebears, one is struck by the inventiveness of our first American music librarians in shaping our profession. In the days before neither cataloging codes nor lists of uniform subject-headings for music had come into existence, and before most of the bibliographic and reference tools which we take for granted today had been compiled, those intrepid pioneers worked more or less independently to organize their collections of *musicalia* into usable libraries for the convenient use of their clients. It is a good thing that they were able to describe their careers and experiences to the next generation of persons who aspired to careers in music librarianship and who were fortunate enough to have worked under their tutelage.

The first professional music librarians with whom I became acquainted were Barbara Duncan, Librarian, and Elizabeth A. Schmitter,

[1]Having recently retired from the librarianship of the Sibley Music Library, a position I held from 1947 to 1984, I have been thinking of the many changes which have taken place in music librarianship during the years of my tenure and have ventured to note some of them here.

Ruth Watanabe is past President of the MLA, and Librarian emerita, *Sibley Library and Professor* emerita, *Music Bibliography, Eastman School of Music.*

Cataloger, of the Sibley Music Library of the Eastman School of Music (University of Rochester), where I began to work as a student assistant in January, 1943. Although as an undergraduate in California I had used the resources of the Los Angeles Public Library, where I had met Gladys Caldwell, head of the Music Department, and as a first-year graduate student I had done a bit of research under the aegis of Edythe N. Backus at the Huntington Library, the Sibley Library was the first research collection devoted to music in which I really felt at home. Between them, Misses Duncan and Schmitter had organized and developed the large collection into an outstanding facility for the use of both performers and scholars, students and public clients. Miss Duncan was in charge of administration and collection development, while Miss Schmitter had charge of cataloging. A half-dozen student assistants, most of us candidates for graduate degrees, took care of circulation, shelving and reshelving, and record-keeping.

Miss Duncan was often at the circulation desk to oversee the activities of her "minions," as she called us, and to chat with us if no clients were waiting for scores or books, which it was our duty to run and fetch. Through those conversations we acquired a high degree of respect, not only for the library, but even more for the two librarians themselves. Neither Miss Duncan nor Miss Schmitter held college degrees, but this was a matter of almost no importance, for their knowledge of the materials of music was awesome.

Miss Duncan was a dignified and duchess-like lady, proud of her association with the Allen A. Brown Collection of Music at the Boston Public Library, where she had attained a formidable reputation as librarian and a large measure of *savoir faire*. She had, as she liked to tell us, been lured away from her beloved Boston by the well-kept promise of opportunities in Rochester to build an outstanding library, with almost complete freedom from financial considerations, for the collection's benefactor, Hiram W. Sibley, was a generous and judicious donor. I can still see her vividly in my mind's eye as she sat in her office behind her large desk piled high with both local and New York papers, which she perused daily for information about musical events. She had as well a formidable pile of publishers' and dealers' catalogs, which she assiduously checked for acquisitions of both contemporary and anti-quarian items.

I remember Miss Schmitter as a full-time cataloger and part-time pianist. Almost every afternoon she left the library with several volumes of piano duets for her sessions of music-making with friends, often members of the Eastman School faculty. She was a completely dedicated and conscientious librarian, who had trained in Northampton and Springfield and had worked previously in New York. Her practical knowledge of music had been enhanced by her work in a music store and by her devoted attendance at many concerts. She was never critical of the performances she heard; instead, she seemed delighted to absorb the music itself. I can still see her painstakingly producing cards for the shelf-list and the public catalog, fulfilling her quota of seven items to be processed *without fail* each day. She cataloged Monday through Friday (which were full-time days) and filed cards on Saturday (the half-day). It was only after she had completed her weekly duties that she took time to talk to us, never failing to extol the virtues of the Cutter system, with which she had "grown up in Northampton."

It was from Miss Duncan and Miss Schmitter that we learned "all there was to know" about music librarianship in the early forties. Miss Duncan spoke, too, of the founding and purposes of the Music Library Association and of its fledgling *Notes*, about which more will be said later. We came to know who her colleagues were, where they held forth, and what they did, so that when I went to my first MLA meetings several years later, I recognized many of the members and felt I had known some of them for a long time. Miss Schmitter impressed upon us the serious responsibility of the cataloger, who prepared the all-important single tool allowing one to gain access to the treasures of the library. We could see that cataloging and classification were a many-sided, demanding process, to test the intellectual mettle of the practitioner. Only Frank Campbell, among all of us student assistants, was allowed to assist Miss Schmitter.

In addition, we read *Notes*.[2] A repository of reports of the accomplishments of music librarians working independently, then pooling their resources, *Notes* contained such items as: plate numbers for the positive identification of editions for cataloging; calls for cataloging codes; lists of music subject-headings, and sub-headings under large, broad main entries; checklists of variant and/or multiple editions of standard works (*e.g.*, Albert Riemenschneider's several lists of editions

---

[2]*Notes for the Members of the Music Library Association*, First Series, consists of fifteen numbers dating from 1934 to 1942. In this essay, the numbers of the First Series issues will be given in Arabic numerals. Series Two, beginning in 1943/4, continues to the present. Its volume numbers will be designated here by Roman numerals, followed by the issue number in Arabic.

of J. S. Bach's works, beginning in No. 2 [Dec. 1934] 6–11, and continuing *passim*. through several subsequent issues); early indexes (No. 4 [May 1936] entirely devoted to Robert Bruce's "Partial Index to the *Encyclopédie de la Musique et Dictionnaire du Conservatoire* of Lavignac"); bibliographies (*e.g.*, Eva J. O'Meara's "Music in Seventeenth- and Eighteenth-Century Periodicals" in No. 2 [Dec. 1934] 1–16, a survey of notices of music and musical events in European journals, principally German); calls for retrospective and current periodical indexing; and descriptions of music holdings in individual libraries.

There was no hard and fast publication schedule for *Notes*. Only when sufficient material had been amassed, to fill some fifteen to twenty pages, did an issue "go to press," and more often than not it did not appear until several weeks or even months after the date designated on its title-page. Each of the fifteen numbers of the First Series was mimeographed and assembled at the several MLA libraries taking turns at production. Sibley Library's turn came during my first year on the student staff. Miss Duncan's secretary typed the stencils and ran them off on the old manually-operated mimeograph until her cranking arm gave out, whereupon I volunteered my services to finish the remaining few leaves. Finally, we all pitched in to collate the pages and to assemble "our" issue, which we regarded with a mixture of relief and pride. This had been, in its simplistic way, a bit of fun and a diversion from fetching and reshelving books as we went about our apprenticeship. As Gladys E. Chamberlain (1944:49) remarked in her article on training:

> Until a few years ago the only answer [to the question of preparation for music librarianship] was to learn by doing. Naturally a general library school course could be advised, but no specific [program] was available and every aspirant had to serve his apprenticeship on the job.

Notices in *Notes* have made it clear that much discussion was taking place in the MLA about training for music librarianship. In 1937, Otto Kinkeldey reported to the American Library Association on the principal requisites for the profession (1937:459–63), and several years later Richard Angell (1940:17–18) elaborated upon Kinkeldey's report.

Briefly stated, a general library education was deemed advisable, together with a knowledge of music history, music theory, and foreign languages. The recommended pre-professional or undergraduate preparation was a liberal arts course leading to a Bachelor's degree with music as the major subject, supplemented by studies in languages,

literature, fine arts, and general history. Professional or graduate education should consist of a library school curriculum leading to the B.S.
degree or its equivalent,[3] with emphasis upon cataloging and bibliography, and including an elective course in music librarianship. To be
covered in the latter would be the materials of a music library, cataloging
and classification of books on music, music scores, and recordings, music
bibliography and reference work, music binding, and equipment for a
music library. Angell added: "The candidate who looks forward to work
in a research music library should include further subject specialization
in his program"(*op. cit.*:18).

In 1941 Dorothy Lawton proposed in *Notes* that a fellowship be
established to provide a means for candidates to gain practical experience in librarianship. Four three-month segments would constitute
one year of work, during which a trainee would assist in: the Music
Division of the Library of Congress, in the first quarter; the Music
Division, Reference Department, New York Public Library; the Music
Library of the Circulation Department, New York Public Library; and
in a library of the student's choice (Lawton 1941:10).

Three programs of study were available in New York City by 1944,
when Gladys E. Chamberlain's aforementioned article was published:
Dorothy Lawton's course, which she first gave at the New York College
of Music in 1935 and was giving independently in 1944; Richard Angell's
course in music library administration, at the School of Library Service,
Columbia University; and Herbert Inch's program at Hunter College's
Evening and Extension Division (Chamberlain, *op. cit.*:49–50).

Upon the retirement of Barbara Duncan in 1947, I was appointed
Acting Librarian of the Sibley Library jointly by John R. Russell,
Librarian of the University of Rochester, and Howard Hanson, Director
of the Eastman School of Music. By then I had some years of apprenticeship under the direction of Misses Duncan and Schmitter, and as a
doctoral candidate in musicology, I had used most of the library's major
reference and bibliographical tools. But although, in the opinion of Mr.
Russell and Dr. Hanson, I had enough background and experience to
"carry on," I had not originally intended to pursue music librarianship
as a career, and I keenly felt the need for some systematic training before
embarking upon the new venture which had surprisingly been offered
to me. It was a formidable assignment to take over the administration

---

[3]In those days the B.S. was the standard graduate degree in library science.

of as vast and as well organized an institution as the Sibley Library, and in any case Miss Duncan's shoes were impossible to fill.

I would have rushed to Miss Lawton's training course, about which I had heard from friends in New York, but it was too late, for Miss Lawton had departed for England during the previous year. Dr. Hanson, though anxious for me to start my new work immediately, agreed to let me go to Columbia University, where Richard Angell's course had been partly taken over by Catharine Miller. It was her class in music bibliography which was my principal reason for enrolling that summer in the School of Library Service. I was a bit taken by surprise to find that I was accepted at the school on the basis of my degrees in English Literature rather than on my degrees in music; in those days most major library schools did not recognize music as adequate pre-professional training, and I wondered how graduates of music schools would manage to receive training at a *bona fide* library school.

Of the several different bibliography courses I had taken in literature and in music at two different universities, Mrs. Miller's was the most practical and informative, as well as the most enjoyable. My two other library courses, cataloging and the survey course, were also helpful, although music was never mentioned. Mrs. Miller was the source of much sage counsel, to whom I put a number of questions, and it was she who encouraged me to visit Miss O'Meara.

Through my perusal of *Notes* and Miss Duncan's conversations I had known of Eva J. O'Meara's work at Yale. I spent a day with her in New Haven, asking a myriad of questions, all of which she answered with perfect grace. In retrospect, it seems to me that some of my queries were laughable, but she was too much a lady to do anything but to satisfy my curiosity. She gave me hours of her precious time, together with advice which I never forgot.

In 1947, when comparatively few music librarians could boast a library degree, I was urged by my two directors to finish my doctorate which would, they assured me, be proof that I was a scholar, capable of developing and using a research collection. (I therefore completed my doctorate in musicology, but not my B.S. in Library Science.) Their charge to me was to concentrate on developing a facility for music research in its many aspects, for which a generous budget would be provided, and to initiate any new programs of service that I deemed appropriate. Building upon Miss Duncan's contacts with publishers, dealers, and antiquarians, and following her custom of perusing their catalogs, I did my best to add to the research collection while stocking as many of the contemporary scores and books as were available. I was fortunate in attracting many gift collections as well. The decades of the fifties and sixties were indeed ideal for collection development, for the information explosion had resulted in an unprecedented amount of research and publication, and the rare-book market in Europe was the source of many treasures.

Those two decades were also years of astounding growth of music libraries. Departments and schools of music throughout the nation were expanding their curricula and their facilities to accommodate their many students: ex-service personnel and, later, the children of the war years. New faculty members were being hired and libraries were burgeoning to meet their classroom and research needs.

At the Eastman School of Music, too, the pressure was on to expand course offerings, especially for graduate students who were enrolling in ever greater numbers. Allen Irvine McHose, appointed Director of the Summer Session in June, 1954, set about at once to increase opportunities for study during July and August, when teachers and students could make the best use of their time. He wished to "provide the best possible applied music instruction for the program offered by the Department of Professional Studies in the Graduate School" (Riker 1963:45), toward which aim he initiated programs for teachers of instruments, voice, chamber ensembles, bands, and orchestras. Believing wholeheartedly in the value of concentrated study and free exchange of ideas among professional people, he established new workshops and institutes for scholars and music administrators.

At his instigation, in 1957, the staff of the Sibley Library planned a summer Music Library Workshop which was, so far as we were aware, the first of its kind in America. Elizabeth Matthews and I were to recall:

> In a spirit of adventure (and not without some trepidation) the announcements of the workshop were sent out to deans of colleges and universities, to directors of public libraries, and to curators of special music collections. . . The response was, as one of the members of the staff remarked, 'just perfect.' The participants, not including the staff of the Sibley Library and the visiting lecturers, numbered twenty-five, an ideal group of librarians and administrators from all parts of the country (Riker 1963:52–53).

The Workshop ran for five days, during which the guest of honor and principal speaker was Harold Spivacke, Chief of the Music Division, Library of Congress. In addition to the members of the Sibley staff, who led discussions in their areas of expertise, there were some half-dozen guest panelists and speakers, including Fred G. Tessin of the C. W. Homeyer Company, Lockrem Johnson, Director of Library Service for the C. F. Peters Corporation, and Charles Hendry, Educational Representative for Associated Music Publishers. Availability of scores and books was a major issue as librarians were engaged in building their collections as rapidly as possible to meet the demands of their patrons. Acquisitions and collection development occupied much of their attention, but other aspects of librarianship, including public service, reference work, music journals, and research were fully discussed. My duties were to coordinate the Workshop and to introduce the topics for consideration. The principal benefit derived from that Workshop, and those which followed well into the sixties, resulted from the free exchange of ideas among the representing many kinds of libraries and expressing divergent opinions. In the course of the years that followed, other speakers and guest panelists participated: Catharine and Philip Miller (who came several times), Sydney Beck, James Coover, Richard Hill, Brooks Shepard, Martha Baxter, and Merle Montgomery, to name a few. With each Workshop the emphasis was upon those problems and issues with which the participants were most concerned at the time: public service, bibliography, staffing, budgeting, furnishings, maintenance of law and order, library fines, and—always—cataloging and classification.

In subsequent years, especially in the late sixties and early seventies, other institutions held similar workshops, some led by former participants of the Sibley sessions. I was often asked to conduct discussions at annual meetings of various organizations, including the one-day session for non-music librarians in Dallas in 1965. During the course of the many Workshops at Sibley, approximately one-third of the then-active membership of the MLA had participated either as members of the group or as featured speakers and panelists. Moreover, many administrators of schools and departments of music, along with librarians, had taken part. Dealers and publishers' representatives were generous with their advice, and Walter Hinrichsen and Walter Bendix of the C. F. Peters Corporation were particularly helpful and contributed scores for the Workshops. Finally, during the seventies, when their usefulness to music librarians had been served, the Sibley Library Workshops were discontinued. It is amazing, however, how much feed-back we still get from participants, after these many years.

Guy Marco, Dean of the School of Library Science at Kent State University during the sixties, designed a special program for music librarians during Kent's summer session, which included a concentrated two-week class in bibliography and another class in music library administration, running concurrently. The first year I was the guest faculty member, followed the next year by Clara Steuermann. The classes were small and the atmosphere relaxed, enabling the students to talk freely. We presumed that the course had been useful, for we did not have the proof of later feed-back in the numbers of responses we received with the Sibley workshops.

At the Dallas meeting of the MLA in 1965, we heard that the School of Library Science at Case Western University was planning a double master's program, offering the M.A. in musicology and the M.S. in Library Science, the required courses to be taken either concurrently or in tandem. Some of us were privileged to see the proposed curriculum, which seemed to be all-inclusive and interesting. This program, one of the several double degree courses offered at Case Western, was initiated soon thereafter and continued to be offered until the library school was closed in the early eighties.

In the meanwhile many library schools added special courses for would-be music librarians. An example was the State University of New York at Geneseo, where a strong department of library science for public school educators had existed for many years. An elective sequence of classes, including music history, music bibliography, and a practicum in music librarianship was instituted, with Dr. John Kucaba, a fine musicologist, teaching history and bibliography, and the Sibley Library being designated as the practicum library, for it was the nearest research and circulating collection of music in the vicinity of Geneseo. I was named Adjunct Professor, "on loan" from the Eastman School, during the summer session of six weeks, to coordinate the practicum, wherein heads of departments at the Sibley Library also taught music binding and conservation, special problems in music cataloging, and reference work. Outstanding contributions were made by Sion Honea, in charge of binding and conservation, and Joan Swanekamp, Head of the Catalog Department. The school at Geneseo also offered special courses in other fields of librarianship, including medical bibliography, taught by Lucretia McClure, Librarian of the Edward G. Miner Medical Library of the University of Rochester. These special courses continued until the closing of the library school in 1983–84.

Within recent years, for many reasons, a number of library schools have been closed, including some outstanding institutions like Case

Western Reserve and the University of Southern California. But simultaneously, to offset the loss, some strong courses in music librarianship have been developed and training for the profession appears to have become more or less stabilized. According to the most recent survey, in July, 1986 there were forty-eight schools in the United States and Canada which offer some instruction in music librarianship (portions of courses in reference, bibliography, and library materials); eight schools offer special bibliography and literature classes concentrating on music; and eight schools have the double degree program, leading to the M.S. in Library Science and the M. A. in musicology (Thompson 1986).

The literature of music librarianship has grown immeasurably during the past four decades. In addition to the MLA's contribution of a lion's share of information through myriad accounts in *Notes*, and practical data in its *Music Cataloging Bulletin* and its series of *Technical Reports*, there are many articles and studies touching upon music librarianship in a number of journals. Because it is beyond the scope of this article, no bibliography of the profession is offered here, although I will cite two publications which are milestones.

Vincent Duckles edited the special issue of *Library Trends*, which appeared in April, 1960, under the title, *Music Libraries and Librarianship*, in which more than a dozen authors contributed articles on music librarianship. Duckles opened the issue with his introductory essay on "The Music Librarian in 1960" (1960b: 495–501), followed by Gordon Stevenson's account of "Training for Music Librarianship: A Survey of Current Opportunities" (1960: 502–9). Individual articles covered such subjects as bibliography, cataloging, reference services, recordings, library administration, and the physical properties of a music library. The issue concluded with Harriet Nicewonger's fine bibliography on music librarianship (1960:614–26).

The MLA's *Manual of Music Librarianship*, edited by Carol June Bradley, Chairperson of the Information and Organization Committee who had wisely pointed out a need for such a work, was published in 1966. It was the first such *enchiridion* to be compiled in the United States and remains today as a unique contribution to the literature of the profession. Subjects treated by the individual authors included the materials of a music library (James Coover); the plant, personnel, and budget (Bennet Ludden); acquisitions for the college library (Walter Gerboth); acquisitions for the public library (Irene Millen); classification and cataloging (Isabelle Cazeaux); binding and circulation

(Catharine Miller); records and tapes (William Shank); sound recordings and sound equipment (Edward E. Colby); performance parts and sheet music (Harry L. Kownatsky); copy and microtext in the music library (Ruth Watanabe); friends of music (George R. Henderson and Dorothy Linder); and museum aspects of the music library (Brooks Shepard, Jr.).

It seems to me now, looking back over the forty years of involvement with music libraries and librarians, that those years were exciting ones of exploration, discovery—usually by trial and error, sometimes by sheer luck—and personal development through knowledge generously shared by others. It is certainly true that we would have gained much in time and effort if there had been the fine courses in music librarianship then that are available now, and we would probably have become more sophisticated than we are at present, but we would have missed the opportunity to contribute our bit to the profession in the piecemeal fashion that was so satisfying and, yes, even thrilling, in the good old days.

REFERENCES CITED

Angell, Richard
>   1940   "Resolution Presented to the Board of Education of the American Library Association," *Notes*, 7:17–18 (May).

Bradley, Carol June, ed.
>   1966   *Manual of Music Librarianship*. Chicago: Music Library Association.
>   1986   "Notes of Some Pioneers: America's First Music Librarians," *Notes*, 43(2):272–91 (Dec.).

Chamberlain, Gladys E.
>   1944   "Courses in Music Librarianship," *Notes*, 1(3):49–50 (June).

Duckles, Vincent, ed.
>   1960a   *Music Libraries and Librarianship*, published as a special issue of *Library Trends*, 8(4):495–625 (Apr.)
>   1960b   "The Music Librarian in 1960," *Library Trends*, 8(4):495–501 (Apr.).

Kinkeldey, Otto
>   1937   "Report [on music library training]," *ALA Bulletin*, 31:459–63 (Aug.).

Lawton, Dorothy

    1941   "Announcement," *Notes*, 7:10 (Apr.).

Matthews, Elizabeth O., and Ruth Watanabe

    1963   "The Music Library Workshop," in Charles Riker, ed., *The Eastman School of Music*, 1947–1962 (Rochester: University of Rochester), pp. 52–53.

Nicewonger, Harriet

    1960   "A Selected Bibliography on Music Librarianship," *Library Trends*, 8(4):614–26 (Apr).

Riker, Charles, ed.

    1963   *The Eastman School of Music, 1947 – 1962.* Rochester: University of Rochester.

Stevenson, Gordon

    1960   "Training for Music Librarianship: A Survey of Current Opportunities," *Library Trends*, 8(4):502–9 (Apr.).

Thompson, Annie F., comp.

    1986   *Directory of Library School Offerings in Music Librarianship.* Second edition. Chicago: Education Committee, Music Library Association.

HISTORY

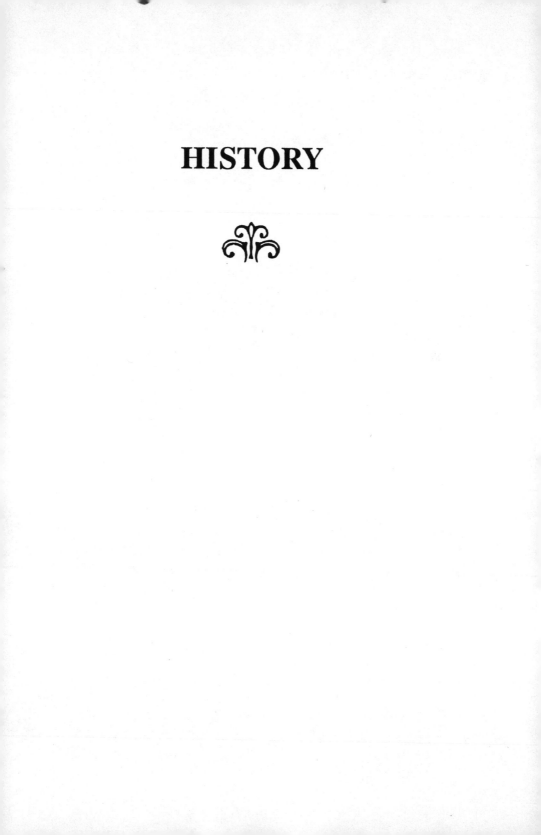

Samuel G. Armistead

CATALAN CHILDREN'S GAMES IN A LOUISIANA SPANISH COMMUNITY

The *Isleños* of St. Bernard Parish constitute a small Spanish speech-island whose origins date back to late eighteenth-century initiatives to colonize Louisiana with immigrants from the Canary Islands.[1] Since 1975, I have undertaken a series of field trips aimed at recording and preserving for future study the fast disappearing Spanish oral literature, folklore, and language, now the exclusive patrimony of elder genera-tions of the *Isleño* community.[2] The small discovery embodied in the present article, which helps to confirm an important feature of Hispanic culture among the *Isleños*, may perhaps not be an altogether inap-propriate contribution to a volume in honor of Carleton Sprague Smith, whose far-ranging scholarship has shed light on both Anglo- and Hispano-American folk traditions.

The *Isleños* are justifiably proud of their community's origins in the Canarian colonization that began in 1778, but, as the study of my

[1]See, especially, MacCurdy (1950); Din (1976; 1988); and Lipski (1990).

[2]See Armistead (1978; 1980–81; 1981; 1982; 1983a; 1983b; 1985; 1989), as well as my forthcoming book (1991).

Samuel G. Armistead is Professor of Spanish and Comparative Literature at the University of California, Davis. His research concerns medieval Spanish literature and modern Hispanic folk literature. He has done fieldwork among the Sephardic Jews, among the descendants of 18th-century Spanish immigrants in Louisiana, and in rural Spain and Portugal.

field tapes has gone forward, other and equally important components of the *Isleño*-Hispanic heritage have insistently come to light. Many an *Isleño* family can recall one or more relatively recent, nineteenth-century ancestors who came to St. Bernard Parish from some area of Spain other than the Canary Islands: Galicians, Santanderinos, Andalusians, Catalonians have all taken part in forming the *Isleño* communities and there have also been on-going contacts with various Hispanoamerican areas. Though geographically isolated in the marsh lands of the Mississippi delta, the *Isleños* never broke off altogether their contacts with the mother country and, up to the early twentieth century, Spanish settlers continued, from time to time, to arrive in the *Isleño* settlements.[3] Sustained contact with the variegated Hispanic traditions brought in by such recent immigrants must have been a powerful factor in renewing and reinvigorating the *Isleños'* Hispanic culture and in reinforcing the strong awareness of cultural distinctiveness characteristic of the *Isleño* worldview, even down to the present day. Rather than solely an isolated survival of exclusively Canarian traditions in a New World setting, the *Isleño* heritage—in terms of both oral literature and language—has emerged, after closer scrutiny, as a richly eclectic amalgam shaped from a variety of different Hispanic traditions. Two brief texts, in which elder *Isleños* recall the games they had played as children in the first decades of this century, confirm the geographic and cultural diversity of Hispanic contributions to *Isleño* folklore.

On February 27, 1981, at Violet (St. Bernard Parish), Mrs. Nisha García and Mrs. Irena González explained to me an *Isleño* modality of "Hide-and-Seek":[4]

---

[3]During my field work in St. Bernard Parish, I was able to interview one informant from Santander—appropriately nick-named "El Montañés"—and two aged Galicians, with one of whom I even exchanged a few words in *gallego*. In his pathfinding article on *Isleño* folktales, Raymond MacCurdy includes three texts provided by an informant born in Galicia (1952:227). The situation of the *Isleño* community, whose Spanish language and culture have been nourished over the years by such diverse contacts with the outside world, can be contrasted with the relatively greater isolation and consequent earlier decline of two other barely surviving Louisiana Spanish-speaking communities of eighteenth-century origin: The *Adaeseños* (of Sabine and Natchitoches Parishes) and the *Brulis* (of Ascension, Assumption, and Iberville Parishes). On *Bruli* Spanish, see MacCurdy (1959); for *Adaeseño*, Armistead and Gregory (1986); Lipski (1986; 1987).

[4]The symbol $\hat{s}$ indicates an aspirated s, which in word-final position coexists in the dialect with the sound's disappearance, reflected in a consequent opening of the preceding vowel (a, e, etc.). See MacCurdy (1950:35–36).

Jugábamos el fet, que yamaban, el roc. . ., el fet. . . Eŝ un juego que te díą y diŝpuȩ́ te dían a buŝcá. Y cuando te jayaban, desía: "¡Ay! ¡Jayé el roc!". . . Lọ niñọ nọ escondíamọ. Uno se eŝcondía. . . Es un. . . se levantó y. . . ah. . . y̓ tenían una pajita. ¿Ve? Y venían echando. . . y el que cogía la pajita era el que se tenía que que'á y los otrọ se dían a eŝcondé. . . Se sentaban tós; tenían. . . cogían una pajita y. . . y día. . . asina, en to'ą lą manọ, hasta que la [daba] a caer en una mano. Y la que tenía la pajita se tenía que que'á pa dí a buŝcá lọ otrọ que le quitaban. . . Cuando le [jayaban], gritaban: "¡Fet!". . . Tenían una pajita, una na más, y se sentaban tọ ayí, diⲐien'o una cosa, *though*. Nunca lo quiría diⲐí. . . No m'acuardo lo quediⲐían.¿Uŝté sabe?. . . Eŝto jugábamọ. . . Eya. . . Y al que le sentaba, cogía la pajita. Pero él . . .ninguno de lọ otrọ. . . La otra [decía]: "Ahora váyanse to'ą a eŝcondése." Y él se tiene que que'á. Y era el que tenía que que'á. Cuando la gente se. . . to'ọ lọ otrọ se escondían. . . to'ọ lọ chiquiyọ se eŝcondían. . . [Era] de noche. ¿Ve? De noche no había lụ ni nada. ¿No? Cualquiera se podía eŝcondé. Y le gritaban: "¡Fet!" De ahí dían corriendo p'ayí, corriendo p'aquí, haŝta que lọ jayaban. . . Y ese juego, eso era el fet.

(*Translation*: We played what they called *fet, roc. . . fet.* It's a game in which you go and then they go to look for you. And when they found you, they shouted: "Oh! I found the *roc*!". . . We children would hide. One would hide. . . Someone. . . stood up. . . and. . . uh. . . and they had a little straw. You know? And they went along dropping. . . and whoever got the straw was the one who had to stay and the others went to hide . . . Everybody sat down; they had. . . they took a little straw and. . . and he went. . . like this in everybody's hands, until he dropped the straw in someone's hand. And the one who had the straw had to stay to go look for the others who left him. . . When they [found] him, they shouted: "*Fet*!". . . They had just one straw and everyone sat there, saying something, *though*. I never wanted to say it. . . I don't remember what they said. You know? We played this. . . She. . . And whoever it turned out to be, got the straw. But he. . . none of the others. . . The other girl [said]: "Now, everybody go and hide." And he has to stay behind. And that was the one who had to stay. When the people. . . all the others hid . . ., all the children hid. . . [it was] at night. You know? There was no light at night or anything. Right? Anyone could hide. And they shouted at him: "*Fet*!" They went out of there, running here and running there, until they found them. . . And that game, that was [called] *fet*.)

At Delacroix Island, on March 23, 1982, Mrs. Malvina Pérez, assisted by Mr. Irvan Pérez, discussed several children's games: two types of marbles, "Hide-the-Stone," and "Hide-and-Seek":

I.P.: Las canicas era de cal. . .

M.P.: El juego se yamava jugar al roc. Cualquiera cosa se escónde y eyos lo tienen que dir a buscá y el que lo jaye. . . El fet. . . en él. . . se tenía que escondé. . . la persona. . . Discué lo otro tenían que buscá'nd'esa persona'staba. . .Pa jayálo. . . Sí. El que me jayaba a mí, él tenía que que'áse, pa'l otro esconderse. . . Cuando jugábamo al fet, cuando yo lo jayaba, yo desía: "¡Lo jayé!" Cuando. . . nojotro no escondíamo; él se que'aba; nojotro gritábamo: "¡Fet!" Entonse él día a buscáno. . .

I.P.: El tor, que yamaban, era el que tiraban. . . con. . .

M.P.: El que tiraban. . .

I.P.: El qu'estaba hecho, más o meno, de. . . de. . . de vidrio. . . de vidrio. . . Sí.

(*Translation*:

I.P.: Marbles (*canicas*) were made of clay. . .

M.P.: The game was called playing *roc*. Some object is hidden and they have to go and look and the one who finds it. . . *Fet*. . . in that [game]. . . you had to hide. . . the person. . . Then the others had to look for where that person was. . . to find him. Sure. The one who found me, he had to stay there, and the other one had to hide. . . When we played *fet*, when I found them, I said: "I found them!" When. . . we used to hide; he stayed behind; we shouted "*Fet!*" Then he went to look for us.

I.P.: What they called *tor* was what they threw. . . with. . .

M.P.: What they threw. . .

I.P.: It was made, more or less, out of glass. That's right.)

In regard to "Hide-and-Seek," the two explanations are at odds: In the first, the word *fet* is shouted when a hidden person is found, but, in the second, the hidden children shout *fet* to inform the child who is "it" that he should start looking for them. This latter explanation is, as we shall see, undoubtedly more satisfactory, in terms of the game's origins. In the first text, the seeker is apparently chosen by being given a straw in connection with some sort of counting-out rhyme long since forgotten. Here, too, "El roc" is confused with "El fet," but, as becomes clear in the second text, "El roc" is undoubtedly a different sort of game, in which some object is hidden and then searched for (something like "Hide-the-Button," in English and Scottish tradition).[5]

The term *fet* is recognized by the informants themselves as not being a Spanish word. The term and the game are undoubtedly of Catalan origin. Compare the following descriptions of the Catalan game:

> *Fet:* Joc de nois, en què tots els jugadors s'amaguen fora el qui paga; quan stán amagats, criden "Fet!," i el qui paga els va a cercar, i en trobar-ne un, aquest paga (Alcover and Moll 1968–69:V, 841b).

> ('*Fet:* A children's game, in which all the players hide except the one who pays; when they are all hidden, they cry "Fet!" ['Done'], and the one who pays goes to look for them and when one is found, he pays.')

> Lo *fet* consisteix en poder atrapar un dels que jugan, que regularment se fa a sort, a los demés que o be s'amagan o fugen ben lluny, desde ahont cridan: *Fet* (Maspons i Labrós 1874:80–81; 1931:73–74).

> ('*Fet* consists in one of the persons who plays—usually selected by lot—being able to catch the others, who either hide or run far away, from where they cry out: *Fet.*')

Clearly our second *Isleño* account is the correct one: *Fet*, shouted by the hidden children, signaled the beginning, rather than the conclusion, of the search. In regard to *roc*, I have so far found no Catalan documentation for a specific game, but the *Isleño* form, especially in association with the obvious Catalanism, *fet*, can be convincingly related to Catalan *roc* 'a small rock.' *Tor*, although its derivation remains problematic, might be seen as a metathesized form of Catalan *truc*: "Joc que consisteix a tirar un còdol o bola contra el del contrincant." (Alcover and Moll 1968–69:X, 560a) ('A game which consists of shooting a pebble or marble against that of one's opponent.') In such a case, the correspondence with the *Isleño* game would be quite exact. In any event, the three terms, *fet*, *roc*, and *tor*—whatever the exact meaning of the last two may be—would seem clearly to be of Catalan origin. Very probably, they were brought in by Catalan immigrants, known to have settled in the St. Bernard communities during the nineteenth century.

[5]See Maclagan (1901:91–92); Gomme (1964:214).

Taken together with an extensive comparative study of *Isleño* and Pan-Hispanic folk poetry, the Catalan terminology of these children's games reinforces our view of the eclectic character of *Isleño* tradition— a tradition that has borrowed extensively and creatively from numerous different Hispanic (and even extra-Hispanic) sources to form its own unique and distinctive Louisiana-Spanish repertoire.

REFERENCES CITED

Alcover, Antoni Maria, and Francesc de B. Moll

     1968–69   *Diccionari català-valencià-balear*. Barcelona: Editorial Moll. 10 vols.

Armistead, Samuel G.

     1978   "Romances tradicionales entre los hispanohablantes del estado de Luisiana," *Nueva Revista de Filología Hispánica*, 27:39–56.

     1980–81   "Spanish Language and Folklore in Louisiana," *La Corónica*, 9(2):187–89.

     1981   "Hispanic Folk Literature among the *Isleños*," in John Cooke and Mackie J.-V. Blanton, eds., *Perspectives on Ethnicity in New Orleans* (New Orleans: University of New Orleans), pp. 21–31.

     1982   "Un corrido de la muerte de Madero cantado en Louisiana," *Anuario de Letras*, 20:379–87.

     1983a   "Más romances de Luisiana," *Nueva Revista de Filología Hispánica*, 32:41–54.

     1983b   "Spanish Riddles from St. Bernard Parish," *Louisiana Folklore Miscellany*, 5(3):1–8.

     1985   "Adivinanzas españolas de Luisiana, in *Homenaje a Alvaro Galmés de Fuentes* (Madrid: Gredos), Vol. II, pp. 251–62.

     1989   "Más adivinanzas españolas de Luisiana," *Homenaje a Alonso Zamora Vicente* (Madrid: Castalia), Vol. II, pp. 25–38.

     1991   *The Spanish Tradition in Louisiana: I: 'Isleño' Folkliterature*. Newark, Delaware: Juan de la Cuesta.

_____, and Gregory, Hiram F.

1986   "French Loan Words in the Spanish Dialect of Sabine and Natchitoches Parishes," *Louisiana Folklife*, 10:21–30.

Din, Gilbert C.

1976 "Spanish Immigration to a French Land," *Revue de Louisiane*, 5(1):63–80.

1988 *The Canary Islanders of Louisiana*. Baton Rouge: Louisiana State University Press.

Gomme, Alice Bertha

1964 *The Traditional Games of England, Scotland, and Ireland*. New York: Dover. 2 vols.

Lipski, John M.

1986 "El español vestigial en los Estados Unidos: Características e implicaciones teóricas," *Estudios Filológicos*, 21:7–22.

1987 "El dialecto español de Río Sabinas: Vestigios del mexicano en Luisiana y Texas," *Nueva Revista de Filología Hispánica*, 35:111–28.

1990 *The Language of the 'Isleños': Vestigial Spanish in Louisiana*. Baton Rouge: Louisiana State University Press.

MacCurdy, Raymond R.

1950 *The Spanish Dialect in St. Bernard Parish, Louisiana*. Albuquerque: University of New Mexico Press.

1952 "Spanish Folklore from St. Bernard Parish, Louisiana: Part III, Folktales," *Southern Folklore Quarterly*, 16:227–50.

1959 "A Spanish Word-List of the 'Brulis' Dwellers of Louisiana," *Hispania*, 42:547–54.

Maclagen, Robert Craig

1901 *The Games and Diversions of Argyleshire*. London: David Nutt.

Maspons i Labrós, Francesc

1874 *Jochs de la infancia*. Barcelona: Frederich Martí y Cantó.

1931 *Jocs d'infants*. Third ed. Barcelona: Editorial Barcino.

Marcos Carneiro de Mendonça

THE *AULA DO COMERCIO* IN THE REFORMS OF POMBAL IN EIGHTEENTH-CENTURY BRAZIL

PREFACE

I had originally intended to add the subtitle "Pombal, Illustrious Reformer-Creator before Becoming Marquis" to point out the fact that the period of the formation of the *Aula do Comércio* ('School of Commerce') corresponds to the time when Pombal was Sebastião José de Carvalho e Mello, Count of Oeiras (1754–1759). In other words, he was not yet the powerful Marquis that we have come to know.

Also I wish to add that the contents of the documents, some of which are gathered here for the first time, led me to conclude that the *Aula do Comércio* probably contributed more that anything else to the development of a Portuguese middle class (with repercussions in Brazil) by providing a solid commercial, economic, social, and financial training ground.

I first became interested in Pombal's *Aula do Comércio* in 1958, when the publisher Anhambi S.A. included the late Prof. Ramos de Carvalho's (d. 1972) "O Ensino em São Paulo" in the collection *Ensaios*

Marcos Carneiro de Mendonça (d. 1988) was an unusual scholar, who was known to many Brazilians as the finest goal tender of Fla-Flu soccer team of Rio de Janeiro. Together with his wife Anna Amelia, their collection of Braziliana in Cosme Velho has long been familiar to connoisseurs of fine arts and scholarship.

Paulistas (1958:600–22). Later on Prof. Betty de Oliveira offered me copies of her two studies, *A Educação Brasileira na Era Pombalina* (1970) and *As Reformas e a Educação no Brasil* (1973). At that time, I had already published the second edition of *O Marquês de Pombal e o Brasil* (1966) and *A Amazônia na Era Pombalina* (1963). Moreover, as a businessman, I realized the great importance of the subject upon discovering that the *Aula do Comércio* was closely related to the contribution of Pombal's regime in Brazil.

Afterwards, while reading and admiring Prof. Francisco da Gama Caeiro's prologue in Prof. Laerte Ramos de Carvalho's *As Reformas Pombalinas da Instrução Pública* (1978:11–23) and Antônio Alberto Banha de Andrade's, *A Reforma Pombalina dos Estudos Secundários no Brasil* (1978), I began to feel that these and other studies about Pombal's important reforms always emphasized his modernization of Coimbra University, without making any reference to Lisbon. After all, it was in Lisbon where the modest *Aula do Comércio* began. The founding of this institution, operating since 1759, was at the root of the great boom of development and commercial wealth that occurred in Portugal and Brazil during the second half of the eighteenth century.

In my opinion, the establishment of the *Aula do Comércio* was as significant as the better known reform of Coimbra University in 1772. It should be noted, however, that the latter was conceived and implemented in Portugal, while the *Aula*, though also a Pombaline innovation, was conceived in Brazil, but founded in Portugal. The *Aula* originated in Brazil because of Governor Francisco Xavier de Mendonça Furtado (d. 1770), who, in February of 1754, proposed the establishment of a *Companhia Geral de Comércio* ('General Company of Commerce'), aimed at saving the region of Amazônia, which he governed, from its condition of extreme poverty.

The pioneering participation of this governor in creating the so-called Pombaline Commercial Companies, can be seen in the private correspondence which the Governor maintained with his half brother on his mother's side, Sebastião José de Carvalho e Mello.[1]

---

[1]The correspondence comprises five important letters (these and other documents were also published in Carneiro 1982):

  a. from Pará (21 November 1751);
  b. from Pará (24 January 1754);
  c. from Pará (30 January 1754);
  d. *Projeto de Estatutos*, from Pará (15 February 1754); and
  e. from Pará (20 February 1754)

The first letter (*Carta do Pará*, dated 21 November 1751) is addressed, as all others, to "The Most Illustrious and Most Excellent Lord, Brother of my heart, "which immediately shows that this correspondence was not meant to be divulged, and therefore of great significance as historical veracity. The key document presented here is the letter (dated 30 August 1770) from the Palacio de Nossa Senhora da Ajuda. In this first letter to his half brother, Governor Mendonça Furtado wrote:

> In this country it is customary to pay one tenth of the value of exports upon embarkation, and nothing is taken aboard ship without first being weighed. Thus, products are assessed a payment of forty percent upon departure, because every *arrôba* (today = fifteen kilos; in earlier times = thirty-two *arráteis*) of cacao, which this year is worth ten *tostões*, is taxed by one *tostão*. Each *arrôba* is taxed an additional ten *réis* for being weighed, which amounts to eleven percent.

> Upon arrival at the *Casa da India* in Lisbon, each *arrôba* is assessed 400 *réis* for custom duty, plus 100 *réis* for miscellaneous charges. This amounts to fifty percent, a sum which, when added to the cost of embarking rights, totals sixty percent.

> At the Consulate in Lisbon, the products brought to this country are charged four percent. If they come from our own country they are also charged five percent at the market, which, upon leaving Lisbon, amounts to nine percent.

> Upon entering customs here, the products, according to the new policy, are assessed ten percent. The charges for export from Lisbon and for import in this town amount to nineteen percent. Together with the sixty charged upon export, this amounts to a total tax of eighty percent on the commerce of this State.

> The clergy does not pay export taxes. Likewise, it does not pay, under the pretext of Missions, neither consulate and market tariffs in Lisbon, nor custom duties in this State. Therefore, since they do not pay fees anywhere, it is obvious that priests make a profit of 100 percent. Lay businessmen are in an entirely different situation. From this your Excellency can deduce that the poor merchants are unable to compete with the Holy Powers, who have an assured profit of eighty percent.

This letter clearly shows why, in Amazônia, in the second half of the eighteenth century, both the government and the settlers, whether merchants or not, were suffering extreme poverty. It is also fairly certain that any reaction to this predicament could easily have served as a pretext for religious persecution.

The fifty-second letter exchanged between both half brothers (dated 24 January 1754) reads:

> Of the many ideas that have occurred to me on how to repair, even partially, the pitiful ruin to which these two Captaincies [Pará and Maranhão] have been reduced, none seemed better than to establish here a commercial company that would introduce a goodly number of negroes to this State, so that our sugar mill and plantation owners would find an accessible fair where they can be purchased for a reasonable price, thus redeeming themselves from ruin.

In the fifty-fourth letter (dated 30 January 1754), Mendonça Furtado wrote:

> I have written Your Excellency extensively regarding the new Commercial Company that these poor residents wish to establish so that they can redeem themselves and strive for this State to prosper.

> Because this Company cannot be founded except under conditions that would benefit those who would invest in it and with the expertise to enable them to manage the operation, I found myself in an unfortunate position, for in this town there is not a single person with knowledge of business practices.

> Since I was certain that the parties with sufficient wealth would not join without first knowing the details of the contract, I decided on the conditions that I am sending you. Inasmuch as they were accepted by everyone, I advised the individuals involved to consult with someone else on this important matter, so that I should not have to bear total responsibility.

> Because I do not have any material at hand that addresses these matters, nor a copy of the regulations of similar enterprises to guide me so that I might adapt them to the needs of the country, I had to rely on conversations and on my own observations in order to produce the enclosed document. At any rate, I explained the circumstances to those interested and, despite their satisfaction, I suggested that they make further inquiries in Lisbon in order to ensure that their assets are as secure as possible.

I have a great interest in this Company, because I would like to see prosperity in this wretched State. I am convinced that this is one of the measures that can be implemented to realize that goal. Nevertheless, whatever His Majesty decides will certainly be the best and most just solution.

In concluding the first part of this correspondence, I transcribed the following letter which Mendonça Furtado wrote from Pará (dated 28 May 1754) to D. Antônio Rolim de Moura, Governor of Mato Grosso:

I have spent two and half years working towards this goal, taking advantage of my residence in the area to convince these people to create a Commercial Company for the introduction of negroes under the enclosed conditions. These exclusive rights, granted as they may by His Majesty, will doubtless enable the mines of Mato Grosso and this State [Pará] to be completely redeemed. Within a few years poverty will be replaced by abundance, and the Royal Treasury will not need to make any major contribution toward providing slaves. Since this territory is so vast, it would not, in any event, be able to do so. On the other hand, this can easily be accomplished through the Company that we would like to establish.

The military has accepted the idea and was the first to join, setting an example without which I could not have accomplished anything. Nonetheless, it was impossible to collect more than 13,000 *réis,* which is an insignificant amount for such a huge endeavor.

The Governor concluded this cycle of correspondence with a letter to the Minister Diogo de Mendonça Corte Real, who had countersigned the impressive Instructions that were sent to him in September of 1751. He wrote:

To create this Company, I did all I could to make these people understand that their entire fortune was dependent on it. They soon realized that I was correct, and each of them contributed whatever little he could. As of now we have raised the sum of 30,000 *cruzados,* an amount which, in truth, is insignificant for an objective of such magnitude as that of supplying both this State and the mines of Mato Grosso with slaves.

In order to increase these meager funds, this Company is now seeking permission from His Royal Majesty to invite the participation of the merchants of Lisbon and Oporto. This would enable us to multiply our stocks. After requesting His Majesty's immediate royal protection, the Company will ask him to grant it the three exclusive rights contained in the enclosed petition. From what I can understand, those rights are in no way prejudicial to His Majesty's Treasury. In fact, they can contribute greatly to the reconstruction of this entire State.

The modest amount that this Captaincy was able to raise represents all that is left of its wealth, and if His Majesty, in all his mercy, does not shield and protect it, surely its residents will experience total ruin, owing to a plan wherein they hoped to find their redemption.

If this Company prospers with His Majesty's protection and assistance, as I am persuaded, all his royal revenues will be increased in proportion to its growth, and all the areas that presently comprise deserted farms and uncultivated soil, will, in a few years, become extremely lucrative sugar mills and very large plantations, leading to expanded commerce. The sterility and poverty in which people live in these lands will be turned into abundance and wealth.

There remains yet another extremely important reason for the creation of this Company to merit the royal attention of His Majesty, for it will provide him the opportunity to put an end to the disgusting and scandalous enslavement of the Indians. The concern of His Majesty is well known. Since, among the residents, there is no one to farm the plantations, it is extremely difficult to intercept and extinguish the wicked black market dealing in Indian slaves. In this respect, what took place in Brazil when there lived men who thought like those who live here now constitutes a good example. These men are treating the Indians with equal savagery in order to unjustly enslave those miserable souls without any justification other than violence and tyranny.

When these facts were presented to the Court [at Lisbon], and when it was pointed out that those innocent, poor ignorant pagans were not only being harassed but completely tyrannized by the ambitious settlers of that State, King D. Sebastião promulgated a law on 20 March 1570 wherein he demanded the total abolition of slavery, permitting it only in specific instances.

When the rule of these kingdoms was later transferred to the Kings of Castile, Philip II was informed that the law of 1570 was not sufficient enough to prevent the Indians from being persecuted unjustly. He then promulgated yet another law on 11 November 1595, restricting even further that of King D. Sebastião. But this law still did not suffice to halt the cruelties done to the Indians.

This matter was brought to the attention of Philip III, who issued another law on 30 July 1609 in which he completely abolished the enslavement of Indians. The same king ordered that a new law be published on 10 September 1611, wherein, besides determining how the Indians should be governed, he authorized slavery once again, though only in the case of rebellion or uprising by the Indians.

After commerce was initiated with the African Coast and negro slaves were brought to this country to cultivate the land, the enslavement of Indians was gradually forgotten. Today there is not a person who would want to buy them even for a very low price.

Because trade from the African Coast was never introduced into this State, and since there was such a relaxed attitude towards the enslavement of the Indians, the settlers became so involved in contraband that they ruined themselves and the entire State as well.

When this Company is firmly established, providing the settlers with an abundance of slaves, the same situation will occur as in the rest of Brazil, for they will eventually forget the unjust slavery of the Indians. Their mills, which are currently abandoned, will thus be put to use: the land will be cultivated, and commerce and tariffs will increase. Thus, rather than having to depend on the Royal Treasury, we will be able to shoulder the expenditures that must be undertaken for the defense of this State, such as the new fortresses that His Majesty ordered to be built. Last but not least, good relations will exist between the residents and the Indians, together with whom we will be able to create new towns so that we may settle in this wilderness, for there is no other way to populate it.

Once again, I tell Your Excellency that, having meditated very carefully on how to restore these two Captaincies [Pará and Maranhão], no other possibility has occurred to me other than the creation of this Company, upon which I am entirely convinced that the interests of this land depend.

May God preserve Your Excellency for many years to come. Pará, 18 January 1754.

Diogo de Mendonça Corte Real

Contrary to the previous letters, which had been exchanged with his half brother, this was a case of official rather than private correspondence. It is important to note the candid manner in which Governor Mendonça Furtado justified the enslavement of Africans, who could provide the needed manpower as a substitute for that of the Indians.

I am certain that the incisive terms of this timely letter contributed to the creation, a year and a half later, of his desired company.

Mendonça Furtado's proposal for the Company was sent to Lisbon from Pará on 15 February 1754. The statutes appeared in Lisbon on 6 June 1754. Beginning with Article 48, their stipulations were quite remarkable: "The stock and capital of the Company will be one million and two hundred *cruzados*, divided into one thousand and two hundred shares of four hundred *réis* each, etc." This amount was underwritten not only with the patriotic participation of individuals from the *Velha Nobreza* ('Old Aristocracy') of Portugal, but also with that of merchants who originally were opposed to the creation of the Company.

To avoid any doubts regarding the influence and participation of Francisco Xavier de Mendonça Furtado in the organization of the first great Pombaline Commercial Company, I will transcribe the initial statement of the organizers of the *Companhia Geral do Grão Pará e Maranhão*:

> Sir: The merchants of Lisbon, whose signatures are affixed below, and those of Your Majesty's vassals residing in this kingdom, being aware of the petition presented to Your Majesty by the residents of the Captaincy of Grão Pará on February 15 of last year, 1754, and encouraged by the hope of rendering a great service to God, to Your Majesty, the common good, and the preservation of that State, have decided to create a new Company that will at once develop its declining commerce and agriculture, and provide for the welfare of its presently decaying population; thus, we hereby request that Your Majesty support the aforementioned Company with the confirmation and concession of the following regulations and privileges.

Hence, it is the organizers themselves who confirmed that the decision to approve the creation of the Company was based on the proposal they sent to Lisbon on 15 February 1754.

Now we shall see how the *Aula do Comércio* was created, on 19 April 1759, as a result of the great Commercial Company of Grão Pará and Maranhão and which can be credited for various important developments, including the appearance of many wealthy *Comendadores*, followed by Barons, Counts, and Viscounts, who formed the high Pombaline bourgeoisie in Portugal.

Among the many documents in the Cosme Velho Archive relating to the creation of the *Aula do Comércio*, the following are of fundamental importance:[2]

---

[2]The documents are translated as follows:
  a) Projected statutes for a General Company of Commerce
  b) Creation of the General Company of Grão Pará and Maranhão.

a) *Projeto de Estatutos* de uma Companhia Geral de Comércio (Pará, 15 February 1754).

b) Instituição da *Companhia Geral do Grão Pará, e Maranhão:* (Lisbon, 6 June 1755).

c) Exposição justificativa, e Relação das pessoas que S. Majestade foi servido nomear para a fundação de uma Junta do Comércio (Belém [Portugal], 30 September 1755).

d) *Estatutos da Junta do Comércio* (12 December 1756).

e) Capítulo XVI dos *Estatutos da Junta do Comércio*, então formada.

f) Alvará com força de Lei, em cujo Capítulo XVI encontra-se declarada a obrigação do comerciante ter, e exibir quando necessário, o *Livro Diário*, de sua escrita contábil.

g) *Estatutos da Aula do Comércio*: N. S. da Ajuda (19 May 1759).

As far as Portugal is concerned, the existence of the *Aula do Comércio* was extremely beneficial to the *Companhia Geral da Agricultura das Vinhas do Alto Douro* ('General Company for the Cultivation of the Vineyards of the Alto Douro'), to the *Real Fabrica de Sedas* ('Royal Silk Factory'), and to the regular implementation of the *Estatutos dos Mercadores do Retalho* ('Statutes for Retail Merchants').

In Brazil's case, this applied not only in reference to the *Companhia Geral do Grão Pará e Maranhão*, but also in relation to the *Companhia Geral do Pernambuco e Paraíba*, created in Lisbon on 30 July 1759. And here I am compelled to question: why Pernambuco and Paraíba and not Pernambuco and Bahia? Could it be that the tense Jesuit problem in Bahia had something to do with it?

The great importance of the *Aula do Comércio* in Portugal can be gathered from the fact that the *Comendadores* of Bahia and Rio de

---

c) Justifying statement and list of the individuals whom His Majesty named for the creation of a Commission of Commerce.

d) Statutes for the Commission of Commerce.

e) Chapter XVI of the Statutes of the Commission of Commerce then formed.

f) Charter with force of law, whose Chapter XVI stipulates that merchants are obliged to keep and present, when petitioned, the daily record of their accounts.

g) Statutes for the School of Commerce.

Janeiro, when visiting the Royal Family upon their arrival (1807–08), suggested to the Prince Regent, D. João, the creation of an *Aula do Comércio*, both in Bahia and in Rio de Janeiro. That is how those schools came to be.

The *Aula do Comércio* was born in Portugal due to the clash of interests involving the marketing of products from Amazônia. These products were commercially manipulated by the Confraria ('Brotherhood') of Espírito Santo and the Society of Jesus. Upon learning of the privileges granted to the great Company of Commerce, they protested vehemently against its existence. The aggressive tone of the government's reaction to these protests can be found in the document (no. 3) of 30 September 1755.

In his research at the Instituto Histórico e Geográfico Brasileiro, Kenneth Maxwell found a document which he translated (1973:8, n. 4). It reads as follows:[3]

> Few or rare were the Portuguese merchants in condition to do business with their own funds and with goods that were not foreign. All the commerce of Brazil was made on credit and the greater part by salesmen of the foreign houses and by *Comissários Volantes* ('traveling salesmen' of today) who brought the goods from Portugal to America [Brazil] and sold them on behalf of the foreigners, receiving a mere commission, and perhaps a bonus when they were particularly successful in serving the interests of the manufacturers of the goods.

This is an example for which Kenneth Maxwell, without meaning to, provides us with yet another proof of the extremely modest business aptitude of the Portuguese merchant of the 1750's. When Sebastião José de Carvalho e Mello became Minister in September of 1750, he confronted this situation as soon as he could and aspired to improve it. The opportunity arose when his half brother, Francisco Xavier de Mendonça Furtado, presented him with a proposal for the creation of the Commercial Company of Grão Pará and Maranhão in February of 1754. This proposal led to the issuance of the Statutes for the new

---

[3]The original text reads: Poucos ou raríssimos foram os Negociantes Portugueses em estado de negociar com os seus próprios fundos; nenhum com fazendas que não fossem estrangeiras. Todo o comércio do Brasil se fez a crédito, e a maior parte dele por caixeiros das própias Estrangeiras, e por comissários volantes que levavam para América as Fazendas e ali as vendião e negociavão por conta dos mesmos Estrangeiros, recebendo uma simples comisão do seu trabalho ou alguma gratificação mais, quando faziam melhor a utilidade dos originários senhores das mesmas fazendas.

Commercial Company on 6 June 1755 and to the Statutes of the Junta do Comércio on 12 December 1756. In Chapter XVI of the latter there is a reference to the creation of the *Aula do Comércio* that, after 1759, led to the great economic, social, and financial boom which is the subject of my humble contribution to this *homenagem*.

I would like to call attention to the provision included in Article 39 of the Statutes of the *Companhia de Comércio do Grão Pará and Maranhão*. Thanks to this measure, the old Portuguese nobility was encouraged to engage in commerce without losing its privileges, as was the case in the past. The same Article also enticed young people of more modest background to work diligently and efficiently to develop the country by promising titles to those who distinguished themselves.

In conclusion, I would like to say once again, that, in my opinion, the overall influence of the *Aula do comércio*, though overlooked in previous investigations, matched the results obtained by the better known reform of Coimbra University in 1772.

REFERENCES CITED

Banha de Andrade, Antônio Alberto

    1978   *A Reforma Pombalina dos Estudos Secundários no Brasil*. São Paulo: Saraiva/EDUSP.

Carneiro de Mendonça, Marcos

    1960   *O Marquês de Pombal e o Brasil*. São Paulo: Companhia Editora Nacional (Bibliotheca Pedagógica Brasileira, Série 5.). [2nd ed. São Paulo:Nacional, 1966 (Brasiliana, vol. 299).]

    1963   (Ed.)*A Amazônia na Era Pombalina; Correspondência inédita do governador e capitão-general de estado do Grão Pará e Maranhão, Francisco Xavier de Mendonça Furtado, 1751–1759*. São Paulo: Instituto Histórico e Geográfico Brasileiro [in Rio de Janeiro]. 3 vols.

    1982   *Aula do Comercio: Nas Comemorações do Bicentenário da Morte de Sebastião José de Carvalho e Mello, 'Marqués de Pombal' (1782–1982)*. Rio de Janeiro: Xerox do Brasil.

Maxwell, Kenneth

    1973   *Conflicts and Conspiracies. Brazil and Portugal 1750–1808*. New York: Cambridge University Press. Transl. into Portuguese by João Maia, *A Devassa da Devassa. A Inconfidência Mineira*. Rio de Janeiro: Paz e Terra, 1977; 2nd ed., 1978; 3rd ed., 1985.

Oliveira, Betty Atunes de

   1970   *A Educação Brasilieira na Era Pombolina.* Unpublished term
             paper (written for a History of Education course, Univer-
             sidade Federal do Rio de Janeiro). Typescript.

   1973   *As Reformas e a Educação no Brasil.* A revision of the former
             work. Published as a brochure in a limited edition. São
             Carlos, São Paulo: Universidade Federal de São Carlos.

Ramos de Carvalho, Laerte

   1958   "O ensino em São Paulo," in *Ensaios Paulistas* (São Paulo:
             Anhambi), pp. 600–22. (Contribuição de 'O Estado de São
             Paulo' às Comemorações do IV Centenário da Cidade).

   1978   *As Reformas Pombalinas da Instrução Pública.* Prólogo por
             Francisco da Gama Caeiro. São Paulo: Ed. Saraiva / Univer-
             sidade de São Paulo.

Francis A. Dutra

THE PRACTICE OF MEDICINE IN EARLY MODERN PORTUGAL

The Role and Social Status of the *Físico-mor* and the *Surgião-mor*

The governance of medicine in Portugal during the sixteenth and seventeenth centuries varied in several respects from practices in the Spanish portion of the Iberian peninsula, but some basic similarities also existed. Michael E. Burke points out in his study of surgery and Spanish medical reform that "Spanish medicine was governed not by universities, guilds or governmental bodies, but rather by the Royal Protomedicato" (1977:27). The *protomedicato* was a board composed usually of three licensed medical examiners appointed by the king. Its responsibility was to examine and license all those wishing to practice medicine of any kind in Spain (Lanning 1985:395). While a formal board of medical examiners did not exist in Portugal until the late eighteenth century, medicine, like its counterpart in Spain, was generally governed centrally, directed by appointees of the king. Instead of a *protomedicato*, the Portuguese had two officials, the chief physician (*físico-mor*) and the chief surgeon (*surgião-mor*), who, in addition to acting as head physician and head surgeon of the royal household respectively, had the authority to examine and license all those wishing to practice medicine or cures in Portugal.

Francis A. Dutra, a specialist in Portuguese and Brazilian history at the University of California, Santa Barbara, is former Chair of the Latin American and Iberian Studies Program.

In contrast to the Spanish *protomedicato* which examined and licensed all practitioners, in Portugal there was a division of labor, with the chief physician generally having jurisdiction over those persons engaged in curing internal diseases and the chief surgeon over those who dealt with external maladies. Both were to supervise apothecaries with the principal responsibility belonging to the chief physician. Although the distinction between the two jurisdictions sometimes blurred, the chief surgeon examined midwives, ophthalmologists and dermatologists in addition to surgeons, barbers, bloodletters, bone setters, and tooth pullers. In short, with certain exceptions, which will be discussed later, no one could practice medicine formally in Portugal without a license from either the *físico-mor* or the *surgião-mor*.[1] Francisco Marques de Sousa Viterbo published seventy-nine royal letters or licenses issued to persons engaged in the field of medicine for the sixteenth and early seventeenth centuries and summarized an additional nineteen (Sousa Viterbo 1893–1915).

As early as the reign of King Afonso IV (1325–1357), the Portuguese monarch ordered that physicians, surgeons, and apothecaries be examined before they practiced their professions (see Gonçalves 1965:71). In an attempt to upgrade medical and surgical practices and to eliminate quackery, other rulers followed this precedent. In 1430 King João I (1385–1433) ordered that all who practiced medicine be examined and approved by his physician, Mestre Martinho. Letters were issued to the successful candidates, signed by Mestre Martinho and sealed with the royal seal. Those practicing without royal permission were to be imprisoned and their properties and wealth forfeited to the crown (*Ibid.*:72–73). King João I's successors continued these practices. However, from at least the reign of Afonso V (1438–1481), professors holding chairs of medicine at the University of Lisbon were exempt from examinations (*Ibid.*:75–76). The *regimento* for the chief physician issued by King Manuel I (1495–1521), in 1515, further exempted doctors and licentiates who received their degrees from the University of Lisbon. But those persons who held degrees from foreign universities had to be reëxamined by Portugal's chief physician (*Ibid.*:76).[2]

---

[1]See the *regimentos* ('standing orders') for Portugal's chief physician and chief surgeon in *Systema, ou Collecção dos Regimentos Reaes* (1818:VI, 338–46). The chief surgeon's *regimentos* are also found in J. J. de Andrade e Silva (1854–59:IV, 233–34 and 248–49).

[2]These provisions were also included in the 1521 *regimento* discussed below. They remained in effect when Portugal's chief university was transferred from Lisbon to Coimbra in 1537.

On 25 February 1521, King Manuel I revised and added to the *regimento* in his instructions to the new chief physician, Diogo Lopes, who was succeeding Manuel Afonso in that post. In it the ruler declared that no physician, Portuguese or foreigner (with the exceptions mentioned above), could practice medicine in Portugal without first being examined by the chief physician and at least two Court physicians chosen by him, although it would suffice if only one were available. The examination was to cover theoretical as well as practical matters. In addition, sworn affidavits testifying to the quality of the practical skills of the candidate were to be obtained. Furthermore, the candidate should have completed two years of practical experience in the company of physicians who had been licensed by Portugal's chief physician. Finally, three or four visitations were to be made to sick patients in the company of the chief physician to insure that the candidate possessed the necessary skills.

After a candidate had completed these requirements successfully, the chief physician issued a license, stating that the required examinations had taken place and which included the names of the examiners. Official letters bearing this information would then be issued by the Royal Chancery and the newly-approved physician would make a payment of a silver mark (*marco da prata*) to the chief physician. Anyone who attempted to practice medicine without such a license and accompanying letters would be subject to punishment. The fine was thirty *dobras de banda*, half disbursed to the chief physician, the other half to the accuser. At the same time, because there were many parts of Portugal which did not have qualified physicians, provisions were made to license others who claimed to have medical skills. Such men and women could present affidavits from local officials testifying to their healing abilities. The chief physician, after examining them, could grant licenses to those who qualified for a fee of two *dobras de banda*. Such licenses would then be issued through the Royal Chancery.

The king ordered his judicial officials to assist the chief physician in apprehending persons practicing medicine without licenses. The chief physician also had authority over apothecaries (*boticários*), who required licenses in order to prepare prescriptions. The candidates were to be examined by the chief physician and other physicians of the Court, along with the royal apothecaries, or, if the latter were not available, a qualified apothecary from the place where the examination was held. The license fee for apothecaries was one *cruzado* ($400) and the penalty for failing to own one was thirty *dobras de banda*. The chief physician had the power to visit apothecary shops together with the royal apothecaries to make sure they had the proper medicines. Worthless medicines were to be publicly burned and those who possessed them were subject to a series of fines. Apothecaries could not dispense certain medicines without prescriptions from physicians nor could they sell medicines at higher prices than allowed for court apothecaries. Finally, King Manuel I gave strict orders that surgeons not interfere in the sphere of physicians and that physicians stay out of that of surgeons.[3]

One of the earliest *regimentos* for the chief surgeon is dated 25 October 1448 and was issued by the young monarch Afonso V to his servant and surgeon, Manuel Gil, who was named chief surgeon for Portugal. Mestre Gil's responsibility was to examine, approve, and issue licenses to all those who wished to practice the "art of surgery". Anyone practicing this art without a license from the chief surgeon was to be imprisoned and to pay a fine of two marks of silver (*marcos de prata*), one to the chief surgeon and the other to his accuser. In the same *regimento*, the king ordered all his judicial officials to apprehend any persons practicing surgery without proper licenses and to detain them until the chief surgeon approved their release. In addition, King Afonso V put three armed men at the chief surgeon's disposal to apprehend the unlicensed miscreants (Andrade e Silva, IV, 248–49).[4] As can be seen from the letters published by Sousa Viterbo, the authority of the kingdom's chief surgeon actually covered all persons who attempted to cure external maladies. Details are found in the *regimento* of 1631, which will be discussed later.

As the sixteenth century got under way, some new influences were affecting the practice of medicine in Portugal. Like other parts of western Europe, Portugal was touched by the Renaissance and the new emphasis on experimentation and practical experience. To aid in the study of anatomy, King João III (1521–1557) ordered that cadavers be supplied to the University of Coimbra.[5] There was also an upgrading in the teaching of medicine at the University. According to the 1559 Statutes of the University of Coimbra, there were six chairs of medicine.

[3]The *regimento* for the chief physician is found in *Systema* (1818:VI, 338–43).

[4]A certified copy of this *carta* was provided by Jorge da Cunha, a scribe at the royal archives of Torre de Tombo, 30 July 1632. See J. J. Andrade e Silva (1854–59:IV, 249). This document is also found in *Systema* (1818:VI, 345–46).

[5]See, for example, the two *alvarás* of 16 October 1546 published in M. Brandão (1937–41:III, 71–72).

The holder of the *prima* chair, which was the most prestigious and which paid the highest annual stipend, taught the works of the Greek physician Galen (200–130 B.C.). The *nona* chair also dealt with the writings of Galen. The *terça* chair was concerned with the writings of the Persian-born Arab philosopher and physician, Avicenna (980–1037 A.D.). The holder of the *vespera* chair, which was the second most prestigious and highest paid chair in medicine, taught the writings of Hippocrates (c. 460–377 B.C.), the Greek physician known as the father of medicine. Among the chairs of medicine, there was also a chair of anatomy which ranked third in prestige as well as the amount of its stipend. Finally there was a chair of surgery (see Leite 1963:93 and 295–302).[6] The professors holding such chairs of medicine were obliged to visit the hospital of Coimbra with their students, so that the latter could have practical experience (*Ibid.*:311–14). A number of Portuguese also studied or taught at foreign universities, such as those of Salamanca (in Castile) and Montpellier (in France) (see Veríssimo Serrão 1977–88:III, 356 and 359). In 1492 the Royal Hospital of All Saints (Hospital Real de Todos os Santos) was established in Lisbon and, as the sixteenth century progressed, it became a major center for the instruction of surgeons (Carmona 1954:9 and 278–86).

Certain changes were also taking place in society. In 1497, King Manuel I forced all Jews in Portugal to convert to Christianity. Prior to that year, many influential physicians, surgeons and apothecaries in Portugal were Jews (Veríssimo Serrão 1977–88:IV, 407).[7] However, with this forced conversion to Christianity—followed in time by the activities of the Inquisition against persons of Jewish ancestry—many of Jewish ancestry, who held university degrees in medicine, emigrated to other parts of Europe. Popular sentiment in Portugal was hostile towards Jews who had converted to Christianity and their descendants. This prejudice intensified as the sixteenth century unfolded and there was a lack of confidence on the part of the general population regarding those who were known as New Christians (Veríssimo Serrão *Loc. cit.*)

By the time Sebastian inherited the Portuguese throne in 1557, greater emphasis was placed on restricting the practice of medicine to those who could claim to be Old Christians. By a law issued on 20 September 1568, King Sebastian (1557–1578) established a scholarship

---

[6]A similar system was followed in Spain in that the chairs were named after the canonical hours. The holder of the *prima* chair taught in the morning and that of the *vespera*, later in the afternoon. See R. I. Kagan (1974:162–64).

[7]See M. J. P. Ferro Tavares (1982–84).

fund called the *partidos dos médicos* for Old Christian students to study medicine, the funds being obtained from various cities and villages in Portugal. The law stipulated that there always be thirty qualified Old Christian students studying medicine and surgery at the University of Coimbra. However, the law does not seem to have been fully implemented (Braga 1892–1902:II, 779–80) and King Philip III (1598–1621) issued a new *regimento* dated 7 February 1604 (Andrade e Silva 1854–59:I, 42–46). By a resolution of 1 September 1622, even those New Christian physicians, who had been reconciled with the Inquisition, were forbidden to practice medicine in Portugal (*Ibid.*:III, 77).[8] In that same year, a law was passed prohibiting New Christians from teaching at the University of Coimbra (Veríssimo Serrão 1977–88:IV, 322).

The concept of nobility was also undergoing some changes. The noble class was being broadened to include, among others, important physicians and surgeons. A number of prominent physicians and surgeons in sixteenth-century Portugal received patents of nobility. For example, physicians attached to the royal household were frequently given such patents and some, like Pedro de Vila Nova—physician and surgeon to Catherine of Austria, queen of King João III—were given a coat of arms.[9] At times leading physicians and surgeons achieved the more exclusive knighthoods in one of the three Portuguese military orders: Christ, Santiago, and Avis. By the beginning of the sixteenth century, one of the most prestigious symbols of social status in Portugal was the possession of a knighthood and habit in one of these orders.[10] Members usually displayed the insignia of their Order in their portraits and were frequently identified as knights of their particular Orders in crown documents, notarial records, and petitions, as well as in genealogies and when they signed their names. As the century

---

[8]On 17 August 1671, Pedro II (1667–1706) gave special orders to his chief physician to make sure that the resolution of 1622 be obeyed (Braga 1892–1902:II, 810–11).

[9]See the letter of 3 February 1538, ANTT, Chancelaria de D. João III, *Doações*, liv. 44, fol. 115ᵛ (reprinted in Sousa Viterbo 1915 [5th series]:187–88).

[10]For knights of military orders, the terms *hábito* ('habit') and *cavaleiro* ('knighthood') may be used interchangeably. All knights in the military orders also received the *hábito* of that Order. However, those members who led a monastic life, or who were priests, received only the *hábito* without the knighthood. According to the Rules and Statutes of each order, the ceremony of knighthood was to precede the reception of the habit. The early seventeenth-century statutes are conveniently reprinted in J. J. Andrade e Silva (1854–59:III, 181–271 [Christ]; III, 272–408 [Avis]; and IV, 1–66 [Santiago]). The latter two orders were established in the twelfth century to help drive the Moslems from Portugal. The Order of Christ, founded in 1319, replaced (in Portugal) the international Order of the Knights Templars, which had been suppressed by Pope Clement V in 1312.

progressed and anti-New Christian sentiment in Portugal increased, membership in the military orders gained further appeal, because the purity of blood statutes of the orders excluded from membership, at least theoretically, persons of Jewish and Moslem ancestry. In the first item of his "Regimento and Statutes Regarding the Reform of the Three Military Orders," dated 6 February 1572, King Sebastian stated specifically that no one descended from Moslems or Jews should be allowed membership in any of the three military orders (ANTT, Chancelaria da Ordem de Cristo, liv. 2, fol. 278ᵛ).[11]

The majority of knighthoods in military orders which were held by members of the medical elite during the period under discussion were in the Order of Christ, the largest and most prestigious of the Portuguese military orders (see Dutra).[12] One reason for this was the crown's ability to use membership in this Order for its patronage purposes for a longer period than the other Orders. In 1496, Pope Alexander VI (1492–1503) gave permission to new knights in the Order of Christ to marry. This dispensation opened the way for the Order to become an important source of crown patronage, especially because the king was master, governor, and administrator of the Order, dating from the reign of Manuel I. The Orders of Santiago and Avis, on the other hand, were headed by Dom Jorge, Duke of Coimbra, the illegitimate son of King João II. From the early 1490's to his death on 22 July 1550, Dom Jorge was master of both orders with patronage largely under his control. In 1551, by the papal bull, "Praeclara Charissimi," issued on 4 January of that year, the kings of Portugal became masters, governors, and administrators of all three Portuguese military orders. Thus the Orders of Santiago and Avis also became important sources of rewards for the crown's use.

During the years between 1500 and 1675, Portugal's chief physicians and chief surgeons were the most prominent among the elite in the medical profession who were rewarded with patents of nobility and habits in the military orders. Royal Chancery documents, notarial records, and parish registers yield up the names of fourteen chief

---

[11]Of course there were exceptions.

[12]Although the military orders' records for much of the sixteenth century are incomplete, it is clear that there were more than 3,000 new knights in the Order of Christ during that century. It is more difficult to estimate the number of new members in the Orders of Santiago and Avis during the same period, but a rough estimate is five hundred to seven hundred new knights for each Order. Between 1601 and May of 1631 there were approximately 1,000 additional new knights in the Order of Christ.

physicians and twelve chief surgeons for the years 1520 to 1675, although a few of these may have served as substitutes. It is clear that eight
of these chief physicians became knights in the Order of Christ and two
became knights of Santiago. Of the chief surgeons, five were knights in
the Order of Christ; of these, one had first been a knight in the Order
of Santiago.

One of the earliest physicians to become a member of one of the
military orders in the sixteenth century was Doctor Diogo Lopes. As
one of King Manuel's physicians in 1518, with a monthly allowance
(*moradia*) of 2$, Lopes in 1521 was named as Portugal's chief physician
(*físico-mor*), succeeding Doctor Manuel Afonso, who had held the
post.[13] In a document issued the following year, Lopes is described as
"Mestre Diogo" and is identified as a commander in the Order of
Christ.[14] There are numerous documents in which he is listed as an
examiner for those wishing to practice medicine in Portugal.[15]

Although several documents concerning Portugal's next chief
physician, Mestre Diogo Franco, have been published, the royal letter
specifically appointing Franco to that post has not been found (Sousa
Viterbo 1893 [1st series]:38). However, it is clear from various records
that Diogo Franco was both chief physician and a knight in the Order
of Christ. One of the earliest documents referring to him, dated 5 July
1526, reports that, on 3 March of that year in the chapel of the University
of Lisbon, bacharel Mestre Diogo Franco was elected professor of the
vespera chair of medicine, replacing Mestre Gil, who had been elected
professor of the *prima* chair. King João III confirmed the results of the
election.[16] Franco is listed among the thirty-two *letrados* and physicians
attached to Dom João III's royal household in 1540 (Caetano de Sousa
1946–54:VI:2, p. 333). It seems that Franco held the post of chief
physician from about 1548 to 1554. In the former year both he and his
wife, Inês Rodrigues, were awarded the annual *quarto de pão*, which his

[13]See *regimento* of 1521 in *Systema* (1818:VI, 345). For 1518, see "Livro da Matricula
dos Moradores da Casa del Rey D. Manoel, do primeiro quartel do anno de 1518," in
A. Caetano de Sousa (1946–54:II[1]:461).

[14]See the letter of 17 June 1522 in ANTT, Chancelaria de D. João III, liv. 51, fol. 187
(reprinted in Sousa Viterbo 1895 [2nd series]:36–37).

[15]F. M. de Sousa Viterbo reprints several, the latest dated 1545 (see 1915 [5th
series]:171).

[16]See ANTT, Chancelaria de D. João III, liv. 36, fol. 129ᵛ (reprinted in F. M. de Sousa
Viterbo 1895 [2nd series]:48–49).

predecessor had during his lifetime.[17] In the latter year, his daughter Barbara Franco, because her father was dead, was granted his annual pension of 20$ by the Order of Christ for the remainder of her lifetime.[18] Although it is clear that Diogo Franco was a knight in the Order of Christ, his name does not appear in the list preserved from the Order's *Livro da Matricula* (see Machado de Faria 1955:36–37).

On 4 May 1554, Diogo Franco was succeeded as chief physician by Leonardo Nunes.[19] A native of the *vila* of Castelo Branco, Nunes had gained a baccalaureate in medicine, when, in 1522, he was given permission by chief physician, Doctor Diogo Lopes, to practice medicine.[20] Fourteen years later, on 22 March 1536, Leonardo Nunes, now with the title of licentiate, was named physician of the Casa da Suplicação with an annual stipend of 24$.[21] In the 1540 list of *letrados* and physicians mentioned above, Licenciado Leonardo Nunes is included as a member of the household of King João III (Caetano de Sousa 1946–54:VI[2], 333). On 19 February 1546, he received the habit and knighthood in the Order of Christ.[22]

It is not clear when Leonardo Nunes died and there seems to be some question as to who succeeded him as Portugal's chief physician. Both Diogo Barbosa Machado and Luis Augusto Rebelo da Silva state that Doctor Tomás Rodrigues da Veiga, noted professor of medicine, held the post of chief physician of Portugal during the reigns of Dom João III and Dom Sebastian, but none of the documents published by Sousa Viterbo support or deny this claim.[23] Rodrigues da Veiga was born

---

[17]ANTT: Chancelaria de D. João III, liv. 55, fol. 53 (reprinted in Sousa Viterbo 1893 [1st series]:38–39).

[18]See the letter of 11 December 1554 in ANTT, Chancelaria de D. João III, liv. 10, fol. 191 (reprinted in Sousa Viterbo 1895 [2nd series]:50).

[19]See the letter of the king in ANTT, Chancelaria, de D. João III, liv. 58, fol. 55ᵛ (reprinted in Sousa Viterbo 1895 [2nd series]:38–39).

[20]See the letter of 17 June 1522 in ANTT, Chancelaria de D. João III, liv. 51, fol. 187 (reprinted in Sousa Viterbo 1895 [2nd series]:36–37). F. M de Sousa Viterbo (*Ibid.*:36–41) also reprinted four documents on the career of Nunes. A brief biographical sketch is found in D. Barbosa Machado (1965–67:I, 132), under his son's name (Ambrósio Nunes).

[21]See the letter of 22 March 1536, in ANTT, Chancelaria de D. João III, liv. 21, fol. 123 (reprinted in Sousa Viterbo 1895 [2nd series]:37–38).

[22]See the extract from the Order's *Livro de Matricula* in A. Machado de Faria (1955:57). See also D. Barbosa Machado (1965–67:I, 332).

[23]See, respectively, D. Barbosa Machado (1965–67:III, 748) and L. A. Rebelo da Silva (1860–71:V, 256). An index of proper names is included in the latter work.

in Evora and studied at the University of Salamanca. He began teaching medicine at the University of Lisbon and moved to Coimbra when the university was transferred there.[24] On 3 January 1558, he took over the *prima* chair of medicine. He was greatly favored by Dom João III, as can be seen from the numerous documents published by Mário Brandão.[25] On 22 September 1558, Tomás received authorization to become a member of the Order of Santiago and, on 2 October, the ceremonies took place at the monastery of Santos in Lisbon. The witnesses were Doctor Diogo de Santiago, a knight in the Order of Avis, and Doctor Diogo Lopes, a knight in the Order of Santiago (see ANTT, Habilitações da Ordem de Santiago, Letra T, Maço 1, número 33). It is possible that the reason Tomás Rodrigues was granted a knighthood in the Order of Santiago rather than that of Christ, was the fact that he was of New Christian heritage. Chapter four of Santiago's 1542 Statutes—added to the Rule of that Order by Dom Jorge—stated that those hoping to enter the Order should be of noble background. Also, neither they, nor their parents, nor either set of grandparents should be Jews or Moslems. However, the statutes continued, if such a person, illuminated by the grace of God, converted to Christianity and could serve or honor the Order, the Master could receive him into the Order.[26] Although this statute was specifically revoked in the reformed 1627 Statutes of the Order,[27] it probably provided the justification for Tomás Rodrigues' knighthood in the Order of Santiago. Rodrigues da Veiga was the author of several commentaries on Galen as well as several other works on medicine. He died in Coimbra on 26 May 1579 (Braga 1892–1902:II, 770).[28] Tomás Rodrigues received favorable mention by

[24]F. M. de Sousa Viterbo (1915 [5th series]:167) reprints documents dated 28 July and 16 October 1540, showing that Rodrigues da Veiga was granted fifteen cruzados for moving and travel expenses. See also M. Brandão (1937–41:I, 259–60).

[25]For example, King João III increased the salary of Dr. Tomás Rodrigues several times, calling him "my physician, professor of the *vespera* chair." See the *alvarás* of 27 September 1546 and 24 November 1551 in M. Brandão (1937–41:III, 45 and IV, 111–12, respectively).

[26]See Chapter IV of the 1542 statutes that are appended to the Order's 1627 *Definições* (Andrade e Silva 1854–59:IV, 20).

[27]See *Definição* III from the Order's 1627 *Definições* in J. J. Andrade e Silva (1854–59:IV, 37).

[28]D. Barbosa Machado (1965–67:III, 748), however, gives 1593 as the date of this death.

his contemporaries as one of the most important physicians in sixteenth-century Portugal.[29]

The next chief physician, explicitly identified as such, was Sebastião Rodrigues de Azevedo, one of the few sixteenth-century chief physicians who apparently did not hold a knighthood in one of the military orders. He had been Queen Catherine's personal physician as well as that of her grandson, King Sebastian.[30] Shortly before Catherine's death in February of 1578, he received an annual grant of 200$.[31] The year in which he was awarded the post of chief physician is not clear, but it was probably about 1569.[32] Rodrigues de Azevedo appears in four documents, dated 1573, 1574, 1575, and 1580, wherein he is described as *físico-mor*.[33]

With the death, in 1578, of King Sebastian at the battle of Alcácer Quibir, followed, in December of 1580, by that of his uncle, the Cardinal-King Henrique, the Portuguese crown passed to King Philip II of Spain and afterward to his son and grandson. During the years from 1580 to 1640 the Court was in Madrid instead of Lisbon, and it becomes more difficult to identify Portugal's chief physicians and chief surgeons. It would seem that Rodrigues de Azevedo was succeeded as chief physician by António Pereira, who is described in notarial records of 1586 as chief physician and a resident of the parish of Santa Catarina de Monte Sinai in Lisbon (*INVTL* 1930–49:IV, 196). However, he may have been an interim chief physician.

[29]For a contemporary opinion of Tomás, see for example, P. de Mariz (1806:II, 104), who described him as follows: "O Doutor Thomaz Rodrigues, Portuguez, na de Vespera, que foi na sua faculdade mais insigne que todos os que em muitos séculos florecerão no mundo" (Dialogue V, Chapter 3). Mariz's *Dialogos* were first published in Coimbra in 1594.

[30]See the letter of 8 July 1570 in J. Veríssimo Serrão (1962:I, 149–50). A second revised edition of this important work appeared in 1987.

[31]See the letter of 4 February 1578 in *ibid.*:II, 198.

[32]See the *alvará* of 14 June 1569 in *ibid.*:I, 100. The Biblioteca da Ajuda (Lisbon), 44–XIV–4, fols. 302v–307v, contains a *regimento* for the chief physician issued in Santarem, 17 February 1569. See A. de Silva Rego (1966:I, 436).

[33]See the letters of 21 January 1574 and 20 April 1580 in ANTT, Chancelaria de D. Sebastião and D. Henrique, *Doações*, liv. 29, fol. 308 and liv. 45, fol. 65, respectively. The former letter granted permission to Maria Fernandes, a widow and resident of Ericeira, to work cures for a period of three years since there were no physicians in her *vila*. However, she could not use purges without the approval of a certified physician. The latter letter gave permission to Joana Colaça Loba, a native of the *vila* of Vimieiro, to cure illnesses of children and women. In both cases, however, they were to be first examined by the chief physician before practicing their cures. Both letters are reprinted in F. M. de Sousa Viterbo (1895 [3rd series]:32–34 and 34, respectively).

At any rate, António Pereira, in turn, was probably succeeded by Fernão Rodrigues Cardoso. Fernão, a native of Viseu, was the son of Doctor Pedro Fernandes and Barbara Fernandes.[34] His brother, Doctor António Dias Cardoso, was an inquisitor at Coimbra and Evora before becoming deputy of the Conselho Geral of the Holy Office (Barbosa Machado 1965–67:I, 256). According to Barbosa Machado, Fernão was admitted as a medical student at the royal college of São Paulo at the University of Coimbra on 6 July 1568. After his graduation, beginning on 22 December 1572, he held a temporary chair (*cathedrilha*), which had been newly created by King Sebastian. On 8 January 1577, he was promoted to the Avicenna chair. The following year, on 1 February 1578, he took over the *vespera* chair, holding it until 1585, when he was called to Lisbon to take over the post of Portugal's chief physician.[35] Two years later, on 10 October 1587, he received authorization to become a knight in the Order of Christ.[36] In documents dated 1602 and 1606, he is described as "professor of the *prima* chair of medicine at the University of Coimbra and chief physician of Portugal."[37] Rodrigues Cardoso was a wealthy Lisbon landlord, and he, his family, his servants and retainers, and his properties are mentioned many times in the parish registers of Lisbon's cathedral.[38] He died on 20 June 1608.[39] Less than two years later, on 15 April, his oldest son, João Henriques Mascaren-

---

[34]The following biographical account is based largely on D. Barbosa Machado (1965–67:II, 52).

[35]He was appointed on 22 February 1585. See ANTT, Chancelaria de D. Filipe I, *Doações*, liv. 8, fol. 113. Philip II of Spain is considered to be Philip I of Portugal. The chancelarias in ANTT are thus given the Portuguese enumeration.

[36]ANTT, Chancelaria da Ordem de Cristo, liv. 7, fol. 97. On 13 August, he was awarded an annual pension of 20$ with the knighthood. See *ibid.*:liv. 7, fol. 138.

[37]See the letter of the king, dated 19 January 1606, in ANTT, Chancelaria de D. Filipe II, *Doações*, liv. 18, fol. 289. In it permission was given to Leonor Dias, an inhabitant of Évora, to cure infirmities of children and women, after being approved by the kingdom's chief physician, Rodrigues Cardoso, on condition that she not use purges or bleedings without the advice of "fisicos letrados." This document is reprinted in F. M. de Sousa Viterbo (1895 [3rd series]:37–38).

[38]See E. Prestage and P. de Azevedo (1924–27). A few examples will suffice: the baptism of his daughter, Juliana, 5 September 1586 (*Ibid.*:I, 269); the confirmation of four of his children on 27 January 1598 (*Ibid.*:I, 222); the death of his younger son, António Cardoso, on 9 May 1601 (*Ibid.*:II, 460); and the death of his wife, Dona Catarina, on 10 August 1603 (*Ibid.*:II, 469).

[39]*Ibid.*:II, 489. See also D. Barbosa Machado (1965–67:II, 52).

has, received authorization for a knighthood in the Order of Christ (ANTT, Chancelaria da Ordem de Cristo, liv. 9, fols. 244v–245).[40]

Baltasar de Azeredo, another professor of medicine at the University of Coimbra, succeeded Fernão Rodrigues Cardoso as the chief physician of Portugal. Together they held the post of chief physician for more than four decades.[41] Azeredo was born in the *vila* of Guimarães and studied at the University of Coimbra. After receiving his doctorate, he became a member of the faculty at the royal college of São Paulo on 4 May 1579. He was professor at the University of Coimbra teaching Galen's *De Crisibus* in 1582. According to D. Barbosa Machado (1965–67:I, 442), he was promoted to the Avicenna chair on 24 December 1583 and rose to the *prima* chair on 12 January 1589. Due to the high quality of his teaching and the length of his service to the university, Baltasar was awarded a knighthood in the Order of Christ and an annual pension of 20$ (the latter to be paid from the revenues of the University). The Mesa da Consciência e Ordens ('Board of Conscience and Military Orders') was informed of this award by a *carta régia* of 16 June 1603 (see Andrade e Silva 1854–59:I, 19).[42] Later that year, the reception of the habit and knighthood took place.[43] The following year he was also awarded the honor of *professor jubilado* for his long years of teaching (Barbosa Machado 1965–67:I, 442).[44] However, the king was becoming impatient with Baltasar's continuing requests for rewards and ordered the Mesa da Consciência and others not to correspond with the crown regarding additional rewards from the treasury or from the university itself for teaching, since professors were already paid for that by the university.[45] In 1609, Azeredo became chief physician of Portugal, holding the post until his death in 1631.[46] Azeredo was married to Dona

[40]On 10 November 1611, João Henriques Mascarenhas was awarded an annual pension of 20$ with the habit of Christ. See ANTT, Chancelaria da Ordem de Cristo, liv. 21, fols. 358–358v.

[41]Though he is called Azevedo by J. J. Andrade e Silva (1854–59) and elsewhere, D. Barbosa Machado (1965–67:I, 442) calls him Azeredo. The Madrid list from the Order of Christ's *Livro da Matricula* also uses Azeredo. See BNM, Ms. 938, fol. 134v.

[42]In the same document, Philip III also informed the viceroy of Portugal that a practice should not be made of giving knighthoods in the military orders to professors and other officials at the University of Coimbra since their salaries were sufficient reward.

[43]See the Madrid List from the Order's *Livro da Matricula*, in BNM:Ms. 938, fol. 134v.

[44]In a letter dated 9 November 1604, he is referred to as *professor jubilado*.

[45]See the letter from the king, dated 9 November 1604, in J.J. Andrade e Silva (1854–59:I, 93).

[46]For his appointment to the post, see ANTT, Chancelaria de Filipe II, *Doações*, liv. 23, fol. 115v. See T. Braga (1892–1902:II, 799).

Maria de Madeireira. He died in Lisbon on 6 January 1631 and was buried in the Jesuit House (*casa professa*) of São Roque in Lisbon.[47] It is possible that Azeredo may not have taken up the post of chief physician immediately upon his appointment in 1609. In several documents dated 1610 and 1611, Duarte Mendes is described as *físico-mor*, probably as a temporary substitute.[48] Mendes had received, earlier in 1604, a habit and knighthood in the Order of Christ.[49] Little else is recorded about him.

With Azeredo's death in 1631, a heated debate took place over who was to follow him as chief physician. One group insisted that his successor be a university professor. Foremost among this faction was Doctor Tomás Serrão de Brito, holder of the *vespera* chair at the University of Coimbra, and the chief university candidate for Azeredo's post. He also sought a knighthood in the Order of Christ. Serrão de Brito claimed (erroneously) that the post had always been given to professors from the University of Coimbra.[50] In a *consulta* of 17 June 1634, Dom António de Ataíde, First Count of Castro Daire and President of the Mesa da Consciência e Ordens, took exception to Serrão de Brito's statements, pointing out that the chief surgeons Manuel Cardim, Francisco Tomás, and Ambrósio Nunes had not been professors at the University of Coimbra. He also pointed out that, although Fernão Rodrigues Cardoso and Baltasar de Azeredo had been professors of the University of Coimbra, some of their predecessors in the post of chief physician—Sebastião Rodrigues, Leonardo Nunes, Mestre Manuel Afonso, and others—had not been.[51]

---

[47]For the above biographical details, see D. Barbosa Machado (1965–67:I, 442).

[48]"Doutor Duarte Mendez, que hora por meu mandado serve de meu *físico-mor*." See the letter of 1610 in ANTT, Chancelaria de D. Filipe II, *Privilégios*, liv. 1, fol. 132v; also, the letter of 14 June 1611 in ANTT, Chancelaria de D. Filipe II, *Doações*, liv.21, fol. 175v. Both letters are reprinted in F.M. de Sousa Viterbo (1895 [3rd series]:46–47 and 48–49, respectively).

[49]His *carta de hábito* and *alvará de cavaleiro* are also missing from the Order's registry books. However, he is listed in the Order's *Livro da Matricula*. See "Lista dos Cavaleiros" in BNM: Ms. 938, fol. 135. See also the *padrão de 20$ de tença com o hábito*, dated 25 April 1607 in ANTT, Chancelaria da Ordem Cristo, liv. 17, fols. 163–163v and the postscript dated 27 March 1608.

[50]See the *consulta* of the of Mesa da Consciência e Ordens, dated 17 June 1634 (reprinted in Braga 1892–1902:II, 800–2). Serrão de Brito's claim is found on p. 800.

[51]*Ibid*. Ataíde's response is found on p. 802.

The post appears to have gone to a compromise candidate—Simão Roubão da Costa, a knight in the Order of Santiago who had served as chief physician in India.[52] Simão was an Old Christian of humble background and a native of Setúbal who had received financial aid from the *partidos dos médicos* and had been awarded a baccalaureate in medicine from the University of Coimbra. In 1604 he was awarded a teaching fellowship to continue at the University.[53] Dr. Roubão da Costa received authorization for a knighthood in the Order of Santiago on 13 March 1622 (ANTT, Chancelaria da Ordem de Santiago, liv. 12, fol. 100v.). However, he needed a dispensation to gain admittance into the Order because his ancestors were fisherfolk (*Ibid.*). He also received permission to have the ceremonies performed in the chapel of the monastery of Santos, the nunnery where the women's branch of the Order of Santiago was housed.[54] The reason for this urgency was his imminent departure for India, where he was to serve as chief physician. The date of his return to Portugal is uncertain; however, it appears that he returned in 1629, for on 30 August of that year he was authorized to make the profession of vows in the Order of Santiago (See ANTT, Chancelaria da Ordem de Santiago, liv. 13, fol. 135).[55] He clearly was in Portugal in 1634, 1636 and 1637, when he is referred to in documents as the chief physician of Portugal who examined two Italians (Francisco Romano and Salvador Palomo) and two Germans (Guilherme Escoph and António Matias) as distillers (*destiladores*), and an Italian (Francisco Galeno) as a practitioner of household remedies.[56] On 31 December 1640, he renounced his post as chief physician in favor of Dr. André

[52]According to M. Roque (1984:127), he was named to the post by Philip IV on 29 April 1634.

[53]See the *consulta* of the Mesa da Consciência e Ordens, dated 28 March 1604 (reprinted in Braga 1892–1902:II, 778–79).

[54]See the marginal note to his *carta de hábito* in ANTT, Chancelaria da Ordem de Santiago, liv. 12, fol. 100v.

[55]There is no indication in his *alvará de profissão* that the ceremony was to take place in India.

[56]The letters for Palomo and Romano are dated 2 March 1637 and 2 December 1636, respectively (see ANTT, Chancelaria de D. Filipe III, *Doações*, liv. 28, fol. 67v and liv. 40, fol. 96; reprinted in F. M. de Sousa Viterbo 1915 [5th series]:168–69 and 96). The letter for Escoph was dated 12 May 1634, and for Matias, 9 September 1637. See *ibid.*, liv. 29, fol. 198v and liv. 32, fol. 374v, respectively (reprinted in F. M. de Sousa Viterbo 1915 [5th series]:52 and 129). The letter for Galeno is found in ANTT, Chancelaria de D. Filipe III, *Doações*, liv. 29, fol. 191v (reprinted in Sousa Viterbo 1915 [5th series]:72).

DOCTORIS
ANDREAE AN-
TONII DE CASTRO, SERE-
NISSIMI BRIGANTIÆ DVCIS, PRO-
thomedici, & Oremſis arcis Præfecti Maximi,

de febrium curatione

LIBRI TRES

QVIBVS ACCESSERE DVO ALII LIBELLI DE
jim, action medicamentorum facultatibus; & alter de qualitatibus alimen-
torum, quæ humani corporis nutritioni ſunt apta.

CVM INDICE RERVM, ET VERBORVM SCITV DIG-
norum locupletiſsimo.

AD IOANNEM OCTAVVM
Ducem Potentiſsimum.

Cum facultate S. Inquiſitionis, Ordinarij, & Regis.

Villauiçoſæ. Apud Emmanuelem Carvalho.
Ducis Typographum Anno. M. DC. LXI .636.

Plate 1: Title page of the treatise *Febrium curatione*, written by André António de Castro, chief physician of D. João, eighth Duke of Bragança and future king of Portugal. It was published in Vila Viçosa in 1636. Castro accompanied his monarch to Lisbon when the duke was proclaimed king and he served briefly as chief physician of Portugal. (Courtesy of the National Library of Medicine, Bethesda, Maryland.)

António de Castro (*INVTL* III, 202–3).[57] Simão Roubão da Costa is listed in Lisbon's notarial records on 23 February 1641 and is described as chief physician, knight in the Order of Santiago, married to Dona Simoa da Veiga and living in Lisbon on Rua Direita da Porta da Cruz (*INVTL* I, 5).

Roubão da Costa's successor as chief physician, Dr. André António de Castro, was Dom João IV's physician in Vila Viçosa when the monarch was then Duke of Bragança. Actually, two men with similar names held the post of chief physician in the 1640's: the above-mentioned André António de Castro and Doctor António de Castro. It is likely that they were related as uncle and nephew.[58] Both were born in Vila Viçosa and, to add to the confusion, both had fathers with the same name: Diogo de Castro. According to Barbosa Machado (1965–67:I, 137), André António de Castro was the son of Doctor Diogo de Castro and grandson of Doctor André de Castro, both of whom were chief physicians of the Dukes of Bragança.[59] In 1586, at a young age, André António de Castro also became attached to the Bragança household. At the urging of Dom Teodósio, seventh Duke of Bragança (1568–1630), André António also made the study of medicine his career, during which he wrote *Febrium curatione* (1636) (see Plate 1). When João, eighth Duke of Bragança, was proclaimed king of Portugal on 1 December 1640, André António accompanied him to Lisbon and was made chief physician of Portugal. According to Barbosa Machado, Dr. André António de Castro was also named *alcaide-mor* of the *vila* of Ourém and given the commandery of Montalegre in the Order of Christ.[60] Santa Maria de Montalegre, located in the archdiocese of Braga, was one of

[57]In this document he was identified as the father of Francisco Roubão, abbot of the monastery of São João de Pesqueira.

[58]António de Oliveira de Cadornega, the seventeenth-century author famous for his *História Geral das Guerras Angolanas*, stated, in his description of the festivities surrounding the 1633 marriage of the eighth Duke of Bragança (the future king João of Portugal) and Luiza de Guzmán (daughter of the Spanish Duke of Medina Sidonia), that near the end of the procession were "Doctor André António and his wife Dona Leonor, he being a commander [in the Order of Christ] and *alcaide-mor* of the *vila* of Ourém, with his nephew, the licenciado António de Castro." Also, in the procession was another physician who would eventually serve King João IV in Lisbon, Francisco Morato Roma, a knight in the Order of Christ (Oliveira de Cadornega 1982:73). A brief sketch of Morato Roma's career can be found in D. Barbosa Machado (1965–67:II, 210–11).

[59]D. Barbosa Machado also mentioned that Dr. André António de Castro had been professor of the *vespera* chair at the University of Coimbra.

[60]For the above biographical details, see D. Barbosa Machado (1965–67:I, 137).

the commanderies over which the Dukes of Bragança had the right of presentation. In 1620 it was appraised at 150$ annually.[61] Unfortunately, the chief physician did not have long to enjoy these awards, for he died in 1642 (*op. cit.*).

Dr. André António de Castro was succeeded by Salvador Vaz de Orta, who held the post of chief physician only briefly, aided by the chief surgeon of Portugal, António Francisco Milheiro, who was called upon to serve also as chief physician.[62] Then, by an *alvará* of 25 June 1644, Doctor António de Castro, who held the post of physician to the Royal Household, was named chief physician of the Royal Palace and of Portugal, and was granted the same *moradia* as Doctor André António de Castro, his predecessor (*LMMCR* 1911–17:II, 332).

Dr. António de Castro, the son of Diogo and Dona Isabel de Castro, was born in Vila Viçosa, and had been a physician for the Braganças before the eighth Duke was acclaimed King João IV of Portugal (*INVTL* III, 329). He held the post of chief physician until his retirement in 1669 (*LMMCR* II, 73).[63] In the *alvará* mentioned above, he is described as *fidalgo* and *médico da câmara*. It does not appear that he ever received a knighthood in one of the Portuguese military orders, possibly because of the long-standing suspicion that he was a New Christian.[64] Two of his sons, however, did receive knighthoods in the Order of Christ.

When Dr. António de Castro retired from his post of chief physician of Portugal in 1669, he was succeeded by Doctor Crispim do Rego.[65] Also a physician in the household of Dom João IV, Dr. Crispim do Rego had been awarded a knighthood in the Order of Christ by a

---

[61]See the Rule and Statutes of the Order of Christ in J.J. Andrade e Silva (1854–59:III, 269).

[62]For Vaz de Orta's appointment, see *LMMCR* 1911–1917:II, 332. For Milheiro's role, see letters of 2 December 1641 and 10 May 1642 (reprinted in Sousa Viterbo 1915 [5th series]:36 and 48).

[63]In "Regimento dos preços por onde os Boticários hão de vender suas mezinhas", dated 20 May 1653, Doctor António de Castro is identified as "Médico da Câmara e Pessoa Real de Sua Magestade, e seu Físico Mor." See J. J. Andrade e Silva (1854–59:VII, 114–17).

[64]Some of the records of the Order of Christ are missing for the 1630's. However, in other documentation he is not described as a member of the Order.

[65]For Castro's retirement see the *alvará* of 5 August 1671 in *LMMCR* II, 73. For Rego's appointment see the *alvará* of 23 September 1669 in *LMMCR* II, 72.

portaria of 2 October 1654 and an annual pension of 40$ (*IPR* II, 34).[66] In the background investigation which followed, it was discovered that his father had been a *caixeiro* ('clerk'). The Mesa da Consciência e Ordens in a *consulta* of 5 November 1654 recommended a dispensation and the king quickly approved (see ANTT, Habilitações da Ordem de Cristo, Letra C. Maço 12, Número 107). The letters authorizing the knighthood, habit, and profession were issued on 6 December 1654 (see ANTT, Chancelaria de Ordem de Cristo, liv. 38, fols. 168–169). On the 24th of that month, permission was granted for the ceremonies to take place in Lisbon.[67] In 1657, because of his service as *médico da câmara* of the Royal Palace, he was given permission to will to his son or sons, 40$ of the annual pension (*tença*) he was receiving from the Casa da Portagem.[68] On 25 June 1659, he was awarded an additional 40$ (for a total of 80$ annually) consigned from the *almoxarifado* of the Casa da Portagem with the right to will 20$ of the second 40$ to his wife or children (*IPR* II, 220). On 23 September 1669, he was named chief physician of Portugal (*LMMCR* II, 72).

The first of Portugal's chief surgeons, in the sixteenth century, to become a knight in the Order of Christ was Mestre Gil da Costa. He held the post of chief surgeon during most of João III's reign (1521–1557) and is listed for 1518 as one of six physicians of King Manuel, receiving a monthly allowance (*moradia*) of 1$500 (Caetano de Sousa 1946–64:II[1], 461). Because Mestre Gil was responsible for examining various practitioners of medicine, his name appears on at least sixteen documents published by Sousa Viterbo, the earliest dated 20 January 1523 and the latest 1551.[69] Mestre Gil is first identified as a knight of the Order of Christ in a document dated 29 January 1530 and in five others in (1532, 1539, 1541, 1542, and 1548).[70] He was married to Monica da Fonseca and had at least two children, including Madre Marta de Cristo,

---

[66]The *padrão de tença* was issued on 27 October 1654. See ANTT, Chancelaria da Ordem de Cristo, liv. 38, fol. 128v. For his medical services at the royal palace, he had previously been granted an annual pension of 100$. See the *alvará* of 20 June 1647 in LMMCR II, 263.

[67]See the postscript to ANTT, Chancelaria da Ordem de Cristo, liv. 38, fols. 168–169.

[68]See the *alvará* of 7 May 1657, *IPR* II, 147.

[69]ANTT, Chancelaria de D. João III, liv. 3, fol. 106v (reprinted in Sousa Viterbo 1895 [3rd series]:31), and ANTT, Chancelaria de D. João III, liv. 64, fol. 196. See F.M. de Sousa Viterbo (*Ibid.*:30).

[70]For the earliest mention, see ANTT, Chancelaria de D. João III, liv. 42, fol. 13 (reprinted in Sousa Viterbo 1895 [3rd series]:17–18).

IV, 248). He died before 1 October 1554, for on that date his son, Gaspar da Costa, was named to succeed him as chief surgeon of Portugal.[71]

At the time of his appointment to his father's post of chief surgeon, young Gaspar da Costa, who possessed a patent of nobility (*escudeiro fidalgo da casa real*), held the degree of Master of Arts, and was still a student at the University of Coimbra. Before he could assume the post of chief surgeon, he first had to receive the degree of *licenciado* in medicine from the University and practice surgery for one year at the hospital of the Spanish monastery of Our Lady of Guadalupe.[72] Meanwhile, as these conditions were being fulfilled, Leonardo Nunes, who already held the post of Portugal's chief physician, would also hold the post of chief surgeon.[73]

Like his father, Gaspar was a physician as well as a surgeon. As chief surgeon, he had to examine and certify not only those who wished to practice surgery, but also those wishing to practice certain other types of cures in the kingdom. On 9 and 12 June 1568, respectively, King Sebastian granted Baltasar Barbosa, an inhabitant of Arrifana de Sousa, and Rodrigo da Costa, an inhabitant of Setúbal, permission to practice their surgical skills throughout his kingdom after they had been examined by Doctor Gaspar da Costa, *físico* and *surgião-mor* (Veríssimo Serrão 1962:I, 44 and 45). In addition to examining surgeons, Doctor Gaspar da Costa was also obliged to examine bone-setters (*algebristas*)—those who worked with broken bones and muscles out-of-joint. The Chancery records of King Sebastian contains documents showing that women often practiced such a calling. On 20 December 1569, the monarch granted Filipa Dias, an inhabitant of Evora, permission to practice her skills throughout the kingdom after she had been approved by the chief surgeon.[74]

Gaspar da Costa received authorization for a knighthood in the Order of Christ on 12 October 1571 (ANTT, Chancelaria da Ordem de Cristo, liv. 2, fol. 83v.). In 1574, he and the chief physician, Sebastião

---

[71]See ANTT, Chancelaria de D. João III, liv. 63, fol. 124v (reprinted in Sousa Viterbo 1895 [2nd series]:4).

[72]*Ibid*. In the sixteenth century, the hospital at Guadalupe had an excellent reputation for medicine.

[73]See the *alvará* of 16 September 1554 in ANTT, Chancelaria de D. João III, liv. 63, fol. 124 (reprinted in Sousa Viterbo 1895 [2nd series]:39–40).

[74]See ANTT, Chancelaria de D. Sebastião e D. Henrique, *Doações*, liv. 26, fol. 9 (reprinted in Sousa Viterbo 1895 [3rd series]: 32).

Rodrigues de Azevedo, prepared and signed a report concerning King Sebastian's illness when the ruler was in Vila Franca de Xira (Veríssimo Serrão 1962:II, 48). Gaspar accompanied Dom Sebastian on the ill-fated North African campaign of 1578 and died with his monarch at the battle of Alcácer Quibir on 4 August (see *INVTL*, IV, 241 and 248).

Some confusion surrounds the post of chief surgeon during the first two decades of Habsburg rule in Portugal. Five men are mentioned in various documents as holders of the post. The first is Cristóvão Dias, son of Gonçalo Dias and a resident of Lisbon. Cristóvão also accompanied Sebastian to Alcácer Quibir. He was wounded in the battle, taken prisoner, and remained in Moslem captivity for two years. Whether he died in captivity or after returning to Portugal is not clear. He left behind a wife (Branca Lopes), three daughters, and a son (see Sousa Viterbo 1898 [4th series]:16–18). He was dead by 21 October 1584, for from that date his wife was to receive an annual pension of 8$.[75] Cristóvão Dias's name does not appear in the registry books of any of the three military orders.

The second, Manuel Cardim Frões, is described in a document, dated 13 November 1590, as physician and chief surgeon of the "kingdom and seigniories of Portugal."[76] Little else is known about him. Upon his death, Manuel was succeeded by Francisco Tomás, also described as a physician and chief surgeon, who was awarded the latter post on 30 May 1592.[77] Earlier, Francisco, a physician of the royal household, had accompanied King Sebastian to North Africa.[78] Because of his services, he was awarded dowries for several of his daughters, one of whom married Alvaro Teles de Meneses and had been awarded, as a dowry, the post of Treasurer of the Casa de Ceuta for three years (ANTT, Chancelaria de Filipe I, *Doações*, liv. 3, fol. 121). Alvaro, a knight in the Order of Christ since 1583, never actually took up this post, but was awarded instead the Order's commandery of São Bartolomeu

---

[75]For his widow's annual pension see the *alvará* of 20 November 1585 in ANTT, Chancelaria de Filipe I, *Doações*, liv. 11, fol. 248 (reprinted in Sousa Viterbo 1898 [4th series]:17).

[76]See ANTT, Chancelaria de Filipe I, *Doações*, liv. 22, fol. 210v (reprinted in Sousa Viterbo 1895 [3rd series]:18–19).

[77]ANTT, Chancelaria de D. Filipe I, *Doações*, liv. 23, fol. 211v. Francisco Tomás's patent is reprinted in F. M. de Sousa Viterbo (1898 [4th series]: 25–26).

[78]See *carta de padrão* of 15 July 1581 in ANTT, Chancerlaria de Filipe I, *Doações*, liv. 2, fol. 80v (reprinted in Sousa Viterbo 1898 [4th series]:21).

TRACTADO
REPARTIDO EN
CINCO PARTES PRIN-
CIPALES,

Que declaran el mal que significa este nombre Peste
con todas fus caufas, y feñales prognofticas, y indi-
catiuas del mal, con la preferuacion, y cura que
en general, y en particular fedeue hazer.

*Dirigido al Excelentifsimo feñor Don Chriftoual
de Mora, Marques de Caftel Rodrigo, Virrey, y
Capitã General en la Corona de Portugal, &c.*

COMPVESTO POR EL DOCTOR
Ambrofio Nuñez Portugues, Cauallero de la Orden, y habito de
nueftro Señor IESVCHRISTO, Medico, y Cirugia-
no Mayor de fu Mageftad, en la Corona de Portugal, Ca-
thedratico de Vifperas de Medicina Iubilado en
la Vniuerfidad de Salamanca.

EM COIMBRA,

*Acabouse de Imprimir, na Officina de Diogo Gomez Loureyro Impreffor
da Vniuerfidade.* Com Licença da S. Inquifição. 1601.

Com Priuilegio Real.

Plate 2: This important treatise was inspired by the epidemic of 1598. Written
by Dr. Ambrósio Nunes, one of the most illustrious men of medicine in
sixteenth-century Portugal and chief surgeon of that kingdom, it was meant to
complement an earlier treatise written by two physicians from Seville, García
de Salzedo Coronel and Tomás Alvares de Castro. Both doctors were invited
to Portugal in 1569 by King Sebastian to help stop the epidemic that was
ravaging the Portuguese capital in that year. For their services they were
authorized to become members of the Order of Christ, in 1570, an honor that
Ambrósio Nunes would later receive. (Courtesy of The Francis A. Countway
Library of Medicine, Boston.)

de Covilhão in the diocese of Guarda appraised at 100$ a year.[79] Francisco Tomás, a surgeon at Lisbon's Royal Hospital of All Saints, wrote a famous letter to Bishop Dom Jorge de Ataide in 1592, complaining about the poor state of medical and surgical practices in Portugal compared to what he described as its flourishing state during the reign of King João III.[80]

Francisco Tomás is mentioned as chief surgeon of Portugal in a document issued as late as January of 1594.[81] It is not clear who succeeded him. In notarial records dated 1597 there is a Heitor Lopes Pinto, who is described as chief surgeon (*INVTL* IV, 100). However, Ambrósio Nunes, in royal letters dated 20 March and 5 April 1596 which contain approvals for licenses for a bone-setter and a midwife, is described as physician and chief surgeon of the kingdoms and seigniories of Portugal, as well as holder of the *vespera* chair of medicine, *jubilado*, at the University of Salamanca.[82]

Ambrósio Nunes was the son of Dona Leonor Coronel and Leonardo Nunes. Leonardo, as mentioned earlier, was *físico-mor* of Portugal, *fidalgo da casa real* and a knight in the Order of Christ. Born in 1526, Ambrósio was given a scholarship by Dom João III to study at Coimbra, where he received his doctorate. He moved to the University of Salamanca, where he held the chair of medicine. Upon his return to Portugal, he was named physician to the Royal Household and chief surgeon of the kingdom. In the meantime, on 11 June 1569, he received authorization to become a knight in the Portuguese Order of Santiago (ANTT, Chancelaria da Ordem de Santiago, liv. 4, fols. 56v–57v). Some decades later he decided to request a change to the Order of Christ—a request that was granted in 1592.[83] In 1601, he published *Tractado*

[79]See the *verba* of 15 July 1593 in ANTT, Chancelaria de Filipe I, *Doações*, liv. 7, fol. 232. For Alvaro's authorization for knighthood in the Order of Christ in May of 1583, see ANTT, Chancerlaria da Ordem de Cristo, liv. 5, fols. 196ᵛ–197. The Order's *Livro da Matricula* has the ceremonies taking place the same year (see BNM:Ms. 938, fol. 122v). For the commandery, see L. de Figueiredo Falcão (1859:230) and Biblioteca da Ajuda (Lisbon), 49–IV–32, fol. 45.

[80]See *Compêndio histórico do estado da Universidade de Coimbra (1771)*. I have used the facsimile edition (Coimbra, 1972:297–98).

[81]See ANTT, Chancelaria de Filipe I, *Doações*, liv. 27, fol. 179 (reprinted in Sousa Viterbo 1895 [3rd series]:35–36).

[82]ANTT, Chancelaria de D. Filipe I, *Doações*, liv. 29, fol. 20 and liv. 30, fol. 66 (reprinted int Sousa Viterbo 1895 [3rd series]:19–20 and 36–37).

[83]His letters of authorization to receive the *hábito* and knighthood in the Order of Christ are missing. However, he is listed in the Order of Christ's *Livro da* [continued]

repartido en cinco partes principales que declaran el mal que significa este nombre peste regarding the great plague of 1598 (Braga 1892–1902:II, 771) (see Plate 2). He died in Lisbon on 11 April 1611 at the age of eighty-five (Barbosa Machado 1965–67:I, 132).

By 1613 Portugal's new chief surgeon was Pero de Barros Pinto. In that year, the University of Coimbra was seeking a replacement for Doctor Barros Pinto, who had been professor of the Avicenna chair before being named chief surgeon (Braga 1892–1902:II, 774–79). In 1618 he is described as physician and chief surgeon for Portugal in a document which licensed André Mendes de Oliveira as a surgeon. André was the son of the royal surgeon, Cristóvão Mendes, who also had been surgeon for the Casa da Suplicação.[84]

Pero de Barros Pinto, in turn, was succeeded by António Francisco Milheiro, who, in more than a dozen documents dating from 1631 to 1642, is described in such phrases as "my chief surgeon" and "who is now serving as *físico-mor*."[85] On 12 December 1631, King Philip IV issued a new *regimento* for the chief surgeon of Portugal. It was addressed to Doctor António Francisco Milheiro, who in that year was also serving as Portugal's chief physician due to the vacancy caused by the death of Baltasar de Azeredo (Andrade e Silva 1854–59:IV, 233). Milheiro was ordered to conduct a visitation of the kingdom and to look into matters covered by this new *regimento*, as well as matters concerning the chief physician.

The chief surgeon was to keep a book in which would be listed all the surgeons of Portugal. A list of penalties followed for those who attempted to practice their surgical skills without a license, followed by the penalties for unapproved bloodletting. Midwives and those who repaired arms and legs, used sweating cures, pulled teeth or attempted to cure the insane or mentally impaired without a license would be fined 2$. In addition, the chief surgeon, along with two other surgeons attached to the royal household, would examine all who wished to practice surgery in Portugal. Those who did not know Latin or who

---

Matricula for 1592; see BNM:Ms. 938, fol. 129v. See also ANTT, Chancelaria da Ordem de Cristo, liv. 8, fols. 128–128v.

[84]See *carta* of 10 June 1618 in ANTT, Chancelaria de D. Filipe III, *Doações*, liv. 1, fol. 4v. Reprinted in Sousa Viterbo (1915 [5th series]:132).

[85]See, for example, the letter of 12 May 1631 in ANTT, Chancelaria de D. Filipe III, *Doações*, liv. 26, fol. 52 (reprinted in Sousa Viterbo 1915 [5th series]:134).

practiced medicine in a local hospital should not be admitted for examination. Those aspiring to be surgeons must present evidence that they practiced surgical skills for four years with a surgeon under whom they apprenticed. Their licenses, when issued, were to contain the names of the examiners. Whether they passed or failed, all who took the examination paid two cruzados to the chief surgeon and one to each of the other two examiners. Those surgeons, who were finally approved, were obliged to pay one mark of silver for letters certifying them as surgeons. After they had been instructed by master bloodletters, those hoping to practice such skills were to be examined by the chief surgeon and a committee of two barbers. After this initial approval, bloodletters were to serve a two-year internship with master barbers or in an approved hospital. Those wishing to be midwives would also be examined by the chief surgeon and two midwives chosen by him. Similarly, those who repaired limbs or pulled teeth would be examined by a committee of two practitioners of those skills and the chief surgeon. They were to pay an examination fee of 600 reis whether or not they passed the exam. Those who successfully completed their examination would be issued a certificate—at a cost of three cruzados (1$200)—directly by the chief surgeon, without going through the royal registry books.

Furthermore, the chief surgeon was not to issue temporary licenses and he was only to issue licenses to barbers in places where there were no surgeons. The chief surgeon could also visit apothecary shops to examine those medicines that pertained to surgery; however, other medicines fell under the purview of the chief physician. Those who were not surgeons, but who knew how to cure scrofula (tuberculosis of lymph glands, especially in the neck), sores (*chagas*), simple wounds and similar ailments, could obtain licenses from the chief surgeon after being examined by him and two others who knew such cures. The fee was one cruzado for the chief surgeon and another cruzado for the two other examiners. The fee for the license itself was three cruzados (1$200) paid directly to the chief surgeon, in the same manner as mentioned above.[86]

António Francisco Milheiro was succeeded in the post of chief surgeon by Francisco Borges de Azevedo. In 1641 the latter was identified as chief surgeon of Portugal and resident of Lisbon, living on Rua Direita do Loreto (*INVTL* II, 166). Borges de Azevedo was followed in the post by Dr. António da Mata Falcão.

---

[86]J. J. Andrade e Silva (1854–59:IV, 233). The *regimento* listed two different fines for bloodletters, who practiced without a license. Earlier in the *regimento*, the fine was 10 cruzados or 4$; at the end, the fine was stated as 2$.

Dr. António da Mata Falcão, a physician in the king's household, who held a patent of nobility as *moço da câmara da casa real*, seems to have held the post of *surgião-mor* of Portugal late in his lifetime.[87] In a document dated 14 August 1664, he is described as *surgião-mor*, living in Lisbon on Rua da Caldeireira (*INVTL* I, 23). One of the earliest mentions of Mata Falcão identifies him as a court physician and an examiner for António de Almeida, *curandeiro*, in 1633.[88] In 1640, King Philip IV awarded Mata Falcão a knighthood in the Order of Christ and a promise of 20$ annually, because of his services and those of his father (Antão da Mata Falcão) in Ceylon, Barcelor, Angola, and Benguela.[89] Mata Falcão, who supported the new monarch João IV, had no trouble receiving his award, being granted the necessary letters of authorization for membership in the Order on 19 January 1641 (see ANTT, Chancelaria da Ordem da Cristo, liv. 34, fols. 98, 373–373v). Because of his work as a physician, he continued to receive numerous rewards from the crown. He was awarded a pension of 40$ in 1649,[90] and in 1654 the annual pension was raised to 60$ to include the 20$ he had been promised in 1640.[91] In 1658, his pension was increased to 100$ because of his services at court and "jornadas fora della."[92] He was dead by 16 February 1668, for on that date he was mentioned in hearsay testimony during the proceedings regarding the annulment of Afonso VI's marriage to Queen Maria Francisca. Henrique Carvalho de Sousa, *provedor das obras e paços* of the king, swore that he had heard Doctor António da Mata, physician of the royal bed chamber (*médico da câmara real*), by then deceased, and whom he described as a great physician, speak of King Afonso VI's impotence due to a childhood disease.[93] In 1669 Mata Falcão was succeeded as chief surgeon by Dr. António Ferreira.

---

[87]See document dated 20 August 1677 in ANTT, Chancelaria de D. Afonso VI, liv. 38, fols. 352v–353v.

[88]ANTT, Chancelaria de Filipe III, *Doações*, liv. 32, fol. 172 (reprinted in Sousa Viterbo 1915 [5th series]:21–22).

[89]See the *portaria* of 4 August 1640 in *IPR* I, 18.

[90]For the details, see the *portarias* of 14 April and 21 May 1649 in *IPR* I, 307 and 313, respectively.

[91]See the *portaria* of 24 October 1654 in *IPR* II, 39.

[92]See the *portaria* of 30 January 1658 in *IPR* II, 171.

[93]See A. Baião (1925:80–81). Furthermore, Carvalho de Sousa swore that he had heard from Dr. António da Mata that the reason why Francisco Nunes, surgeon of the royal bedchamber, had been beaten to death was because he had given the same medical opinion as Dr. António Mata.

Just as writers have understandably confused Doctors André António de Castro and António de Castro, both of whom served as chief physicians in the early 1640's, so, too, there is a problem with the António Ferreira, who eventually became chief surgeon of Portugal beginning in 1669. There were at least two physicians or surgeons by the name of António Ferreira who were attached to Portugal's royal house by the 1660's. To complicate matters, both of them served in Lisbon's Royal Hospital of All Saints, both received knighthoods in the Order of Christ, both were named to accompany Catherine of Bragança to England for her marriage to Charles II, and both made depositions regarding King Afonso VI's medical state in that monarch's marriage annulment case against Queen Maria Francisca of Savoy.[94] The more famous of the two António Ferreiras was the author of the important treatise on surgery, *Luz Verdadeyra* (1670) (see Plate 3) and, because of this, merited a biographical sketch by Barbosa Machado in his *Bibliotheca lusitana* (1965–67:I, 274).

Because Barbosa Machado has described this António Ferreira as Catherine's chief surgeon, there has been a tendency to identify him as the chief surgeon of Portugal. It is now clear, however, that it was the other António Ferreira, the physician, who was the chief surgeon of Portugal from 1669 to 1690. When and where this other António Ferreira was born is not known, although he was about fifty-eight years old, in 1668, when he testified in Afonso VI's marriage annulment proceedings (Baião 1925:107). His father was João Alvares.[95] Because of his services at Lisbon's Royal Hospital of All Saints, this António Ferreira was named, by an *alvará* of 16 June 1644, a palace physician (*médico do paço*) in order to fill the vacancy left by Dr. António de Castro, who had been promoted to the post of chief physician of Portugal.[96]

When Francisco Borges de Azevedo, chief surgeon of Portugal, retired in 1659, António Ferreira was promoted to the post of physician of the royal bedchamber (*médico da câmara*) with an annual salary of 100$.[97] He was married to Marta de Booz (Bos) and by her had a number of children, including João Ferreira de Booz (Bos). In 1662, he was

---

[94]António Ferreira testified on 23 February 1668. For the two sets of depositions (*i.e.,* both António Ferreira's) *on Afonso VI's medical state, see A. Baião (1925:107–9, 118–26, and 155–62).*

[95]See the *alvará* of 16 June 1644, *LMMCR* II, 332.

[96]*Loc. cit.* He was also granted a monthly stipend (*moradia*) of 2$.

[97]See the *alvará* of 6 August 1659 in *LMMCR* II, 332.

L U Z
VERDADEYRA,
E RECOPILADO EXAME
DE TODA A CIRURGIA,
DEDICADO
A' AUGUSTA, E REAL MAGESTADE
DEL-REY
D. PEDRO II.
NOSSO SENHOR:
AUTHOR
O LICENCIADO ANTONIO FERREYRA,

Cirurgiaõ da Camera do dito Senhor, sua Guarda, & Hospital Real,
dos Carceres do Santo Officio, & Familiar delle, & do Tribunal
da Relaçaõ desta Corte, Cavalleiro professo da Ordem de
nosso Senhor JESU Christo:

ACRECENTADO NESTA QUARTA IMPRESSAM COM HUMA
Nova Pratica do mesmo Author, com todos os accidentes, que podem sobrevir às feridas.

LISBOA,

Na Officina de VALENTIM DA COSTA DESLANDES,
Impressor de Sua Magestade, & à sua custa impresso.
Com todas as licenças necessarias, & Privilegio Real.
ANNO M. DCCV.
Vende-se na rua da Ferreira.

Plate 3: Title page of the 1705 edition of the widely circulated treatise originally published in 1670. António Ferreira was one of the most famous surgeons
in seventeenth-century Portugal. However, due to the bias against surgeons,
he never attained the post of chief surgeon. That honor went to his colleague,
a physician with the same name, António Ferreira. (Courtesy of The Francis
A. Countway Library of Medicine, Boston.)

named to accompany Catherine of Bragança—as her physician—to England and because of this was granted numerous rewards. By a *portaria* of 10 February 1662, in which he is identified as *médico da câmera*, he was awarded a knighthood in the Order of Christ and an annual pension of 40$. On the same day, he was also awarded a *foro de fidalgo* (see *IPR* II, 318).[98] Three days later, on 13 February 1662, António Ferreira's patent of nobility of *cavaleiro fidalgo* was officially upgraded to *fidalgo cavaleiro* (*LMMCR* II, 122). Also because of his appointment as Queen Catherine's physician, there were further rewards for his family. His son, João Ferreira de Booz (Bos), was awarded a knighthood in the Order of Christ on 10 February 1662. In a *consulta* of 17 April 1662, the Mesa da Consciência e Ordens brought to the king's attention the need for a dispensation (ANTT, Habilitações da Ordem de Cristo, Letra J, Maço 90, Número 16). On 25 April António Ferreira set sail with Catherine for England. He did not remain there long, having returned to Portugal later that year (Castello Branco 1971:460). While in England, he also had under his care, Portugal's ambassador Francisco de Melo, the Marquês de Sande.

Theresa M. Schedel de Castello Branco, in her study of the Marquês, quotes from letters sent to the Portuguese crown, in 1662, which stated that, in the professional opinion of Dr. António Ferreira, the ambassador had been gravely ill, suffering from a variety of ailments, including a lingering fever, chest pains, gout, and kidney stones. Ferreira recommended a change of scenery and a return to Portugal (*loc. cit.*). In 1668 he testified in the marriage annulment case of King Afonso VI and Queen Maria Francisca of Savoy (see note 94). On 26 March 1669, he and his wife, Dona Marta de Bos, are listed in notary records as having purchased a *juro de tença* of 40$ (see *INVTL* I, 45). In an *alvará* of 17 June 1669, he was appointed chief surgeon of the royal palace to succeed Doctor António da Mata Falcão (*LMMCR* II, 73). In notary records ten years later, Dr. António Ferreira, described as *fidalgo*, knight in the Order of Christ and chief surgeon, appears again, having purchased some houses on the Rua da Lagem and on the Beco do Chancudo (*INVTL* II, 30). On 4 January 1683, the chief surgeon approved Simão Pinheiro Morão's *Trattado Unico das Bexigas e Sarampo*, dedicated to D. João de Sousa, *mestre de campo* of Pernambuco, and published in Lisbon later that year. Ferreira pointed out that Morão discussed the causes, symptoms, and cures of the diseases of smallpox

---

[98]The *carta de padrão de tença de 40$* can be found in ANTT, Chancelaria da Ordem de Cristo, liv. 18, fol. 45.

and measles with "great erudition" and emphasized that the book should have great value, especially for the inhabitants of Brazil.[99] Mário Roque (1984:128), without citing his source, states that this António Ferreira was alive in 1690 having served as chief surgeon of Portugal from 23 May 1669 to his retirement on 2 December 1690.

The post of chief surgeon would endure for almost another century after Ferreira's retirement.[100] Then it, along with the post of chief physician, fell victim to the centralizing and reforming winds of the Enlightenment. It seems that, despite the promising developments in medicine and surgery in the early and middle sixteenth century, by the end of that century there were frequent complaints about the quality of medicine being practiced in Portugal. Teófilo Braga argues that medicine went into decline in Portugal for complex reasons. Among them was the persecution of New Christians which brought about the emigration of a significant number of talented men of medicine. Also important was the role of the Jesuits and the Counter-Reformation in stifling experimental research which challenged authority. Another factor was the abuse in the issuance of licenses to those without university training (*médicos idiotas*) by the chief physician and chief surgeon. Because fees were involved, there were charges that these licenses were being sold to unqualified practitioners of medicine. Still another factor was the comparative lack of prestige in the medical profession, which encouraged university students to study civil and canon law and theology instead of medicine (see Braga 1892–1902:II, 770–71).[101] By the early seventeenth century there was difficulty filling several of the chairs of medicine at the University of Coimbra (Braga *ibid.*:II, 776).

A major reform and reorganization of Portugal's governance of medicine came about in the late eighteenth century during the reign of

---

[99]See the license page reproduced in G. Osório de Andrade and E. Duarte (1956:77). Morão anagrammatized his name on the title page: Romão Môsia Reinhipo. A short biographical sketch for Morão can be found in D. Barbosa Machado (1965–67:III, 720), and a more complete one in S. Pinheiro Morão (1965:viii–x). Morão died in 1685 not 1686, as can be seen from his tombstone in the cloister of the Third Order church of São Francisco in Recife. See G. Osório de Andrade and E. Duarte (*Ibid.*:4). A drawing of the inscription is found opposite page 4.

[100]C.R. Boxer (1974:203), citing Manuel Gomes de Lima's *Memorias chronologicas e criticas para a história de cirurgia moderna* (Porto, 1762), points out that "it had become customary in Portugal to appoint a physician as *cirurgião-mor*, a practice which blighted the prospects of promotion for surgeons to the highest office, and further emphasized their subordination to physicians." As can be seen from the examples in this study, such was also the case for the sixteenth and seventeenth centuries.

[101]Similar problems existed in Spain. See R. I. Kagan (1974:217–18).

Maria I (1777–1816). Because of abuses and lack of knowledge on the part of many physicians and surgeons, as well as the gross ignorance of many apothecaries and problems in apothecary shops both in Portugal and overseas, the queen, on 17 June 1782, abolished the posts of chief physician and chief surgeon and replaced them with the *Junta do Protomedicato*. The *Junta* was initially composed of seven deputies— five physicians and two surgeons, all members of the royal household— with the most senior deputy serving as president.[102]

REFERENCES CITED

Andrade e Silva, José Justino de

1854–59   *Collecção Chronológica da Legislação Portugueza*. 10 vols. [Lisbon: Imprensa de J.J.A. Silva, Vols. I (1854), II–III (1855); Imprensa de Francisco Xavier de Sousa, Vols. IV–V (1855), VI–VIII (1856) and IX (1859?); Imprensa Nacional, Vol. X (1859).]

[ANTT] Arquivo Nacional de Torre do Tombo (Lisbon)

Baião, António, ed.

1925   *Causa de nulidade de matrimónio entre a Rainha D. Maria Francisca Isabel de Saboya e o Rei D. Afonso VI*. Coimbra: Imprensa da Universidade.

Barbosa Machado, Diogo

1965–67   *Bibliotheca lusitana histórica, crítica, e cronológica* [Coimbra, 1741–59]. Third edition. Coimbra: Atlântida Editora. 4 vols. [Vols. I (1965), II–III (1966), and IV (1967).]

Biblioteca da Ajuda (Lisbon)

[BNM] Biblioteca Nacional (Madrid)

Boxer, Charles

1974   "Some Remarks on the Social and Professional Status of Physicians and Surgeons in the Iberian World, 16th–18th Centuries," *Revista de História,* 50(100):197–215 (São Paulo).

[102]See "Lei, pela qual S. Magestade mandou crear a Junta do Protomedicato, extinguin-do os empregos de Fysico mór, e Cirurgião mór," in *Systema* (1818:VI, 355–57).

Braga, Teófilo

1892–1902 *História da Universidade de Coimbra nas suas relacões com a Instrucção Pública Portugueza*. Lisbon: Academia Real das Sciencias. 4 vols. [Vols. I (1892), II (1895), III (1898), and IV (1902).]

Brandão, Mário, ed.

1937–41 *Documentos de D. João III*. Coimbra: Por ordem da Universidade. 4 vols. [Vols. I (1937), II (1938), III (1939), and IV (1941).]

Burke, Michael E.

1977 *The Royal College of San Carlos. Surgery and Spanish Medical Reform in the Late Eighteenth Century*. Durham: Duke University Press.

Caetano de Sousa, António

1946–54 *Provas da história genealógica da Casa Real Portuguesa* [Coimbra, 1739–48]. Second edition. Edited by M. Lopes de Almeida and Cesar Pegado. Coimbra: Atlântida-Livraria Editora. 6 vols in 12. [Vols. I(1–2)(1946), I(3)–II(1)(1947), II(2)– III(1)(1948), III(2)(1949), IV(1)–IV(2)(1950), V(1)– V(2)(1952), and VI(1)– VI(2)(1954).]

Carmona, Mário

1954 *O Hospital Real de Todos os Santos da Cidade de Lisboa*. Lisbon: Boletim Clínico dos Hospitais Civis de Lisboa, 1954.

[This study orignally appeared in the *Boletim Clínico dos Hospitais Civis de Lisboa*, 18(1–4): 408–608 (Lisbon, 1954).]

Castello Branco, Theresa M. Schedel de

1971 *Vida de Francisco Mello Torres, 1º* Conde da Ponte Marquês de Sande. Soldado e diplomata da Restauração, 1620–1667. Lisbon: Oficina Gráfica.

1972 *Compêndio histórico do estado da Universidade de Coimbra* [Lisbon, 1771]. Facsimile edition. Coimbra: Por ordem da Universidade.

Dutra, Francis A.

(in press) "Membership in the Order of Christ in the Sixteenth Century: Problems and Perspectives," in *Portuguese Language and Culture throughout the World*, Proceedings of the 1983 Colloqium, Jorge de Sena Center for Portuguese Studies.

Ferro Tavares, Maria José Pimenta

1982–84   *Os judeus em Portugal no século XV.* Lisbon:Universidade Nova de Lisboa/Instituto Nacional de Investigação Científica. 2 vols.

Figueiredo Falcão, Luis de

1859   *Livro em que se contém toda a fazenda e real patrimonio dos Reinos de Portugal, India e Ilhas adjacentes e outras particularidades.* Lisbon: Imprensa Nacional.

Gomes de Lima, Manuel

1762   *Memorias chronológicas e críticas para a história da cirurgia moderna.* Porto: Na Of. Episc. do Capitão Manoel Pedros Coimbra.

Gonçalves, Iria.

1965   "Físicos e cirurgiões quatrocentistas. As cartas de exame," *Do Tempo e da História,* 1:69–112 (Lisbon).

[INVTL] Index das notas de varios tabelliães de Lisboa, entre os anos de 1580 e 1747.

1930–49   Lisbon: Biblioteca Nacional. 4 vols. [Vols. I (1930), II (1931), III (1934), and IV (1949).]

[IPR] Inventario dos livros das portarias do reino

1909–12   Lisbon: Imprensa Nacional. 2 vols.

Kagan, Richard I.

1974   *Students and Society in Early Modern Spain.* Baltimore: The Johns Hopkins University Press.

Lanning, John Tate

1985   *The Royal Protomedicato. The Regulation of the Medical Profession in the Spanish Empire.* Durham: Duke University Press.

Leite, Serafim, ed.

1963   *Estatutos da Universidade de Coimbra* [Coimbra, 1559]. Coimbra: Por ordem da Universidade.

[LMMCR] Inventario dos livros de matrícula dos moradores da Casa Real.

1911–17   Lisbon: Imprensa Nacional. 2 vols.

Machado de Faria, António.

1955   "Cavaleiros da Ordem de Cristo no século XVI," *Arqueológia e História* 6:13–73 (Lisbon).

Mariz, Pedro de.

1806   *Dialogos da varia historia* [Coimbra, 1594]. Fifth edition. Lisbon: Impressão Regia.

Oliveira de Cadornega, António de.

1972   *História geral das guerras angolanas* [Lisbon, 1680]. Lisbon: Agência-Geral do Ultramar. 3 vols [Facsimile of earlier edition. Vols. I–II (1940) edited by José Matias Delgado; Vol. II (1942), edited by Manuel Alves de Cunha.]

1982   *Descrição de Vila Viçosa*. Edited by Heitor Gomes Teixeira. Lisbon: Imprensa Nacional.

Osório de Andrade, Gilberto, and Eustáquio Duarte, eds.

1956   *Morão, Rosa e Pimenta. Notícia dos três primeiros livros em vernáculo sbre a medicina no Brasil*. Pernambuco: Arquivo Público Estadual.

Pinheiro Morão, Simão

1965   *Queixas repetidas em ecos dos Arrecifes de Pernambuco contra os abusos médicos que nas suas capitanias se observam tanto em dano das vidas de seus habitadores*. Edited by Jaime Walter. Lisbon: Junta de Investigações do Ultramar.

Prestage, Edgar, and Pedro de Azevedo, eds.

1924–27   *Registo da Freguesia da Sé desde 1563 até 1610*. Coimbra: Imprensa da Universidade. 2 vols.

Rebelo da Silva, Luis Augusto

1860–71   *História de Portugal nos séculos XVII e XVIII*. Lisbon: Imprensa Nacional. 5 vols. [Vols. I (1860), II (1862), III (1867), IV (1869), and V (1871).]

Roque, Mário.

1984   "Físicos, cirurgiões, boticários, parteiros e barbeiros que na sua maior parte viveram em Lisboa nos séculos XVI e XVII," *Anais da Academia Portuguesa da História,* II series, 29:121–36 (Lisbon).

Silva Rego, António de, ed.

1966   *Manuscritos da Ajuda (Guia)*. Lisbon: Centro de Estudos Históricos Ultramarinos.

Sousa Viterbo, Francisco Marques de.

1893–98 *Noticia sobre alguns medicos portuguezes ou que exerceram a sua profissão em Portugal.* Lisbon: Imprensa Nacional. [1st series (1893); 2nd series (1895); 3rd series (1895); 4th series (1898); and 5th series (1915). The first four originally appeared in the *Jornal da Sociedade das Sciencias Medicas de Lisboa.]*

1915 *Notícia sobre alguns médicos portuguêzes ou que exerceram a sua profissão em Portugal.* 5th series. Porto: Tipografia a vapor de "Enciclopédia Portuguesa." [Appeared posthumously in *Arquivos de História da Medicina Portuguesa.*]

Systema, ou Collecção dos Regimentos Reaes [Lisbon, 1783–1791].

1818 ed. Lisbon: Typografia Lacerdina. 6 vols. [1st ed. Edited by José Roberto Monteiro Campos Coelho e Soisa (Lisbon, 1783–1791): Vols. I (1783) and II (1785). Lisbon: Na Officina de Francisco Borges de Soisa (*sic!*); Vol. III (1785). Lisbon: Na Officina Patriarcal de Francisco Luiz Ameno; Vol. IV (1785). Lisbon: Na Officina de Simão Thaddeo Ferreira; Vols. V (1789) and VI (1791).Lisbon: Na Officina Patriarcal de Francisco Luiz Ameno.]

Veríssimo Serrão, Joaquim.

1962 *Itinerários de El-Rei D. Sebastião (1568 – 1578).* Lisbon: Academia Portuguesa de História.2 vols. [A second revised edition of this important work appeared in 1987.]

1977–88 *História de Portugal.* Lisbon: Editorial Verbo. 10 vols. [Vols. I–II (1977), III (1978), IV (1979), V (1980), VI (1982), VII (1984), VIII–IX (1986), and X (1988).]

Américo Jacobina Lacombe

THE TERM *BANDEIRA* IN THE HISTORY OF BRAZIL

Something should be said about the term *bandeira* (literally 'flag'), which has provoked so much discussion. There are people who think that the name comes from the insignia adopted by the *sertanistas* ('backwoodsmen'). That they carried insignias is indisputable: the Spanish missionary Jesuits, Fathers Justo Mansilla Vansurk and Simon Maceta, said that, as far as they could see, they contained neither symbols of Spain nor Portugal. Alfred Ellis Júnior (1944:148) remarked that they might well be a symbol of independence, but Jaime Cortesão (1958:179) suggested that they were perhaps the coat of arms of the *donatário* ('concessionaire').

Certainly it was not because of the insignia that the troops employed such a name, even though it was always displayed. In the beginning the generic term *entrada* was used to describe incursions upon the Indians or for geographical verifications. Father Antônio Vieira (1608–1697) did not use any other word when speaking of the expeditions in the State of Maranhão, as for example "entradas ao sertão," "entrada do pe. Manuel Nunes," "entrada para o interior" (Vieira 1951:I, 157, 189, and 201, resp.). The same term is used many times by the São Paulo city council (*câmara*) in various decrees: "entrada" by Fernão Dias. But Father Vieira himself, when referring to

Américo Jacobina Lacombe is Brazil's foremost authority on the Brazilian jurist, writer, and statesman, Ruy Barbosa (1849–1923). Among his innumerable historical writings is included the Introduction to the Study of Brazilian History *(1974). He is a member of the Brazilian Academy of Letters.*

groups that were accompanied by military units, applied the term *companhia*: "Companhias de soldados brancos ('Companies of white soldiers')," and "45 soldados com um *capitão* ('forty-five soldiers with a captain')" (*Ibid.*:I, 189 and 201, resp.).

The term *bandeira* is equivalent to that of *companhia*, and its application is strictly military and of Italian origin. It is discussed fully in the *Enciclopedia Italiana di Scienze, Lettere ed Arti* (Rome, 1929–37) edited by Giovanni Treccani. *Bandiera*, according to this outstanding encyclopedia, means a specific number of soldiers organized under the same insignia:

> *Bandiera di Fanti*, all'epoca delle compagnie di ventura, indicava una squadra di fanti affidata e aggruppata sotto un capo. Le bandiere furono di forza variabile. In una scrittura o patto fra Piero Vanni da Santa Maria e la repubblica fiorentina del 1377, il Vanni si obbliga de condurre una bandiera de 27 uomini balestrari, egli compreso, fra i quali dovevano esservi il banderaio e un ragazzo.
>
> In un altro patto del 1395 un Malvolta Giovanni di Firenze si obbliga per una bandiera di 25 fanti e 2 cavalieri, egli compreso fra questi e tra i fanti dovevano esservi: 12 balestrieri, un ragazzo, un tamburino e un banderaio; in un altro de 1438, Gregorio Ricci dà 30 fanti in una bandiera, egli compreso, ecc.[1]

From Italy the term travelled to Spain, where it appears in the *Enciclopedia Universal Ilustrada Europeo-Americana* (Madrid, 1905–33) under *bandera*:

> El mismo nombre se daba en los tiempos de la Casa de Austria á las compañías que formaban los tercios, por tener cada una su insignia.[2]

---

[1]Translation: A *bandiera di fanti*, in the time of the campaigns of the soldiers of fortune, indicated a squadron of infantrymen (or foot soldiers) grouped together under the command of a leader. The number of infantry men in a *bandiera* varied. In a written agreement or pact of 1377, between Pietro Vanni da Santa Maria and the Florentine Republic, Vanni undertook to lead a *bandiera* of twenty-seven archers, including himself, among whom would also be the flag bearer and a boy.

In another pact of 1395, a certain Malvolta Giovanni di Firenze agreed to provide a *bandiera* of twenty-five infantrymen and two cavalrymen, one being himself; and the infantrymen were to include twelve archers, a boy, a drummer, and a flag bearer. In another pact of 1438, Gregorio Ricci agreed to furnish a *bandiera* of thirty infantrymen, himself included, etc.

[2]Translation: In the time of the Hapsburgs (Casa de Austria) the same name was given to the companies which formed the infantry regiments, each one having its own insignia.

From Spain the term moved to Portugal, where, during the Middle Ages, it meant:

> Um conjunto de cinco ou seis lanças, abrangendo na designação de lança: o homen de armas, o seu escudeiro, o pagem, dois arqueiros ou besteiros e um cutileiro. Ao todo uma bandeira compunhase de trinta e seis homens. Um certo número de bandeiras completava a companhia de homens de armas (César 1929:II, 534).[3]

As part of a *companhia*, the term *bandeira* became a synonym for it. During the reign of Dom Manuel (1469–1521), the organization of *tropas de reserva* were known as militias and ordinances. Their military laws are not known. Cortesão believes that the term *bandeira*, as a synonym for *companhia*, dates from this period.

However, during the reign of Dom Sebastião (1557–1578), the famous *Regimento dos Capitães-mores e mais capitães e oficiais das companhias de gente de cavalo e de pé* ('*Regimento of the captains-in-chief and other captains and officials of the cavalry and infantry*') was formalized, in 1574, in the *Provisão sobre Ordenanças* ('*Regulations concerning the Ordinances*'). Under the title *Regimento das Ordenanças*, this legal document figures prominently in the six-volume compilation, much utilized in the time of the Empire, by José Roberto Monteiro de Campos Coelho e Souza, entitled *Systema, ou Collecção dos Regimentos Reaes* and published in Lisbon between 1783 and 1791.[4] In this work, *bandeira* and *companhia* are treated synonymously. Each *bandeira* comprised two hundred and fifty men, with ten squadrons of twenty-five each. Each *companhia* had a captain, a warrant officer, a sergeant, a legal official, and a record keeper. Each captain had a flag, entrusted to the warrant officer, and a drummer. All the regiments were called either *bandeira* or *companhia*.

The reserves, called the ordinances or third line, were formed by civilians in all the municipalities. When these forces were organized in such a manner, the expression *fazer bandeira* ('to create a *bandeira*') was used:

---

[3]Translation: A group of five or six lances, including, in this designation of lance: the armed man, his squire, his page, two archers or crossbowmen, and a cutler. In all, a *bandeira* was composed of thirty-six men. A certain number of *bandeiras* made up a company of armed men.

[4]This compilation was well known and is referred to in the official communication no. 115 (dated 21 August 1826) of the imperial minister Visconde de São Leopoldo. This *Regimento* appears in Carneiro de Mendonça (1972:I, 157 and 161).

> E no lugares em que houver menos de 250 homes se ajuntará com eles a gente das aldeias e casais do termo para *fazerem uma bandeira* de 250 homens, contanto que não estejam em distância de mais de uma légua das cabeças, nem possam por si *fazer bandeira*.[5]

The *bandeira* was prepared for war and practiced military exercises periodically; "cada oito dias, em domingo ou dia santo" ('every eight days, Sundays or holidays'). In each there was a *capitão-mor*, who was the commander-in-chief of the ordinances. He was assisted by a *sargento-mor*, who led the captains of the *bandeiras*.

Cortesão (*loc. cit.*) cites an example from Diogo do Couto's *Soldado prático*, wherein these terms can be verified as current in Portuguese India. The Governor General Manuel de Sousa Coutinho, writing to the king on 10 December 1588, states that it is impossible "reduzir a soldadesca da India *a bandeiras* por não haver dinheiro para se lhes pagar" (*Boletim da Filmoteca Ultramarina Portuguesa*, 1960:549, n. 77).[6]

The term was also current in Brazil, as Cortesão proved from a letter written by Father Henrique Gomes; transcribed by Father Serafim Leite (1945:VI, 324). This same author mentions, in addition, various documents existing in the Jesuit archives wherein it can be verified that *fazer bandeira* and *levantar bandeira* ('to raise a *bandeira*') were genuine military expressions according to the law at the time. Furthermore:

> Certifico eu Francisco da Costa Barros, Provedor. . . que os moradores da Capitania de S. Vicente, em especial os da vila de S. Paulo, costumam ir ao sertão formando para isso companhias, *levantando bandeiras* a nomeando capitães e todos os mais ofícios militares . . .[7]

---

[5]Translation: In places with less than 250 men, there shall be assembled people from the villages and hamlets of the district to make a *bandeira* of 250; however, these people should not be situated more than one league away nor be able to organize a *bandeira* by themselves.

[6]Translation: To reduce the number of troops in India only to *bandeiras*, because there is no money to pay them.

[7]Translation: I, Francisco da Costa Barros, Provedor, certify that the inhabitants of the Captaincy of São Vicente, especially those of the village of São Paulo, are accustomed to travelling to the interior, forming for that purpose companies, raising *bandeiras*, and appointing captains and all other military officers. . .

It is worth mentioning that they organized themselves militarily according to the regulation concerning the ordinances. The same author transcribed another letter:

> Certifico eu Pedro Homen Albernaz, Governador, Provisor e Vigário Geral. . . que os moradores de S. Paulo, como outros doutras capitanias. . . levantam capitães e oficiais de milícia, com *bandeiras* e tambores.[8]

Father Manuel Pacheco is even more explicit:

> Que os sertanistas de São Paulo. . . fazem capitães, alferes e sargentos e os mais oficiais de milícias, com *bandeira* e tambor. O pe. Antônio Gomes fala tambem em "capitães, e mais oficiais de guerra, com suas *bandeiras* e tambores." O pe. Francisco de Oliveira usa até a expressão "*levantando companhias*, capitães, com todos mais ofícios que costumam servir nas milícias, com bandeiras e tambores."[9]

Father Vieira, in a letter to King D. João in 1554, stated that established companies of white soldiers should go on "jornadas do sertão ('journeys to the interior')" and not those "criadas de novo ('created anew')," but, with captains and soldiers (1951:I, 189). It should be noted that all these expressions are from the *Regimento das Ordenanças*, which was the source of the terminology. Moreover, Cortesão cited a deposition to the Holy Office in Bahia wherein one Francisco de Barbuda, who was a captain in one of the companies of ordinances, qualified as *capitão de uma bandeira*. This occurred in 1618 (*Anais da Biblioteca Nacional* 1936:114).

Yet from Maranhão, in 1624, we possess descriptions of military operations by Brother Cristóvão de Lisboa wherein he utilized several times the term *bandeira*:

---

[8]Translation: I, Pedro Homem Albernaz, Governor, Treasurer, and Vicar General. . . that the inhabitants of São Paulo, like others from other captaincies. . . raise captains and militia officers, with *bandeiras* and drums.

[9]Translation: That the *sertanistas* of São Paulo make captains, second lieutenants, sergeants, and the other officers of the militia with a *bandeira* and a drum. Father Antônio Gomes also mentions "captains and other war officers, with their *bandeiras* and drums." Father Francisco de Oliveira even uses the term "raising *companhias*, captains, together with all the other officers who usually serve in the militia, with *bandeiras* and drums."

Father Serafim Leite attributed the term *bandeira* more to an insignia than to a military unit. However, now we see that the term indicated not only the insignia, but the unit itself, which was the *companhia*.

> Mandou [o governador] uma *bandeira* sendo avisado que saíam pela terra dentro. Esta *bandeira* se atemorizou. . . e se desencontrou com o inimigo. . . Antônio de Albuquerque que ia por capitão da *bandeira* (Melo 1954:25).[10]

In 1640, Henrique Dias, writing to the Count of Bagnuolo, referred to his troops as *bandeiras*: "Saltei no porto da Pipa com três bandeiras d'El-Rei" (*Documentos históricos* 34: 84, n. 6).[11]

In a dreadful document, in which the *paulistas* ('people of São Paulo') are accused of being rebels and disrespectful to the laws of His Majesty, because under the governor's orders they conquer the peaceful pagans of the villages, the Governor Antônio Luís Gonçalves referred to the military organization of his *tropas de paulistas* ('Paulist troops') with *capitães-mores* and *sargentos-mores*. The term *tropas dos paulistas* is used exactly as the currently employed term *bandeirantes*. "Os paulistas saem de sua terra e deitam várias tropas por todo o sertão" (*Ibid.* 33:345).[12] Here *tropa de paulistas* supersedes the term *bandeira*.

The same governor, who was not sympathetic to the *paulistas*, referring to an armed expedition against the Indians organized in the time of Governor Mathias da Cunha, said that it was composed of "soldados paulistas" (*Ibid.* 33:451) and did not fail to mention the soldiers' extraordinary capacity for resistance while fighting in the forests, because—and these are his words: "os paulistas quando 'embrenhados,' são mais destros que os mesmos bichos" (*Ibid.* 33:337).[13]

In the same year (1640), there was an uprising of mercenaries in Bahia due to a delay in payment. This is how the same governor described it: "encostaram-se à casa da pólvora dizendo que lhes pagassem o que deviam, que logo tornariam para as suas *bandeiras*."[14] When

---

[10]Translation: [The governor] sent a *bandeira*, being informed that it was leaving for the interior. This *bandeira* was frightened. . . and failed to meet the enemy. . . Antônio de Albuquerque was the captain of the *bandeira*.

[11]Translation: I landed at the harbor of Pipa with three of the king's *bandeiras*. (Letter to His Majesty, 8 August 1693.)

[12]Translation: The *paulistas* leave their places and take their troops everywhere in the interior. (Letter of 19 June 1691.)

[13]Translation: When in the forests, the paulistas are more ingenious than the animals themselves.

[14]Translation: They leaned against the powder house saying that they should be paid the amount due or they would return to the *bandeiras*.

the rebels were paid, "se vieram a meter debaixo das suas *bandeiras*" (*Ibid.* 33:337).[15]

In all administrative acts and correspondence from the mid-seventeenth to the eighteenth century contained in the collection of *Documentos Históricos*, the term *bandeira* was not used anymore; *companhia* was the preferred term. Expeditions are *jornadas*. All the provisions, regulations, and orders designate captains for the *companhias*. The expeditions, whether exploratory, for prospecting mines or for quelling the wild Indians, are designated as *entradas* or *jornadas* even when composed of Paulist draftees.

In 1658, Governor Francisco Barreto, for example, appealed to the *paulistas* to free Bahia from the furious attacks of the Tupi Indians (*tapuias*). The expeditions sent up to that time, composed of local ordinances, failed because the Bahian troops "menos costumada a penetrar o sertão que os moradores daquela capitania [São Vicente] cuja experiência em *jornadas* a diversas conquistas os têm tão notoriamente habilitado para maiores empresas" (*Ibid.* 3:397).[16] Even on this occasion, the term conferred on the *paulistas* is captains of the conquest; but, the term *bandeira* was not used anymore. The terms are always *companhias de ordenança*, *capitães*, and *soldados sertanistas* (*Ibid.* 5:520).

In the extensive explanation made in the Bahia report, in 1669, Governor Alexandre de Sousa Freire, in order to declare fair the war against the *tapuias*, mentioned the armed expedition under the command of the *paulista* chief, Domingo Barbosa de Calheiros, as follows:

> Se resolveu mandar vir da capitania de S. Vicente e S. Paulo a gente e cabos mais experimentados que ali havia nas *jornadas* do sertão, em que preferem todos os do Brasil.[17]

Calheiros's title was that of *capitão-mor* ('expedition captain'), leading the chosen infantry (*Ibid.* 4:203). The same title and the expedition's classification as *jornada* appeared in the similar expedition,

---

[15]Translation: They returned to serve under their *bandeiras*.

[16]Translation: [Bahian troops] were less accustomed to penetrate the interior than the inhabitants of that captaincy [São Vicente], whose experience in *jornadas* and various conquests have so notably equipped them for major enterprises.

[17]Translation: It was decided to send from the captaincy of São Vicente and São Paulo, the most experienced people and corporals, selected from all parts of Brazil, that were in the *jornadas* of the interior.

which departed in 1671, under the command of another *paulista*, Sergeant Major Antônio Rodrigues de Arção (*Ibid.* 4:209). Estêvão Ribeiro de Baião Parente, departing that same year, acquired the title of *capitão-mor* "da conquista dos bárbaros ('of the barbarian conquest')" and the expedition is classified as an *entrada*. Still, in the concluding agreement with the city of São Paulo for the execution of the undertaking, the expedition is classified as a *jornada* (*Ibid.* 3:110).

In a letter to the *Capitão-mor* of the captaincy of São Vicente regarding that expedition and referring to the *grande alvoroço* ('great revolt'), while awaiting the arrival of the expert *paulistas*. . ., the Governor General referred only to the "*companhias* de infantaria" (*Ibid.* 3:227). And, in 1654, Dias Adorno himself departed with a *companhia* (*Ibid.* 8:384).

Yet in 1673, in a letter to Brás Rodrigues de Arzão, congratulating him on the victories against the Indians (*bugres*) and praising "a glória dos paulistas ('the glory of the *paulistas*')" who showed themselves to be more interested in the conquest than in the immediate interests, the Viscount of Barbacena already employed the term current in São Paulo: "a respeito da *bandeira* que tinha mandado a buscar as relíquias dos tupis" (*Ibid.* 8:385).[18] However, in the following year, when referring to Fernão Dias Pais, "que tinha encarregado há tempos o descobrimento da prata na serra de Sabarábuçu,"[19] the Viscount again used the term *tropa* with reference to the *paulista* expedition.[20]

It can be asserted therefore, that the term *bandeira*, as a military force of the third line, called ordinances, almost fell into disuse during the seventeenth and eighteenth centuries, except in São Paulo, to indicate an armed expedition to the interior. The term reappeared in the nineteenth century. The Governor-General used it, referring to the *paulistas* only, and already in the nineteenth century, the royal letter of Prince D. João resorted to it:

[18]Translation: With respect to the expedition that has been sent to bring back the Tupi relics.

[19]Translation: Who had supervised the discovery of silver in the Sabarabuço mountains.

[20]In the description of the battle with the French in Rio in 1710, now in the Biblioteca da Ajuda, we read: "metendo-se *uma bandeira* por trás da Igreja do Carmo ('*a bandeira* placing itself behind the Church of Carmo')," "correndo com as *bandeiras* franceses ('running with the French *bandeiras*')." In the report of the Senate of Rio to the king (Pizarro 1821:I, 119), it is said that the "inimigo veio à campanha com onze *bandeiras*, em que vinham 1400 homens ('enemy came to the campaign with eleven *bandeiras*, in which there were 1,400 men')" (Ennes 1944:I, 241).

> Quando seja obrigado a declarar guerra so índio, que então proceda a fazer e deixar fazer prisioneiros de guerra pelas *bandeiras* que ele [Governador de S. Paulo] primeiro autorizar a entrar nos campos, sem esse permissão nenhuma *bandeira* poderá entrar.[21]

Here again the term *bandeira* was restored, be it for troops, militiamen, or civilians (Malheiro 1944;I, 303).

A note in the *Proceedings* of the Instituto Histórico e Geográfico, in 1839, probably written by the secretary, the erudite Canon Januário Barbosa da Cunha, found it necessary to supply an explanation of the term *bandeira*:

> Dá-se *em Minas Gerais*, o nome de bandeira a uma reunião de indivíduos que voluntariamente se ajuntam a fim de explorar os sertões ainda não conhecidos (*Revista do Instituto Histórico e Geográfico Brasileiro* 1908:202).[22]

According to Affonso d'Escragnolle Taunay (1927:III, 343), the term was common in São Paulo in the eighteenth century. It appears in a *regimento* passed by the Count of Alvor, *Capitão-general da Capitania*, in 1740. According to an observation by Paulo Prado (1925:121), it is registered in Aires de Casal (1943: I, 248).

That the organization of *bandeiras* in São Paulo had a military basis, can be deduced from the abundant *paulista* documents that were published. As Cortesão remarked, in the work we have been following, the captains of the *entradas*, *jornadas*, or *bandeiras* are exactly the captains of the commanding battalions organized in the captaincy.

Thus, in 1592, Afonso Sardinha, the so-called "proto-bandeirante" was "capitão da gente da vila de S. Paulo." According to the *Registro Geral* (I, 51, 59), he was appointed to lead the raid that year. In 1599, according to Cortesão (*Ibid.*), D. Francisco de Sousa named Antônio de Proença "capitão da gente cavalo desta vila de S. Paulo [ordenança] e das entradas que nela se fizerem." In 1601, the city council elected Garcia Rodrigues as "capitão de milícias." The governor, who most

---

[21]Translation: When he is obliged to declare war on the Indians and then proceeds to take and allows the *bandeiras* to take prisoners of war which he [the governor of São Paulo] authorizes upon entering the interior, without this permission no *bandeira* can enter.

[22]Translation: In Minas Gerais the name *bandeira* is given to a group of individuals who voluntarily join together to explore the unknown interior.

devoted himself to bringing about *bandeirismo*, was exactly the same who best organized the militia forces, promoting a strictly military recruitment that included Indians.

During the sixteenth century, the militia battalions were always organized with their men, captains, and their maneuvers. Impressed by the arrival of the Dutch in Bahia, preoccupation about defense resurfaced. The names of the captains, in 1624, were the same as the important military officials of the *bandeiras*: Pedro Vaz de Barros and Antônio Raposo Tavares.

One can still find in the *Registro Geral* (I, 494–96) a document with references to "*companhias* que foram ao sertão; o signatário daquele documento é o mesmo que dirá mais tarde, em outro documento, que partiram várias *bandeiras* contra os índios no sertão" (Cortesão 1958:77).[23] A *Câmara* announcement in 1635 employed both terms in the same period, ordering "os capitães de ordenanças fossem *com suas bandeiras* assistir no porto da vila de Santos ('the commanding captains to go *with their expeditions* to help out at the Port of Vila de Santos')" (*loc. cit.*).

That the expeditions maintained military organizations during their operations has been stated expressly by Alcântara Machado (*op. cit.*:260) and we have the proof in the Montova testimony, which states:

> El suplicante y otros religiosos sus compañeros los han visto varias veces por aquelles campos marchar con mucha orden de guerra, en que estan muy ejercitados: y tanto en andar a pie y descalzos, que, como pudieran andar por las calles de esta Corte, caminan por aquellas tierras, montes e valles, sin ningun estorbo, trescientas y quatrocientas leguas (Cortesão 1958:157).[24]

Among the works presented to the doctorate program on *bandeirismo*, administered by Prof. Waldemar Ferreira of the Law School of the University of São Paulo, in 1955, two deal specifically with the meaning of the word *bandeira* (Hecht 1955 and Gola 1955). It is curious

---

[23]Translation: Battalions that went to the interior; the signer of that document is the same who will say, later on in another document, that various *bandeiras* ('expeditions') departed to the interior to fight the Indians.

[24]Translation: The supplicant and other religious persons, who are his companions, have at various times seen them in the fields marching in a military manner, for which they are well drilled, and so many are walking barefoot, as they do in the streets of this Capital, that they are able to walk 300 or 400 leagues across these lands, mountains, and valleys without any difficulty.

that, in the last pages of the latter work, the author only quoted the military definitions of Dom José Mirales and General José Maria Latino Coelho from the *Enciclopedia Universal Ilustrada Europeo-Americana*, but did not consider this concept fundamental.

In the famous plan of the *bandeiras* included by Paulo Prado in his *Retrato do Brasil* (1928:67), Capistrano de Abreu generalized the term by applying it to *entradas* of various geographical origins: *bandeiras* paulistas, *bandieras* baianas, *bandeiras* pernambucanas, *bandeiras* maranhenses, and *bandeiras* amazônicas.

The well-known *paulista*, José Bonifácio Andrade e Silva (1763–1838), in his essay "Apontamentos para a civilização dos índios bravos" (1963:II, 108), restored the term *bandeira* to its original context, exactly as that of an expedition destined to search for Indians. But here he suggested that the expeditions acquired a more civilized meaning. Thereafter, the term has been applied as a synonym of *campanha*, a cultural and moral expedition.

REFERENCES CITED

Aires [Ayres] do Casal, Manuel

    1943   *Corografia brasílica. Relacão histórico geográfica do reino do Brasil*. São Paulo: Ediciones Cultura. 2 vols. [First published in São Paulo, 1817.]

Anais da Biblioteca Nacional (Rio de Janeiro)

    1936   Vol. 49.

Andrade e Silva, José Bonifácio de.

    1963   *Obras científicas, políticas e sociais*. Coligidas e reproduzidas por Edgard de Cerqueira Falcão. Santos: Grupo de Trabalho Executivo das Homenagens ao Patriarca. Vol. 2.

Boletim da Filmoteca Ultramarina Portuguesa (Lisbon)

    1960   No. 15.

Carneiro de Mendonça, Marcos, ed.

    1972   *Raízes da formação administrativa do Brasil*. Rio de Janeiro: Instituto Histórico e Geográfico Brasileiro / Conselho Federal de Cultura. Vol. 1.

César, Victoriano José

    1929   "Elementos constitutivos do exército nosprimeirostempos de monarquia," in Damião Peres, ed., *Historia de Portugal* (Barcelos: Portucalense Editora), pp. 533–51.

Cortesão, Jaime

1958   *Rapôso Tavares e a formação territorial do Brasil.* Rio de
        Janeiro: Ministério de Educação e Cultura, Servício de
        Documentação (Colecção "Vida Brasileira," No. 11).

Documentos Históricos (Bibliotheca Nacional, Rio de Janeiro)

1928   Vol. III
1928   Vol. IV
1928   Vol. V
1929   Vol. VIII
1936   Vol. XXXI
1936   Vol. XXXIII
1936   Vol. XXXIV

Ellis Júnior, Alfredo

1944   *Rapôso Tavares e sua época.* Rio de Janeiro: Livraria José
        Olympio Editora.

Ennes, Ernesto

1944   *Dois paulistas insignes.* São Paulo: Companhia Editora
        Nacional. Vol. I (Biblioteca Pedagógica Brasileira, Série 5ª,
        vol. 236).

Gola, Waldemar

1955   "A bandeira e sua origem vocabular," *Revista da Faculdade
        de Direito,* 50:319–43 (São Paulo). [Actually printed in 1956.]

Hecht, Johannes Dietrich

1955   "A origem vocabular e o conceito histórico de bandeira,"
        Revista da Faculdade de Direito, 50:249–71 (São Paulo). [Ac-
        tually printed in 1956.]

Leite, Serafim

1945   *História da Companhia de Jesus no Brasil.* Lisbon: Livraria
        Portugalia / Rio de Janeiro: Civilização Brasileira. Vol. 6.

Malheiro, Agostinho Marques Perdigão

1944   *A escravidão no Brasil: Ensaio histórico-jurídico-social.*
        Facsmile ed. São Paulo: Cultura. Vol. 1. [Original edition.
        Rio de Janeiro: Typographia Nacional, 1866].

Melo, José Antônio Gonsalves de

1954 *Henrique Dias: Governador dos pretos, crioulos e mulatos do Estado do Brasil*. Recife: Editora Universidade.

Pizzaro e Aráuno, José de Sousa Azevedo

1821 *Memórias históricas do Rio de Janeiro*. Rio de Janeiro: Imprenta Nacional. Vol. 1 [Reprinted: Rio de Janeiro: Imprenta Nacional, 1945.]

Prado, Paulo

1925 *Paulística: História de São Paulo*. São Paulo: Companhia Graphico-Editora Monteiro Lobato. [2nd augmented ed. Rio de Janeiro: Ariel Editora Limitada, 1934].

1928 *Retrato do Brazil*. 2nd ed. São Paulo: Duprat-Mayença.

Registro geral (São Paulo: Arquivo do Estado)

Revista do Instituto Histórico e Geográfico Brasileiro (Rio de Janeiro)

1908 3rd edition. Vol. 1.

Taunay, Affonso d'Escragnolle

1927 *História geral das bandeiras paulistas: 1641 – 1651*. São Paulo: Typographia Paulista / H.L. Canton. Vol. 3.

Vieira, Antônio

1951 *Obras escolhidas*. Prefácio e notas de Antônio Sérgio e Hernâni Cidade. Lisbon: Livraria Sá da Costa. Vol. I. Cartas.

Kenneth Maxwell

SPAIN AND PORTUGAL

Contrasts and Comparisons Over the Past Decade

Spain and Portugal share the same peninsula, and, in the full flood of renaissance self-confidence, both also believed they could divide the world between them. Indeed, the Treaty of Tordillias of 1494 ratified this presumption. Africans, Asians, and Amerindians, needless to say, were not consulted. It is important to remember, however, that when some Europeans still debate how "European" the Iberian nations really are, that, for almost two centuries, to the rest of the world, Europe itself signified little more than Spain and Portugal; that for three centuries nothing passed in Europe without Spanish involvement; and that Portugal as a nation-state predates Germany and Italy by seven centuries. Moreover, Columbus's encounter with America, in 1492, and Vasco de Gama's with India, in 1498, began the extraordinary process of conflict, destruction, and recreation which made the world what it is today.

The competition of the age of the discoveries was, of course, symptomatic of much which passed between Spain and Portugal over the centuries. But it must be said at the outset that the relationship has always been both competitive and symbiotic, and each nation shares at least as much as divides them. The Peninsula's geographical and physical makeup have produced similar ecological and social patterns on both sides of the frontier. The Minho in the north of Portugal shares many characteristics with its immediate Spanish neighbor, Galicia, not to

Kenneth Maxwell is Senior Fellow for Latin America at the Council on Foreign Relations in New York and founder of the Camões Center at Columbia University.

mention a similar language. The pattern of migration, agriculture, use of remittances, and religiosity of Northern Portugal is not unlike that of the northern Atlantic provinces of Spain.

Yet each country is, nevertheless, very distinctively its own self and has its own personality. The reasons for these differences are sometimes more easy to describe than to explain. Portugal's self-identity was, of course, formed largely in opposition to Castilian attempts to establish an Iberian hegemony. The very word "Iberianism" in Portugal is one which provokes controversy—being identified with Peninsula-wide federalism, rather than being the neutral geographical and descriptive word as it is in English usage. Outsiders also tend to lump Spain and Portugal together with disregard for history and sometimes divergent national interests, in a way which irritates both Spaniards and Portuguese. Certainly Portugal sought, and, for much of its history, succeeded to protect its independence by seeking alliances with Spain's enemies, by turning its back on the interior of the Peninsula and looking overseas for its resources and national vocation. The entrance of both nations into the Common Market in 1986, coming after the end of Portugal's overseas engagements, was without question a historical turning point, requiring the Portuguese to come to terms with their old enemy Spain.

In Spain itself, Portugal remains something of an unknown quantity, despite the fact that it receives a very substantial number of Spanish tourists each year. Serious scholarly interest is virtually non-existent despite the fact that there have been many parallel developments during the recent history of each country. Both were dominated for a substantial part of this century by right wing authoritarian regimes. In Portugal, Dr. Antonio de Oliveira Salazar ruled from the late 1920s until his incapacitation in 1968, and his system survived his demise until the military *coup d'état* of April 25, 1974. Salazar's regime, like General Franco's, was fundamentally opposed to liberal democracy, no less than to communism, and reflected many of the right wing authoritarian tendencies of the 1930s in Europe. The most overtly fascistic elements of the Portuguese new state (the secret police, the labor legislation, the youth movement, press censorship among them) was, however, balanced by the strong influence of Catholic traditionalism. Salazar was a man of small town rural background and was always sensitive to the deeper religious sentiments of the northern peasantry (reflected most dramatically at Fátima). Franco likewise tamed the more fanatical elements among his supporters by turning the *Falange* into a bureaucratic appendage of the state and by starving the army which had put him into power of modern material equipment. By the 1950s he had skillfully eased Spain, via arrangements with the United States, back into a state of international tolerance, if not respectability, by embracing the geopolitical cause, if not the liberal proclivities of what he had once called the "putrid democracies."

The normalization of political life in the Iberian Peninsula, brought about by the establishment of democratic regimes in both Spain and Portugal in the 1970s, had, of course, some important implications for the United States. Above all else these changes make questions of international affairs legitimate ones for public debate in each country. Thus, unlike the situation which prevailed under the dictatorships, many more actors are entering an arena long the exclusive preserve on the Iberian side of closed bureaucracies. The result is to make bilateral negotiations more complicated and more subject to parliamentary and press debate. Public opinion is engaged in ways it was not previously and governments will not hesitate to play cards with public, parliamentary or electoral politics in mind.

The United States has strategically important bilateral military relations with Portugal and Spain: with Portugal it goes back to the Second World War and involves access to facilities in the Azores by the United States Armed Forces; with Spain it dates from the 1950s, when the United States obtained naval and air bases. Both these bilateral agreements remain in effect and are periodically renewed in negotiations, which have been progressively more difficult, and, from the United States point of view, increasingly expensive. The NATO referendum in Spain incorporated a commitment on the part of the Spanish government to reduce United States military personnel in Spain. These negotiations have not been easy. The geo-strategic dimension of Spain and Portugal's insertion in the western Alliance (especially Spain's) is, in fact, considerably more controversial than is the economic rapprochement involved in membership within the EEC (European Economic Communities); this is partly the result of historical circumstances.

Spain's isolation from the European mainstream was longer and more complete than Portugal's. Lisbon remained neutral during the Second World War, but had participated in the First World War and was a founding member of NATO. During the final decades of his rule, Salazar also increasingly opened up the country and its colonies to international trade and investment. Portugal joined EFTA (The European Free Trade Association) and its isolation, by the late 1960s, was more a function of the wars in its African territories than of any lack of participation in the international economy. The African conflicts, however, meant that Portugal's active NATO participation was negligible. The major part of its armed forces until 1975 (numbering at the time almost 200,000) was deployed in Mozambique, Angola, and Guinea-Bissau. The burden of supporting this armed struggle, and the threat of military defeat in Guinea-Bissau, in particular, led to the *coup d'état* of 1974 and the consequent tumultuous revolutionary period, out of which the current regime in Portugal emerged.

Spain, of course, had been a major component of the European state system prior to the Napoleonic period. But following the collapse of the French imperium, Spain retreated into a prolonged isolation. As northwestern Europe industrialized and modernized, Spain was increasingly left behind in the nineteenth century and preoccupied with its own internal struggles. During the 1820s, Spain also lost its colonies on mainland South and Central America, and at the end of the century, in a traumatic confrontation with the United States in Cuba, lost its remaining Caribbean and Pacific colonies, including, in addition to Cuba, Puerto Rico and the Philippines—an historical event United States policy makers would do well to remember on occasion.

The twentieth century saw Spain neutral in the First World War, followed by colonial adventures in Morocco and the Western Sahara. The Moroccan engagement served to emphasize again Spain's military debility and led to a concern, among Spanish military thinkers, with North Africa (which continues to this day to be seen as a greater threat to Spain's security than any potential conflict with the east).

After 1931, the second Republic's relationships with the Western powers was never easy; they were complicated by the consequences of the great depression, disputes over the role of foreign interests in Spain, and fear by the governments of London and Washington of the political complexion and power of Spain's leftists. During the Civil War, the Western democracies pursued a policy of "non-intervention" as sanctimonious as it was porous, being successful in preventing any assistance to the Republic in its death struggle with Franco's nationalists, while failing to prevent the forces of international fascism, nazism, and communism from intervening at will. Spain was again neutral throughout World War II, and diplomatic and economic boycotts followed the War's end (1948–1951). The longevity of the Franco regime perpetuated Spain's isolation from post-war Europe and its process of economic reconstruction and integration. Recuperation from the devastation of the Civil War was painfully slow. It was not until the late 1950s that Spain regained the levels of economic activity it had sustained before the Civil War broke out in 1936.

Yet by the 1970s Spain had been dramatically transformed from the essentially agrarian society it was in the 1930s. Living standards, urbanization, levels of education, and health approximated the Western European norm. In a series of calculated liberalization measures and economic plans, Spain participated increasingly in Europe's growth, benefiting especially from tourism and immigrant remittances.

Despite the elaborate corporative structure General Franco created, based on the right wing authoritarian models of the 1930s, but imposed *de facto* by the victorious coalition, which formed the Nationalist side in the Civil War, this institutional framework became, by the 1970s, an archaic shell, within which modern Spain awaited the right moment to assert itself. Thus, while Spain had attempted, without success, to fasten advanced liberal institutions over a traditional society for much of the nineteenth and twentieth centuries, by the mid-1970s the opposite situation prevailed, wherein social and economic development had superseded archaic institutions.

Paradoxically, until the mid-1970s, it was politics that kept Iberia out of the European community; after the mid-1970s, it was economics. With Franco's death, in 1975, and the overthrow of the old regime in Portugal a year before, the European community no longer had the excuse of the two Iberian dictatorships to prevent serious negotiations with Portugal and Spain over accession. By 1974, all the Western European economies were suffering the consequences of the energy crisis, recession, and growing unemployment. Thus, despite much rhetoric about democratic solidarity, when it came to the bargaining table, disputes arose over more mundane issues: fish, olive oil, wine, migration and so on, *ad infinitum*. Spain and Portugal's desire for quick accession was thwarted by protracted and, at times, acrimonious negotiations. In addition, Spain and Portugal found themselves at loggerheads—especially over fishing rights and trade. Eventually, when the political cost of further procrastinations had become too high to risk yet another postponement of the date of accession, an accord was finally agreed to in March of 1985, with barely time left for the Treaty documents to be signed and approved by the respective European Parliaments.

In the community, considerable reservations remained (and remain) concerning Europe's ability to absorb the Iberian economies, especially Spain's. The decision was seen as being one of political expediency. But in Spain accession signified much more than a question of resolving technical issues. The accession treaty, above all else, was seen as bringing Spain back to the European mainstream it had left in 1815, and in Madrid accession was celebrated as such. Lisbon chose to mark the signing of the treaties of accession at the Jeronomite monastery of Belém, a vast Manueline pile constructed to house the corpse of Vasco da Gama and to commemorate his opening of the route to India. The choice of site was not accidental. For Portugal, accession to the European community marked the termination of a multi-secular pattern in Portugal's international posture—a posture which, since 1415, has been oceanic, directed overseas, turning away from Europe and, above all, away from Spain. The end of overseas involvement, which the *coup d'état* of 1974 brought about, no less decisively than it did the end of dictatorship, thus marks the beginning of a formal continental arrangement, which constitutes an important turning point for Portugal.

Spain had joined NATO precipitously in the final months of the centrist government led by Leopoldo Calvo Sotelo in 1981. As with the EEC's attitude towards Spanish membership, the NATO decision was seen as being at least as much a political as a security need. Spain does not, on the whole, feel threatened by the Soviet Union, and tends to worry more about the potential for conflict with Morocco over the two Spanish enclaves, Ceuta and Melilla. Some saw NATO as a means of keeping the army out of domestic politics. The Socialists fought their victorious election campaign in 1982 with an anti-NATO plank; yet, faced with a *fait accompli*, they promised a referendum on the issue and found themselves in the awkward position of having to convince the public, which was (or had been according to the public opinion polls) opposed to participation in the Alliance by a substantial majority.

With active campaigning by Felipe González, the government won the NATO referendum, but with conditions which have since caused strain in United States–Spanish relations, and leaves ambiguous the exact nature of Spain's *de facto* integration in Western European defense.

The NATO issue also has major significance for Spain's relationship with Portugal. Lisbon fears that its own role will be overwhelmed by Spain's involvement, and the Portuguese military still tends to view Spain more as a potential enemy than as potential ally. They categorically reject serving in any capacity under a Spanish-based unified Iberian command. The Gibraltar question also complicates the NATO issue for Spain. Negotiations to resolve the dispute have resumed, but should Spain decide to fully integrate into the NATO military structure, this could, as with the Portuguese fears of Spanish dominance, create major problems regarding the composition of NATO force commands. Thus, although the past years have seen significant ratifications of the Europeanization of Iberia, by its accession to the European Community and its integration into the Western Alliance, on the economic and strategic front and in bilateral relations with the United States, the prospects for disagreements with new and old partners were greater than was recognized. Nor had much attention been given the potential economic and political impact of EEC membership and the changing demands of Alliance participation on both countries.

The year 1986 saw major domestic developments in each country. In Spain, the Socialists under the charismatic Felipe González, after a successful term as the first Socialist government since before the Civil War, were reelected with a new majority. And, in a narrow electoral victory in Portugal, the former Socialist leader Mario Soares succeeded General Ramalho Eanes as the first civilian president Portugal has known since 1926. The civilianization of the Portuguese presidency marked an end to the transition from dictatorship to a fully Western European representative system.

Yet, despite the fact Portugal has, since 1976, never come close to the type of military putsch which threatened Spain in 1981, nor has it in any way been subjected to the scale and virulence of terrorist assaults, such as those perpetrated by Basque separatists in Spain, many in Portugal, in striking contrast to the optimism in Spain, remained deeply concerned about the state of their democracy and its survivability. Unlike Spain, no government had been able to sustain itself in office for its elected term, no party has been able to gain an overall majority, and the President and successive Prime Ministers have found themselves at loggerheads. The last Socialist-led coalition government, of which Mario Soares was Prime Minister, had collapsed in 1985, forcing general elections in advance of the scheduled presidential election. In these parliamentary elections, the social democratic party, for the first time since free elections were instituted in Portugal in 1975, surpassed the Socialists. Outgoing President Ramalho Eanes was thus obliged to call on Professor Cavaco Silva, the Social Democratic leader, to form a minority government. Incoming President Mario Soares was, in consequence, faced with a Prime Minister who leads a party which is the major competitor of the Socialist Party he had founded, and a government whose parliamentary position depends, to an important degree, on the good will of his presidential predecessor, General Eanes, with whom Soares' relationship was, to put it mildly, glacial. Professor Cavaco Silva, moreover, had, on being elected to the head of the Social Democratic party in 1985, broken up the coalition government which Mario Soares headed as Prime Minister, leading directly to the Socialists' crushing defeat in October 1985. If all this is confusing to the reader, it is also confusing to the Portuguese. As one Lisbon observer put it: "the Portuguese did not need novelists to write 'magical realism' for them; all they had to do was to read the newspaper's political columns each morning." Ironically the deadlock proved to be a major breakthrough. In 1986 new elections gave the Social Democrats a majority.

In comparative perspective, two important elements are notable in Spain. First, the role of the King in Spain's process of consolidating democracy. Second, the significance of the emergence of a strong, moderate, and majoritarian Socialist Party PSOE (*Partido socialista obrero español*). Neither of these phenomena was inevitable. In the case of the PSOE, the role of the Felipe González-Alfonso Guerra leadership group, in facing down maximalist demands and placing electoral over mass politics, was, of course, critical. The situation in Portugal during the transitional period, in contrast, saw power slip into the streets, at least for six to nine vital months, and all the Portuguese political parties felt pressure from the extreme left. Portugal also, unlike Spain, had no continuity at the top. Yet had anyone suggested, even as late as 1974, that a Spanish monarch, especially Juan Carlos, would or could play the vital role he did in consolidating Spanish democracy, the very idea would have been dismissed as mildly demented. This situation is worth noting, since, for almost two generations, historians and social scientists have been telling us that individuals are less important than collectivities, events less significant than long term cycles, and aggregated statistics better indicators than politics in understanding change.

The fact is that both Iberian dictators, General Franco and Dr. Oliveira Salazar, died natural deaths, and it was the skill or lack of skill of their successors that did much to determine subsequent developments. In comparative perspective, therefore, the failure of Salazar's successor, Marcello Caetano, to liberalize, something the Spaniards were able to achieve between 1975 and 1977, meant that the Portuguese missed the opportunity to negotiate a transition without "*ruptura*" in the immediate aftermath of Salazar's death in 1970. The modernizing elements within the old regime in Portugal were unable to form alliances with the democratic opposition, and after the *coup d'état* of 1974, lost whatever leverage they exercised within the state apparatus. It is probable, therefore, that any chance of a "*reforma pactada*," that is, of a 'negotiated reform' of the Spanish type, had been lost in Portugal as early as 1972, a situation made worse by the continuing wars in Africa and the growing disaffection within the military institution which was called upon to fight them.

Hence, the forces of the center and the right had a small role in determining the shape of Portugal's new regime. Since a large part of the Portuguese population is intensely conservative and traditional, this has created severe problems for the legitimacy of the new constitutional structure which emerged from the revolutionary turmoil of 1975 and the substance of which few now defend except the Communist Party.

The Portuguese Constitution of 1976, in fact, reflected very much the circumstances which surrounded its writing. Here again, the contrast with Spain is striking. Spaniards were very conscious of the failures of the Republican regime of the 1930s and self-consciously built in mechanisms to make the fall of governments difficult. The Parliament delegated the writing of the constitution to a broadly based but small group of experts, who worked in total privacy, and who all placed compromise high on their agendas. When disagreements could be covered by obscurities, they chose obscurities. In Portugal, the constituent assembly acted as a magnifying agent for maximalist posturing. Elected on 25 April 1975, the constituent assembly worked throughout the period of leftist triumphalism, their labors conditioned by a pact imposed on the political parties by the Armed Forces Movement, faced (and on one occasion besieged by) massive mobilizations in the streets and in the countryside. Thus, incorporated into the constitutional text were provisos which made the expropriations and nationalizations of March, 1975 inviolate, and declared Portugal to be engaged in a "transition towards socialism." There was confusion, however, over the allocation of power within the 1976 constitutional settlement. Both President and Prime Minister had popular and elective mandates.

It was partly because of the diffusion of power between President and government and the lack of conciliation of the social forces, which had provided the basis for the revolutionary and counterrevolutionary camps during the 1974–75 period, that the task of consolidating the democracy in Portugal has not been easy.

But why was the contrast with Spain's democratic transition so striking? The impressive economic and social change in Spain is by no means sufficient explanation for the particularities of the transition to democracy, or the cause for the contrast with the Portuguese case. Certainly, the economic growth of Spain increased the gap between the two Iberian countries dramatically. But it is also important to note that Franco never locked his regime into the impossible position which Portugal faced, by 1974, with respect to its pretentions in Africa. In effect, the old regime in Spain, unlike that in Portugal, was able to alter its dictatorial nature, while at the same time restructuring and democratizing its character. It was not, as some argue, a democratization from the top down, but a democratization from the inside out. Certainly the break was less traumatic than it was in Portugal, and was the result of a gradual transformation that the Franco elite and the democratic opposition to Franco negotiated in Spain between Franco's death on November 20, 1975, and the ratification of the constitutional monarchy by national referendum on December 8, 1978. The role of the Spanish opposition was, of course, critical to the success of this enterprise, since only the opposition could bring democratic legitimacy to the change. The Francoist past was thus rejected without, at the same time, rejecting a large segment of the Francoist elite. In essence, what occurred was that the legalistic transformation of the old regime in Spain succeeded in carrying into the new era the army and bureaucracy of the past, while encouraging the emergence of democratic institutions that gained their legitimacy from their acceptance by the opposition to Franco and were then ratified by elections.

Unlike the situation in Portugal, this compromising atmosphere was facilitated by the fact that the two symbols of previous polarizations, as well as the two organizations with the capacity to make polarization a politically effective force, had each moved toward the center. In Portugal, where the Church and the Communists moved toward the extremes in the turmoil of 1975, in Spain, the Church and the Communists moved toward the center. Santiago Carrillo, then the Spanish Communist leader and a leading exponent of Eurocommunism, had broken with Moscow and had embraced a parliamentary path. The Church, for its part, had embraced democracy, or, more important, provided no cover or legitimacy for the enemies of democracy. The Portuguese Church also embraced democracy, to be sure, but it did so belatedly and less by reason of democracy's merits than in the course of a campaign against the Communists. Moreover, Alvaro Cunhal, the Portuguese Communist leader, was, of all West European Communists, Moscow's staunchest henchman—looking always to the "sun" of the international Communist movement, which is how he described the position of the Soviet Communist leadership.

There was another striking difference between the Iberian transitions. In Spain, the army stood moodily on the sidelines between 1977 and 1979, whereas in Portugal the army held center stage from 1974 to

1976. In Portugal the army created the opening for democracy; in Spain it was a threat to democracy. In Spain the army was a force of the Right; in Portugal a force of the Left. Yet the important point in the end was that Spain's army accepted the transition. There were rumblings of discontent to be sure. But when a group of Civil Guards and army officers took over the Parliament and held the government hostage for several hours in February 1981, the armed forces as a whole rallied to the constitutional order. The King is, of course, the key to this phenomenon. The Spanish transition faced no discontinuity at the top, or disruption in the lines of authority. It was by providing this continuity that the King's role thereby became central in Spain—central in protecting democracy under challenge, and central, because, by guaranteeing authority in the midst of transition, the King was able to carry the forces of order with him while embracing the forces of change.

In summary, four general points might be suggested in comparative perspective. First, it must be remembered that the opportunity for democracy in Portugal was created by means of a *coup d'état*. It is important to emphasize this point since it serves to demonstrate a very important difference between the Portuguese case and the other democratic transitions of the 1970s and 1980s in Europe and Latin America. In every other case a vital element in the process of democratization was the extraction of the military (in most cases a military regime) from power. By contrast, in Portugal it was the military which destroyed a fundamentally non-military authoritarian system. The desire to disengage from Africa as rapidly as possible became a key element in the first months of the new regime and one which served in combination with domestic instability to propel Portugal to the left. As a result of this temporary combination of external and internal pressures, Portugal in a little over a year swung from being the oldest right-wing dictatorship in Europe to become the first European nation, since the 1940s, wherein a communist takeover seemed for a time possible. In the event, however, the Portuguese rejected the power grab during 1975 by the authoritarian left as firmly as they had welcomed the demise of the authoritarian right in 1974. But in both the swing to the left and in the anti-communist counter *coup* of November 1975, it should be remembered that the military was central to the process.

Secondly, it should not be forgotten that Portugal came close to civil war in 1975. The seriousness of this threat is often underestimated by analysts, but not by any of the military men involved in the November confrontation of 1975. Portugal was then a divided country with highly mobilized forces on both sides of the political spectrum, drawing support from regionally based social forces. The revolution in Portugal had been one which provoked real changes in Portuguese society and economy—expropriation of the great estates in the South, nationalization of industry, banks, and insurance companies, the jailing and purging of individuals. The role of the Communists in all this was important, but so too was the collapse of the state's authority and a social movement among the poor and the landless.

The social movement in the cities and southern countryside was sufficiently threatening to the small landowners in Central and Northern Portugal that, after many decades of acquiescence and demobilization, they were propelled into organization and counteractions, which provided a solid social backing for those in the military and in the democratic political parties who sought to establish a Western European system of representative government. It is fundamental, therefore, to any understanding of where Portugal stands today, to recognize the depth of the discontinuity which occurred in 1974, and the threat perceived by large numbers of Portuguese in the events of 1975.

Thirdly, the importance of the role of the Communists in the immediate aftermath of the *coup* must be emphasized. Unlike Spain, where the Communists were an important partner in both social and political pact-making during the critical transitional period, and were in any case marginal to the political forces grouped at the center of the political spectrum, in whose hands the political initiative lay in the period, in Portugal the political initiative rapidly escaped the centrist politicians and soldiers, and the PCP (Portuguese Communist Party) found itself the dominant force. This strategic difference was partly conjunctural and partly organizational, in that the PCP alone had reliable cadres, clear ideological positions, and rapidly assessed the importance of the MFA (*Movimento das Forças Armadas*).

In one particular aspect the Spanish Communists faced some important problems not suffered by their Portuguese colleagues. The behavior of the Spanish Communists during the Civil War, especially towards their competitors on the left, had a significant impact during the period of the reemergence of the Spanish Communist Party from clandestinity after Franco's death. This memory helped the Socialists. The bitter internal history of the left in Spain meant that the Communists could not claim an unambiguous purity, of opposition to oppression, a factor which did much to fortify the credibility of the Marxist-Leninists in the immediate post-dictatorship circumstances in Portugal.

Fourthly, again, unlike Spain, it must be noted that, with the exception of the Communists, all the political groups in Portugal, including the Socialists, were new and lacked organization. The old establishment, even the most modern-minded elements within it, meanwhile, found themselves out-maneuvered, discredited, and as authority shifted into the hands of the younger officers and their leftist allies, increasingly intimidated, purged, and even jailed. No Spanish UCD-type (i. e., *Unión de Centro Democrático*) centrist coalition emerged in Portugal. The Portuguese Socialist Party's roots lay more in a Republican and liberal intellectual opposition than in the type of trade union and historically Marxist tradition so important to the century-old PSOE. Hence, Portugal stands in striking contrast to the transitional situations, not only in Spain, but elsewhere in Europe and Latin America, all of which found the initiative in the hands of long-standing and organized political forces, most led by men with governmental experience, many representing the conservative constituencies. In this sense, the Portuguese experience, at least in the year following the *coup d'état* of 1974, is more like Nicaragua in the 1980's than like Spain (or Greece, Argentina, and Brazil, for that matter).

Finally, it is important to stress one external factor, which deserves attention, especially in comparative perspective. Because of the role of the Communists, the social turmoil in the country and radicalization of the military, Portugal was, in 1975, high on the international agenda. Unlike other transitional situations (again excepting Nicaragua), wherein no major geostrategic threat was perceived, Portugal not only became embroiled in East-West discussions, but also provoked considerable, if discreet, intervention by outside forces. Spain, which had been at the very fulcrum of such international intervention in the 1930s, almost totally avoided it in the 1970s.

It is also worth noting, in passing, that it was Portugal which underwent the process of democratization first and, although Spaniards are loath to admit they can learn anything from their neighbor, they did draw several important, if negative lessons from the transition in Lisbon. King Juan Carlos, in particular, who had spent his earliest years in Portugal, speaks Portuguese well, unlike most Spaniards, and had many Portuguese friends, saw very clearly how important decisive action was to anticipate events and not follow them if breakdown was to be avoided.

Yet, if the plots in Spain and Portugal were different, the outcome in each case was a new, and, despite problems, resilient democracy. We are in the end therefore talking of success stories, two of the more remarkable success stories of the past decade.

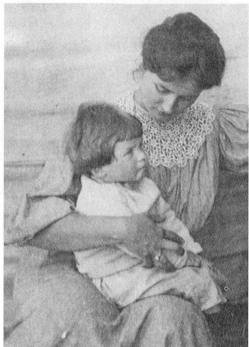

Carleton at eighteen months, with his mother, Catharine Cook Smith (1879–1961) [left], and at age seven (below).

Carleton and Elisabeth [Cowles Sperry] in a wedding photo, Geneva, Switzerland, June 30, 1934 (left), and upon their arrival in São Paulo, Brazil, 1940 (below).

At Stanford University (1935) with Mrs. Elizabeth Sprague Coolidge, the Roth String Quartet, and unidentified musicians (above). A group of participants at the International Congress of Musicology, held in New York, September 10 to 16, 1939. Back row (from left to right): Harold Spivacke, Otto Kinkeldey, Otto Gombosi (Hungary), Knud Jeppesen (Denmark), Fernando Liuzzi (Italy), and Gustave Reese. Front row (from left to right): Edward J. Dent (Great Britain), Carleton Sprague Smith, Curt Sachs, Alfred Einstein, and Dayton C. Miller (below).

In 1940, at the Biblioteca Municipal (São Paulo, Brazil) with Elisabeth, Oneyda Alvarenga, distinguished bibliographer, and the librarian Rubens Borba de Morães (above), and with Aaron Copland and Darius Milhaud (Tanglewood, 1942, below).

As flutist (above), and with the Interamerican Music Board (Washington, D. C., 1962). Carleton is in the second row, third from the right.

With Adlai Stevenson and Senator William Benton at the fortress city of the Incas (Machu Picchu, Peru, 1960).

With Henry Allen Moe of the Guggenheim Foundation (above), and
with Dave Winfield (among the recipients of an honorary doctorate at
Syracuse University, 1987).

DIPLOMACY

Luiz Heitor Corrêa de Azevedo

CARLETON SPRAGUE SMITH AND BRAZIL

Carleton Sprague Smith represents the pure essence of qualities of the East Coast, New England, Harvard man. The embodiment of religious (Christian) and civic values (liberty and democracy), absolute confidence in individual initiative without dependence on government, and an attachment to European culture—which does not exclude the acceptance of that which is typically American without Old World precedents—are the qualities that are intrinsically related to his personality and background. They have not hindered other facets of his personality, the artistic, scholarly, nor even his receptiveness to the outside world— beyond the boundaries of his country—a receptiveness greatly enhanced by his innate gift, which has been the ability to speak foreign languages. Carleton is profoundly American and broadly international. In his internationalism, Brazil occupies a position of privilege very close to his heart.

His intelligence and sensibility, while basically Anglo-Saxon, is a harmonious blend of French, Germanic, and Hispanic cultures. Later amorphous elements of Portuguese America were added, which the successes of an energetic and busy existence enabled him to know so well and to form bonds of friendship and intellectual affinity. Music was

Luiz Heitor Corrêa de Azevedo, a foremost Brazilian musicologist, was titular professor at the Escola Nacional de Música (Rio de Janeiro) and founder of its ethnomusicology program. He moved to Paris in 1947 where, until 1965, he was music program specialist for UNESCO and also taught at the University of Paris (1954–68).

an element in the bonding—not an exclusive one, but certainly a dynamic one.

I first met Carleton Sprague Smith in Rio de Janeiro in 1940. The vicissitudes of our pilgrimages throughout this world were such that we saw one another many times north and south of the equator, and on one side or the other of the Atlantic. Being of equal age, we saw each other grow older, relating, each time we met, the positive and negative events which the years had brought our way. It is principally these impressions of the past, rather than a systematic account of what Carleton gave and received from Brazil, which make up the substance of this account.

In 1940, public opinion in the United States under the presidency of Franklin Delano Roosevelt was hostile to the idea of intervention in the European conflict and had to be turned away from isolationism. National solidarity was essential, and those in the White House felt that it was necessary to develop an active policy of close ties to other republics in the hemisphere, especially in the areas of culture in its various forms of expression. Music, naturally, was a part of this policy. Therefore, a conference, sponsored by the United States State Department, was organized, in October, 1939, for the purpose of planning musical events which would further inter-American relations. As a result of this conference, in which approximately two hundred delegates participated, numerous groups travelled throughout the three Americas in order to better acquaint themselves with musical resources and available possibilities. During this and later periods, tours by artists were arranged and grants and scholarships were funded, the result of which was a better understanding of Latin America and its values.

During this period, I was librarian of what was then called the National School of Music of the University of Brazil (today called the Federal University of Rio de Janeiro). I received many of these "emissaries" of a new ideal; they came to Brazil in order to become acquainted with its people, discover its culture, and to form bonds of hemispheric solidarity. Carleton was among those "emissaries" whom I was fortunate to meet in Rio, and which included, among others, Lazare Saminsky (1882–1959) and Evans Clark. When Nicolas Slonimsky (1894–) passed through Rio de Janeiro in 1941, I was then in the United States, thus did not meet him personally. I also came to know William Berrien, Charles Seeger (1886–1975), and Gilbert Chase (1906–), but my relationship with Carleton went beyond a simple friendship. With the exception of Charles Seeger, who was older than I, we were men of the same generation.

Carleton spent the war years (1942–1945) in Brazil and formed strong ties with Brazilian intellectuals and artists, especially musicians. He was often with Lidy and Francisco Mignone, Antonio Sá Pereira, and Mário de Andrade. In 1944, when he moved to São Paulo, our personal contacts became less frequent. However, our collaboration became more active in 1947, in Paris, when I became director of the musical section of UNESCO. From his lengthy residence in Brazil, Carleton retained profound life-long impressions as a result of the friendships he made and the knowledge he acquired of Brazilian life and history, which were mirrored in his published writings, as well as the activities in which he was engaged.

I recall his first visit (1941) during a scheduled conference, at which he wished to read his paper in Portuguese. He had translated his text and practiced reading it aloud (at this time he did not, as later, speak flawless Brazilian Portuguese) to Egydio Castro e Silva, who was, at that time, my collaborator at the Research Center of the School of Music on Rua do Passeio. Mercedes Reis Pequeno, who was also a member of my circle of fellow workers and was responsible for assisting me in the final version of *Bibliografia Musical Brasileira*, which appeared under the joint authorship of Cleofe Person Mattos and myself, was the person who assisted us in the same kind of work when Carleton returned, in 1942, with his wife, Elisabeth, and daughter, Damaris, commissioned by the authorities in Washington, D.C., to develop cultural and political ties between the two countries. Due to the efforts of Carleton, Egydio Castro e Silva was the beneficiary of a grant which made it possible, in the years that followed, to go to the United States and graduate with a degree in music from Yale University. It was on the faculty of Tulane University that he ended his professional career as an excellent pianist and possessor of impressive literary and artistic knowledge. Thanks to assistance obtained through Carleton, Mercedes Reis Pequeno, so well known today among music librarians, graduated from Columbia University (New York). In 1956, Mercedes was named Chief of the Music Section of the Bibliotéca Nacional in Rio de Janeiro, a position she still holds, and renders impressive service to that institution and to all who request needed documentation for their current research projects.

In São Paulo, which has always been an important and dynamic musical center, Carleton and his wife became a vital part of its important musical events, and Carleton also participated as an eminent flutist, having studied with Louis Fleury in Paris and Georges Laurent in Boston. The catalog of works of more than one Brazilian composer of this period exhibits titles or works written for or dedicated to him. Camargo Guarnieri, in particular, who at this time was at the height of his creative maturity, was one of the composers most closely associated with Carleton in São Paulo (1944–1945). On his first trip to the United States, he performed the *Sonatina for flute and piano*, with Carleton as flutist and himself as pianist.

For many years Dr. Smith's apartment on East 65th Street in New York became a meeting place for innumerable Brazilian intellectuals, artists, and musicians who were visiting New York or had come to stay for some time. The Smiths continued to welcome their old friends, with whom they shared so much that there seemed to be no barriers between the man from North America and his friends from South America.

Carleton returned several times to Brazil to meet other generations of Brazilians and to experience the transformations taking place in Brazil's vast territory and among its people. I remember meeting him in Bahia in 1954, at one of the Colloquiums of Luso-Brazilian Studies, and at a Colloquium at his Alma Mater, Harvard University, in 1966, and at other Colloquia.

In his writings and lectures, as well as in his teaching at New York University, where he was associated for many years and where he continued to study Brazilian subjects, Carleton stimulated the interest of his audiences and students in the country to which he had formed a strong attachment.

In 1956, he organized a special supplement on Brazil, entitled *Perspectives on Brazil*, for the *Atlantic Monthly* (Vol. 197, no. 2), then in its ninety-eighth year of publication. It comprised seventy-four pages of text, prose, and poetry of Brazilian authors translated into English. Among the authors were Mauricio Nabuco, Gilberto Freyre, Mário de Andrade, José Cândido de Andrade Muricy, Erico Veríssimo, Alceu de Amoroso Lima, Alcântara Machado, José Valladares, Lúcio Costa, Rubem Braga, Antônio Cândido, Jorge Amado, Afonso Arinos, Décio de Almeida Prado, Monteiro Lobato, Vinicius de Morais, Augusto Frederico Schmidt, Cecília Meireles, Manuel Bandeira, João Cabral de Melo Neto, and Carlos Drummond de Andrade—a constellation of Brazilian intellects of the post-war period. In his introduction, Carleton observed that "no one who aspires to a knowledge of twentieth-century culture should ignore Portuguese-speaking Brazilian America." And in broad strokes he painted the picture of Brazilians:

> They are independent of mind and intelligent, extremely courteous, reflective, patient and generally non-violent even in their revolutions.

Cordial and friendly—the *abraço* ('embrace') between men being very common—their large families tend to make them hospitable, even to strangers. Brazilians are more tolerant in human relations than North Americans. They have a natural dignity and Christian spirit which is impressive.

In Volume VI of the *Boletín Latino-americano de Música* (1946), he published an article of eight pages on musical relations between Brazil and the United States (originally in Portuguese), wherein he presented and analyzed a curious piece, *Favorita Waltz Brasilense para Piano Forte Com Accompanhamento de Flauta, Clarinete e Violin* [*sic!*] by Pedro Weldon, published in 1809 in New York (E. Riley Engraver, 31 Day Street). The waltz was dedicated to "His Royal Highness, Prince Regent of Portugal and Brazil," that is, the future Dom João VI (1816–1826), who, in the preceding year, had fled to Rio de Janeiro with his mother, a mental invalid, and his court in order to escape the invasion of Lisbon by Napolean's troops under Marshall Andoche Junot (1771–1813). Upon João's arrival, Rio de Janeiro became the capital of the Portuguese Empire. The frontispiece of this edition of the waltz of Pedro Weldon (who was a good musician, pianist, violinist, conductor, composer, organizer of concerts, and whose name appears with a certain frequency in lists of works of the period) shows a picture representing the "Disembarkation of the Royal House of Bragança in Rio de Janeiro harbor, with a view of the city and the port." The title is printed in Portuguese and English, side by side. In 1942, when Carleton came to Brazil, he presented me with a copy of the curious piece, which was later used to illustrate his article in the *Boletín* and which today is in the possession of Francisco Curt Lange.

Carleton discussed the curious problem of the melodic relationship which this early nineteenth-century "Brazilian Waltz," bears to the well known religious song, "Ave, ave, ave Maria," addressed to the Virgin at Lourdes, traditionally sung by the pilgrims who walk before her image in the famous grotto of Missabielle. Written in 3/8 meter, on a descending arpeggio figure, the flute melody in the Brazilian waltz is the same, with a small change in the last measure, as the song of praise to the Mother of God, universally-known today. Carleton asked if "some Brazilian, traveling to the place of miracles" might have taken the "melody with the intention of, once cured, commemorating the event with the sound of the music of a native dance." Imagine him "throwing away his crutches" and dancing!

Even more important more developed and more solidly documented, although in a field foreign to musicological matters, was
Carleton's contribution to the series of conferences presented at
Vanderbilt University in Nashville, Tennessee during the 1949–1950
academic year, on which occasion he spoke on "William James in
Brazil." His lecture was published, along with those of others, in 1951,
by this university under the title, *Four Papers presented in the Institute
for Brazilian Studies*. Using ample documentary evidence, and with
quotes taken from the correspondence of the philosopher and his
followers, Carleton's essay recounts the travels of the young William
James in Brazil in 1865 as part of the scientific expedition organized by
the Swiss scientist Louis Agassiz (1807–1873)—an expedition which
began from New York in March of that year. In order to write his essay,
Carleton obtained the important James papers (from the archives of the
famous philosopher at Harvard University). To conclude his essay, he
quoted what James had written before leaving Brazil, after several
months of fieldwork with his old teacher from Harvard University, Louis
Agassiz: "When I get home I am going to study philosophy all my days."
Carleton judiciously observed that "the twenty-three year old lad made
a decision at the time for which the world may be thankful," adding that
"Brazil contributed more than she knew to the history of American
thought." While in Brazil and as a result of his experience there, William
James discovered his true vocation "not to go on exploring expeditions,"
as he wrote in a letter to his father, "but to engage in speculative
philosophy."

In 1967, Carleton came upon two copies of Luis Antonio Rosado
da Cunha's *Relação / da entrada que fez / o excellentissimo, e reverendis-
simo senhor / D. Fr. Antonio / do Desterro Malheyro / Bispo do Rio de
Janeiro, em o primeiro dia deste presente Anno de 1747...* ('*Account of
the Entry Made by the Most Excellent and Most Reverend Dom Antonio
do Desterro Malheyro, Bishop of Rio de Janeiro, on the first day of the
present year of 1747...*'). His training as a historian would not allow such
an important discovery to go unnoticed. Thus, Carleton provided the
historical setting, together with a discussion of the minute differences
of both editions, the first carrying a title page with the erroneous date
1247, the second with the corrected title page - 1747, in his article "Two
copies of the First Book Published in Brazil at the New York Public
Library" in Helmut Lehmann-Haupt, ed., *Homage to a Bookman* [Hans
P. Kraus] (Berlin: Mann, 1967), pp. 187–94.

Those who want to see in Carleton Sprague Smith only the multi-lingual aristocrat from New England, the urbane man whose naturalness and supreme elegance make him more of a dilettante than a true musician and scholar, are wrong. Hidden beneath an affable exterior appearance with a friendliness which has been helpful to so many artists, who were the beneficiaries of his social prestige, Carleton has always demonstrated a curious and structured mind and a capacity to achieve, which mark the innumerable endeavors with which he has been as-sociated—as was the case, in 1966, on the occasion of the aforemen-tioned International Colloquium of Luso-Brazilian Studies and the admirable concert conceived and organized by him at the Hispanic Society of America in New York.

The gentleman from Waldingfield Farm, the family estate, in a rustic setting in Connecticut, has been a professor, encourager of musical enterprise, active musician, has taught in various universities, fulfilled official functions for his country, and appeared on the concert programs of famous ensembles, including the Lener Quartet, and others. He was one of the founders of the International Council of Music of UNESCO in 1949, and I know this for a fact, because at that time I was responsible for the music program of this agency of the United Nations, and it was through Carleton's intercession that Serge Koussevitzky was able to present to this organization his project of creating an international fund for providing help and incentives to composers, which, with some changes, continues to exist, under the very active leadership of Yehudi Menuhin. It is the Musicians International Mutual Aid Fund (MIMAF) which has its headquarters at UNESCO in Paris.

It can be said, with some justification, that during a sizeable portion of this life, Carleton Sprague Smith was connected with Brazil. It is appropriate that in the celebration of his octogenarian status, he be remembered by a Brazilian.

Goodwin Cooke

THE STATE AS IMPRESARIO

One of the high points of my tour as Ambassador to Central Africa was the visit to Bangui of the McLean Family Bluegrass Band, sponsored by the U. S. Information Agency. The McLeans proved to be people of parts, talented and delightful musicians, and Mr. McLean is a scholar and teacher of American folk music. We turned the Residence into a theatre, and watched with bemusement as two hundred francophone Africans, with hardly a word of English among them, went into foot-stomping rapture at: "Good-bye girls, we're going to Boston." (Won't we look pretty in the ballroom, early in the morning!)

After my retirement from the Foreign Service, my wife and I went to a theatre in Newark, New Jersey, to watch a ballet troupe from Ivory Coast led by Marie Rose Giraud, for whom I had arranged a Fulbright award some years earlier. Ms. Giraud has since appeared with Alvin Ailey and other American dance ensembles. On this occasion there was an instant and exciting rapport between the largely black American audience and the vigorous, lively dancers performing to traditional West African music.

I have attended many other, less successful, cultural exchange presentations, including the time when the blues singer got hold of the Ambassador's gin and fell from his stool during "St. James Infirmary." But what all these episodes suggest is the extent to which cultural

Goodwin Cooke is Vice-President of International Affairs at Syracuse University and Adjunct Prof. in the Maxwell School of Citizenship and Public Affairs. He served the Department of State for twenty-five years and was a former Ambassador to the Central AfricanRepublic.

exchange, singers, dancers, art exhibits, poetry readings, basketball teams, and what-have-you, have become part of our diplomacy, an accepted and valued element in our relations with other countries. Few would deny that the support of the McLean Family and the grant for Ms. Giraud were useful and rewarding. But it may not be easy to define precisely to what use they were put and what the rewards were.

How does cultural exchange promote the national interest? The United States government spends millions of dollars each year to finance thousands of performers traveling between the United States and other lands. One can gauge the temperature of U.S.-Soviet relations by the number of cultural presentations offered by the U.S. Information Agency in Moscow and by the visits of the Bolshoi or Ukranian ballets to New York and Los Angeles. Cultural Affairs Officers at Embassies from Belgrade to Brazilia to Bujumbura sponsor visiting artists and exhibits. Equally, they seek out local artists of promise and help them to visit the United States, either with official funding like the Fulbright Program or through contact with interested American private institutions. But the purposes served by these activities are not clearly defined, and there are no standards against which the long range success of the programs can be measured.

If asked, most Cultural Affairs Officers, and Ambassadors, would say that cultural exchange serves to advance U.S. Policy objectives; and I suspect a Soviet cultural attaché would say the same. But even this bland formulation is dubious. Foreign policy objectives are usually selected to enhance and defend the national interest, which in turn is traditionally defined as the security and prosperity of the state and its people. Thus the dominant objective of U.S. foreign policy for the past forty years has been the containment of Soviet expansionism. It is not at all clear what role the art exhibit or the string quartet can play in this context. Indeed, too close an identification of cultural exchange with containment policy can be detrimental. Some Cultural Affairs Officers still recall the visits made to the U.S.I.A. libraries by Senator Joseph McCarthy's aides, Roy Cohn and David Schine (known at the time as Rosencohn and Guildenschine) to weed out possibly subversive material. Edmund Bator, a highly competent Cultural Affairs Officer, was savagely attacked by the late Congressman John Rooney for having sponsored a play in Yugoslavia that included language Mr. Rooney found objectionable. The attempt to put the best face on America can be stultifying and counterproductive, but it is tempting to those who tie cultural exchange too closely to foreign policy objectives.

Cultural presentations in the Soviet Union are often selected to show the Soviets the blessings of the American way of life, thence the modern kitchen in which Vice-President Nixon and Chairman Krushchev held their famous debate. But though the Russians are fascinated by American culture and are often avid for American blue jeans and rock music, it is hard to demonstrate any palpable weakening of the Soviet regime which can be traced to cultural exchange. At this writing there are vast and confusing changes going on in the U.S.S.R., but to suggest that *glasnost* is an effect of American cultural activities would be presumptuous at the least. In the other direction, Soviet presentations have been very well received here, but the most important political result has been the well-published defection of important Soviet artists. Indeed, the U.S. Government has tried to use artistic or athletic defectors to demonstrate the superiority of the American way, often perhaps, to the detriment of U.S.-Soviet relations.

It is sometimes said that cultural exchanges help to win the hearts and minds of people in the Third World, again suggesting that the Cultural Affairs Officer is essentially a soldier in the Cold War. I think this argument is short-sighted, and will not stand up under scrutiny. The McLean Family won the hearts and perhaps the minds of their audiences in Africa, and on trips in other parts of the world, but it is unlikely that any votes in the United Nations General Assembly were changed by the highly successful tours. It might be argued that the *withholding* of cultural or athletic presentations from South Africa or other states with appalling records on human rights, may help to persuade dictatorial governments of the error of their ways, but the evidence is scanty.

I would like to suggest that the attempt closely to ally government-sponsored cultural programs with short-range U.S. foreign policy objectives is unwise, but that the programs themselves are of enormous value. And I think this apparent paradox derives from too narrow an interpretation of the national interest. The national interest of a great democracy goes far beyond the traditional definition of security and prosperity. Nor is it particularly well-served by a sort of chest-thumping self-aggrandizement: Look how splendid we are, we have fine singers and dancers and basketball players, and visiting artists defect to be part of our society. This kind of attitude is not particularly convincing and rarely well received. I believe that an open, democratic society's interests are served when people throughout the world are able to learn about, and share in, the cultural achievements of other societies than their own. Thus baldly stated, that sounds like something of a truism, but the thought may lead to unexpected ramifications. It suggests that cultural exchange should continue when political or economic relationships are antagonistic or even confrontational, and that the cessation of government-sponsored cultural activities to demonstrate official displeasure may not be in the national interest over the longer run.

During the early years of the Reagan Administration, when relations with the Soviet Union were at a nadir, cultural exchange dropped to zero. Indeed, following the invasion of Afghanistan, President Carter ordered a boycott of the Moscow Olympic Games, and the Soviets refused to participate at Los Angeles in 1984. In retrospect it is not apparent that the freeze on cultural relations conveyed any benefit to the United States. Because a government votes against us in the UN, or seeks an economic formulation different from own, does not mean that the culture and society that government represents is devoid of interest or importance. It may be in the national interest to continue an exchange even with people under oppressive regimes.

This line of reasoning is perhaps most directly and dramatically challenged by contemporary South Africa. The outrage and revulsion with which most Americans justifiably regard the apartheid system makes it difficult to imagine sponsoring cultural programs in Johannesburg or Pretoria. But a symphony or a play need not imply approval for the government of the state where it is performed. To the contrary, such a presentation can be chosen to reflect the values which the South African regime rejects, and, of course, one can insist on choosing one's audience. This may go against the grain of the current trend to consider the isolation of South Africa as the only way to move its government towards reform, but that policy has yet to demonstrate its effectiveness.

At this writing the Bulgarian women's choir is singing to packed houses in New York. This fascinating, strange polyphonic music, much of it centuries old, has a marvelously contemporaneous sound. Applause for the choir, however, in no sense means support for the regime of Todo Zhivkov! And this, perhaps, brings up another point of interest. Cultural exchange should not be limited to areas of proven popular appeal. Artists whose work is experimental, or controversial, should, where possible, be included. Such programs can raise conservative hackles. I can recall an Ambassador in a European capital outraged at a presentation of contemporary American painting—but the local critics and audiences were entranced. This in turn implies that those who select programs for official sponsorship, in Washington or abroad, must be people of sensitivity and taste, profoundly aware of America's cultural wealth, eclectic in enthusiasm, and at ease in other societies. The role of the Cultural Affairs Officer can be, and should be, demanding and rewarding, one which only the rare bureaucrat can fulfil. It may be that cultural programs, which surely are of enormous value to the national interest as most broadly defined, would profit from further involvement of distinguished scholars of special talent, called upon to serve temporarily in areas for which they are particularly well equipped. The contributions made by Carleton Sprague Smith as a Cultural Affairs Officer during World War II are a powerful argument for this suggestion.

Clinton J. Everett

THE SPANISH INSTITUTE, NEW YORK
(1966–1982)

The Spanish Institute, founded in 1954, is a private, non-profit organization whose aim is to promote understanding, broaden communication and strengthen ties between Spain and the United States.[1] In 1966, it moved its headquarters from a room in a building, occupied principally by the French Institute at 22 East 60th Street, to a handsome town house located at 684 Park Avenue. Superbly located, it is flanked by the Americas Society on one side, the Italian Cultural Center on the other, and across the street, the Council on Foreign Relations and Hunter College. The move was due to the generosity of a number of dedicated patrons, particularly Margaret Strong Rockefeller de Larrain, Marquesa de Cuevas.

In the following year, Dr. Carleton Sprague Smith became its new Director. He had been a board member since 1964, and in 1970 he was named Vice-Chairman. His knowledge of Spain, and familiarity with Iberian studies, together with his experiences in international relations, including the founding of the Brazilian Institute at New York University, made him an excellent candidate.

[1]The original founders of the Institute included Lucrezia Bori, Angier Biddle Duke, W. Randolph Montgomery, George S. Moore, Beatriz Bermejillo Moore, Edward Larocque Tinker, and Dr. Ramón and Cynthia Castroviejo.

Clinton J. Everett III is both a linguist and a musician. Currently he teaches Spanish at the Trinity School in New York and does extensive work as a free-lance percussionist.

The celebration for the opening of the new building took place in 1969, when, during a two-day symposium, dozens of renowned personalities, both from Spain and the United States, participated.[2] The festivities culminated in a banquet hosted by the adjacent Center for Inter-American Relations.

In those early days, when it was sometimes known as the Center for American-Spanish Relations, the Institute sponsored programs that appealed to a small but enthusiastic public. With the relocation of the Institute on Park Avenue, and under the supervision of the Director, Carleton Sprague Smith, new facilities were added. They included the Lucrezia Bori Auditorium, the Hastings Gallery, the Edward Larocque Tinker Library, a bookstore, a large reception room, a terrace, office space, cooking and catering facilities, and much needed storage room. In these new quarters, recitals, concerts, dance programs, art exhibits, conferences, symposia, language classes, lecture courses, and social gatherings took place.

The Institute provides a very special forum in the United States, stimulating interest in many facets of Spanish intellectual life, history, economics, literature, the arts, film—annual film festivals—and especially Spain's changing silhouette in the modern world. This latter aspect had been accelerating in recent times as Spain's economy has become one of the fastest growing in Western Europe. With a relatively small administrative staff and a tight budget, the Institute has achieved a good deal more than what was envisioned during the early years.

Dr. Smith played a central role in realizing the Institute's achievements, insisting upon a breadth of activities for the membership and providing the appropriate resources for bringing to them information on Spain and on Spanish-American relations. The Institute became the home for students and teachers of varied disciplines related to Spain, who were eager to meet outside their own academic circles and whose cooperation the director sought for the dissemination of all aspects of Spanish culture. Its bookstore sold Spanish publications at discount rates, and its research library specialized in twentieth-century Spain. After the death of Francisco Franco, in 1975, the library's acquisitions grew at a much faster pace.

---

[2]Among them were Mr. Lora Tamayo, former Secretary of Education, Prof. Martin de Riquer, Prof. Julián Marías, Mr. Joaquín Calvo Sotelo, Prof. Otis Green, Prof. Aurelio Espinosa, Prof. Lewis Hanke, and others.

EVENTS AND PROGRAMS

To highlight some of the special events that took place at the Spanish Institute during Dr. Smith's tenure, we must certainly mention the following:

—Dinner in honor of His Excellency King Juan Carlos I and Her Majesty Queen Sofia, on June 4, 1976, jointly sponsored by the Spanish Institute and Spain-United Stated Chamber of Commerce. This event marked their first official visit to the United States. It was followed by a series of appearances of the leading political personalities of Spain's transition government.

—Dinner and seminar for the Members of the Spanish Academy of Letters.

—The outstanding *tertulia* series administered by Mrs. Mercedes Tangui Orbón. *Tertulias* are an old Spanish tradition emulating the French literary *salons* of the seventeenth and eighteenth centuries. Some eighty meetings were convened, beginning with "Miguel Servet and the Spanish Reformation," by Prof. Angel Alcalá, and included "García Lorca: Playwright and poet" (given by Mildred Adams); "Spain and the American Revolution" (James Cortada); "Saul Bellow y España" (José María Carrascal); "Don Quijote como actor o el 'como si' de su locura" (Prof. Angel Alcalá); "España y America: Vivencias de un poeta" (Eugenio Florit); "La idea del sueño en *La vida es sueño* de Calderón de la Barca" (Prof. Antonio Regalado); "La censura literaria en España" (Prof. José A. Hernández); "La nueva frontera del teatro español" (José Ruibal); "El teatro barroco hispanoamericano" (Carlos Miguel Suarez Radillo); "Quevedo, volcán florecido" (Prof. Amelia Agostini de del Río); "La Odisea de Hernando de Soto" (presented the Spanish Ambassador Miguel Albornoz); "La prensa española durante la Guerra Civil" (Rafael Abella); "El exilio español de 1939: consecuencias culturales y políticas" (José Luis Abellán); and "La imagen de Eugenio Florit desde su poesía" (Prof. Rosario Hiriart).

—The Institute's celebration (Nov. 18–19, 1977) of the awarding of the Nobel Prize for Literature to Vicente Aleixandre, in cooperation with Hunter College, and the outstanding Spanish writer, Ramón Sender, who was nominated for the same prize at the culmination of a symposium entitled "Two Days with Sender" (May 11–12, 1979). An active campaign followed co-sponsored by dozens of American colleges and universities around the world. Their answers and the text of the official nomination by Prof. Angel Alcalá was sent, in January 1980, to the Swedish Academy in Stockholm. Unfortunately Ramón Sender died just a few months later.

—The inauguration of the Hastings art gallery was made possible by the Hastings Foundation, and for some years the exhibits were donated and directed by Mrs. Elizabeth Peterfreund with help from the Edward Larocque Tinker Foundation.

—The lecture series, included two outstanding writers: "José Ortega y Gasset y sus fuentes germánicas," a book presentation by Nelson R. Orringer, and "Federico García Lorca: Muerte en Granada" by Humberto López Guerra.

—Over the years memorable musical performances by such renowned artists as Andrés Segovia, Alicia de Larrocha, Victoria de Los Angeles, and Federico Mompou were presented either at the Institute or other auditoriums throughout the city.

—In connection with the poetry series, it was my pleasure to work with Dr. Smith in bringing the poet Rafael Alberti to the Institute in 1981. This came on the coattails of a week-long event held at Dartmouth College in honor of the fiftieth anniversary of the formation of the Spanish Republic to which Alberti had been invited—his first trip to the United States—and where he read extensively from his vast collection of poetry. Visiting him in Hanover, New Hampshire, we were able to persuade the poet to extend his trip to give readings both at the Institute and New York University. With the renewed fervor that surrounded Rafael Alberti during those first years following his return to Spain, after nearly forty years in exile, his presence and his work provoked wide enthusiasm and a reinvigoration of his poetic vision on this side of the Atlantic.

—Among the felicitous events held at the Institute were an International Symposium on the *Cantigas de Santa Maria* of Alfonso X, el Sabio (1252–84) in commemoration of its 700th anniversary year (1981) organized by Profs. Israel J. Katz and John E. Keller, and a Symposium celebrating the 300th anniversary of Calderón de la Barca (1600–1681), organized by Prof. Antonio Regalado and Angel Gil Orrios of the Teatro Real Español.

—Finally, among the academic courses planned by Dr. Smith was one entitled "Twentieth-Century Spain: The Political Economy of the

Country Today (1939–1979)," in conjunction with New York University. I was enrolled as a student of this course, and can vouch for the fact that it was fundamental for understanding present-day Spain.[3]

CONCLUSION

In the early 1950's, the Spanish philosopher José Ortega y Gasset presented the case, at the Aspen Institute in Colorado, for a broad-based liberal education as an antidote to the fearsome age of over-

---

[3]The course commenced on February 4, 1980, and included the following subjects and lecturers:

1) Feb. 4: **General Introduction:** Spain's Political Economic and Social Evolution in the 20th Century / by *Carleton Sprague Smith*

2) Feb. 11: **The Modern Spanish State:** Forty Years under Franco and the Transition to Democracy / by *Edward Malefakis* (Columbia University)

3) Feb. 25: **Constitution:** The Laws (written and unwritten); Courts and Judges; Citizens' Rights; Foreigners' Rights / by *Antonio Garrigues Walker* (Garrigues Walker and Associates)

4) Mar. 3: **Political Parties:** Christian Social Democracy, Syndicalism, Republicans, Marxists, Communists, Foreign Influence / by *Richard Gunther* (Ohio State University)

5) Mar. 10: **The Police, Army, Law and Order** / by *Stanley Payne* (University of Wisconsin)

6) Mar. 17: **The Problem of Inflation:** Financing Foreign Investment; Multinational Corporation; Technology Transfer / by *John Coverdal* (Northwestern University)

7) Mar. 24: **Population and Regionalism:** City, Suburban and Agricultural Zones; Minorities; Foreign Colony / by *Juan Linz* (Yale University)

8) Mar. 31: **Spanish Labor:** mostly Christian-Socialist, Marxist-Socialist and Communist / by *Clara Lida* (SUNY at Stony Brook)

9) Apr. 7: **The Church:** Anti-clericalism; Education; Opus Dei; Conservative and Radical Clergy / by *Angel Alcalá* (Brooklyn College, CUNY)

10) Apr. 14: **The Economy:** Industrial Development; Transportation (Railroads, Buses, Aviation, Shipping) / by *Gabriel Torella* (University of Pittsburgh)

11) Apr. 21: **Spain's Economic, Monetary and Trade Policies:** The Spanish Stock Exchange / by *Juan Toribio* (Banco Urquijo, Barcelona)

12) Apr. 28: **Spanish Elections:** Local Power; Citizens' Rights; Civic Responsibility / by *Benjamin Martin* (Carnegie Endowment for International Peace, Washington, D.C.)

13) May 5: **Foreign Capital:** European, Japanese and Arab capital in Spain / by *Wells Stabler* (former Ambassador to Spain)

14) May 12: **Possible Future Changes in the Political Basic Economy of Spain** / by *Frank Moreno* (New York University)

15) May 19: **Summary:** Spain's International Role in NATO and the Common Market: Attitude toward Arab Countries; Spain and the United States / by *Drew Middleton* (The New York Times)

specialization, which he viewed as the most imposing threat to the future of contemporary society. If his assumptions were correct, then even well-educated, cultured men and women were running the risk of becoming progressively alienated from one another, precisely due to the exigencies of their professional lives, wherein the striving for perfection demanded all of their time, attention, and energies. Ortega was keenly aware of these forces in the post-industrial age of the mid-twentieth century which threatened to dominate even the best and brightest with an unrelenting momentum that was impossible to forestall.

Specialization and overspecialization, he argued, had already encroached upon our collective conscience, driving us apart from one another intellectually and spiritually, and were, per force, the inherent enemy of his more favored antithesis, namely, a worldview founded on a broad-based education from an early age, an appreciation and even love of an integrated world spanning many disciplines, and stretching from the arts through the sciences—an intellectual decentralization process filled with feeling and appreciation for diversity itself. What could be done, then, to stem the tide against this?

Those of us who have worked with our versatile humanist Carleton Sprague Smith soon discovered that he was a model of what the Spanish philosopher had in mind when he clamored for the reinvigoration of the broad-based generalist. Carleton's vision has always focused on communication among individuals, transcending borders of specialties with the goal of peoples becoming the beneficiaries of that interaction—bettering personal lives and, in the process, making people happier, while setting the stage for deep mutual understanding. It is a public loss when people grow alienated and are no longer interested in communicating because they have forgotten how, lacking a common ground of experience and an appreciation for life itself.

The foregoing litany of Carleton's accomplishments during his years with the Spanish Institute can be viewed essentially as a string of events which he organized and produced for the benefit of those interested in Spanish culture, and for which he provided one of the most distinguished forums in the United States—not previously enjoyed in its essential dedication to an understanding of Spain, a country only recently emerging from the American mind as a land limited to sunshine, toreadors, castanets, and dancers, and in a city which García Lorca noted, in 1929, "had no notion of Spain." To this end the Institute and all of its members and friends, and certainly this writer, owe a great debt to Carleton Sprague Smith, a man of rare vision and lucidity.

Ernest A. Gross

U. S. INTEREST IN UN DIPLOMACY

Prologue: Carleton and I were college classmates and, I am proud to think, friends ever thereafter. Inasmuch as we often discussed the substance of the following remarks, I have less trepidation in dedicating them to my good friend with gratitude for having shared his thoughts.

* * *

Exponents of power politics tend to disregard moral force as an actual component of power. To some extent the error reflects confusion between "morality" and "moralizing." The primary mistake, however, may consist in faulty appraisal of the political and strategic consequences of the newfound power in the Age of the Atom and the Individual. The human society—like the nucleus of the atom—contains within itself forces which tend to disintegrate as well as those which tend to unite. The major cohesive force of a community, at any level, is a sense of common interest and common purpose. To the degree that such an attitude is strengthened in the city, the nation, or the world, relative stability can be maintained. The essential function of the United Nations and, indeed, its highest reason for existence, is to serve as an instrument to accomplish this purpose. Its value to our own national interest is measured precisely by our success or failure in thus using it.

Ernest A. Gross is Counsel to the New York law firm Curtis, Mallet-Prevost, Colt & Mosle. He is Chairman of the United Nations Development Corporation. From 1949 to 1953 he served as the Deputy U.S. Representative to the U.N. with the rank of Ambassador and also as a U.S. Representative on the U.N. Peace Observation Commission.

The original grand design of the United Nations stressed its integral character. Mankind was aware that other efforts to keep the peace had always failed. The most recent failures had produced the two bloodiest wars ever known. Reaching for collective security was, therefore, born of the greatest "collective insecurity" of history—the Thirty Years' War of our times. The attempt after the first World War to find peace through the League of Nations proved unsuccessful, but not because of mechanical weaknesses in the structure of the League. Nations were, and still are, unprepared to delegate to a world organization supranational attributes. Just as the veto was built into the Charter, so each member of the League of Nations was free to decide whether the Covenant had been violated in a particular case. If it decided in the affirmative, it was nevertheless under no legal duty to aid the victim of aggression. The series of irretrievable losses—Manchuria, Ethiopia, Spain, China, Soviet Union, and Nazi Germany—threw the League into bankruptcy and the world into war.

Nevertheless, the fault is not to be found in mechanical or juridical weaknesses of the Covenant. When the hour came for the dissolution of the League, the French leader Paul-Boncour voiced a general sentiment: "It was not the League that failed. . . It was the nations which neglected it. It was the Governments which abandoned it." In other words, the League did not collapse merely because it lacked power to make binding decisions, it died from the disregard by member states of their moral duty to *carry out their own recommendations*.

The United Nations Charter has been called "preatomic." The implication is that it is obsolete for the atomic age. True, the Charter was signed some weeks prior to Hiroshima. But it was not ratified by any country until afterward. Indeed, it did not come into force until late in October, 1945, by which time the impact of the release of atomic energy had been appraised in every corner of the globe. The need for organization had become all the more apparent, the sense of urgency heightened. Obviously, the United Nations has been beset by all the questions of life and death which the atom poses. Nevertheless, as time goes by, the value of the Charter's flexibility becomes increasingly apparent. It was this very quality which made it acceptable to the United States, in line with our own tradition that basic compacts must be adaptable in order to endure. In this sense the Charter is no more preatomic than is the Constitution of the United States.

The two instruments can be compared in still another respect. Both are premised upon the worth and dignity of the individual human being. It was no accident, but in fact the result of American leadership, that the character of the Charter is stamped by the identical opening phrase of our Constitution: "We the people. . ."

POSSIBILITIES OF STRENGTHENING THE UNITED NATIONS

As war becomes more terrible and the wells of conventional diplomacy threaten to run dry, governments will perforce rely increasingly upon the United Nations as a sort of diplomatic reservoir.

It may be that peace, and the future of civilization itself, will depend upon the extent to which recommendations of the United Nations can be endowed with moral compulsion. The moral component of power is frequently ignored or minimized by the advocates of power politics. I believe it to be self-evident that although moral force cannot move mountains, it moves people—and people can move mountains.

In short, talk about strengthening the United Nations is hollow unless it squarely faces the central issue: how can the United Nations be effectively used as a means of infusing into the faltering community of the free, a sense of *common interest*?

The United Nations is potentially one of the most effective instruments of diplomacy man has ever fashioned. The opportunities it affords for timely consultation, bilaterally or in groups, are unexampled. The forum offers unique advantages for constant personal contacts among delegates versed in political and economic affairs. The open debates and public statements before the microphone account for a small proportion of the work done. Debate may serve as a means of pressure and an adjunct of diplomacy. But it is not, and never can be, a substitute for negotiation.

In order to serve its highest purposes as a means of conducting foreign policy, however, the United Nations must be employed imaginatively, in close conjunction with bilateral and regional negotiation. Above all, it should be fashioned as a tool for democracy rather than as a weapon for recrimination.

The first and most important policy for strengthening the United Nations would be for us to enable the United Nations to place larger resources and energies at the service of those vast populations which are determined to achieve higher standards of well-being and freedom. It is natural that high among our concerns should be the threat of Communist imperialism. But the threat to us is all the more reason to take into account problems which are at the top of the agenda of those peoples who are prime targets of Communist subversion. The Atom, in both its peaceful and destructive aspects, is considered by many people the primary issue in the world today. Yet its priority would be challenged by such an expert as Raymond W. Miller of the Harvard Business School, who has written: "Hunger is the most important fact in the world today. The real challenge of the 20th century is the race between man and starvation." Surely, the pressures for national independence and free institutions are not very far behind, nor is the insistent drive for the promotion of human rights and freedoms.

In the competition for the allegiance of the multitudes who are the real targets of the cold war, these are the vital issues. If we stand neutral or unaligned with respect to them, we have little chance when we seek their interest in our own agenda of national security.

Some of these problems can be dealt with adequately through bilateral or regional procedures. Our mutual aid programs are basic and indispensable. Yet many of the most pressing issues of general or universal concern are manageable (and even there, with difficulty) only in a general or universal forum. Moreover, they have little to do with the cold war as such. Their solution would be just as imperative if the Soviet Union were by some miracle to be turned overnight into a model parliamentary democracy.

Like all basic documents, the Charter is broadly drawn—on the one hand breeding controversy as to its meaning, on the other, defying rigid codification. It is a dilemma familiar to us at home, inescapable in the legal framework of a democratic structure. However, in view of the deep concern for human rights steadfastly proclaimed by the responsible leadership of every continent, our attitude concerning the scope of the Charter becomes increasingly a testing point of our leadership in the United Nations, and therefore in the world.

In short, the diplomatic instrument of the United Nations should be used as a forum for announcing and explaining objectives, principles, and the general nature of programs. Public understanding is built thereby, and public pressures are created to serve as a ballast for negotiation. This search for solutions is the true function of debate. But there is no reason to forget the mutually supporting role of good old-fashioned diplomacy as well. It is the only means by which effective negotiation has ever been, or can ever be, carried out. What passes for negotiation in United Nations forums tends too often to become a word game, in which debating points are scored and a premium is paid for every headline won. Returning debate to true negotiation is one important way to strengthen the United Nations.

It is illuminating to reflect that no major crisis is likely to arise—no new Suez, no new Hungary, no flaring up of hostilities in the Middle East—in which the first urgent recourse would not be to the United Nations.* There is some self-deception in attacks upon the United Nations merely because, in the face of crisis it cannot do enough or because its members talk too much and act too little. The answer is that the sense of common interest, upon which collective security depends, must be strengthened.

This is precisely where American vital interests and American leadership are interconnected. Without the latter, the organization—that is to say, the rudimentary system of world order—breaks into fragments.

American delegates to the United Nations often observe the intense preoccupation with which foreign diplomats—friend, foe and neutral alike—gauge and report home American attitudes on important issues. American public opinion is one of the greatest forces in the world. Thomas Jefferson said "opinion is power." In his own circle of influence, Carleton exemplified the truth of that aphorism.

*Epilogue: In reviewing this tribute to Carleton, which I wrote prior to the Gulf War, I am reminded that the United States indeed did resort to the United Nations as the fountainhead of collective action against the aggressor.

Joseph John Jova

THE IMPORTANCE OF THE BI-NATIONAL AND MULTI-NATIONAL CONCEPT IN WORLD CULTURAL RELATIONS

Among the many noteworthy cultural interests of Carleton Sprague Smith is one which coincides with a strong interest of my own, one that has, in fact, culminated in my presidency of Meridian House International (MHI) in Washington, D.C. MHI is, in many ways, the quintessence of a concept that Carleton has been working toward for many years, that of multi-national centers.

In my own experience as a Foreign Service Officer and then as an Ambassador to several countries and to the Organization of American States, I became convinced that the bi-national or multi-national concept, along with exchange of persons programs, is among the most important tools available to public diplomacy. Of the approximately two hundred cultural centers that the United States Information Agency (USIA) maintains or assists world-wide, some ninety-three are bi-national centers. Such organizations, although partially supported by the USIA (as opposed to American Cultural Centers, which are totally funded by USIA), are autonomous institutions governed by a board of local citizens and resident Americans. They are not directed by the U.S. Embassy and, in fact, while they collaborate in most matters, they remain fiercely independent. Most of the staff of these centers is hired locally,

Joseph John Jova is President emeritus of Meridian House International. Previously he served as U.S. Ambassador to Honduras, the OAS, and Mexico. He retired from Foreign Service in 1977, when elected President of MHI, where he served until 1989.

although some of the positions are sometimes staffed by USIA personnel on detail. These institutions are a uniquely important means of communication, as they reach out to explain and demonstrate the cultures of the two countries involved in an effort to increase mutual understanding. I saw this type of exchange work successfully in a great many places during my years in the Foreign Service. There is no doubt in my mind that a more open approach, which avoids the patronizing aspect of presenting solely one's own culture, is the formula for mutual enrichment.

As President of MHI, a position I accepted immediately after retiring from the Foreign Service in 1978, the importance of these concepts and activities has been reinforced, for MHI is a multi-cultural institution. Located in Washington, D.C., its twofold mission is to introduce foreign visitors to the culture and values of the United States, while at the same time to serve as a window on the world, introducing Americans to the culture of other nations. In structure, it is most similar to bi-national or multi-national centers. Not a government agency, it is owned and operated by its own Board of Directors, themselves drawn from a wide variety of private sector backgrounds.

While the concept of government-owned and operated cultural centers is an old one, that of truly bi-national or multi- national centers, with mixed boards and based on collaboration in an "arms length" manner with the Embassy cultural section, but still independent from it, is more recent. The idea of a two-way street for the enhancement of mutual understanding gained more general acceptance after World War II.

Carleton Sprague Smith was already an authority on this concept, having pioneered the effort to create one of the earliest bi-national centers in Brazil. The international approach was illustrated in a series of lectures under the sponsorship of the French Ambassador to Brazil. The subject of the series was "Les relations culturelles entre la France et les Etats-Unis."

It was natural then that the State Department would call upon Dr. Smith to head an evaluation mission on the subject in Germany in 1950. (Carleton took his doctoral degree at the University of Vienna.) In that year, France, England, and the United States were phasing out the military occupation and turned back the control of government of West Germany and the Allied West Germans over to the people. Germany was no longer the enemy. A year and half of thorough study was made which clearly demonstrated that a multi-national effort, with the cooperation of England, France, the United States, and Germany would be an enlightening, efficient, and workable project.

The Germans, who wished to reenter the new internationalism, felt drawn to the concept of Europe and New World programs in the same headquarters. The Germans were to undertake the major role. Included would be an international library, an auditorium, and attractive reading rooms. As an effective and efficient center, the American Education Service in Nuremberg was by far the best. For a time Germans, French, British, and Americans carried out their activities in the same building and each nation had separate staffs to carry out specific tasks, while working together as a team. The geographic proximity saved a great deal of time and diminished the rivalries of England, France, and the United States. Despite the recommendations of the educational experts, Messrs. Allen (U.K.), Spitzmüller (France) and Koopman (U.S.), that the Education Service Center in Nuremberg "be continued, encouraged and constantly studied," that center was not given a chance to function. It was a propitious time and it could have a close relationship with NATO. In short, although the Europeans were in favor of testing the idea, Washington bureaucracy was not sufficiently enthusiastic. And, although there was enthusiasm for Carleton's plan in Europe, it did not come to fruition at the time, due to the many complicated issues that existed. Carleton still believes very much in the approach he then recommended, particularly in today's highly complicated and technical world. The pooled efforts of small countries in many areas of the world could probably have more effect than what each could achieve on its own.

Some years ago, during a visit to the Spanish Institute in New York and later in Washington, D.C., Carleton expressed his gladness that the multi-national approach has flourished at MHI in Washington. In retrospect, he felt that in 1952 there were a number of people who could have carried out the concept and given the program a whirl.

Let me list some of the many activities which took place during a typical week at MHI in 1988:

> 1) nationwide itineraries and appointments with experts were arranged for an Australian television journalist, a Jamaican pediatrician, and Italian professor of English and American Constitutional law, two economic journalists from the Peoples Republic of China, the dean of the College of Social Sciences in Addis Ababa, a group marketing director for a British publishing company, the director of the National

Society of Fine Arts of Portugal, the project manager of Operation Hunger in South Africa, a fourteen-member group of Bundestag staff assistants, and a three-member Japanese team studying programs for minorities in the United States. (These programs for USIA-sponsored visitors are arranged by MHI's Visitor Program Service.)

2) an orientation to American culture was conducted for thirty-eight rural development specialists from Guatemala, nineteen women in a Department of Labor group studying women in the American labor force (representing Bangladesh, Barbados, Burkina Faso, El Salvador, Grenada, India, Liberia, the Philippines, Tanzania, and Tobago), twenty Costa Rican community leaders, a twenty-member group of Japanese studying contemporary American society and the U.S. economy, and a sixteen-member group from Costa Rica, Oman, Jordan, Morocco, Bolivia, Yugoslavia, and Korea. (These week-long orientation sessions, primarily for AID-sponsored visitors, are conducted by MHI's Washington International Center.)

3) foreign tourists, who know about us from guidebooks printed overseas, were assisted at Dulles Airport on arrival flights from Frankfurt and Paris. Accommodations were found for visitors from France and for an Australian who was surprised at the cost of American hotels! (Foreign language assistance was provided by volunteers via telephone and other services were rendered by MHI's International Visitors Information Service, which assists the privately-sponsored visitor and tourists.)

4) a volunteer committee met to discuss arrangements for the Christmas party to be given by Mrs. Reagan at the White House for diplomatic children, while another seventy-one-member volunteer committee met to discuss the schedule of programs and exhibition tours for diplomats for the coming season. (Services to the Diplomatic Corps and their families are provided by MHI's Hospitality and Information Service.)

5) a program was developed for foreign students to attend mid-winter seminars held around the country during the holiday season. Also during that week:

a) final arrangements were made for a seminar with the Honorable Beryl Sprinkel, chairman of the President's Council of Economic Advisers. In addition to the sixty people signed up for it, this seminar was attended by seven Venezuelan economists, for whom simultaneous translation was provided.

b) plans were completed for an exhibition highlighting MHI's restoration of the John Russell Pope-designed building next door, recently purchased for program expansion. This house was once the residence of Ambassador Henry White, and of Mr. and Mrs. Eugene Meyer.

c) the Boston Council for International Visitors called to report a record number of international visitors for the year.

d) a local council for international visitors was trained on the nationwide computer network linking agencies and organizations serving international visitors and, typically, troubleshooting needed to be done on another council's computer system.

e) a member exchange on organizational development was set up between Los Angeles and Minnesota. (Programs and assistance to local international visitors councils are provided by MHI's National Council for International Visitors.)

f) five hundred guests celebrated the joining of our two house museums—MHI and the White-Meyer mansion—at a reception held in the evening.

Although my own knowledge of Germany was superficial, I knew of Carleton's work there and, in fact, I carried out a somewhat similar evaluation mission in France in 1958, when I was named to an interagency team to study joint U.S.-French cultural efforts throughout France. More recently, I have had the opportunity to observe and admire at first hand Carleton's work in connection with the Spanish Institute of New York, an important force in the cultural life of the city, with which he has been involved for many years. There is no question that he has been a pioneer in a field which becomes more important each year as our planet shrinks. Complemented by exchanges of persons and other international efforts, the multi-national and bi-national center concept pursues the goal of reaching people whose attitudes and opinions need both to understand and to be understood. It is the contributions of people like Carleton Sprague Smith that have shown us how to establish and achieve these goals.

Jordan M. Young

THE BRAZILIAN INSTITUTE, NEW YORK
(1958–1963)

Carleton Sprague Smith represents the deep ties that seem to bind all of us who have had our lives and careers altered in some way by becoming involved with Brazil. My comments about him are simply those of one of the many people who have touched and been touched by him over the many years. Brazil was our common link.

The reverse is also true. Carleton played an important role as an American cultural missionary in Brazil, explaining and demonstrating to many Brazilians that there was a lively and demanding intellectual curiosity on the part of many professors and scholars in the United States to know more about their country. His contacts with anthropologist Gilberto Freyre, Brazilian historian Américo Jacobina Lacombe, and former Foreign Minister Afonso de Melo Franco, among many others, were, because of his personality and style, given an opportunity to see the depth of interest and commitment on the part of many Americans to Brazilian research.

When I began to pull my facts and data together, I was surprised and pleased to discover that it had been more than forty years ago when I first crossed paths with him. In 1941, I was an undergraduate student at the University of Illinois and had decided to take my junior year at

Jordan M. Young is Executive Director of the Institute of Brazilian American Business Studies at Pace University (New York). he is also Professor Emeritus in Residence and teaches the course on Brazilian Civilization. He has written three books on Brazil. Brazil: Emerging World Power, *2nd edition, will appear in 1991.*

the University of São Paulo. Someone told me that I must go to the New York Public Library and speak to Carleton Sprague Smith, a musicologist who was quite knowledgeable on Brazil. I remember being led to what seemed to be a wire cage like office in the bowels of the library, where together we had an exciting half hour conversation which fired up an even greater enthusiasm for my impending Brazilian adventure.

I enrolled in the Universidade de São Paulo Faculdade de Ciencias e Letras as an *ouvinte livre* ('auditor') and at the Largo São Francisco, where I registered for classes at the Escola Livre de Sociologia e Política. A little later on, I learned, much to my surprise, that Carleton had lectured at the Escola Livre.

It was during the early 1950's, when I was working for Chase Bank in Rio de Janeiro, that he broke up a solemn affair at the Universidade de Brasil. The occasion was the awarding of honorary degrees to him and a few other distinguished scholars. It was a warm afternoon in Rio and Professor Pedro Calmon, noted for his histrionic speeches, had overwhelmed the audience for more than forty minutes before it was time for Carleton to speak. When Carleton approached the lecturn, instead of delivering another long and solemn oration, he, instead, took out his flute and performed a beautiful two minute rendition of Claude Debussy's "Syrinx" to an astonished audience. The following speaker, the Brazilian Foreign Minister, Negrão de Lima, was a bit chagrined and apologized for not having brought along his ukulele. But it sure awoke us and endeared Carleton to us forever.

The next and most exciting phase, in my opinion, of Carleton's contribution to Brazilian-American relations was his impact on the Brazilian Institute of New York University, which was established in 1958. He was one of the major driving forces in the structuring and programing of this ambitious Institute. He was joined by Dr. Ernesto Da Cal, Professor of Portuguese at New York University. Carleton took over the directorship from 1959 to 1961.

An important event that he helped organize was the three day conference that New York University sponsored in December of 1958 as part of the founding of the new Institute. The gala conference was presided over by Governor Nelson Rockefeller, along with the Brazilian Minister for Foreign Affairs, Francisco Negrão de Lima, and Mayor Robert Wagner of New York City. The stimulating affair had over 600 invited delegates. Among the many extraordinary "happenings" was the world premier work of the Brazilian composer, Heitor Villa-Lobos, who was Carleton's colleague in music.

A very important function of the Institute, which Carleton recognized as indispensible, was the establishment of short orientation courses for men and women with business and professional interest in Brazil.

The early sixties were exciting times for Brazil because the Juscelino Kubitschek administration instilled in the nation a feeling that it could accomplish anything its people set their minds to do. American corporations were also experiencing this feeling and large investments were made in Brazil.

Carleton, early in his career, realized that there was no substitute for deep information and knowledge, thus, as Director of the Brazilian Institute, he was keenly aware of the importance of the 1960 presidential elections in Brazil. He brought together a group of Brazilian and American scholars to discuss "Brazil's New Administration." Joining us for those discussions were, among others, Professor Hermes Lima, who was later appointed to Brazil's Supreme Court, Berent Friele, then vice president of IBEC (International Basic Economy Corporation), Mr. Frank Nattier, a man with many years of Brazilian experience and a distinguished international lawyer and partner of Nattier and Anderson, and João Roberto Suplicy Hafers, Director of the Brazilian Coffee Institute. Many of the problems that Brazil would face were pinpointed and analyzed by the distinguished panelists.

In January of 1963, Carleton again organized an Orientation to Brazil Program for the business community which included such outstanding Brazilian specialists as Dr. Reynold Carlson, the Ford Foundation Representative in Brazil, Professor Preston James, Chairman of the Geography Department of Syracuse University, and Dr. Charles Wagley, the dean of all Brazilian specialists who was then Chairman of the Anthropology Department at Columbia University. I was also a participant, who presented an historical dimension to this event.

An exciting example of the type of programs that Carleton was able to generate concerns the Champion Paper and Fiber Corporation. They had decided to invest heavily in Brazil and to construct a modern factory to produce paper and pulp products. The Champion people turned to the Brazilian Institute for help in setting up an off campus orientation training operation for their Brazil program. For seven months New York University professors familiar with Brazil worked closely with families of Champion employees, who were to be transferred to their Brazilian facilities. Carleton's deep understanding of the

Brazilian culture was invaluable in helping these people avoid the culture shock that normally accompanies the transfer of nationals from one culture to another.

Many of these employees were born and had spent their entire lives in North Carolina, and Carleton and the Brazilian Institute had a real job ahead of them to acquaint these people with Brazil. The Institute brought together historians, language specialists, musicians, Brazilian diplomats, and businessmen to give them what was undoubtedly one of the greatest cultural experiences of their lives. Thanks to Carleton and the team he assembled, they knew what to expect when they arrived in Brazil.

One anecdote, which I remember well, concerned my wife, who is from Belém do Pará, and though she speaks English fluently, she also has a very definite Brazilian accent. One officer of the Champion Corporation, born and bred in the hills of North Carolina, asked my wife what sort of accent she had and from what country did she come. After she explained she was from Brazil, she, in turn, inquired politely about his exotic accent, which she had never heard before. Reverse culture shock.

Among the many innovative programs put into operation by the Brazilian Institute under the stewardship of Carleton was the junior year program in Brazil. Anyone who has worked in junior year programs knows what mountains of details have to be mastered to make them work successfully. But work successfully they did. Carleton once again was able to attract world famous scholars, researchers, graduate students, and diplomats.

For a man who has had such a wide ranging and fascinating career as Carleton Sprague Smith, the Brazilian Institute remains a beacon for many of us who continue to work for closer, warmer, and deeper ties between Brazil and the United States. We tip our hats to Carleton. And send a warm *abraço*.

PERFORMING ARTS

Angel Alcalá

"AQUESTA INMENSA CITARA"

An Aesthetics of Musical Ecstasy in Fray Luis de Leon's (1527–1591) *Ode to Salinas*

Marcelino Menéndez Pelayo (1856–1912), the foremost critic of Spanish letters, stated, in 1881, that besides San Juan de la Cruz, "whose songs do not seem at all to be written by a man, but by an angel, no Castilian lyrical poet may be compared with Fray Luis de León" (1941:94). For Menéndez Pelayo, Fray Luis's incomparable *Ode to Salinas*, the subject of the present study, includes the most beautiful expression of Plato's aesthetic system (1940:65). It has been similarly evaluated as perhaps the most beautiful ode written in the Spanish language (León Tello 1962:550) or, "perhaps more modestly, as one of Fray Luis's best poems" (Rico 1970:180). Its high praise among literary critics is unanimous. This explains the abundance of more or less useful essays devoted to its commentary and to the unveiling of the many problems that its text and theme still pose.[1]

[1] I am happy to mention the following in particular: D. Alonso (1962:172–92), L.J. Woodward (1962:69–77), O. Macr (1970:105–14 and 134), and F. Rico (1970:170–89). Several convergences and dissonances from some of them, as well as from other critics, will be mentioned later on. Inaccessible has been T. O'Reilly, "The Ode *[continued]*

Angel Alcalá is Professor of Spanish Language and Literature at Brooklyn College, CUNY. He is editor, translator, and author of more than a dozen books and of several articles on literary, theological, and historical topics.

According to Azorín (1874–1977), the great Spanish writer, "there has never been in Spain a more perfect poet, one who has added a more profound and philosophical concept of life and of the world to a vigorous and delightful vision of reality" (1977:87), especially for his verbal exactitude, his concise expression, his lofty thoughts, and his "thrilling sensitivity, like a burning spirit" (García, in León 1951:1401). Regarding this ode, any one who has searched through the jumbled forest of poems about music in various languages would undoubtedly call it the best in the genre. The greatest number of poems on music either describe external circumstances, or praise musical experiences, instruments, or composers, or limit themselves to the lyrical expression of the emotion felt when listening to a melody or a singer's voice, or when recalling the atmosphere of a concert.[2]

This ode excels for quite different qualities. Some of its poetic terms, like "dulcísima armonía" or "mar de dulzura," apparently mere literary commonplaces, will evidently have some correlation with, for instance, Shakespeare's "sweet harmony" or George Herbert's (1593–1633) "sweetest of sweets," and others, such being the continued strength of traditional rhetoric in this as in other topics.[3] But in the *Ode to Salinas* all this rhetorical baggage has been transferred to a transcendent level of meaning due to two distinct factors: 1) the entire poem stands on a well-known Neoplatonic aesthetics common to the diverse national manifestations of the European Renaissance, even though some of its connotations do not seem to have been sufficiently explored,

---

to Francisco Salinas," in S. Bacarisse *et al.*, eds., *What's Past is Prologue. A Collection of Essays in Honor of W.J. Woodward* (Edinburgh, 1984), pp. 107–13, mentioned by C. Thompson (1980:264). This valuable book, by one of the best contemporary Luisian scholars, does not add any new insights to our present topic, and it rather seems that O'Reilly follows Woodward's interpretation.

[2]This conclusion resulted from research undertaken in compiling an anthology of poems about or dedicated to music in five languages (English, French, German, Italian, and Spanish).

The most valuable collections of poems in English about music appear to be those by H. Patten (1905), E.J. Howard (1927), E.W. Naylor (1928), R.H. Schauffer (1935), A. Jacobs (1948), and J. Bishop (1968). Oddly enough, none of them mentioned nor perhaps knew Fray Luis de León or his *Ode to Salinas*.

[3]"How sour sweet music is / when time is broke and no proportion kept" (Shakespeare, *Richard II*, V, 5). "And let the sounds of music / creep in our ears: soft stillness, and the night / becomes the touches of sweet harmony" (*Idem., The Merchant of Venice*, V, 1). "Those dulcet sounds in break of day (*Ibid.* III, 2). George Herbert in the poem, "Church Music" (Howard 1927:17).

in spite of its being the object of a number of critical studies; 2) contrary to so many anecdotal or utterly sentimental poems about or devoted to music, all of it—ten brief stanzas, comprising only fifty verses—evokes the sudden *ascensus* to a strictly musical ecstasy and then laments the inevitable *descensus* to life's troubles.

Since this famous ode is quite unknown outside literary circles, it is gratifying to present here, alongside one of its best critical texts, one of its best English versions, in homage to a true friend whom—as Fray Luis would perhaps say—"a quien amo sobre todo tesoro."[4]

El aire se serena
y viste de hermosura y luz no usada,

The air becomes serene
and robed in beauty and an unknown
[light,

Salinas, cuando suena
la música extremada
por vuestra sabia mano gobernada.

Salinas, when the unseen
deep music soars in flight,
governed by your hand that is wise
[and right.

A cuyo son divino
mi alma, que en olvido está sumida,
torna a cobrar el tino
y memoria perdida
de su origen primera esclarecida.

Before that holy song
my soul, submerged in its oblivion,
recovers sense and long
forgotten memory in
its dazzling and primordial origin.

Y, como se conoce,
en suerte y pensamiento se mejora:
el oro desconoce
que el vulgo ciego adora,
la belleza caduca engañadora.

And having knowledge of
itself, it comes alive in thought and fate,
and has contempt, above
all, for mere gold, the bait
of blind mobs, or beauty in its false state.

Traspasa el aire todo
hasta llegar a la más alta esfera,
y oye allí otro modo
de no perecedera
música, que es de todas la primera

Piercing the air, the soul
reaches into the very highest sphere
and there it hears a whol-
ly different mode: imper-
ishable music, first and without peer.

Ve cómo el gran maestro
a aquesta inmensa cítara aplicado,

It sees the way the grand
master works the immense zither, and
[the way

con movimiento diestro
produce el son sagrado
con que este eterno templo es
[sustentado.

he shapes the holy strand
of sound with dexterous play,
by which that deathless temple is
[sustained.

[4]The great Hispanist and musicologist, Carleton Sprague Smith, for whose homage volume this essay has been written, has distinguished me with his precious friendship as far back in the early seventies at the Spanish Institute (New York), where until our joint abandonment from that institution in 1981, I cooperated with him in his activities and dreams for an actively cultural *hispanismo*.

Y como está compuesta
de números concordes, luego envía
consonante respuesta,
y entrambas a porfía
mezclan una dulcísima armonía.

Aquí la alma navega
por un mar de dulzura y, finalmente,

en él ansí se anega,
que ningún accidente
extraño y peregrino oye o siente.

¡Oh desmayo dichoso!
¡Oh muerte que das vida! ¡Oh dulce
[olvido!

¡Durase en tu reposo,
sin ser restituído
jamás a aquesta bajo y vil sentido!

A aqueste bien os llamo
gloria del apolíneo sacro coro,
amigos, a quien amo
sobre todo tesoro,
que todo lo demás es triste lloro.

¡Oh! Suene de contino,
Salinas, vuestro son en mis oídos,
por quien al bien divino
despiertan los sentidos,
quedando a lo demás amortecidos.

It is composed, then, by
concordant numbers that accompany
a consonant reply.
and both work stubbornly
to mingle lost in sweetest harmony.

Here the souls sails around
inside a sea of sweetness, and
[finally wheels

about and then is drowned
so that it hears or feels
nothing that foreign accident reveals.

O happy deep collapse!
O death conferring life! O sweet
[oblivion!

Now let me never lapse
into the low, vile run
of senses! Let my rest in you be won!

I call you to this good,
the highest glory of Apollos's holy
choir, friends, whom I do
love beyond all wholly
vain wealth, for all the rest is just sad
[folly.

O Salinas, let me hear
the music of your fingers as it rings
constantly in my ear,
my senses wakening
to holy grace and dulled to earthly
[things.[5]

[5]The Spanish text comes from Fray Luis's *Poesias*, edited by A.C. Vega (León 1975:15–17), considered better than O. Macrí's (1970), especially the former's critical edition (León 1955). Although there are many English translations, none can be perfect. That furnished alongside the Spanish, by W. Barnstone (1979:44–47), is more faithful to Fray Luis's original, though less poetic and less abundant in antiquated English expressions than the famous translation by A.F.G. Bell, published by E.L. Turnbull (1962:175–79), which follows:

Calm grows the air around
arrayed in beauty and unwonted light,
Salinas, at the sound
of music exquisite
that thy skilled hand cunningly indite.

And at that sound divine
my soul, that in forgetfulness had lain.
with a new light doth shine
and unto memory plain
of its first splendid origin attain.

No complete commentary on this famous poem is to be expected here. Our discussion will concentrate on the two above-mentioned issues which seem rather to have been overlooked by the critics. But first we shall provide a summary sketch of its author and of Salinas, as well as its internal structure.

I. THE POEM

It is unlikely that scholars will ever reach a consensus on the poem's date. Those who tend to think of it as an homage to Salinas's *De Musica Libre Septem* (Salamanca, 1577) seem to have forgotten that verses which praised books, frequently of little poetic value, were usually printed at the beginning of such books; in this case Fray Luis would have published his poem in Latin or Greek, as those by authors unknown to this writer at the opening of Salinas's volume. Salinas himself dates his dedication to Rodrigo de Castro, Bishop of Zamora, in the same year 1577, which tells us that it was not reviewed by the royal censor, Juan

---

For this new knowledge then
its noble thoughts and destiny restores,
of gold, vain lure of men,
which the blind crowd adores,
the perishable beauty it ignores.

Up through the fields of air
it wings, till in the highest sphere, it
                              [dwells,
and a new music there
it hears, music that wells
undying and all other kinds excels.

The great master it sees,
his hand upon the mighty lyre, with
                              [train
of skillfull cadences,
create the holy strain
that this eternal temple doth sustain.

And since in sweet content
those numbers flow symphonious, reply
concordant is soon sent,
and both together vie
in a mixed power of softest harmony.

Through sea of melody
in rapture sweet the soul doth onward
                              [glide
and sinks there finally,
until whate'er betide
beyond it to its senses is denied.

O heavenly ravishment!
Life-giving death! Oblivion's sweet
                              [defense!
O might my life be spent
in thy calm rest, nor thence
ever return to this vile earthly sense!

To such bliss I entreat
you, glory of Apollo's sacred choir,
o friends for whom doth beat
my heart beyond desire
of treasures that bring tears and
                              [sorrows dire.

O evermore to hear
thy heavenly music, Salinas, be mine;
through whom awaking clear
to holy thoughts incline
the senses, to all else dull and supine.

López de Velasco, who signed his approval in Madrid on 17 September 1575, "porque es obra muy aventajada de lo que hasta agora está escrito en la facultad (Salinas 1958:fol. 8).[6] Fray Luis was freed from the Inquisitorial jail on 15 December 1576, which would have allowed him time to write his poem in praise of the book. Yet the fact that he does not even mention it, proves that the poem's motive and topic was not the famous publication, but rather the music performed by Salinas, or music in general. This being one of the *quaestiones minores* about the poem, the most one can say is that this ode already belongs to a period of maturity in the poet's artistic creativity.[7]

The little we know of Salinas's life comes from his long *Praefatio* and other parts of the book, as well as from entries in the *Libros de claustros de la Universidad de Salamanca*:[8] his birth, in Burgos, probably 1 March 1513; his blindness—perhaps not total—since he was eight or ten; his protection by his relative, Pedro Gómez Sarmiento, the Archbishop of Santiago de Compostela, who took him to Rome in 1538, when he was created Cardinal; his friendship there with musicians of the stature of Francesco da Milano, Giulio Segni, Orlando Lasso, and Palestrina (Fernndez de la Cuesta 1983:8–9); his positions as organist at the chapel of the Viceroy of Naples—then the Duke of Alba; his appointment as organist at the Cathedral of León in May of 1563, after almost twenty-four years in Italy; and his achievement through competition of the Music Chair at the University of Salamanca on 29 June 1567. He retired at seventy-three and died on 13 January 1590.

It is a pity that Salinas's book, always mentioned but little read, could hardly have influenced theoretical musical studies in Spain, in spite of its innovations and of attaining the highest place in musicology of the Spanish Renaissance. A convinced humanist and devoted

[6]Hispanists and musicologists with minimal proficiency in Latin will find most useful the Spanish translation of Salinas's *De Musica* by Ismael Fernández de la Cuesta (1983), who also provides a much better introduction than the short note about Salinas by Kastner at the end of his facsimile edition.

[7]The period classification of Luisian poetry advanced by Menéndez Pelayo is reproduced by C. Cuevas (1982:33), but he, like A.F.G. Bell, and others, cautions us about considering it a solved problem. Contrary to what O. Macrí, and many other critics have thought, it is also difficult to be precise about determining whether any particular poem was written before or after the poet's imprisonment, with the exception of those with clear allusions to it in their text or context. Concerning aspects of this influence on other non-poetic works by Fray Luis and on this works in general, see C.P. Thompson (1980 and 1988:70–78, respectively).

[8]The compact text of the *Praefatio* is eight pages long. Several documents from the *Libros* are translated as appendices by F.J. León Tello (1962:687–95).

teacher, Salinas had to write it in an abstruse Latin for the benefit of his students. The book, published after his retirement, reproduced his lecture notes. The noted Spanish writer on music of the second half of the eighteenth century, the Jesuit Antonio Eximeno y Pujades (1729–1808), records this fact with a grain of graceful irony through one of the characters in his *Don Lazarillo de Vizcardi*: "Los músicos nos hallamos algo enredados en el latín de Salinas, porque no es latín de breviario" (1873;I, 44; cited by León Tello 1962:553). It is to be even more lamented that none of his musical compositions have been preserved, a fate that Salinas would have shared with his contemporary, also blind and from Burgos, Antonio de Cabezón (1510–1566), had the latter's son, Hernando (d. 1602), not committed his works to print. Quite apart from Cabezón, Salinas will not have his Baciero.[9] Besides the unforgettable tribute of this ode, no written record of Salinas's own music appears to exist, except for some scattered testimonies of three or four contemporaries who were among his fortunate listeners.[10]

Our Augustinian friar was among them. A text published by Velázquez's father-in-law, printed opposite his impressive portrait of Fray Luis, tells us much about his love of all the arts: "Fue la mayor capacidad de ingenio que se ha conocido en su tiempo para todas las ciencias y artes. . . Estudió sin maestro la pintura i la exercitó tan diestramente que entre otras cosas hizo (cosa difícil) su mesmo retrato" (Pacheco 1599:69) (see Plate 1, p. 254). Our Fray Luis was an amateur painter! Born in Belmonte, near Cuenca, he studied in Salamanca and Alcalá de Henares, and returned to the former, in 1561, to become the living symbol of a moderately progressive Humanism, soon to be opposed by some of his colleagues who were still entrenched in an unshaken and stony Scholasticism. In love with the classics, a philosopher, theologian, moralist, and Biblical scholar, but above all a poet, he found

[9]Antonio Baciero (b. 1936) has recorded the complete keyboard works of Cabezón.

[10]The historian, Ambrosio de Morales (1513–1591), nephew of the great humanist Hernán Pérez de Oliva, wrote: "Con mucha razón le llamo insigne varón, pues tiene tan profunda intelligencia en la Música, que yo le he visto, con mudarla tañendo y cantando, poner en pequeño espacio en los ánimos diferentíssimos movimientos de tristeza y alegría, de ímpetu y reposo, con tanta fuerça, que ya no me espanta lo que Pythágoras escriven hazía con la música, ni lo que Santo Augustín dize se puede hazer con ella" (1586:liv. XV, cap. 25). The novelist and musician Vicente Espinel (1550–1624), remembered his student years in Salamanca: "Vi al abad Salinas, el ciego, el más docto varón en música especulativa que ha conocido la antigüedad" (1618:Parte I, descanso XI). Nicolás Antonio (1617–1684), the famous bibliographer, repeated Morales's statement with slight modifications (1783–84:I, 473).

Plate 1. The portrait of Fray Luis de León in Francesco Pacheco's *Libro de descripción de verdaderos Retratos de Illustres y Memorables varones* (Seville, 1599).

in the contemplation of nature and in music the inducement for spiritual detachment that his sensitive and tormented soul needed. When jailed, more for his enemies' envy than for his scholarly doctrines, old Salinas testified before the Inquisitorial Tribunal on his behalf on 27 January 1573. He was León's friend, he confessed: "Venía muchas veces a casa de este testigo, y oyó deste testigo la (música) especulativa, y comunicaba con este testigo cosas de poesía y otras cosas del arte."[11] Our Fray Luis was also an amateur musician! This detail is the key for understanding why he qualifies musical ecstasy as "sweet oblivion," and music—if our interpretation is correct—as the "glory of Apollo's sacred choir," the highest culmination of the Muses' gifts. Fray Luis, like every sensitive writer, possessed a poetic universe with its own system of expressions, wherein allusions to music are constant:

> "Pasar la vida en música es pasarla en contento, porque es compañera de la alegría ('Music is a companion to joy')." "Los oídos se alegran en la suave armonía." "Como se hace en la música, hizo una provechosa y dulce armonía." "El canto y las cosas de música, a las cuales va aneja naturalmente una fuerza que excita el ánimo a los cosas celestiales y tranquiliza y compone los afectos," etc.[12]

In this context, it is a mistake to interpret the Luisian concept of *música extremada* as synonymous with 'exquisite,' 'unseen,' or other adjectives produced by the usual translators.

John Stevens (1961:64) has noted that:

> The most notable fact about the musical theory of the fifteenth and early sixteenth century is the complete absence of the very thing we are looking for—an account of music as an expressive agent, as speaking the 'language of the heart.' This is not to say that the medieval theorist

---

[11]See the *Proceso original que la Inquisición de Valladolid hizo al maestro Fr. Luis de León, religioso del "Orden de S. Agustín* in *Colección de documentos inéditos para la historia de España* (Madrid, 1847:XI, 302–3). At the end of the short testimony two secretaries, Benito Rodríguez and García de Malla, stated: "Y esto declaró," y es verdad para el juramento que hizo; y por defecto de ser ciego no pudo firmar, y ansí lo dijo, y en ello se afirmó" é ratificó" (*Loc. cit.*). The manuscript of the proceedings (no. 12749) is now at the Biblioteca Nacional (Madrid). Salinas's testimony is on folio 602. A critical edition of the entire Ms by this writer, as well as a new biography of Fray Luis, is scheduled to appear in 1991.

[12]The texts cited here for immediate consultation were taken respectively from *Exposición del libro de Job, Los nombres de Cristo, La perfecta casada,* and *Opera* IV, 234, according to A.F.G. Bell (1927:280, n. 27).

saw no connection between music and human feelings. On the contrary, he knew that music affected people powerfully in a way that might be good and might be bad.

Music among the Classical philosophers was considered as an educational factor, so that nothing could offend Plato and Aristotle more strongly than basing music on the mere principle of pleasure.[13]

Augustine and Boethius, in their respective *De Musica*, transmitted this tradition which reached the Renaissance and our Fray Luis. One of the former's finest points is his idea about music as *scientia bene modulandi*; the latter divided music into *instrumentatlis*, *humana*, and *mundana*, and looked upon human voices and instruments merely as tools for the soul to recover its own harmony, thus attuning itself to the eternal song of the universe.[14] Only *música extremada*, perfect in its proportions, will be able to achieve so lofty a goal.

---

[13]Both philosophers express their opposition to music as pleasure in various works. Plato (1961), especially, in *Laws* II, 555b, 659a–c; III, 700; and in *Timaeus*, 47d, where he wrote: "Music as is adapted to the sound of the voice and to the sense of hearing is granted to us for the sake of harmony. And harmony, which has motions akin to the revolutions of our souls, is not regarded by the intelligent votary of the Muses as given by them with a view to irrational pleasure, which is deemed to be the purpose of it in our day, but is meant to correct any discord which may have arisen in the courses of the soul, and to be our ally in bringing her into harmony and agreement with herself." Aristotle in *Politics* VIII, 1339b. The Platonic *Dialogues* will be quoted from the edition by E. Hamilton/H. Cairns (Plato 1961), and *Politics* from that by Sir E. Barker (Aristotle 1946).

[14]Augustine: "Poterat omnino nulla de hoc verbo controversia fieri, ut jam musicam sublato eo quod positum est, bene, tantum *scientia modulandi* definiremus" (1845:1086; *De Musica*, I, 6). "Musica, id est, *scientia sensusve bene modulandi*" (1845a:726; Epist. 166, 13), in a context wherein he speaks of the universal concert comprising everything and even small events, thanks to the predefined *modulatio* infused in them by a God-Artist *in hoc labentium rerum tamquam mirabili cantico*, a sentence rightfully translated as 'this wonderful song of succeeding events... in harmony with the control of the universe' (1955:19). The translator of *De Musica*, after cautioning about the difficulty of a correct translation of *modulandi*, since "to modulate" has now a different technical meaning, elects "Music, that is, the science or *perception of mensurating well*" (1847:172, n. 4), while the translator of Augustine's *Letters* (1955:19) gives us "music, that is, the science or *perception of rhythm.*" Recently, other American musicologists have translated it either as "the knowledge of making *controlled variations of sound* in the right way" (La Croix 1988:4) or as "of regulating or *measuring the components of melody*" (Bowen 1988:45; W.R. Bowen deals extensively with this point). Boethius's triple distinction of music is to be found in his *De Musica* I, 2 (1847:1171). Concerning this, see G. Pietzch (1929:40ff.) and L. Spitzer (1963:31).

These concepts were, of course, well known in the Renaissance. Their mention by Fray Luis can be seen in T.E. May and E. Sarmiento (1954:183–92), L. Spitzer (1963:112–15), and F. Rico (1970:178).

The Spartan moralist within Plato's mind tersely differentiated the various levels of musical quality depending on their educational purpose, so that the criteria of the majority must yield to those of critics and of teachers of good upbringing:

> Any unregulated pursuit of music is infinitely improved by being subjected to a system, even without any addition of musical sweetmeats; delight is something which can be provided by all styles alike. If a man has from childhood to the age of sobriety and discretion been familiar with austere, classical music, he is repelled by the sound of the opposite kind and pronounces it unmanly; if brought up on music of the popular, cloying kind, he finds its opposite frigid and displeasing . . . And there is the additional consideration that the one regularly makes those who are brought up on it better men, the other worse (Plato 1961: *Laws*, VII, 802c–d).

The old axiom, *mens sana in corpore sano*, is thus translated into 'gymnastics for the body, and music for the soul,' and 'attuning the harmonies of the body for the sake of the concord in [the] soul' (Plato 1961: *Republic*, II, 37e; IX, 591d). Many pages in Plato's *Dialogues* insist on this need for rhythm and harmony in all human life, both personal and social, because virtue is similar to musical harmony, therefore the harmony of individuals and of society must be obtained by correcting the course of their lives in accordance with "the harmonies and revolutions of the universe, thus renovating their original nature."[15]

It may perhaps sound strange to present day musicologists to hear Fray Luis, as quoted above, speak of "a certain force that elevates the soul, *naturally* attached to music." The old Classic tradition resounds here. Not only Plato, but also Aristotle mentions the common pleasure which all men derive from music—a pleasure indeed, which is natural and instinctive, and which explains why the use of music appeals to all ages and all types of character. . . In listening to more imitative sounds, where there is no question of time or tune, all men are moved to feelings

---

[15]"Viewed from here it (justice) bears more likeness to a kind or concord and harmony than the other virtues did" (Plato 1961: *Republic*, IV, 430e). "Each man. . . by learning the harmonies and revolutions of the universe, should correct the courses of the head which were corrupted at our birth. . . renewing his original nature" (Plato 1961: *Timaeus*, 90d). A Platonic, as well as Stoic concept is the similarity between harmony and temperance, hence the term "to temper" or "a well-tempered instrument." These ideas are aptly resumed by P. Friedländer (1964:16): "Rhythm and harmony penetrate the soul and appease it; the goal of musical education is *eurhythmy* and integration of the soul."

of sympathy. He even says that this musical pleasure is not produced immediately, but as a reflection of the virtuous pleasure aroused by it, or perhaps because, on listening to rhythms and melodies, we assimilate

> the image of anger, and of calm; images of fortitude and temperance, and of all the forms of their opposites; images of the other states— which come closer to their actual nature than anything else can do. This is a fact which is clear from our experience; to listen to these images is to undergo a real change in the soul (Aristotle, *Politics,* VIII, V, 15, 17, and 18:134a; 1946:342–44).

As is well known, it was precisely Eduard Hanslick who opposed this doctrine of natural correlation between music and its spiritual effects, although some of his statements were extreme formulations in the heat of the polemics they produced. One would, however, agree with him that only musical ideas are truly "the subject of music" and that emotions in no way can be strictly represented by them: "The essence of music is sound and motion" (Hanslick 1957:48). However, no aesthetics has succeeded in determining the exact mechanisms through which "music has never ceased to accompany the most tender and profound affections of the human mind" (*Ibid.*:126).

The acerbic discussions and criticisms to which Hanslick's theories were subjected are presently of no further interest to us, nor were rigid doctrines of importance to Fray Luis when he required a *música extremada* to trigger the ecstatic state. He simply postulated some kind of technical musical perfection as a condition to facilitate the musical trance—an austere, serene music—so that air may "grow calm and [be] robed in beauty and unwonted light." This, the first effect of musical audition, prerequires not only the *virtuoso* 'government' [that is, 'mastering'] of the instrument by a 'skilled hand,' but also a certain quality of the music itself: neither all music is an aesthetic object, nor does all "raise the soul to heavenly things" or "calm and soothe our feelings."

This Platonic presupposition, that music produces moral, not only aesthetic emotions, was commonly held in the Renaissance. Not to rely exclusively on Spanish writers, the following text by Pierre de Ronsard (1524-1584) in old French seems worthy of mentioning:

> Car celuy, Sire, lequel oyant un doux accord d'instruments ou le douceur de la voyx naturell ne s'en resjouit, ne s'en esment point et de teste en piedz n'en tressault point, comme doucement ravy, et si ne scay comment derobé hors de soy, c'est signe qu'il a l'ame tortue,

vicieuse, et depravée, et duquel il se faut donner garde, comme de celuy qui n'est point heuresement né.[16]

Prof. Francisco Rico is correct in stating that "it would be an insult to look for direct sources for these ideas of Fray Luis presupposed by him without the need of documenting undiscussed concepts shared by all cultivated people" (1970:179). Not a single one of the theoretical premises of this *Ode to Salinas* is original; all are common to the European Renaissance culture, saturated with Neoplatonism, revived by its transmitters in the Middle Ages and especially in the Quattrocento. One of the Neoplatonist leaders, Marsilo Ficino (1433–1499), who perhaps was not read by our poet (a point which remains unstudied) does not speak of music too often, although he has many important remarks scattered in his *De Triplici Vita* and *Timaeus Commentary*, which is a true paradox, if compared with so many musical texts in Plato. Ficino also admits an affinity between music and the soul; both are for him *spiritus*, "kinds of air, moving in a highly organized way. Since the ear contains air set deep within it. . . sounds being moving, animated air, must combine directly with the *spiritus aereus. Cantus. . . ferme nihil aliud est quam spiritus alter*" (Walker 1953:131–50; now more readily accessible 1985:VIII, also in 1958:6–8, based on Aristotle, *De anima*, 420a; Augustine, *De Musica*, 6.5.10; Ficino, *Theologia Platonica*, 7.6; and Allen 1984:25–26).

It seems convenient to interject here a brief allusion to another secondary topic, namely the discussion about the relative superiority of the eye or of the ear to "awaken" the soul "that forgetfulness had lain." Plato taught that "when the soul uses the instrumentality of the body, whether through sight or hearing or any other sense. . . it is drawn away by the body into the realm of the variable, and loses its way and becomes confused and dizzy," but when it passes "into the realm of the pure and everlasting and immortal and changeless, and being of a kindred nature,

---

[16]From the "Préface au Roi François II," in Ronsard's *Livre des Meslanges contenant six vingts chansons* (1550), quoted by H. Weber (1956:148). It was therefore normal that Count Baldassare Castiglione (1478–1529) would summarize those Renaissance suppositions in a response to someone who qualified music as an effeminate and vain profession: "Non dite; perch'io v'entrarò in un gran pelago di laude della musica; e ricordarò quanto sempre appresso gli antichi sia stata celebrata e tenuta per cosa sacra, e sia stato opinione di sapientissimi filosofi, il mondo essere composto di musica, e i cieli nel moversi far armonia, e l'anima nostra pur con la medessima ragione esser formata, e però destarsi e quasi vivificar le sue virtú per la musica" (C. Butler, 1937:I, xlvii; 117). Confer the English edition by G. Bull, *The Book of the Courtier* (New York: Penguin, 1967), 94–95.

when it is once independent and free from interference . . . remains constant and invariable. And this condition of the soul we call wisdom" (*Phaedo* 79d). One would tend to think that Fray Luis had these words in mind when praising, in *Vida retirada*, another famous ode, "los pocos sabios que en el mundo han sido ('those few wise men who have been in the world')."

Ficino did not hesitate to subordinate sight to hearing.[17] Of the three kinds of beauty, the mind captures the beauty of the soul, the eyes the beauty of the corporeal forms, and the ears the beauty of sounds, so that the three "s'appartengono a lo Spirito" (Ficino 1973:16): "Il cibo dello Animo é la veritá,. . .ma la bellezza é lo splendore del volto di Dio" (*Ibid.*:62, 66). However, visual impressions produce in the spirit a less powerful effect than those of hearing: musical sound, being "spiritual" or "aerial" in itself, captivates and holds the whole person, even though—or rather because—its forms are spiritual, therefore intangible. Its dynamism holds primacy, for the better souls, over the tyranny of vision. *Música extremada* requires a particular mental concentration: "Such a music can no longer be heard except by the inner ear of intelligence." When music has reverberated in a kindred soul and has tuned it up to the universe, it pushes it upwards, and the soul "rises at the climax to rapturous incantation, achieving an effect approximate to that of a religious rite" (Allen 1984:52, 54).[18]

The internal structure of the *Ode to Salinas* becomes obvious once we realize that there are only three attributive subjects in its fifty verses: Salinas's music, the soul, and "the grand master," *i.e.*, three harmonies integrated into one. The poem, thus from this limited point of view, appears to be an exemplification of the three levels of music expounded by Boethius:

	Musica	
instrumentalis		*mundana*
(Salinas)		(Grand Master)
wise, skilled hand		dexterous, skillful play,
holy song, sound divine		holy strain of sound
serenity, beauty, light		the very highest sphere

---

[17]The most complete study of Ficino's ideas on art seems still to be that of A. Chastel (1954).

[18]Both D.P. Walker and M.J.B. Allen mention as sources of these Ficinian ideas Plato's *Timaeus* 67a, as well as *Problemata* 19 and 30 by the Pseudo-Aristotle.

humana
(soul)

recovers sense and memory	hears a new mode of music
self-knowledge, nobler thoughts	this immense zither
wings through the fields of air	sees it sustain this temple
concordant numbers	consonant reply
sweetest harmony	sea of sweetness

the soul sails, glides, sinks—drowns, nothing hears or feels
ravishment, collapse, sweet oblivion, bliss, life-giving death
glory of Apollo's sacred choir
Salinas: *your sound*   in *my ears* is   *the divine good*

Any fleeting and superficial reading of the poem could, perhaps, show that Fray Luis wished to give us not only "a description of the effects that music produced in him, restoring in his soul the memory of its origin," what we admit, but also that "it moved him to God's contemplation, the divine musician whose music is the universe" (Jones 1974:164). Contrary to Jones's latter suggestion, the main point of this essay is to reject any strictly speaking mystical connotation in this poem. This apparent mysticism aside, one can, nevertheless, see that the "four cardinal points of the ode are ravishment, sublimation, ecstasy, and return to life" (Vega, in León 1955:17, n. 7). Therefore:

1) the first stanza describes the impression of physical, environmental change (serenity, beauty, luminosity) upon listening to *música extremada*: a *physical* change.

2) the second and third concentrate on the *psychical* change of the soul and its *moral* improvement, to which it invites the listener, and which is not too dissimilar from the first step of the mystical *ascent*, usually called *via purgativa*, nor too alien to what Hegel called "sounding inwardness" of the aesthetic musical experience.[19]

---

[19]"A musician does not abstract content from each and every thing (like a sculptor), but rather finds content in a text that he sets to music, or else, more independently, clothes some mood for himself in the form of a musical theme, which he proceeds to work out further. But the real field of his composition remains a more formal inwardness, pure sounding. And his penetration into the content proceeds not as an outward constructing, but rather as a retiring into the inner life's own freedom. It is a voyaging of the composer within himself" (Dahlhaus 1982:46, quoted from Hegel's *Aesthetics* 1975:II, 266).

3) the fourth, fifth and sixth stanzas—in part analogous to the same kind of *via illuminativa*—summarizes a *philosophical and musical aesthetics* of Pythagorean origin and of a typically Platonic and Augustinian development; it was the ideological foundation of the artistic and poetic interpretations characteristic of Renaissance culture.

4) the seventh and eighth, contrary to some superficial and hasty readings of the ode, do *not* express any strictly speaking mystical ravishment, but rather a sublime, delightful *aesthetic ecstasy* of a non-religious nature *per se*, which is similar to other ecstasies triggered by other aesthetic, or contemplative experiences.

5) the last two stanzas invite us to share that supremely glorious kind of music and its resulting bliss.

Having thus unveiled some of the issues implicit in the first three stanzas, let us now concentrate on the rest. Their content may be summarized under the following two headings, comprising the remaining parts of this essay: the aesthetics and the ecstasy.

II. THE AESTHETICS

As seen in the preceding diagram, the soul is the gravitational center of the ode. It is the soul that "recovers its lost memory and self-knowledge, becomes better and nobler, soars, hears, sees, sends a consonant reply, and then sails on and drowns in that sea of sweetness." In other words, this *Ode to Salinas* is a poetic description of the Platonic concept of the soul, of its position as an intermediary between the ideal and the phenomenal worlds, and its ability to integrate both within its inner self.

Those familiar with Plato's doctrines will not doubt that his most radical idea was the discovery of the soul.

> The soul is invisible and partakes of reason and harmony, and, being made by the best of everlasting and intellectual natures, is the best of things created (1961: *Timaeus*, 37a). Being itself akin to the divine and the immortal and to the eternal being,... consider what it might be if it followed the gleam unreservedly and were raised by the impulse out of the depths of this sea in which it is now sunk (1961: *Republic* X, 661e). Listen then, all ye who but now gave ear to our dis,course... Of all a man has—after his gods—the divinest thing, and the most truly of his own, is his soul (1961: *Laws,* V, 726).

This intermediary position of the soul in the Luisian ode makes it the echo of the cosmos.

No other writer did more than Augustine, after Plato and Plotinus, to clarify and expand this doctrine; his philosophy is dominated by such concepts as *homo interior, acies mentis, memoria*, and requires a process of psychical interiorization as the means to reach the truth—*Ab exterioribus ad interiora, ab interioribus ad superiora* (cf. Alcalá 1957–58:*passim*). No better formulation than this has been found for the Platonic idea expressed by Aristotle in *De anima* 41b, that "anima est quodam modo omnia" ('the soul is in some way every thing'), since its goal is *"per corporalia ad incorporalia* quibusdam quasi passibus certis vel per venire vel ducere."[20] Therefore, when seeking out possible sources of Fray Luis's poem to music, there is no need to go far; besides suspecting that he might have had direct access to Plato and Plotinus, and perhaps to Ficino or other Renaissance Platonizing writers, one should look for his sources in the works of the founder of the religious order, of which he was a member.

Augustine developed his transmission of the ancient theories on music in several treatises; not only in *De Musica Libri Sex,* but in several pages of *Confessiones, De ordine, De Trinitate*, and *Enarrationes in Psalmos*, well known to Fray Luis. He shares many aspects of this ancient theory of music: the role of music in character development, a certain psychologism, the distinction between sense appealing and sense and mind appealing music, and between creator musician and mere—frequently venal—executor, the rules and norms for public singing that Augustine adapted to his ecclesiastical purpose, etc. Carl Johann Perl points out that it was Augustine, who, within the new, joint Platonic and Christian orientation, proposed for the first time "a concept of music that has metaphysical rules. . . therein lies its mystery. For Augustine, creation was not a finite event, but a continual process. Music, creating order from chaos, the new from nothingness, continues the process, and especially if it is 'well done'. . ." [*bene modulandi*] (1955:501).[21] Perl goes on to say that, according to Augustine, music contributes to the highest possible human activity, namely, restoring the universal harmony originally broken since the fall of the angels. Even more, if according to

---

[20]Augustine, *Retractationes* I.6 (1845:592), translated by Sister M. I. Bogan as "desiring, by definite steps, so to speak, to reach things incorporeal through things corporeal and to lead others to them" (Augustine 1968:21). Menéndez Pelayo (1940:II, 209) thought that these words summarize most aptly the Platonic *Symposium*.

[21]It is perhaps convenient to remember that C.J. Perl translated Boethius's *De Musica* into German for the first time (published in Strassburg in 1937). Concerning Augustine and Music, the new book edited by R.L. La Croix (1988) is highly recommended.

Wisdom 11:21, God "arranged all things by measure and number and weight," *in mensura et numero*, the genesis of music preceded Creation, since the proportions of music have already been utilized by the Creator of all things when He made the world. Music was thus created before time!" (*Ibid*:504). It is a sad paradox, therefore, that the musical ecstasy, which some music may cause, lasts only temporarily.

> Music becomes a symbol of time, time a symbol of life. The great Saint himself found no more apt an icon for the meaning of the world than music, according to the principle on which the world itself was created. The order present in the world, which shall be complete only in eternity, transforms itself in sound and becomes the art of humanity. The paradox that music is the oldest of the arts and yet passes irretrievably with time, cannot reduce its stature, since it is the only art that will remain unto eternity (*Ibid.*:510).[22]

An interesting difference within this philosophy, or rather theology, of music may be found between Ambrose of Milan and Augustine of Hippo, rightly noted by Spitzer. Though it is true that the concept of harmony of the universe, based on one of the beginning sentences in the Bible, *et vidit Deus quod erat bonum* (Gen. 1:18 and 25), is common to most Church Fathers, Ambrose prefers, says Spitzer, the richness and plenitude of the cosmos to be expressed in the polyphony (*sic!*) of the beautiful hymns composed by him for his church, while Augustine, who, in part, owed his conversion to Ambrose, stresses the monodic response, the manifestation of the cosmic order in the lineal succession of time. This premise would have inspired Augustine to use Pythagorean theories, to be sensitive to a tragic conception of the rise and fall of civilizations, to emphasize memory and duration—long before Bergson—that only memory can embrace the totality of what is in itself discursive, temporal, like an event, a poem, a melody, and reduce them to internal unity. However, it is possible that Spitzer went too far in hinting a double vision and dimension of Western culture: the Ambrosian view, more visual, more theatrical, would have culminated in the great works of Baroque and Romantic taste by Calderón and

---

[22]"As a matter of fact, Augustine is one of the most comprehensive sources for information concerning neo-Pythagorean number theory, and he misses few opportunities to discuss the science" (Hopper 1969:79). One of the best works on this topic is C. Butler (1970), who devotes successive chapters to the Greek, Patristic, and Renaissance periods, to the case of Johannes Kepler (1571–1630), to the scientific numerology and its aesthetic presuppositions, and to modern numerical symbolism (cf. Werner 1966).

Wagner, while the more auditive Augustinian view would have found its climax in writers and composers who are more inclined "to live in the cell of meditation." It seems doubtful that such an hypothetical "vigor of the basic polarity Augustine-Ambrose" has ever taken such a strong place in history. Anyhow, those who admire Fray Luis will find it rewarding to read how the great German philologist, on comparing the *Ode to Salinas* with other Luisian texts, concludes by stating that it has "the technique of synesthesia of Ambrose plus the unification and inwardness of Augustine; in this classic Spanish mystic (*sic!*) of the sixteenth century, Ambrose, Augustine, and the new humanism with its regained sense of worldwideness converge" (Spitzer 1963:28, 32–33, 115).

This welcome convergence may, perhaps, also be noticed in the use of other poetic term in the ode: "inmensa cítara" and "eterno templo." While the former suggests Augustinian inspiration, the latter makes Fray Luis an heir to the Ambrosian vision of world as spectacle. One should relate other Luisian odes with this more ecstatic conception, especially those entitled *Noche serena* and *A Felipe Ruiz*. The same basic attitude adds nostalgia to the realization of the abyss between the beauty of the heavens and the vulgarity of daily struggle, the soul, always the soul, being in the middle: "Las almas inmortales /hechas a bien tamaño/ ¿podrán vivir de sombras y de engaño?." But the terminology of both odes repeatedly uses verbs like *ver* and *mirar* ('seeing' and 'looking') as an invitation either to contemplate the nocturnal spectacle–"Ay, levantad los ojos /a esta celestial eterna esfera!"-or to effect a moral betterment –"¿Quién es el que esto mira / y precia la bajeza de la tierra?"–or even more to try to solve the great cosmic enigmas precisely *viendo*, seeing "la verdad pura sin duelo." On the contrary, the *Ode to Salinas* offers a conjunction between *oir* and *ver* ('hearing' and 'seeing'): the universe, for Fray Luis, is at the same time "this immense zither" whose "imperishable music" the soul *hears*, and "this eternal temple" that the souls *sees* sustained by it. The inner laws of cosmos are, therefore, of musical, numerical, and mathematically dynamic nature. The soul *hears and sees*.[23]

[23]A pertinent comment by P. Friedländer (1958:188): "This combination of astronomy with music is a special exemplary case—already recognized by Pythagoreans and most important for Plato" of the unity and kinship among the individual sciences, the *methods* of which lead to the final goal. The souls see and hear this cosmos of sidereal revolutions and pure sounds in the world beyond. And thus they are near the highest kind of knowledge. The vision of the highest images themselves is reached in the *Phaedrus*. In the *Republic* it is only suggested in a reference to what the soul of the good man beholds in its journey to heaven: 'views of inconceivable beauty' (615a)."

It is well known that this Pythagorean concept continued well into the Renaissance.[24] But a remarkable point, often forgotten by the critics, refers to the fact that Fray Luis does not mention in this ode the so-called "music of the spheres"; he only speaks of the imaginary trip of the soul "piercing the air" till it reaches "the highest sphere" and there sees and hears the "great master" play. It seems that what he took from the aesthetic substratum of so many Renaissance treatises and poems was indeed sufficient to give his literary creation a flavor of the period, a common source of inspiration. On the other hand, several studies have emphasized the correlation between the system of poetic atmosphere and the structure of this ode, on the one hand, and those of parallel texts in other of his works, on the other. Fray Luis did not only look for the soul's harmony and order to attune it to the body's, if the latter is also attuned to itself and to nature; the whole of his work is like a great symphony whose *leit-motifs* return time and again. For Fray Luis the world is a "temple of clarity and beauty" (*Noche serena*), but also a chain, an imprisonment, and a jail from which the soul must free itself.[25] It is even more important to note that many sentences in his best works, *The Names of Christ* and the *Exposition of the Book of Job*, are so similar to the concise poetic expressions in this *Ode to Salinas*, that many critics

---

[24]For instance, to quote a text from a book as frequently mentioned as seldom read, those pages by León Hebreo [= Judah Abravanel (c.1460–c.1521)] (1947:92–93), where he speaks of the common nature and essence of heavens, planets, and stars that "en sus movimientos y actos se corresponden con tanta proporción que de diversos se hace *una armonial unión*," so that "Pitágoras decía que, moviéndose los cuerpos celestiales, engendraban excelentes voces, correspondientes la una a la otra *en concordancia armoniana*" [italics are mine]. There is perhaps no better book on the whole topic of Renaissance Pythagoreanism than the remarkable exploration done by S. K. Heninger, Jr. (1974), with the only regret of its extremely poor knowledge of Spanish representatives, as though Spain had indeed been a country without a Renaissance.

[25]F. Rico coincides with A. Guy (1960) in stating that the following famous text from *The Names of Christ* is "todo Fray Luis": "The perfection of all things is that each one of us strives to be a perfect world so that in this way, I being in everything and everything being in me, and I having my being, we all embrace and link this whole universal mechanism and reduce the multitude of differences to a unity, and so without being mixed we touch each other, converse, harmonize, and being many we are not, showing and displaying before us variety and diversity so that unity may conquer, rule, and place its domination in all" (1984:44; Spanish text in García 1951:396 and in Cuevas 1982:155). O. Macrí tries to reduce to a system some of those typical expressions in the odes, like "You broke my chain," "Break, Queen of heavens, this chain," "Breaking the pure air," "Free from this prison," "In this low jail," etc. (1970:86–87). Well-known antitheses, like *suelo-cielo* or *mar-puerto* ('earth-heaven, sea-port') are characteristic of the Luisian poetry and of his prose style as well.

believe all three were written at about the same time or that some chapters in *Names* and *Job* are a deliberate commentary on the latter.[26]

What was said above concerning Fray Luis's limited use of certain ancient concepts—more poetic than scientific—can and must be applied to the verse, wherein "extreme music" awakens the soul from oblivion of its "splendid origin" to memory. It would be preposterous to associate this idea of Platonic inspiration with the old doctrine of the preëxistence of the soul, even with the modification proposed by Augustine's theory called *traducianismus*. Augustine transmitted to Christian tradition the Platonic idea that man is, above all, soul: "Homo anima rationalis est, mortali atque terreno utens corpore." To better explain the generative transmission of original sin he proposed the hypothesis that each soul is like an offshoot of the soul of the parents, like a light which is rekindled by another: "tamquam lucerna de lucerna," and thus the parents pass to their offsprings, by generation, the sin of Adam as well as a soul (Fraile 1955:II, 220, 222). Fray Luis, a great Scholastic, but modern Catholic theologian, could not harbor any doubt about God's immediate creation of each individual soul. Consequently, the Luisian "memory of its primordial origin" may not be associated with the *anamnesis* so dear to Plato's theory of ideas, a myth upon which he tried to solve some hard problems of metaphysics of knowledge.[27] It is evident that in the second and third stanzas of the ode Luis can only allude—though with some Neoplatonic hints—to the psychological self-concentration and inwardness, a precondition for the invitation to

---

[26]M. Menéndez Pelayo (1940:II,102) says that his text in praise of peace in *The Names*, "Prince of Peace (León 1984:212; 1951:585) looks like a commentary to his *Ode to the music of the blind Salinas*" (sic!); this is repeated by D. Alonso (1962:185), L. Spitzer (1963:113); and C. Cuevas (1982:406). It is interesting to compare with the ode these two prose texts: "A cornerstone is a sound contribution to a building, and a string properly tuned helps an instrument played by a clever musician and the whole sound is sweet and harmonious. In the same manner our soul at peace with itself harmonizes with God and helps create a climate of peace and goodwill among all of us" (*The Names* 1984:221; 1951:594; 1982:416–7). "And [Job] calls silent nights '*music from heaven*,' because, when the day noise hushes and all things pause, clearly we see and in some way hear their admirable concert and harmony, and I don't know how it resounds in the secret depths of the heart that it becomes quiet and calm" ("Expos. del libro de Job" in León 1951:1244, my own translation and italics).

[27]Plato deals with knowledge—or universal, necessary, and abstract thinking—as *reminiscence* in *Meno*, 81, *Phaedus*, 249b-c, *Phaedo*, 72c-75, and *Republic*, 476a and 507b.

moral betterment, that is induced by good, *extreme music*.[28] Literary critics with no theological training tend to point to some of Plato's texts as the main sources of certain Luisian expressions, while the best of his moral inspiration, and, to some extent, his terminology is to be found in Augustine.

"This immense zither." Why zither and not lyre? Again, for a series of influences: arcane readings, or perhaps a certain tradition in selecting a term that might be deemed poetically capricious. In this detail, as in others, critics have established predecents that run from the prestige of Apollo's zither as symbol of the universe—Apollo's mention as mythical father of Pythagoras having been so frequent—to either direct or indirect impact from the Pythagorean or Platonic traditions, like the verse "Tu coelum totum canora cithara temperas" from an Orphic hymn translated by Ficino in his *Theologia Platonica*, or readings from Macrobius, Boethius, or others.[29] The Greek concept of interplanetary spaces as musical intervals and their correlation with the sound of the

---

[28]It is for this reason that recent attempts, as A. Huerta's (1979:669–78), to interpret the climax of this ode as an incipient catharsis or moral purification, appear incorrect. If music for Fray Luis would only serve the same pedagogical or educational purpose as it did for Plato or Aristotle, we should not bother to waste our time in the present commentary or in so many others.

[29]See some of these sources in F. Rico (1970), O. Macrí (1970) and E. Orozco Díaz (1954). Regarding Macrobius (fl. c. 400 A.D.), it has been written by W. S. Stahl (1952:10) that his In somnium Scipionis, a commentary on the famous piece by Cicero, was, even more than Cicero's work, "the most important source of Platonism in the Latin West in the Middle Ages"; similar was the influence of his *Saturnalia*, especially II, 3, and other texts. One instance: after identifying Apollo with the Sun, it is said in I, 19, 7 that "as Apollo presides over the Muses, so speech, a function of the Muses, is bestowed by Mercury"; and in I, 19, 15: "In the seven strings of Apollo's lyre one may see a reference to the movements of the seven celestial spheres, which nature has placed under the control of the Sun" (Cicero 1969:134–5). Contrary to what F. Lázaro says (1979:II, 283), quoting another scholar, it is very possible, as insinuated by O. Macrí (1970:332), that Fray Luis could have familiarized himself with Macrobius from a commentary to it by his colleague Bartolomé Barrientos published in Salamanca in 1570.

A secondary problem of textual criticism will not affect us here: whether the stanza about the "great master" is authentic or not. Its absence from some important manuscripts (listed in O. Macrí 1970:113)) has always worried critics .Perhaps, according to Macrí, the poet himself suppressed it because some readers could see in it an allusion to Plato's concept of a demiurgic architect in *Timaeus*, "too risky if meaning *Deus sive natura*, a divine being Pythagorically immanent in the matter of an eternal world." A more simple hypothesis could do: somebody—perhaps Fray Luis himself—felt that this stanza, though extremely beautiful, interrupted the rhythmic flow and the grammatical sequence of the poem between the preceding and following ones. Anyhow, most current critics admit this stanza as being authentic, and it is usually printed as such.

lyre's strings led, on one hand, to formulate the poetic theory of "the music of the spheres," and on the other, to think of those strings as analogous with the harmony of the universe. A little known precedent could also be Plato's predilection in Greek tragedies for the zither over the flute, considered by him extremely exciting and unconducive to peacefulness (Plato 1963:*Gorgias*, 501e; *Republic* III, 399d).

But Fray Luis's use of "immense zither" seems to recall Augustinian reminiscences. One of the most curious speculations in Christian antiquity postulated that the verticality of the lyre should exclusively allegorize the soul's rapid ascent to God, while the zither's curvature, as well as the difference of its material, would better symbolize a tortuous one: the struggle of spirit and flesh and its commitment to the meaning of creation and even incarnation, since the zither's strings and body form the sign of a cross. This theory by Hippolytus was opposed by Prosper of Aquitaine and our Augustine, both of whom taught that the lyre should be used to accompany music conceived for God's glorification, and the zither for music reflecting man's earthly existence. They even suggested the zither's exclusive use for penitential songs, while the lyre was more appropriate for songs in divine praise.[30] Therefore, we should not arbitrarily narrow nor widen the meaning of "zither" in this immortal ode, since a poet as exact as Fray Luis does not write blindly: "Aquesta inmensa cítara" and "this eternal temple" of the universe comprise everything created, from the created human nature

---

[30]M. F. Bukofzer (1942:168). Pertinent quotations are: "Aes nimirum in cithara et lyra inferius resonat adversus plectrum; psalterium autem ejusmodi, superius harmonici numeri habet causas, ut nos etiam supera quaerentes commentemur, neque musicae delectatione abripuamur ad carnis affectionem" (Hyppolytus, In *Psalmos*, VI;1857:715–18). "Psalterium est de superioribus laudans Dominum; cithara est de inferioribus laudans Deum, tamquam de coelestibus et terrestribus, tamquam eum qui fecit coelum et terram. . ., cithara lignum inferius habet" (Augustine, *Enarrat.* in Ps. l50,3; 1845b:1964). "Ut psalterio coelestia, cithara autem terrestria laudentur, quia cavum illud lignum supra quod chordarum resultat extensio, in psalterio superius, in cithara habetur inferius" (Prosper, *Psalmus 150*; 1846:425). C. J. Perl (1955:499) documents some of these allegorical imaginations, and quotes a beautiful Augustinian text from *Enarrat. in Psal. 56*. In this context, we should perhaps not be too concerned with some confusions between lyre, zither, and psalter in the quoted texts.

Nancy Van Deusen has recently dealt with this exotic topic (1988). It might be true that Cassiodor (c.490–c.585), contrary to Augustine—always intent to stress the universal 'concert of the universe'—"emphasizes the separate and distinct qualities of each particular instrument and the materials out of which instruments are made" (p. 91), but she herself gives us a text by Cassiodor, who in fact was a compiler of Augustinian doctrine, that shows him sharing the Augustinian concept of the cithara: "Psalterium ad morum pertinet probitatem, cithara ad afflictionem corporis et dolorem, per haec ostendens et actus laudabiles et gloriosissimam passionem" (p. 83).

of the incarnated Word to the miseries of human existence, excited and invited by the serene audition of *música extremada* to join the cosmic harmony played by the *gran maestro*.

But who is this "grand master"? The classic opposition between composer and executor, equivalent to that between *poietés*, creator, and *demiourgós*, craftsman, technician (Spitzer 1963:8) found in the Middle Ages its correlation in the opposition between theologian and *lector* or reader. It is not strange to find texts, like one by Tinctoris (1455–1511)(1978:IIa, 10), the Flemish musicologist at the service of the Naples king, Ferrante, where Christ himself is called *summus ille musicus*, or in others, *doctor in arte citharisandi* (Stevens 1961:59 and 71). However, it would even exceed the Luisian systematic Christocentrism to put Christ himself as the grand master of the cosmic zither. Accepting the Augustinian allegory for the poem in no way implies Christ either as "poet" or "technician," at least not in the exclusively aesthetic level where the ode functions and works. The whole of its language is only meaningful within a certain systematic aesthetics, and, as it will be shown, it carries the soul to an aesthetic, not to a religious, supernatural, nor mystical ecstasy. This "grand master" is, therefore, God at the natural level of the harmonious natural laws. It is enough that Fray Luis's hypersensitive soul has been moved to such a musical ecstasy after *seeing* and *hearing* them reflected in his friend's *extreme music*.

Some attention should now be devoted to this curious "wholly different mode" of music, that the soul *hears* "in the very highest sphere." It would simply be misunderstood by translating it as just 'a new kind of music.' *Mode* is a technical term in musicology. Its concept and history have been rather confused and Fray Luis, a disciple of Salinas in "música especulativa," must have known this well.

It should not be forgotten that Plato himself, who looked upon the Ionian and Lydian modes of the music of his time as effeminate, approved of the Dorian and Phrygian as virile and apt for adolescent education (Plato 1963: *Republic*, III, 398e–399a).[31] Mode and tone, clearly differentiated by Ptolomy, were then confused by Boethius, and this confusion affected the majority of Medieval theoreticians, as Salinas wrote in plain language: "Quos recentiores vocant tonos magis proprie dicendi sunt modi" (Salinas 1958:185). According to him, for

---

[31]See also, for instance, his various allusions to the myth of the charioteer in *Phaedrus* 246, 251, 255c; and M. Ficino 1973:47.

instance, the octave transposition of a melody does not bring about any strict difference in mode or in musical effects: "Mutatio sola secundum tonum non inmutat animi affectionem" (*Ibid.*:199). Another concept of *mode* is that employed in Gregorian chant, which retained the same melodic classification of eight, but each based on a different *finalis* than those employed by Boethius. During the Ars Antiqua the rhythmic modes were divided into six: "Modus in musica est debita mensuratio temporis, scilicet per longas et breves," according to an anonymous writer (Waite 1954:13). But here another perspective is even more important: *otro modo* can not but mean the concept of the ancient theory coming from Pythagoras, Plutarch, Nichomacus, and Macrobius, and expanded in the Renaissance by Ficino and countless writers— whether directly read by Fray Luis or not is still pending investigation— according to which each of the planets produced a particular musical "mode," and a different identifying note, under the influence of a different Muse, all of whom are presided by Apollo (Walker 1953:144; now 1985:VIII, 144; Heninger, Jr. 1974:178–81). By stating that "the soul hears an entirely different mode of music produced by the playing of 'el gran maestro,'" Fray Luis hints that "el gran maestro" is also a particularly different kind of God.

One may conclude, then, that this "otro modo de música" and this "son sagrado," which are *heard* and *seen* by the triggering of "música extremada" and by the psychic and moral effects it produces, is undoubtedly a "new mode," one which perhaps was not suspected by Salinas, who accepted and taught Glareanus's theory which differentiated nothing less than twelve modes, and which did not take the octave as its criterion, but rather the internal division in 5ths and 4ths or in 4ths and 5ths (León Tello 1962:617). That this "otro modo" may constitute a different mode for Salinas, does not bear the same meaning for Fray Luis, because the ontological analogy of the "son sagrado" that sustains nature's "eterno templo" essentially implies "números concordes." The analogy of concordances between Salinas or any good musician's *musica instrumentalis*, *musica humana*, and that "other mode" of *musica mundana*, is the ultimate reason for the ecstasy produced by their integration in a universal concert. Thus, one may see that this *Ode to Salinas* rests on a complicated aesthetic of an ancient origin, typical of the Renaissance, but difficult if not impossible to define, the core of which was provided for Fray Luis by the writings of Plato, Augustine, and Salinas himself. Fray Luis was familiar with the spirit and the letter of the remote sources of his wise musician colleague in Salamanca before the latter published his *De Musica Libri Septem*.

III. THE ECSTASY

Whether Fray Luis deserves to be considered as one of the great sixteenth-century Spanish mystics has been much discussed. It is astonishing to realize that critics without a technical theological education tend to affirm, even with some grain of obstinate aggressiveness, that he was one of the greatest, while those endowed with such an education, hesitate or sound more moderate. "It is evident," one of his best biographers wrote, "that he was one of those who went farthest up in mysticism, so that the number of Spaniards deserving to be called mystics must be greatly restricted if his works don't qualify as such" (Bell 1927:249).

Of course, it must be restricted, in the same way as is the concept of mysticism itself or rather of mystical experience. Strictly speaking, a person's mystical experience is the consciousness that he or she has of an essential and immediate union of his or her soul with God, a spiritual state that—in the West and in the East, where its object is either a personal God or the totality of nature conceived as divine—is usually expressed in erotic terms. Several critics with some taste for these topics confuse mysticism with simple religiosity, and mystical literature with literature that is just religious literature. The above-mentioned discussion originated in the equivocal use of these terms. Fray Luis never tells us explicitly whether he was ever an experimental mystic, whether he ever reached those experiences; of course, he is not merely an ascetic writer, because they are described in many of his writings in Biblical, Patristic, and even philosophical terms as clearly as anyone can— which makes him an important theoretical mystic writer. Although certain passages in his writings hint at personal mystical experiences, this matter is never completely clear; and though this is also true of two or three of his odes, it does not apply to our *Ode to Salinas*.[32]

Most mystic writers did, of course, employ a terminology of love very similar to that of Fray Luis in the climax of this ode: bliss, ravishment, oblivion, collapse, death, and others; but it would be a grave mistake to take them at their face value as a definitive criterion of

---

[32]Easily accessible information on this matter can be found in E.A. Peers (1942–3), C. de Jesús (1942), D. Gutiérrez (1976), M. Durán (1971:81ss.), and in several chapters of A.C. Vega (1963).

mystical experience. Our ode does have some expressions similar to some in *The Dark Night* and *The Living Flame of Love*, those sublime poems by the best mystical poet ever, St. John of the Cross (d. 1591): both oversensitive poets strive to speak of the ineffability of an ecstasy in their own way and in analogous terms at their reach, but this similarity does not show that both deal with a mystical ecstasy. An overly equivocal concept of ecstasy has added confusion to the usually equivocal concept of mysticism. It is for such an analogous use of similar terms that our ode "smacks of" mysticism to some critics not well versed in these matters. Mysticism does not have anything to do with the transcendent power attributed to music by the aesthetic tradition that this ode evokes, or vice versa. Like every literary text, including those mystical poems by St. John, our ode must be studied in its own terms, although it is both licit and necessary to trace its links to Fray Luis' total philosophical, religious, and poetic system.[33]

Fray Luis, therefore, has synthesized in this ode his personal experience of a musical ecstasy, though sharing terms used by dozens of philosophers, poets, and mystics of his time for different purposes. No poem about music, either in Spanish or in any other language, not even those that have the same aesthetic presuppositions, is as ecstatically explicit. What for so many poets of his time, and afterwards, was just a cathartic culmination—like in "To Musik" by Robert Herrick (1591–1674) (Howard 1927:33)—or a mere assumption of worn out common places—like verses as "From harmony, from heavenly harmony, / this universal frame began" in "Song for St. Cecilia's Day" by John Dryden (1631–1700) (Noyes 1946:107–9)—is transcended by Fray Luis as just an initial step in his ascensional flight towards his "desmayo dichoso," towards his Petrarchically paradoxical "life-giving death" and "sweet oblivion." The same conclusion may be reached by comparing this poem with others written by strict contemporaries of Fray Luis.[34] World litera-

[33]It is in this respect that a recent book by José C. Nieto seems worth mentioning: *San Juan de la Cruz, poeta del amor profano* (San Lorenzo de El Escorial: Swan, Avantos & Hakeldama, 1988). It supersedes his previous, important work, *Mystic, Rebel, Saint: A Study of St. John of the Cross* (Geneva: Droz, 1979) as well as the amplified Spanish edition, *Místico, poeta, rebelde, santo: en torno a San Juan de la Cruz* (Mexico: Fondo de Cultura Económica, 1982).

[34]For instance, Maurice Scève (c. 1501–c.1564) addressed to music the following verses, from a fragment of *Le microcosme* quoted by A.-M. Schmidt (1939:153), that L. Spitzer (1963:145)—fortunately for Spanish literature—valued "among the most beautiful verses in French poetry," nothing less:

Musique, accent des cieux, plaisante symphonie,
par contraires aspects formant son harmonie. *[continued]*

ture has never produced a poem to music that, to admirable poetic qualities, adds such a personal confession of ecstasy. For this reason, the fact that the best critical commentaries, even in Spanish, have either completely omitted this essential dimension of the *Ode to Salinas* or not stressed it enough, constitutes a rather strange and scandalous paradox.[35]

The literary expression of this ecstatic musical experience has, of course, antecedents that may have inspired Fray Luis, independent from the originality of his thinking and the authenticity of his bliss. One must go back to the frequent mention by Plato of the four *enthousiasmoi* or *furores* that can seize the soul, either individually as steps of elevation to the divine, or historically as periods of its revelation. Omitting now the different order in which they were enumerated in *Phaedrus*, *Ion*, and *Symposium* studied by M. J. B. Allen (1984:47), those spiritual steps or moments of enthusiasm, furor or *madness* are for Plato: the poetic and musical, the prophetic, the hieratic or mysterial, and the amorous, love ecstasy always at the top of all Platonic values, summit of all the experiences of the soul and of human progress. These successive degrees of ascension allow men to reconquer the interior unity of their soul broken by its descent at the time of its incarnation and incarceration in matter.

Plato himself proposed what his foremost Renaissance propagandist, Ficino, translated, amplified, and systematized: among other points, the dependence of each of those *furori* upon a provident god. Mercury is, thus, to be credited with the stimulus to inquire, Apollo with the light to see profoundly, Minerva with the strength to attain, Dionysus with making possible that souls *mentes excedere videantur*, while the muses inspire the harmonious order of the universe, and Venus incites to love (Allen 1981:119, text of *Commentarium in Phaedrum*, cap. X; Ficino 1973:149, from *Sopra l'amore*, VII, 14). On the other hand, the supremacy attributed by Ficino to hearing moves him to confer artistic primacy to music and ecstatic priority to the *furor*

De discordant accord mélodieux tesmoins
par les proportions des mouvements celestes
soulageant icy bas nos cures plus molestes.
[35]This is particularly true of the book by O. Macrí (1970), not so much of F. Rico (1970), because the latter, intent to show the Spanish fortune of the idea of man-microcosm that, as we have also proved, stands as the nucleus of this ode, ends his commentary in the sixth stanza.

poeticus associated with it. Prophecy belongs to knowledge, mystery to imagination, and music to hearing, thus being subsequent to prophetic revelation and to priestly function:

> Whoever feels overwhelmed by the divine, just because of the vehemence of the emotion and the plenitude of its jerk, overflows, bolts out, breaks forth, and exceeds human limits and habits *(finesque et mores humanos excedit)*. . . But none of those furies remains a mere word. They burst into chants and songs, so that any of them—either the fateful, or the mysterial, or the amatory—rightly seem to resolve into poetry just because all of them culminate in music. And since poetic song and all verse require harmony, and since harmony is reduced to the nine muses, therefore they were rightly consecrated to them (Ficino, *Ibid.*, cap. IV, p. 85).

It is also known that the muses were usually called Apollo's choir, following writers like Macrobius and Fulgentius's *Mythologiae*, since a double role was attributed to him, leader of the muses and ruler of the planets (Seznec 1961:177–8). Graphic illustrations of this, such as Franchino Gafori's in his *Practica Musicae* (Milan, 1496), reproduced by Jean Seznec (p. 135) and by S. K. Heninger, Jr. (1974:182–3) (see Plate 2), were extremely popular, so much that, as the latter says (p. 368), a "visual image of the nine muses under the direction of Apollo was a conventional depiction of cosmic harmony."[36]

All this Platonic doctrine will make it possible to explain both the selection of terms used by Fray Luis in the last stanzas of his ode and the traditional roots of the musical ecstatic experience that it describes.

Ecstasy is another term which has an unclear and nondistinct meaning. For a certain author it is "in the broad sense, any excited condition of the emotions," and therefore, according to an eloquent text by Nietzsche that he does not document, poetry will not be possible at all without some kind of ecstasy; poetry is the literature of ecstasy, so

---

[36]In this respect the coincidence of Fray Luis with another French contemporary of his is very curious. Pontus de Tyard (c.1522–1605), a rather popularizing poet of La Pleiade, wrote in *Solitaire Premier* (sic) *ou prose des Muses et de la fureur poétique:* ". . . Et de ce faire est pour son peculier devoir la fureur poétique chargée, resveillant par les tons de Musique l'ame en ce qu'elle est endormie, et confortant par la suavité et douceur de l'harmonie la partie perturbée: puis par la diversité bien accordé des Musiciens accords chassant la dissonante discorde, et enfin reduissant le desordre en certaine égalité et proportionnement mesurée et compartie par le gracieuse, et grave facilité des voix compassez en curieuse observance des nombres et mesures" (quot. by H. Weber 1956:34).

that every literature produced in an emotive manner is in itself poetic.[37] A much more restricted and precise meaning is offered in the famous, pioneering book by Marghanita Laski, for whom ecstasy comprises "a range of experiences characterized by being joyful, transitory, unexpected, rare, valued, and extraordinary to the point of often seeming as if derived from a preternatural source" (1961:5). Fray Luis did not err in confessing that the stimulus—what Laski calls *trigger*—of his musical ecstasy was sensing or experiencing that air itself became serene and "robed in beauty and unknown light." Plato said that the soul has wings (*Phaedrus* 246, 251, 255c: various allusions to the myth of the charioteer): its wings are those four ecstasies—enthusiasms, furies, madnesses—that make it fly "through the fields of air," that quadruple divine fury that, according to Ficino, "innalza l'uomo sopra l'uomo e in Dio lo converte" (1973:147). Music is one of those wings, being, as we saw, the culmination of the muses, the most sublime perhaps. Nietzsche (1968:614) meant this in another of his eloquent texts, even though— because written in praise of Wagner, whom he afterwards repudiated— it might just have circumstantial value: "Has it been noticed that music liberates the spirit? gives wings to thought? that one becomes more of a philosopher the more one becomes a musician?—The gray sky of abstraction rent as if by lightning; the light strong enough for the filigree of things;the great problems near enough to grasp; the world surveyed as from a mountain" (*Ibid.*).

It is from these old perceptions, coming at least from Plato and transmitted by Ficino, but sifted through centuries of theological rumination on Christian mysticism, that four fields can now be specified wherein recurrences of ecstatic attitudes can be easily differentiated: the contemplative, mystical, aesthetic, and erotic. Their triggers would be respectively: 1) the silent, especially deep reflection (mental contemplation, absorption in scientific research, etc.); 2) the feeling of an essential union between soul and God overpowering the basic religious feeling of divine transcendence and of human depen,dence; 3) the intuition of cosmic connections implicit in some extreme works of

---

[37]A. Mordell (1969:23 and 170). Nietzsche's text reads: "To the existence of art, to the existence of any aesthetic activity or perception whatsoever, a preliminary psychological condition is indispensable, namely ecstasy" (quoted by Mordell, *Ibid.*, 28). Such a radical conclusion is then summarized in these terms: "Neither verse poetry, nor the prose literature of ecstasy is the highest literature necessarily. . . When we have a description of emotions, we have poetry or the literature of ecstasy" (*Ibid.*, 178). It has been impossible to verify the accuracy of Nietzsche's quotation.

art—especially in the realm of music, painting, and poetry—and in nature, such as being enraptured by a particularly moving landscape; and 4) certain cases of human love in sexual surrender by mutual consent.

A more complete treatment of this point should stress that these four ecstasies, being dimensions or attitudes of the highest possible spiritual accomplishment, must necessarily share common existential aspects and touch some common human ground, which, in turn, explains why those writers, who have described one or the other ecstasy, have always used—as if in a synaesthetic manner—terminologies and descriptions taken from descriptions of other ecstasies. For instance, mystics use erotic terms, and not only *courtly love* poets, but all love poets, use mystical expressions. Now, it is obvious that both music and poetry fall within the ecstasy mentioned in the third category, both of which offer unlimited possibilities for triggering ecstatic ravishment. In his ode, Fray Luis employs certain words common to the poets of love as well as to mystic writers such as Saint John of the Cross, but his trigger was neither an introspective contemplation nor a feeling of losing himself in the sea of divine or human love. *Música extremada* was enough to make him sail in "a sea of sweetness."[38]

Much to the point, and worth mentioning, is Marghanita Laski's distinction between ecstasy of intensity and of withdrawal, that is, the *desmayo dichoso*, the *dulce olvido* of our Fray Luis. She also mentions a certain text wherein Freud speaks of an *oceanic feeling*, of a certain ecstatic experience of seeming to float in water, which she associates with ecstasies of withdrawal more than with those of intensity (1961:69 and 54). Behold, again, the exact Luisian expression. Luis's soul sails in this sea, wherein it sinks so much so that it "hears or feels nothing that foreign accident reveals." As has been rightfully observed by most critics, Fray Luis maintains the same technical terminology—so expressive and useful because of its metaphorical value—when dealing with the strictly mystical ecstasy of the spouse soul upon reaching the *summum* pleasure of its union with God. Few of his texts could be more eloquent than his moving description of this mystical ecstasy in certain

---

[38]Prof. E. Rivers, the eminent hispanist and Renaissance scholar, is quite right in pointing out in his beautiful booklet (1983:65) that the word *allí* ('there') of v. 18 changes to a significant *aquí* ('here'), in v.26, thus giving a feeling of immediacy with the music played by the "grand master"; but, if the present analysis is correct, he would be wrong in insisting, like most critics, that this *mar de dulzura* is "a new metaphor of mystic rapture." Rapture, yes, but not mystic.

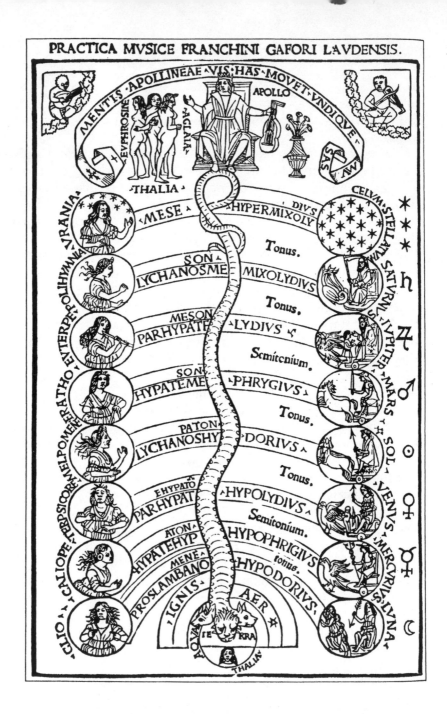

Plate 2. Frontispiece of Franchino Gafori's *Pratica Musice* (Milan, 1496)

pages of the most beautiful book he ever wrote, the dialogue entitled *The Names of Christ*:

> Such a pleasure is so subtle that it is not easy to describe. . . Perhaps this in itself is the best proof of the rare and exalted quality of such an experience. The ones that know it the best are the ones that refuse altogether to talk about it. When we experience it we become speechless: Our whole soul is busy and occupied by such intense feeling that we have time for nothing else. . . We seem to withdraw inside ourselves and our limbs and tongue become useless. The same takes place in the mystic rapture (1984:247–48, name "Husband"). . . The marriage of God and our soul is a source of pleasure, delight, and bliss, that nothing can surpass. . . Therefore the Holy Scripture makes use of several images and metaphors when it tries to describe such a unique experience.

He then proceeds to enumerate some: hidden manna, wine, breasts full of milk, sleep, banquet, drunkenness and faint (*embriaguez* and *desmayo*),

> because God's presence in us so overwhelms us that we feel, say, and do things that are not reasonable and are similar to what a drunken person might feel, say, and do. . . The soul is like a vessel with huge sails filled by the winds of love, sailing a sea of honey (*un mar de dulzor*) burning in secret fire (*Ibid.*:252–53).

Any attentive reader may have noticed the confluence of expressions of those great poets of ecstasy, Luis and John of the Cross. Expressions such as "faint, life-giving death, sweet oblivion, [and] extreme music" in the Luisian ode coincide with John of the Cross' "I don't know what," "night sunk in a profound," "music without a sound," "a solitude of cries," "a supper of light hearts," or other metaphors in *The Spiritual Canticle*; with "all senses in oblivion drift away," "among the lilies falling and out of my mind" in his *Dark Night*; and with "O cautery that freshens! O treasure of a wound! O lamps of fire!" in his *Living Flame of Love*.[39] Analogous poetic terms enabled both poets to express,

---

[39]The English version is by J.F. Nims in Saint John of the Cross (1968:6, 21, and 23). The corresponding Spanish expressions are 'un no sé qué,' 'noche sosegada,' 'música callada,' 'soledad sonora,' 'cena que enamora'; 'y todos mis sentidos suspendía,' 'entre las azucenas olvidado'; 'cauterio suave,' 'regalada llaga,' 'lámparas de fuego.' Expressions like these, descriptive of strictly mystical ecstasies, are not rare in several works by Fray Luis, but it would be a gross mistake to interpret the *Ode to Salinas* as mystical, and even as religious, because of the similarity of these expressions.

as far as possible, similar states of spiritual experience, although of different nature, trigger, and content; for Fray Luis an aesthetic musical ecstasy, and for St. John, a mystical one. As far as possible, because such is the eternal paradox of art, especially of poetry and music, which do not handle material, visible, tangible elements, they begin from and end with silence. Both are also exorcists of our inner silence, "the spellcasters who can exorcise *the unbearable silence within us*" (Peterkiewicz: 1970:5). Both proceed, like mysticism, first with the *via negativa* of excluding superfluous factors, then with the *via illuminativa* of activating the passivity of the senses so that "the other side of silence" is revealed *(Ibid.:*97); both culminate in sounds and rhythms that fill up silences and, if they trigger our ecstasies, wind up, in a kind of *via unitiva*, by opening for us a mysterious world of silent sounds, by communicating with them for a moment, making it impossible to describe them to whoever has not experienced them, and finally by returning us to our solitude, which comprises both sound and silence: "Like solitude in the Spanish concept of *soledad*, silence resembles a listening companion rather than a place emptied of all sounds" *(Ibid.:*69).

This inevitable and lamentable *descensus*, the tedious return to noise and company, *mundanal ruido, triste lloro*, and to *aqueste bajo y vil sentido*, had also been described by Plato and Ficino as the loss of soul's wings *(amittere pennas)* and as man's limited duration (Allen 1981:161, text from *Comment. in Phaedrum*, cap. XXIII). "Durase en tu reposo!" ('Now let me never lapse!'). Impossible illusion of the musically ecstatic Fray Luis! Even "música extremada" is not eternal, not like the "no perecedera música" of this "eternal temple." The most he may hope for is to hear it as often as possible, so that his senses being deadened for all else, he might have an illusion of eternity, and then, faithful to the Greek saying, *bonum est diffussivum sui* (quoted by Aquinas in his *Summa* I,5,4), to invite his dear friends to listen, feel, fly, hear, see, and personally, inwardly, and untransferably share *such bliss* *(bien divino)*.

And who are these friends? Commentators keep repeating, without much critical embarrassment, what long ago became popular:those friends of Fray Luis are his Salamancan circle, the so-called *escuela salmantina*, especially Prof. Francisco Sánchez de las Brozas or Brocensis, Juan de Almeida, the rector of the University, Alonso de Espinosa, the imitator of Fray Luis's poetry, and others (García, in León 1951:1438; Macrí 1970:314; Cuevas 1982:42ff., 294, etc.). But is this necessarily true?

First, the traditional reading *amigos*, in plural, seems to be favored, though Mayans in the eighteenth century, then Coster, and recently Woodward almost alone, still read *amigo*, as if addressed only to Salinas. It would be preposterous, however, to affirm with the latter that, although Plato and Augustine have supplied the conceptual framework to Fray Luis for this ode, it is not at all a Neoplatonic poem to music, or "simply a eulogy of musical harmony as such." This topic would be "unremarkable," unworthy of his fame. For Woodward, this is a poem to friendship:

> The movement of the poem now seems to be, schematically: Earthly music/symbolizing friendship leads to heavenly music/symbolizing Divine friendship. . . The theme of the poem is the love of God which embraces the love of a friend. . . In heaven fray Luis has experienced the joy of 'friendship' of God. . . *Vuestro son* (your sound) is not only organic music; it is the harmony of friendship, both human and divine, etc. (Woodward 1962:69, 71–72, and 76).

None of these conclusions can be supported by any strict textual or contextual analysis.

Second, Fray Luis must not have been unique among Salinas's friends to hear him play. If they had the same opportunities, why should the poet invite them—even rhetorically—to attend those celebrated concerts? This unnecessary redundance makes it compelling to widen the circle of his own friends so that it includes the readers of his poem, as well as all lovers of music. Only in this restricted sense could this ode be interpreted as a poem to friendship. Fray Luis calls us all, his friends, to "such bliss." But there is much more, and here one may notice again the usual routine commentary of the verse "glory of Apollo's sacred choir," that has usually been understood as referring to those same friends of Fray Luis' Salamancan circle. Were it so, there would be here not only a "tremendous hyperbole," even more shocking than when saying next that he loves them "sobre todo tesoro" (Woodward *Ibid.*:70). The meaning of the context itself, and of the text, would be broken if such a reading remained. This *bliss*—the musical ecstasy—is the *glory of Apollo's choir*: the muses can never offer us a better gift, no other aesthetic ecstasy is comparable to musical ecstasy, no other bliss from Apollo—the god of the sun, light, intelligence, art—and his choir of muses can be more glorious. And what is even more: though one could agree that Fray Luis may have remembered, in passing, the Biblical passage, "qui amicum invenit illum, invenit thesaurum" ('he that has found one [faithful friend] has found a treasure')(Ecclus. 6:14) one could even feel the temptation to interpret the disputed, hyperbolic "a quien amo sobre todo tesoro" as referring, not to friends, but to "such bliss, glory of Apollo's choir." The lack of a strategic comma after "os llamo" ('I call you') in an important, but rather late, manuscript of the ode could perhaps substantiate this revolutionary claim.[40] Were this interpretation to be admitted, a literal translation and the true meaning of this penultimate stanza would be: "Friends, I call you to this good, glory of Apollo's sacred choir that I love beyond all treasure, because every thing else is a sad crying."

Almost at the end, we should pose a question: In order to start the soul's flight and reach the musical ecstasy, to which Fray Luis calls us, is it indispensable to share the theoretical framework on which he seems to have based his poem? Did he himself believe in it?

Of course not! Let's not forget that the Pythagorean theory of "the music of the spheres" began to be doubted long before the Renaissance, so that musicians and poets alike soon spoke, not of its physical audition that was criticized by Aristotle in his *Politics*, but just of its spiritual, intellectual audition.[41] Ficino himself indicated that Plato assumed that his theories and myths should be interpreted on a poetic, rather than on a philosophical level.[42]

---

[40]Allusion to the so-called Jovellanos Ms, now at the Royal Academy of History in Madrid, according to the facsimile reproduction in A. Barasoain (1973:176). That comma is, nevertheless, grammatically convenient to separate a noun (*bien*) and its first propositional apposition (*gloria*). For the same grammatical justification,it does not seem that the "hyperbole" should be applied to "amigos," but to "este bien, gloria": the following *quien* did not mean only 'who' in ancient Spanish, but also 'what' or 'that,' valid for persons and things; and in "*que* todo lo demás" (meaning 'since everything else') the first word means 'because,' thus making a very clear antithesis between "bien-gloria" and "triste lloro." The reading of "todo lo visible" instead of "todo lo demás—that many good critics hold"would greatly enhance Fray Luis' delicate allusion to Salinas' blindness, as well the importance given to hearing over "lo visible," just seeing.

[41]This interpretation became common among Medieval writers such as Roger Bacon, Johannes de Grocheo, Walter Oddington, and Jacobus de Liège, who said that he maintains this "metaphorica locutio" just "ad excusationem antiquorum," for the excuse of the elders (Bukofzer 1942:166). Similarly, Aurelianus de Reome, a monk of mid-ninth century, ironically wrote that although there is some *harmonia modulationis* in the sky, that sound does not reach our ears, "ad aures nostras sonus ille non pervenit" (León Tello 1962:42). The skepticism might come *from Boethius himself, who in the very text where he speaks of musica mundana* wrote: "Ad nostras aures sonus ille non pervenit, quod multis fieri de causis necesse est." He, nevertheless, did not doubt that the ordered motion of the spheres must produce some musical sound.

[42]According to M.J.B. Allen (1981:75 and 161), who several times stated that Plato wrote "poeticis quibusdam ambagibus," "non tam philosophicam quam poeticam agit personam," "poetica licentia," etc.

The same is, of course, valid for Fray Luis. He uses the Renaissance Neoplatonic aesthetics because of its current poetic, cultural value. As René Wellek wrote in his prologue to Spitzer's book:

> The *musica humana*, the well-tempered man, was or tried at least to be in harmony with the great *musica mundana*, while the *musica instrumentalis* was a means of reconciling microcosm and macrocosm, man with nature—the work or even the composition of God. Without succumbing to superstition or sentimentality we may feel this even today in our deepest experience of music and poetry (Spitzer 1963:ix).

Fray Luis, as a student of music with Salinas, did not ignore that his colleague and teacher adopted in his *De Musica*—probably still in manuscript when this great ode was written—a totally skeptical attitude towards the "no perecedera música, que es de todas la primera" (Salinas 1958:2).

Therefore, the final conclusion is clear: no particular aesthetics is either necessary nor sufficient to make us plunge into the *dichoso desmayo* of an inner, ecstatic musical experience. Why and how is this possible, why and how certain musical compositions and certain poems of 'extreme' perfection captivate the spirit of disparate listeners and readers, either educated or ignorant, why and how music and poetry can transport us into ecstasy, are mysteries that no aesthetic theory has been able to unveil. It is enough to apply to this *Ode* what was most wisely written with regard to the extremely beautiful prose in Fray Luis's *The Names of Christ*: "What we hear, if only our ears are properly attuned to León's sweet words, is music: music from the lofty spheres, heavenly music" (Durán 1971:131).

This ode by Fray Luis about music which entices us all, his friends, to fly with him on the wings of the best available music and to ravish with him in ecstasy, is truly—at least for me—a celestial music.

REFERENCES CITED

Alcalá, Angel

1957–58   "Interioridad y conversión a través de la experiencia de San Agustín," *La Ciudad de Dios* (El Escorial), 120(1957):592–624; 121(1958):375–418

Allen, Michael J. B.

1981   *Marsilio Ficino and the Phaedran Charioteer.*
            Berkeley:University of California Press.

1984   *The Platonism of Marsilio Ficino. A Study of his 'Phaedrus,' Its
            Sources and Genesis.* Berkeley: University of California
            Press.

Alonso, Dámaso

1962   *Poesía española.* Madrid: Gredos.

Antonio, Nicolás

1783–84   *Bibliotheca Hispana Nova.* Madrid: Ibarra.

Aristotle

1931   *De anima* in J. A. Smith, ed., *The Works of Aristotle.* Oxford:
            Clarendon Press.

1946   *The Politics.* Transl., with an intro., notes and appendices by
            Sir Ernest Barker. Oxford: Clarendon Press.

Augustine, Saint

1845   *Retractationum libri duo, De Musica libri sex* in Jacques Paul
            Migne, *Patrologia Latina.* Paris: Migne. Vol. 32.

1845a   *Epistolarum* in *Ibid.,* Vol. 33.

1845b   *Enarrationes in Psalmos* in *Ibid.,* Vol. 37.

1947   "On Music," in *Writings of Saint Augustine.* Vol. 2. Transl. by
            Robert Catesby Taliaferro. New York: Cima.

1955   *Letters* in *Ibid.,* Vol. 4. Transl. by Sister Wilfrid Parsons,
            S.N.D.

1968   *The Retractations* in *Ibid.,* Vol. 6 Transl. by Sister Mary Inez
            Bogan.

Azorín (Martínez Ruiz, José)

1977   *Los dos Luises y otros ensayos.* 4th ed. Madrid: Espasa-Calpe.

Barasoain, Alberto

1973   *Fray Luis de León.* Madrid: Júcar.

Barnstone, Willis

1979   *The Unknown Light. The Poems of Fray Luis de León.* Albany:
            State University Press.

Bell, Audrey F. G.

    1927   *Luis de León. Un estudio del Renacimiento español*. Barcelona: Araluce.

Bishop, John

    1968   *Music and Sweet Poetry*. London: John Baker.

Boethius, Anicius Manlius Severinus

    1847   *De Musica libri quinque* in Jacques Paul Migne, *Patrologia Latina*. Paris: Migne. Vol. 63.

Bowen, William R.

    1988   "St. Augustine in Medieval and Renaissance Musical Science." In Richard L. La Croix, ed. *Augustine on Music* (Lewiston, New York: Mellon), pp. 29–51.

Bukofzer, Manfred F.

    1942   "Speculative Thinking in Medieval Music." *Speculum*, 17(2):165–88

Butler, Christopher

    1970   *Number Symbolism*. London: Routledge & Kegan Paul.

Castiglione, Baldassar

    1937   *Il cortegiano*. In G. Pressolini, ed., *B. Castiglione - G. della Casa. Opere*. Milano: Rizzoli.

Chastel, André

    1954   *Marsile Ficine et l'Art*. Genève et Lille: E. Droz.

Cicero, Marcus Tullius

    1969   *Somnium*. Ed. by Percival Vaughan Davies. New York: Columbia University Press.

Cuán Pérez, Enrique

    1978   "Oda de Fray Luis de León 'a Francisco Salinas': una expresión de unidad y amor," *Religión y Cultura*, 24:701–12

Cuevas, Cristóbal

    1982   *Fray Luis de León y la escuela salmantina*. Madrid: Taurus.

Dahlhaus, Carl

    1982   *Esthetics of Music*. Transl. by William W. Austin. London: Cambridge University Press.

Durán, Manuel
    1971   *Luis de León*. New York: Twayne.

Espinel, Vicente
    1618   *Relaciones de la vida del escudero Marcos de Obregón*. Madrid:
                Juan de la Cuesta.

Eximeno, Antonio
    1873   *Don Lazarillo de Vizcardi. Sus investigaciones músicas con
                ocasión del concurso a un magisterio de capilla vacante*.
                Madrid: Sociedad de Bibliófilos españoles. 2 vols.

Fernández de la Cuesta, Ismael, transl.
    1983   *Francisco de Salinas. Siete libros sobre la música*. Primera
                versión castellana. Madrid: Editorial Alpuerto.

Ficino, Marsilio
    1973   *Sopra lo amore o ver Convito di Platone* [1474?]. Ed. by
                Giuseppe Rensi. Milano: Celuc.

Fraile, Guillermo
    1955   *Historia de la Filosofía*. Madrid: Editorial Católica. Vol. 2

Friedländer, Paul
    1958   *Plato. I. An Introduction*. New York: Pantheon.
    1964   *Plato. II. The Dialogues*. New York: Pantheon.

Gutiérrez, David
    1976   "Fray Luis de León, autor místico." *Religión y Cultura*,
                23:409–33

Guy, Alain
    1960   *El pensamiento filosófico de Fray Luis de León*. Madrid:
                RIALP.

Hanslick, Eduard
    1957   *The Beautiful in Music*. Transl. from German by Gustav
                Cohen. New York: Liberal Arts Press.

Hebreo, León (Judah Abravanel)
    1947   *Diálogos de amor*. Transl. by Inca Garcilaso de la Vega.
                Madrid: Espasa-Calpe.

Hegel, George Wilhelm Friedrich
  1975   *Aesthetics: Lectures on Fine Arts*. Transl. by Thomas Malcolm
          Knox. Oxford: Clarendon Press.

Heninger, S. K., Jr.
  1974   *Touches of Sweet Harmony. Pythagorean Cosmology and
          Renaissance Poetics*. San Marino, California: Henry Hun-
          tington Library and Art Gallery.

Hopper, Vicent Foster
  1969   *Medieval Number Symbolism*. New York: Cooper.

Howard, Esme J. H. S.
  1927   *Music in the Poets*. New York: Brentano.

Huerta, Alberto
  1979   "Katharsis musical en la *Oda a Salinas*." *Religión y Cultura*,
          25:669–78

Hyppolytus
  1857   *In Psalmos*. In Jacques Paul Migne, *Patrologia Graeca*. Paris:
          Migne. Vol. 10.

Jacobs, Arthur
  1948   *Music Lover's Anthology*. London: Winchester.

Jesús, Crisógono de
  1942   "El misticismo de Fray Luis de León." *Revista de
          espiritualidad*, 1:30–52

John of the Cross, Saint (San Juan de la Cruz)
  1968   *The Poems of St. John of the Cross*. English version by John
          Frederick Nims. New York: Grove Press.

Jones, R. O.
  1974   *Siglo de Oro: prosa y poesía*. Barcelona: Ariel.

La Croix, Richard R., ed.
  1988   *Augustine on Music. An Interdisciplinary Collection of Essays.
          Studies in the History and Interpretation of Music*. Lewiston,
          New York: Mellen.

Laski, Marghanita
  1961   *Ecstasy. A Study of Some Secular and Religious Experiences*.
          London: The Gresset Press.

Lázaro Carreter, Fernando

1979 "Más observaciones sobre la estrofa quinta de la *Oda a Salinas.*" In *Estudios sobre literatura y arte dedicados al Prof. Emilio Orozco Díaz.* Madrid: Gredos. Vol. 2, pp. 279–86.

León, Fray Luis de

1891–95 *Magistri Luysii Legionensis. . . Opera.* Ed. by M. Gutiérrez. Salamanca: Ep. Calatravae Collegio. 7 vols.

1951 *Obras completas castellanas.* Ed. by Félix García. Madrid: Editorial Católica.

1955 *Poesías.* Ed. by Angel Custodio Vega. Madrid:Saeta.

1975 *Poesías. Poesías originales.* Translation of the *Eglogas* of Virgil and of the Songs of Solomon. Ed. by Angel Custodio Vega. Barcelona:Planeta.

1982 *De los nombres de Cristo.* Ed. with an intro. by Cristóbal Cuevas. Madrid: Cátedra.

1984 *The Names of Christ.* Transl. and intro. by Manuel Durán and William Kluback. New York: Paulist Press.

León Tello, Francisco José

1962 *Estudios de historia de la teoría musical.* Madrid: Consejo Superior de Investigaciones Científicas.

Macrí, Oreste

1970 *La poesía de Fray Luis de León.* Salamanca: Anaya.

Macrobius, Ambrosius Aurelius Theodosius

1952 *In Somnium Scipionis. Commentary on the Dream of Scipio.* Ed. and transl. by W. H. Stahl. New York: Columbia University Press.

1969 *The Saturnalia.* Transl. with an intro. and notes by Percival Vaughan Davies. New York: Columbia University Press.

May, T. E. and E. Sarmiento

1954 "Fray Luis de León and Boethius." *Modern Language Review,* 49:183–92

Menéndez Pelayo, Marcelino

1940 *Historia de las ideas estéticas en España.* In *Obras completas.* Madrid: Consejo Superior de Investigaciones Científicas. Vol. 2.

1941 *Estudios y discursos de crítica literaria. Ibid.,* Vol. 7.

Morales, Ambrosio de

1586   *Los cinco libros postreros de la Crónica general de España que continuara Ambrosio de Morales.* Córdoba: Gabriel Ramos Bajarana.

Mordell, Albert

1969   *The Literature of Ecstasy.* Port Washington: Kenmikat Press.

Naylor, Edward Woodall

1928   *The Poets and Music.* London: J. M. Dent and Sons.

Nieto, José C.

1979   *Mystic, Poet, Rebel, Saint. A Study of St. John of the Cross.* Geneva: Droz.

1982   *Místico, poeta, rebelde, santo: en torno a San Juan de la Cruz.* Mexico: Fondo de Cultura Económica.

1988   *San Juan de la Cruz, poeta del amor profano.* San Lorenzo de El Escorial: Swan, Avantos & Hakeldama.

Nietzsche, Friedrich Wilhelm

1968   "The Case of Wagner." In *Basic Writings of Nietzsche.* Transl. and ed., with commentaries by Walter Kaufmann. New York: The Modern Library.

Noyes, Alfred, ed.

1946   *The Golden Book of Catholic Poetry.* Philadelphia and New York: J. B. Lippincott.

Orozco Díaz, Emilio

1954   "Sobre una posible fuente de Fray Luis de León. Nota a la estrofa quinta de la *Oda a Salinas*" *Revista de Filología Española*, 38:133–50.

Pacheco, Francisco

1599   *Libro de descripción de verdaderos Retratos de Illustres y Memorables varones.* Seville.

1985   *Ibid.* New ed. by P. M. Piñero and R. Reyes Cano. Seville: Diputación Provincial de Sevilla.

Patten, Helen

1905   *The Music Lover's Treasury.* Boston: D. Ester and Co.

Peers, Edgar Allison

1942–43   "Mysticism in the Poetry of Fray Luis de León." *Bulletin of Hispanic Studies*, 19/20:25–40

Perl, Carl Johann

1955   "Augustine and Music." *Musical Quarterly*, 41:446–510 [Transl. from the German by Alan Kriegsman.]

Peterkiewicz, Jerzy

1970   *The Other Side of Silence. The Poet and the Limits of Language.* London: Oxford University Press.

Pietzch, Gerhard

1929   *Die Klassifikation der Musik von Boethius bis zu Ugolino von Orvieto.* Halle: M. Niemeyer.

Plato

1961   *The Collected Dialogues of Plato.* Ed. by Edith Hamilton and Huntington Cairns. New York: Pantheon.

Prosper of Aquitaine

1846   *In Psalmos.* In Jacques Paul Migne, *Patrologia Latina* (Paris: Migne). Vol. 51.

Rico, Francisco

1970   *El pequeño mundo del hombre. Varia fortuna de una idea en las letras españolas.* Madrid:Castalia.

Rivers, Elias

1983   *Fray Luis de León. The Original Poems.* London: Tamesis.

Salinas, Francisco

1958   *Francisci Salinas Bvrgensis. . . in Academia Salmanticensi Musicae Professoris, de Musica Libri Septem, in quibus eius doctrinae veritas tam quae ad Harmoniam, quam quae ad Rhythmum pertinet, iuxta sensus ac rationis iudicium ostenditur, & demonstratur* (Salamanca, 1577). Edited by Macario Santiago Kastner. Kassel: Bärenreiter.

Schauffer, Robert Haven

1935   *The Magic of Music.* New York: Todd, Mead and Co.

Schmidt, Albert-Marie

1939   *La poésie scientifique en France au XVIᵉ siècle.* Paris: Editions Albert Michet. Reprinted. Paris: Rencontre, 1978.

Seznec, Jean

1961   *The Survival of the Pagan Gods. The Mythological Tradition and its Place in Renaissance Humanism and Art*. New York: Harper & Row.

Spitzer, Leo

1963   *Classical and Christian Ideas of World Harmony. Prolegomena and Interpretation of the Word Stimmung*. Ed. by Anna G. Hatcher. Baltimore: John Hopkins University Press.

Stahl, William Harris, ed. and transl.

1952   *Macrobius. Dream of Scipio*. (See Macrobius 1952.)

Stevens, John

1961   *Music and Poetry in the Early Tudor Court*. London: Methuen and Co.

Thompson, Colin P.

1980   "La huella del proceso de Fray Luis de León en sus propias obras." In A. M. Gordon and E. Rugg, eds., *Actas del Sexto Congreso Internacional de Hispanistas celebrado en Toronto, 1977*. Toronto: University of Toronto Press.

1988   *The Strife of Tongues. Fray Luis de León and the Golden Age of Spain*. London: Cambridge University Press.

Tinctoris, Johannes

1978   *Opera Theoretica*. Edited by Albertus Seay. American Institute of Musicology (Corpus Scriptorum de Musica, 22).

Turnbull, Eleanor L., ed.

1962   *Ten Centuries of Spanish Poetry*. Baltimore: Johns Hopkins University Press.

Van Deusen, Nancy

1988   "Medieval Organologies: Augustine vs. Cassiodor on the Subject of Musical Instruments." In Richard R. La Croix, ed., *Augustine on Music*. Lewiston, New York: Mallen, 53–94

Vega, Angel Custodio

1963   *Cumbres místicas: Fray Luis de León y San Juan de la Cruz*. Madrid: Aguilar.

Waite, William G.

1954   *The Rhythm of Twelfth-Century Polyphony*. New Haven: Yale University Press.

Walker, Daniel Pickering

    1953   "Ficino' *Spiritus* and Music." *Annales Musicologiques*, 1:131–50

    1958   *Spiritual and Demonic Magic from Ficino to Campanella.* London: Warburg Institute (Studies, vol. 22).

    1985   *Music, Spirit and Language in the Renaissance.* Edited by Penelope Gouk. London: Variorum Reprints.

Weber, Henri

    1956   *La Création poétique au XVIe siècle en France de Maurice Scève à Agripa d'Aubigné.* Paris: Nizet.

Werner, Eric

    1966   "The Last Pythagorean Musician: Johannes Kepler." In Jan LaRue, ed., *Aspects of Medieval and Renaissance Music: A Birthday Offering to Gustave Reese.* New York: W. W. Norton, pp. 867–82.

Woodward, L. J.

    1962   "Fray Luis de León's *Oda a Francisco Salinas.*" *Bulletin of Hispanic Studies*, 39:69–77

Howard Boatwright

AN ENCOUNTER WITH SOUTH INDIAN VIOLIN PLAYING

In August, 1958, I received a letter from Srimati Lilavati Munshi, Vice-Chancellor of the Bharatiya Vidya Bhavan in Bombay, asking me if I would be interested in coming to her institution as a guest professor. I thought the idea was fascinating, though I knew almost nothing about India or its music. The friend I thought of immediately who might advise me about it was, of course, Carleton Sprague Smith. I talked to him about the project, and when the time came to send letters of recommendation for a Fulbright grant, he wrote one for me, though he cautioned me by saying: "Once you get involved with Indian music, you'll never get away from it." To show that Carleton was right, I am now writing for the first time, twenty-six years later, about one of the most fascinating aspects of that year, my encounter with South Indian violin playing.

Shortly before I was to leave for India in 1959, a colleague at Yale called me to say that an old friend of his was attending his class reunion in New Haven, and that I should have a talk with him because he had been a missionary in India for more than thirty years. I went to see the Rev. Emmons White in his temporary quarters at Davenport College, and indeed was given a new idea for a project in India.

The Rev. White had with him a volume called *108 Kritis of Sri Tyagaraja*, notated in Devanagari script (Sanskrit letters) by C. S. Ayyar,

---

Howard Boatwright is Professor of Music Emeritus, Syracuse University. He is a violinist, composer, and writer on music theory, Indian music, and twentieth-century composers.

retired Accountant General of Madras.[1] He was a brother of Sir Chandrasekhara V. Raman, who was awarded the Nobel Prize in physics in 1930, and the father of Subrahmanya Chandrasekhara, who received a Nobel Prize in physics in 1983. From the time of his retirement until his death in 1960, C. S. Ayyar worked on notating the music of Tyagaraja. A second volume brought out in 1959 contains an additional 120 *kritis*. Ayyar himself played these pieces on the violin (South Indian style, which I will describe later), and his hope was that Western violinists might learn to play from his book. He sent it to many libraries, and to Yehudi Menuhin, whose interest in Indian music was already well-known at the time. But, according to the Rev. White, no Western violinist had tried to unravel the notation and perform them, much to Ayyar's disappointment. Since I was a violinist, would I try to learn some of them? With this hope, the Rev. White gave me his own copy of *108 Kritis*.

My Fulbright grant was to an institution in Bombay, but to complete this project, I would need to go to Madras to see C. S. Ayyar. The Rockefeller Foundation gave me a grant to make that possible. However, as soon as I arrived in Bombay in July, 1959, I began to transcribe some of the pieces from *108 Kritis* into Western notation. This proved relatively simple as far as the basic pitches and rhythmic values were concerned. The Indian equivalent of our *solfa* system used the Sanskrit letters representing *sa-ri-ga-ma-pa-da-ni-sa*. Rhythmic values were shown by underlining the letters for diminution, and by the use of typewriter-available signs, such as the comma and semicolon, for the expansion of time values. The Hindi typewriter was the only tool necessary, with special signs for ornaments.

The main problems arose with the interpretation of the ornaments, so necessary to idiomatic performance—a problem not unlike that which nineteenth-century pianists faced in understanding the claveçin ornaments of Couperin and Rameau.

I wrote to C. S. Ayyar on August 7, and only two days later received a long typewritten response to my first questions. Thus began a correspondence which was to continue until I went to Madras for the festival concerts of the Madras Music Academy between Christmas and

---

[1]Published by the author, Madras 1955.

New Year's Day, 1960. During that time I had my first meetings with Sri Ayyar.

The transcriptions I had made till then (of ten of the *kritis*) followed Ayyar's suggestion, in his book, that the Indian *sa* (corresponding to our *do*) should be represented by the letter C. Also, from the book, it was unclear to me how these pieces were to be played on the violin. The first thing I learned from watching Ayyar play them was that the basic sa was not C, but rather the pitch of the second string of the violin (the "A" string, though it was not tuned to 440 cycles or any other standardized pitch). Furthermore, the lowest string ("G") was also tuned to *sa*, an octave below the second string. The top string ("E") was a 5th above *sa*, called *pa*; and the next-to-the bottom string ("D") was tuned a 5th above the low *sa*, also called *pa*. Keeping the lowest strings of a Western violin tuned to G and D, the upper strings would have to be brought down a whole tone to g and d. This tuning, then, had the strings harmoniously related in octaves and 5ths, without the 9ths formed in Western tuning (G–a, D–e).

The pitch location of the melodies played on the violin was mainly on the upper two strings, with the lower two more rarely used, though they gave some sympathetic resonance to the upper strings because of the octave relationships in the tuning. In notating the pieces in the Western treble clef, my first thought was to write the actual pitches with *sa* as G. But since the tuning of the top strings was one tone lower than on the Western violin, the fingerings would also be different, making the pieces more difficult for a Western violinist to read. The solution to this problem was one which had already been applied in Western music during the baroque period. The viola d'amore had its four upper strings tuned in many ways, the most common being d–f-sharp–a–d. Since the fingerings with these unstandardized tunings would be difficult for violinists to find (because they were used to G-D-a-e), the notes were written not as they sounded, but in the places where the violinist, thinking of his own tuning, would normally put his fingers. This practice of varied tunings (*scordatura*) and a compensating notation was used notably by Attilio Ariosti (1666–ca. 1740) in his *Lezione* for viola d'amore (London 1728), and by Heinrich Franz Biber (1644–1704) in his *Biblical Sonatas*.

To apply the principle here, one would write a and e for the two upper strings, knowing that the sound would come out as g and d. This is the same, in fact, as the transposition for the clarinet or trumpet in B-flat. Employed on the violin, this notation would mean that the very commonly-used note an octave above the second string, *sa*, would be played on the top string by the first finger in what Western violinists call "third position." This is where Indian violinists play that note. Therefore, the transposed notation of the upper strings would lead the Western violinist to play all the notes in the same places on the fingerboard as his Indian counterpart. But solving the notation problem does not tell us what fingers the Indian violinist would choose to press down the string in those places, because, in that respect too, they have a very different technique, and special ornamentations lead to finger manipulations that have no parallel in Western playing.

For an understanding of the ornaments (*gamakas*) and the signs used for them in his book, Ayyar sent me to his daughter, Mrs. Vidya Shankar, a well-known teacher and veena player in Madras. From this very helpful lesson, I was able to make a table of twelve distinct ornamental formulas used in South Indian music. But Mrs. Shankar's demonstrations of them on the veena, often pulling the string sideways to raise the pitch, did not help me to relate them to violin playing, in which such string-pulling is not idiomatic.

One of the experts on Indian music attending the Music Academy meetings and concerts was Narayana Menon, then Director General of the All-India Radio, whom I had met earlier in New Delhi. I told him about my work with C. S. Ayyar, and he immediately suggested that I work instead with one of the younger professional violinists. While Ayyar's notations were basically sound, Menon said that his playing of them was that of a good amateur, and that the versions would lack some of the richness and finesse in ornamentation of a professional violinist. The best of these in South India at the time was T. N. Krishnan, and he would try to bring me together with him. We were introduced at one of the concerts of the festival, and we set a date for our first working session.

I was staying at Chesney Hall, the old Governor's residence made over into a residential hotel. I had a two-room suite in a ground floor side wing, off a veranda. Krishnan came with his violin and played, while sitting on a mat on the stone floor, as I watched and listened from my chair, taking down exactly what he played in Western notation, writing out each ornament and slide with the fingering and bowing I could see him using. After each phrase, I would try to play it back to him for corrections. Because Krishnan had great respect for Ayyar as the notator of the pieces, he kept the book before him, and chose, at the beginning, some of the pieces I had already transcribed from the book. But his playing of those pieces included much that Ayyar's notation did not reflect, so that the reason Narayana Menon wanted me to go to Krishnan was clear; the ornamentation had an element of spontaneity (which, of course, might be different with each performer) that had to be seen and heard, not transcribed from a book.

The ornaments demonstrated by Mrs. Shankar as string-pulling were now seen on the violin as slides made by one finger. In fact, the South Indian left hand technique of violin playing was developed to produce the typical connections from tone to tone of the human voice by sliding the fingers between the main notes.

In a situation such as this, recording the Indian violinist would never give a complete account of the style, since without *seeing* how the sounds were produced, one could not notate them exactly, and certainly one could not reproduce them in playing. Transcription, then, has to include exact fingerings and bowings, the latter reflecting, by the use of slurs, the articulation of the syllables of the text. *Kritis* are all basically vocal pieces, though they are played by violinists in solo concerts without singers; the audience will usually know the words to the more famous pieces.

The Indian violinist uses mainly his first (index) and second fingers, sometimes the third in fast passages, and almost never the fourth. To be able to execute rapid passages by sliding one finger requires a very loose grip on the neck of the instrument, with little counter-pressure from the thumb. For a Western violinist, this is difficult because the violin is held in the air, and the thumb must play some part in supporting it; also, the thumb has to exert counter-pressure for the fourth finger, if it is to be used.

The position of the violin for the Indian player is related intimately to his left hand technique. The left hand is totally free from the task of supporting the instrument, because in a sitting position the violin is held firmly between the front (not the top) of the shoulder and the ankle of a crossed leg. The head of the player never touches the instrument. Many instruments have a Western-style chin rest, but it is only a decoration since no chin ever touches it. The downward angle of the left arm leaves it in position to execute small slides with wrist and hand movements alone. The forearm needs to move only in going to high positions, which is a relatively rare occurrence. For a Western player, with his erect position, these same sliding movements may involve the entire forearm, making them much clumsier to execute. This is true even if the left hand is kept free of support responsibilities by the use of a shoulder rest.

In bowing, the Indian violinist holds the stick not at the very end as the present day Western violinist does, but higher up as baroque violinists used to do. Since the tuning is often well below our modern pitch for G, being sometimes as low as E or E-flat, the string tension is much less than in European tuning (as it was in the baroque period). Short-holding the bow eliminates some of the weight of the nut end, and this suits lower string tension better than the greater weight of the whole stick (normally about two ounces, more or less).

The instrument of which we speak is a true Western violin, and most of those that I have seen were of Western manufacture imported into India at some time. They are said to have been first introduced in Madras and Tanjore by members of British bands during the time of Governor George Pigot (1755–63; 1775–77) (Raghavan 1948:65). So the present violin in India is an import, not a descendant from the Arabian *rabab* within the subcontinent, though within Europe the violin can be traced to such instruments through the medieval *rebec*. The modern Indian descendant of the *rabab* is the *sarangi*, which in North India is a bowed instrument played with a sliding technique somewhat similar to that used on the violin in South India. However, in the construction of its body, the *sarangi* is far removed from the Western violin.

In South India, the violin, in spite of its Western origin, is treated so differently as to make it now an authentic and standard vehicle for Indian music, and its use has spread to North India as well. The tuning, the positions for holding the violin and the bow, and all the details of fingering are suited to rendering the melodic characteristics of Indian music in the most expressive way.

Here follow some brief examples from one Tyagaraja *kriti* which was part of my study project. The piece is no. 17 of Ayyar's *108 Kritis*. Example 1 shows this portion of the piece reproduced from Ayyar's notation. The information at the top of the example announces the name of the raga, *Pantuvarali*, the *mela* number, 51 (an Indian method of classifying the scale types), and the *tala*, which is *Adi* (sixteen beats in the cycle). The thirteen boxes show the placement of the notes in this *mela* from the low *sa* to the octave above. The boxes are a semitone apart, so that the notes (if C is *sa*) are C–D-flat–E–F-sharp–G–A-flat–B–c

Example 1: C. S. Ayyar's notation in Devangari script (using Sanskrit letters) of No. 17 in the *108 Kritis of Sri Tyagaraja*.

Example 2 shows a literal transcription allowing the value of an eighth-note for each pulse of the *tala*. A full barline marks the end of the cycle of sixteen pulses. The line of text and the musical phrase have the duration of one cycle. It is performed three times, each time with variations in the ornamentation, and the last note of the third phrase is stretched to fill an entire cycle, because this is the end of the first section of the piece. This first section is called *Pallavi*, indicated by the Indian letter for "p" placed just to the lower left of the encircled no. 17 in Ayyar, and indicated as *PA* at the beginning of Example 2.

Example 2: A literal transcription of the first section (*Pallavi*) of No. 17.

17.8 x 2 = 16 Adi (medium tempo) Mela 51

The two special signs above the staff are for *veena* ornaments involving pulling the string, producing oscillations of the pitch.

Example 3 shows the same segment written out in violin notation, as described above, with the violin "A" string treated as *sa*. The ornaments, fingerings, and bowings are as played to me by T. N. Krishnan. A line following a fingering number in this example means that the same finger is used until a new number occurs. Note that in Krishnan's version, each of the three variants of the phrase is played twice (indicated by the repeat signs).

Example 3: The previous example given in violin notation.

PA *VADERA DAIVAMU.*   *Pantuvarali.*   *Adi.*

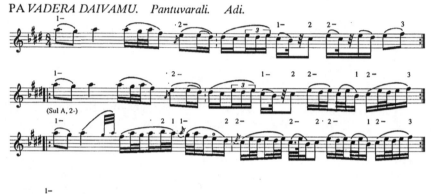

I completed four *kritis* with Krishnan before I left Madras in January, two more during his visit to Bombay in early March, and in May, I returned to Madras, where all the earlier pieces were given a final scrutiny, and four more were added to the set.

The encounter with an artist such as Krishnan, who is at present head of the Department of Music at the University of Delhi, was a rare experience, made all the richer by his extraordinary generosity in sharing his art with a Westerner who, in spite of a lifetime commitment to violin playing, found himself a bungling amateur when confronted with the complex subtleties of South Indian violin playing.

REFERENCE CITED

Raghavan, V.

    1948   "The Indian Origin of the Violin," *Journal of the Madras Music Academy,* 19:65–70.

Joseph Braunstein

CONCERNING BEETHOVEN'S *GRANDE FUGUE,* OP. 133

It is generally known that the *Grosse Fuge* originally constituted the last movement of the *Quartet in B- flat Major,* Op. 130, and that after the first performance on March 21, 1826, Beethoven had yielded to the suggestion of the publisher, Matthias Artaria, to write another *finale*— since, according to the general consensus, the blame for the lack of an unqualified success of the Quartet was placed particulary on the immense fugal *finale*. We are told that Beethoven agreed reluctantly to Artaria's removal of the *finale*, which the publisher proposed as an independent composition to be issued as a four-hand piano version. Beethoven himself undertook the task, since the four-hand piano arrangement made earlier by Anton Halm (1789–1872) did not meet with his approval. However, the publication of the separated *finale* required a title, for which Beethoven decided on *Grande Fugue, tantôt libre, tantôt recherchée*. Both the quartet *finale* and the piano version were published posthumously (issued on May 10, 1827 by Artaria), with the respective opus numbers 133 and 134, and the dedication to Beethoven's one-time theory student, the Cardinal Archduke Rudolph (1788–1831). The dedication is of biographical and artistic significance

---

Joseph Braunstein, a former member of the Music Division of the NYPL (1950 – 57), taught at Mannes College of Music (1957–72) and the Manhattan School of Music (1958–91). Since 1975, he has been senior program annotator for the Chamber Music Society of Lincoln Center. He holds a Ph.D. in musicology from the University of Vienna.

inasmuch as nearly all works of contrapuntal (fugal) nature, created during Beethoven's last years, were dedicated to the musical Hapsburg Prince: the *Piano Sonata in B-flat Major*, Op. 106; the *Missa solemnis*, Op. 123, and the *Grande Fugue*, whose piano version (Op. 134) was Beethoven's last work for that instrument.

Discussing the *Grande Fugue*, and in order to realize its scope, we have to proceed from its original position in the B-flat Major quartet (Op. 130), which forms, with its sister works, the A minor (Op. 132) and C-sharp minor (Op. 131) quartets, an artistic unit. Closely bound together by means of a basic motif, in manifold alterations, and displaying polyphonic techniques in chorale variations (Op. 132), fugue and canon (Op. 131), and double fugue (Op. 130), these quartets clearly manifest Beethoven's intentions to expand and modify the traditional forms without giving up the frame work (sonata) which—in spite of all—Beethoven deemed basically unalterable and still usable for a new and revolutionary means of expression. And with the *Grande Fugue* he launched an experiment, whose historic and formal significance could hardly be grasped in 1826.

The three Quartets in B-flat Major, C-sharp minor, and A minor were not completed according to the arithmetical order of their respective opus numbers. The actual sequel is Op. 132, 130, and 131. And, if we consider their respective keys in A minor, B-flat Major, and C-sharp minor, we discover an alphabetical order which may or may not be coincidental. Of greatest significance, however, is their thematic link. A sketch book used, in 1824, chiefly for studies on the *String Quartet in E-flat Major*, Op. 127, shows also the first attempts related to Op. 132 and Op. 130. Working on the *finale* of Op. 127, Beethoven jotted down a short phrase with a motif from which the introductory passage to the opening movement of the A minor quartet was developed (see Ex. 1):

Example 1. Op. 132 (Nottenbohm 1887:548)

The same sketch book shows that Beethoven left the region of A minor (see Ex. 2):

Example 2. Op. 132 (Nottebohm 1887:550–51)

Here we recognize the basic theme of the *Grande Fugue*. I shall refer to this motive as the key motif. Its basic form contains three intervals, in succession: up a minor 2nd, up a minor 6th, and down a minor 2nd. We notice in the opening *Assai sostenuto* of the A minor quartet the inversion of the key motif: down a minor 2nd, down a minor 6th, and up a minor 2nd. Moreover, the motif permits six additional permutations as follows:

		Minor 2nd	Minor 6th	Minor 2nd
1.	Original form	up	up	down
2.	Inversion	down	down	up
3.	"	up	down	up
4.	"	up	down	down
5.	"	down	up	down
6.	"	down	up	up
7.	"	up	up	up
8.	"	down	down	down

Beethoven used all of them in Op. 130, 131, and 132, varieties 7 (mm. 233–72) and 8 (mm. 273–338) in the third section of the *Grande Fugue*. The interconnection of Beethoven's last creations is amazingly demonstrated in the *Scherzo* of the E-flat Major quartet (Op. 127), in which he anticipated the key motif (Ex. 3*a*), and the rhythmical quality of the countersubject in the double fugue of Op. 133 (Ex. 3*b*).

Example 3a. Op. 127, mm. 57–60 (Edition Peters, no. 3032*c*)

[cresc.] – *ff*

Example 3b. Op. 133, mm. 30–32 (Edition Peters, no. 3032*d*)

The most interesting alteration of the key motif—the augmenta-tion of the ascending 6th to a diminished 7th—occurs in measure 75 of the first movement of the A minor quartet (see Ex. 4), and this alteration resulted in the formulation of the basic idea of Op. 133:

Example 4. Op. 132, mm. 75–82 (Ibid.)

Varieties of the key motif appear in the B-flat quartet in the prefatory *Adagio* passage and subsequent repetitions (see Ex. 5):

Example 5. Op. 130, mm. 1–2, 21–22, and 94–95 (Edition Peters, no. 3032*c*)

Space forbids a demonstration of the use of the key motif in the C-sharp minor (Op. 131) and F Major (Op. 135) quartets. The metamor-phosis of this motif reached its last stage in the Rondo, which replaced the original *finale* of Op. 130 (see Ex. 6):

Example 6. Op. 130, mm. 133–38 (*Ibid.*)

When Beethoven, in the last phase of his creative life, decided to compose a string quartet in six movements, he approached or reverted to the formal pattern of a genre he had cultivated during his early Viennese years, but which he definitely abandoned in 1800. It was the multi-movement *divertimento* as such. Haydn and Mozart wrote many works of this kind and Mozart's *Divertimento for String Trio in E- Flat Major*, K. 563 (1788), served Beethoven as a model for the *String Trio in E-flat Major*, Op. 3 (1792), and the famous *Septetto*, Op. 20 (1800). Beethoven's B-flat quartet (Op. 130) displays, to a certain extent, the *divertimento* character in the number and diversity of its movements, and the inclusion of two dance movements. Here the similarity stops.

There is no cheerfulness nor serenity in the quartet. The opening movement requires fifteen metrical and fourteen tempo changes, unthinkable in any sonata movement before that time. It demands five key signatures (B-flat Major – B-flat minor – D-flat Major – G Major – E-flat Major). All these features foreshadow what was going to occur in the *finale*. The fluctuating harmony, however, was anticipated in another *Grande Fugue*, also in B-flat, in the *Piano Sonata*, Op, 106 (composed in 1818), usually referred to as the *Hammerklavier* sonata.

The second movement of the quartet, though not entitled *Scherzo*, fulfills the function of a *Scherzo cum Trio*. It is rather short, running 106 measures, the *da capo* included. This movement differs fundamentally from the symphonic *scherzo* of the *Quartet in E-flat Major*, Op. 127 (1824), and the imagery of the corresponding movement of the A minor quartet. By the same token, in the B-flat Major quartet, there is no match to the inwardness of the variations of Op. 127 and to the loftiness of the *Heiliger Dankgesang* ('Holy Song of Thanksgiving') of Op. 132. Even the *Andante* of Op. 130 should be played *quasi scherzoso*. The *scherzoso* element, prevalent in the *danza tedesca*, is strongly contrasted with the *Cavatina*, the only movement of the quartet in which the deepest feeling is expressed, and it is significant that Beethoven did not achieve it in a broadly designed *Adagio*, but chose instead a short operatic form. Yet the *Cavatina* fits the general plan of the middle movements and avoids large scale structures that are paramount in the two preceding quartets (E-flat Major and A minor).

The opening movement of Op. 130 is 234 measures long, while all four middle movements amount to 410. This situation called for a substantial *finale* in order to achieve architectural balance. The enormous length of the *finale*, running 741 measures and even exceeding the combined total number of measures of the other movements (644), was a foregone conclusion. The quartet, to use a term coined by Alfred Einstein, was to be a "*finale* quartet." As such it is unique in Beethoven's entire quartet output and the *finale* parallels in some way that of the Ninth Symphony.

Discussing the B-flat Major quartet, we have to pay attention to the testimony of Beethoven's first biographer, Anton Felix Schindler (1795–1864), who called himself "Beethoven's confidential secretary without salary." Schindler called the B-flat quartet a *monstrum*. There is a specific Austrian or Viennese touch in this expression, which implies a bit of depreciation meaning something "awful," "awkward," and "uncouth," and, in using this word, Schindler wanted not only to characterize the quartet, but also to denounce it. He disliked its over-dimensional shape and considered it abnormal in style. Reporting on its first performance in the third edition of his *Biographie von Ludwig van Beethoven* (1860:II, 114), Schindler quoted at length the anonymous correspondent of the *Allgemeine Musikalische Zeitung* (1826:310–11), published in Leipzig, and represented in Vienna chiefly by Ignaz Xaver Seyfried (1776–1841), a pupil of Mozart and conductor at the Theater an der Wien, who was always on the best terms with Beethoven. Malevolence and bad intention on the part of the *Zeitung*'s correspondent could not be expected. The paper pointed to the success of the *Scherzo* and *danza tedesca* which caused such enthusiastic applause that both movements had to be repeated. But, in discussing the *finale*, the anonymous reporter felt compelled to think less in musical and more in geographical terms by confessing:

> But this writer does not dare to interpret the meaning of the fugue-*finale* which was to him incomprehensible and rather Chinese. If the instruments advancing into the regions of the North- and South Poles are faced with enormous difficulties, if each of them has to work out passages in a difficult way and they all are mingled together *per transitum irregularem* producing an immense number of discords: if the players mistrusting themselves fail to get the right pitch, then the

Babylonian mess is at hand and there will be a concert which would be a pleasure perhaps to Moroccans [*translation mine*].

Suppressing his geographical fancy, the reporter continued:

Some pages would perhaps not have been written if the master would be able to hear his own creations. But we do not want to condemn him hastily, for maybe the time will come when what now appears dim and confusing, at the first glance, will be recognized as clear and well shaped.

It speaks for this critic that he publicly confessed his inability to grasp the work emotionally, as well as formally, and he revealed a deep sense of responsibility to the composer and his own artistic conscience by speaking of future possibilities which might supersede the viewpoint of his day.

Schindler took a different attitude. He did not contradict this report, but gave its correspondent credit for having described the general impression correctly. Nonetheless he went so far as to deny any artistic value of the fugal-*finale* of the B-flat quartet:

This composition appears to be an anachronism. It should have been created in those grey old times when musical relations were determined by mathematical calculations. Without hesitations one may regard such combinations as the greatest errors of the speculating intellect, and the impression we get from these errors will cause a Babylonian mess, probably forever. As for this composition there can never be spoken of obscurity in contrast to clarity [translation mine](Schindler 1860:II, 115).

Thus spoke the master's "confidential secretary," who had claimed for himself the infallibility in Beethovenianis.

To understand fully the implications in this paragraph, one has to bear in mind that these sentences were not written and the conviction expressed therein was not communicated to the musical world in 1826 after the performance of Op. 130, but more than thirty years later. For the third edition of Schindler's biography of Beethoven was published in 1860. These curious pages clearly prove that Schindler did not understand the language and problems of Beethoven's last creations, and, in 1860, he found himself still on the same musical level as in 1826.

Beethoven was not the first composer who concluded a quartet with a fugal movement. In Haydn's quartet series, Op. 20, called Sun Quartets, written in 1775, there are three with fugues as finales. The double fugue in the F minor quartet, no. 5 of the series, anticipates the *Kyrie* fugue in Mozart's *Requiem*. Haydn wanted to distinguish himself before amateurs and professional musicians by displaying his contrapuntal dexterity in this set also called Great Quartets. Mozart concluded his Quartets in in F Major (K. 168) and D minor (K. 173) with fugues. Haydn repeated this experiment in the F-sharp minor quartet of Op. 50, no. 4 (1787). Yet it is significant that neither Haydn nor Mozart included fugues in their later quartets, wherein, of course, *fugato* passages are not lacking. The regular fugue was apparently deemed improperly suitable to the refined classical quartet style and relegated to the *fugato*. It is, therefore, erroneous to call the final movement of Beethoven's C Major quartet (Op. 59, no. 3) a fugue. It is a regular sonata movement with exposition, development, recapitulation, and coda, to which fugal technique is applied. The fluctuating harmony in the development section, particularly in the portion wherein all the instruments, that follow each other soloistically in D minor – B-flat Major – F minor – C minor – G minor – C minor and F minor (mm. 154–97), reflect the unlimited harmonic freedom of the classical sonata and symphony. The scale-like passages of the main theme anticipate the fugal subject of Op. 106 and the harmonic treatment foreshadows that applied to this sonata and the *Grande Fugue*.

Analytical essays and the customary program notes point out that the *Grande Fugue* is "prefaced" by a thirty measure-long section entitled *Overtura*. Modern editions bear this title above the tempo indication *Allegro* at the head of the score. The description of the original manuscript by expert authorities reveals a different picture. Martin Gustav Nottebohm (1817–1882), who was in the position to study the autograph of the B-flat Major quartet when it was still in the hands of Artaria, simply remarked that "the autograph has the title *Overtura*" (1868:127). This was fully confirmed by Wilhelm Altmann (1862–1951), head of the Music Division of the Prussian State Library—known earlier as the Royal Library—which had acquired the Beethoven manuscripts that were owned by the Artaria family. In his comments to the pocket score edition of the *Grande Fugue,* published by Eulenburg in 1930, Altmann stated: "The manuscript of the fugue... was called *Overtura*." Yet the general opinion considered the heading *Overtura* as pertaining to the opening thirty measures, all the more so, as the beginning of the fugue is designated *fuga* (m. 30). In doing so, Beethoven followed precisely the procedure he had initiated in Op. 106 and continued in the *finale* of the *Piano Sonata in A-flat Major*, Op. 110.

That the creator of the overtures to *Coriolanus* and *Egmont* should place a thirty-measure passage in the same category as the 641–measure long overture to *Leonore*, is difficult to accept. Yet the situation appears in a different light when considered in the context of the B-flat Major quartet. Here we observe three consecutive movements with titles:

4. *Alla danza tedesca*: *Allegro assai*

5. *Cavatina* : *Adagio molto espressivo*

6. *Overtura*: *Allegro*

Hermann Deiters, who edited the material left by Thayer for concluding the fourth and fifth volumes of *Ludwig van Beethovens Leben*, quoted from a conversation book of March 1826 a question of Karl Holz (1798–1858): "Does the term *Overtura* remain (Thayer 1908–23:V, 295)?" According to Thayer, this conversation took place at the time of the rehearsals of the B-flat quartet, during which Holz participated as second violinist. Since the performers' parts were copied from the manuscript, Holz was aware of the matter. Unfortunately we do not know Beethoven's answer. That the *finale* of the quartet, which later became the *Grande Fugue*, was originally entitled *Overtura*, is beyond question.

Hugo Leichtentritt (1874–1951) was the first among modern authorities to give a clue to the master plan upon which Op. 133 was built. In his *Musikalische Formenlehre* (1927:130), he described the *Grande Fugue* "as a series of fugal variation fantasies welded together along the formal pattern of a sonata." His theory was actually not entirely new, but I am inclined to assume that Leichtentritt was not aware of the fact that, as far back as 1859, a Viennese musician, composer, teacher, and editor, Leopold Alexander Zellner (1823–1894) had come to the same conclusion. One year older than Bruckner, as his superior at the Vienna Conservatory, Zellner had made Bruckner's life difficult at this institution, from 1868 onward, through pettiness and animosity.

Zellner described the *Grande Fugue* as "almost a quartet in one [continuous] movement. It is not a fugue of book learning, but rather it comprises several rhythmically different parts, representing Introduction, First Movement, *Andante*, and *Finale*, based on a principal subject manifoldly varied."[translation mine]. Zellner (1859) explained this idea in the *Blätter für Musik, Theater und Kunst*, a Viennese periodical which he edited.[1] This was a publication of local importance and under these circumstances Zellner's article was condemned to sink into oblivion without having any effect in the musical world at large.

Yet it came to the attention of Wilhelm von Lenz (1809– 1883), well known through his *Beethoven et ses trois styles* (St. Petersburg, 1852), who, recognizing the novelty as well as the soundness of Zellner's analysis, incorporated a brief summary of Zellner's article in the fifth volume of his *Beethoven: eine Kunststudie* (1860:290–92). Zellner's idea was preserved, but shelved in a remote place, where even the most diligent student comes across only by mere chance. Leichtentritt did not refer to Zellner, neither did Thayer nor his editors, Hermann Deiters and Hugo Riemann, of the German edition.

No detailed analysis of the *Grande Fugue* will be given here; however, the piece will be discussed as the *finale* of the B-flat quartet in terms of its interpretation as a three-movement complex, or, so to speak, as a quartet within a quartet, indicated graphically:

First movement:	Allegro (4/4) in B-flat	158 measures
Second "	: Meno mosso (2/4) in G-flat	73 "
Third "	: Allegro molto (6/8) in B-flat	510 "
	Total	741 measures

The musical material, however, is based on that characteristic musical idea which stems from the Quartet in A minor and appears here with its varied descendants (see Ex. 7):

Having stated the basic theme in a broad shape, the prefatory passage offers a table of contents by introducing three varied versions of the basic theme which differ in rhythm, key, and tempo. There is a certain parallelism to the Ninth Symphony. In the first pages of the *finale*, themes of the preceding movements are quoted, while the introduction to the *Grande Fugue* prepares us for things to come. But here the themes are presented in a sequence contrary to the order in which they are later developed. That is to say, the version of the basic theme, which is used in the third section of the *finale*, is stated first and then follows those that are worked out in the second and first sections of the entire complex.

---

[1]The periodical was published from 1855 to 1874, covering 33 forty volumes, up through number 104. From 1866 (Vol. 12) on, its title was changed to *Blätter für Theater, Musik und bildende Kunst*. From 1874, it continued under the title *Deutsche Musikzeitung* (see K. Kirchner 1977:246).

Example 7. *Grande Fugue* (Edition Peters, no. 3032*d*): a) *Allegro* (mm. 2–10); b) *Allegro* (mm. 11–13); c) *Meno mosso* (mm. 17–25); d) *Allegro* (mm. 26–30)

The first section, treated as a double fugue, constitutes the first movement of the quartet within the quartet. The first fugal exposition corresponds to a sonata exposition, the second constitutes the development section, while the third can be defined as recapitulation and coda. The double fugue is unique in Beethoven's *oeuvre*, because of the harshness and aggressiveness of its musical language. There is not a single phrase that is played *piano*. Constant *forte* prevails and more than 250 *fortissimo, forte,* and *sf[orzando]* marks appear in 158 measures. In several passages, accents are required on every beat. This music, demanding considerable physical strength from the players, appears to have been conceived in terms of orchestral dynamics.

For the opening section of the double fugue, Beethoven had established a remarkable precedent in the fugal portion of the overture to *Die Weihe des Hauses* ('*The Consecration of the House*') (composed in 1822) (see Ex. 8a).

These passages (*Allegro con brio*) anticipate the mood of the first section (movement) of the *Great Fugue*, the rhythmical and dynamic qualities, as well as the forcefulness (see Ex. 8b).

The ensuing *Meno mosso e moderato* in G-flat (2/4) provides the greatest contrast imaginable. This section represents the middle movement in the *finale* complex of Op. 130. There is soft legato playing and tenderness prevails. The fugal elaborations continue on a reduced scale.

Example 8a: *Die Weihe des Hause*, mm. 89–92 (Edition Peters, no. 5537)

Example 8b. *Grande Fugue*, mm. 30–33 (Edition Peters, no. 3032*d*)

The choice of key (G) justifies a brief remark. Beethoven did not choose the dominant of B nor the sub-dominant, but the flattened sub-mediant—though it involves intonation difficulties, because G-flat rules out the use of open strings. In doing so, however, he consistently maintained a stylistic feature significant in his last important instrumental works, except for the E-flat Major quartet (Op. 127): the application of mediant and sub-mediant keys to the slow movements. Witness the *Ninth Symphony* (D – B-flat), and the quartets in A minor (Lydian in lieu of F), C-sharp minor (A), B-flat (D-flat and G Major), and finally the F Major quartet (D-flat). Summing up, the influence of the harmonic concept, characteristic of the last symphony and quartets, can be observed in the middle movement of the quartet within a quartet.

The tenderness of this lyrical intermezzo is rudely disturbed by a bang (*ff*), which opens the last movement of the quartet within Op. 130. It is cast in 6/8, which the esthetics of the eighteenth century associated with the hunt. This meter was used chiefly in final movements and Beethoven employed it in the D Major (Op. 18, no. 3) and F minor (Op.

95) quartets. The opening passage mirrors a gay and somewhat humorous touch which is pushed aside briskly in the following pages in A-flat. It is in this substantial section wherein the motto *tantôt libre, tantôt recherchée* finds its forceful realization.

Beethoven designated the final movement of the B-flat sonata (Op. 106) a *fuga con alcune licenze*. This is actually an understatement. In Op. 130 or 133, if you please, the *licenze* becomes a permanent feature in conjunction with the multiplied "sought out" (*recherchée*) elements. The fugal and canonical elaborations are interrupted by a surprising resumption of the *Meno mosso* in A-flat. Divested from the tender lyrical character, the basic theme conveys a forceful proclamation, the seriousness of which is intensified by obstinate *forte* accents on each one of the thirty-six beats of the eighteen-measure statement. The injection of this episode, *libre* and *recherchée*, is not animated by the spirit of the fugue as such, but betrays the pervasive influence of the sonata which henceforth prevails until the gay ending. To determine the form of this sub-*finale*, I submit the following breakdown:

Exposition	B-flat non fugal meas.		232–272	A
Development	A-flat	"	273–413	B
	E-flat	"	414–442	AB
	A-flat	"	453–492	A
Meno mosso	A-flat	"	493–510	C
Bridge		"	511–532	
Recapitulation	B-flat	"	533–662	A
Coda		"	663–741	

The rondo design clearly emerges which conveniently suits the traditional 6/8 meter.

The *finale* of the B-flat Major quartet was a noble and adventurous experiment. According to Thayer, Beethoven made the following statement to Karl Holz (ca. 1817 or later): "To compose a fugue is not a great artistic achievement. I have made dozens of them in my student years. But fancy wants also its rights to exert and nowadays a new and really poetic element must be infused into the old traditional form" (1908–33 23:IV, 76). Passing over the questionable downgrading of the technical side of fugal composition, we must ask: How was Beethoven's demand for fancy and poetry fulfilled in the *Grande Fugue*? Fancy can be seen in the diversity of the musical pictures and metrical qualities

(4/4, 2/4, and 6/8), the free harmonic treatment, and the variegated shape of the basic theme. The poetic element, however, can hardly be detected or felt.

Beethoven wanted to climax his B-flat quartet with an extraordinary *finale*. The means he chose to achieve this aim were those of the intellect and the absence of the poetic element, which proved to be a very stable stumbling block for the audience that Beethoven befriended with the second *finale*. We are told that Beethoven had consented reluctantly to the removal of the fugal movement, yet this often very stubborn man was also a pragmatist. He demonstrated this attitude by consenting to revise the opera *Leonore* (1805) after a long session with friends and supporters. He had probably realized that the audiences of 1826—and it turned out also in later decades—could not understand the language he spoke in the *finale* of the B-flat quartet. Still he wished this work to be accepted by the musical world at large, and consequently, he accepted Artaria's proposition and wrote instead another *finale*. He did not consider this task a chore. In spite of the most adverse circumstances to which he was subjected in the Fall of 1826, he wrote this movement in good spirit and even penned it with gusto.

Beethoven's Op. 133 remained a *noli me tangere* through almost a century while the last quartets became a part of the public musical life, thanks to Joseph Joachim (1831–1907) and Lucien Capet (1873–1928). I was exposed to Beethoven's quartets by the group led by Gustav Mahler's brother-in-law, Arnold Rosé (1863–1946), who followed strictly the Joachim tradition. That is to say, he played the B-flat quartet, as published, as Op. 130, with the rondo *finale*. I heard the work when the Capet Quartet played it in Vienna. In more than seventy years of concert going, I have received the strongest impression from a performance of the *Grande Fugue* in the adaption for string orchestra by Felix Weingartner, under his direction. I still recall the overwhelming first entrance of the double basses (ten players) in the double fugue. Adolf Busch, the *primarius* of an internationally renowned quartet ensemble, led an orchestral presentation of the *Grande Fugue* in New York, in the 1940's.

How should the Quartet in B-flat and the *Grande Fugue* be performed? More recent younger quartet ensembles have seen fit to dismantle Op. 130, replacing the rondo *finale* by the *Grande Fugue*. This practice violates Beethoven's clearly expressed intention by the publication of the Quartet Op. 130. This situation worsens when the rondo *finale* is being played detached from the Quartet Op. 130 within another program, artistically an inadmissable procedure. As for Op. 130, I am pleading for the published version as sanctioned by Beethoven, and wholeheartedly advocate the inclusion of Weingartner's arrangement for string orchestra of the *Great Fugue* in the program of orchestral concerts.

REFERENCES CITED

Altmann, Wilhelm

1930   *Grosse Fugue.* London–Zurich–New York: Eulenburg.

Anonymous

1826   "Nachrichten: Am 21sten, im Salle des Vereins, eine von Hrn. Schuppanzigh zum Schlusse der diessjährigen Abonnement-Quartetten veranstaltete Abendunterhaltung. . ." *Allgemeine Musikalische Zeitung,* 28(19): 310–11 (Leipzig, May 10).

Beethoven, Ludwig van

n. d.   *"Ouverture Die Weihe des Hauses,* Op. 124," in *Beethoven Overturen.* Edited by Alfred Dörffel. Leipzig: C.F. Peters. (Edition Peters, no. 5573)

n. d.   *Quatuors für 2 Violinen, Viola und Violoncell,* Opus 95, 127, 130. Edited by Joseph Joachim and Andreas Moser. Leipzig: C.F. Peters. Vol. III. (Edition Peters, no. 3032c)

n. d.   *Quatuors für 2 Violinen, Viola und Violoncell.* Opus 131, 132, 133, 135. Edited by Joseph Joachim and Andreas Moser. Leipzig: C.F. Peters. Vol. IV. (Edition Peters, no. 3032d)

Kirchner, Joachim, ed.

1977   *Die Zeitshcriften des Deutschen Sprachgebietes von 1831 bis 1870.* Mit einem Titelregister von Edith Chorherr. Stuttgart: Anton Hiersemann.

Leichtentritt, Hugo

1927   *Musikalische Formenlehre.* 3rd edition. Leipzig: Breitkopf & Härtel.

Lenz, Wilhelm von

1860   *Beethoven: eine Kunststudie.* Vol. V: Kritischer Katalog sämmeltlichen Werke Beethovens mit Analysen derselben. Periode Op. 101 bis Op. 138. Hamburg: Hoffmann & Campe.

Nottebohm, Martin Gustav

  1868   *Thematisches Verzeichniss der im Druck erscheinenen Werke
            von Beethoven.* 2nd edition. Leipzig: Breitkopf & Härtel.

  1887   *Zweite Beethoviana.* Nachgelassene Aufsätze. Leipzig: Ver-
            lag von Reiter-Biedermann.

Schindler, Anton Felix

  1860   *Biographie von Ludwig van Beethoven.* 3rd edition. Münster:
            Aushendorff. 2 vols.

Thayer, Alexander Wheelock

  1908–23   *Ludwig van Beethovens Leben.* Nach dem original-Manuskrit
            deutsche bearbeitet. Neu bearbeitet und ergänst von Her-
            mann Deiters. Revision von Hugo Riemann. Leipzig: Breit-
            kopf & Härtel. 5 vols.

Zellner, Leopold Alexander, ed.

  1859   *Blätter für Musik, Theater und Kunst,* 5 (Vienna)(see W. von
            Lenz 1860:290–92).

Wiley L. Housewright

MUSIC OF THE SIXTEENTH-CENTURY FRENCH SETTLEMENT IN FLORIDA*

The Bulls of Pope Alexander, in 1493, awarded most of the Western hemisphere to Spain, the remainder to Portugal.[1] But Frenchmen in pursuit of power, wealth, position, and security were not intimidated by proclamations. French kings in the sixteenth and seventeenth centuries explored and founded colonies in the New World. In 1523, Francis I (1515–1547) sent the Florentine navigator Giovanni da Verrazano (ca. 1480–1527?) to explore the eastern coast of North America from the land then called Florida to Newfoundland. In 1534, he sponsored the exploration of Canada by Captain Jacques Cartier (1491–1557). While these two explorations gave France tenuous claims to North America, no actual settlement in the New World was attempted until after mid-century. The first of these was in Brazil, the second in Florida (see Plate 1).

Religious wars and political intrigue had sapped the energy of many Frenchmen, so that they were not eager to leave the comforts of

---

[1]Francis I, with tongue in cheek, asked to see the will of Adam, so that he might learn of this division of the world. See García Arias (1954–56), quoted in Lyon (1971:1–24).

Wiley L. Housewright, long-time dean and professor at Florida State University, was a member of the academic music advisory panel to the U.S. Department of State's Cultural Presentations Abroad Program.

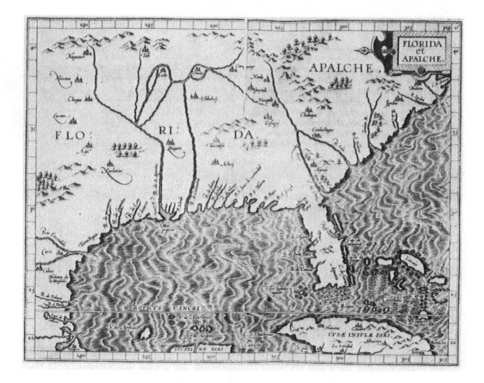

Plate 1. Map of the Province of Florida by the French cartographer Jacques
Le Moyne (1591) (Courtesy Library of Congress).

their homeland to endure the rigors of establishing an overseas colony.
They had no scruples that interfered with the ambitions of wealthy
patrons who influenced the kings, but they needed a good reason to risk
their lives while crossing the ocean. Adventure, greed, or curiosity would
have been reasons enough to satisfy some men, but Gaspard de
Châtillon Coligny (1519–1572), admiral and advisor to the king, found
a better one: religion. Coligny was head of the French protestants, and
it was his intention to establish retreats for the faithful of the new
religion who were persecuted in France.

For his first colonization, King Henry II (1547–59) sent an expedition in 1555 to Brazil led by Nicolas Durand, Chevalier de Villegagnon
(c. 1510–1571). Villegagnon and John Calvin (1509–1564) had been
fellow students at the Sorbonne. Calvin encouraged French poets to
write metrical versions of the psalms and composers to set them to

music. Villegagnon was an avowed Huguenot. He arrived in Brazil on November 10 "singing praises and giving thanks to the Lord" (Lescarbot 1907:155). Then he wrote the Calvinists for help, asking that they send ministers to indoctrinate the Indians. The second group to support Villegagnon arrived in Brazil on 26 February 1557. It included 230 men, six lads to learn the language, and five young girls for propagation. On March 7, they reached Rio de Janeiro and were greeted there by Villegagnon. The company then entered a small hall and sang the Fifth Psalm in the translation by Clément Marot (1496?–1544):

Aux paroles que Je veu dire,
Plaise toy l'aureille prester:
Et a congnoistre t'arrester
Pourquoy mon coeur pense et souspire,
Souverain Sire (Pidoux 1962:I, 9).

In continuance of the Genevan custom, the Calvinists held an hour's service every week-day and two services on Sunday. It is presumed that the tradition of the sect in singing metrical psalms was continued as well. Jean de Lery, a student of the Brazilian colony, wrote that on one occasion he was so moved by the beauty of the scene that he sang the metrical setting of Psalm 104, "Sus, sus mon ame, il to faut dire bien" (Baird 1885:I, 37).

However, the strength of psalm singing and the sermons of Minister Richer were not great enough to hold the colony together. Disagreement over religious issues were heated and frequent. Finally, Villegagnon publicly disavowed the Calvinist doctrine and returned to Catholicism. On 4 January 1558, fifteen of the colonists boarded a ship for France and others followed. The dissenter's colony was permanently broken. Their psalms were replaced by the chants and hymns of Portuguese Catholics just as in Florida, where they were soon to be replaced by Latin hymns and services of the Spanish Catholics.

After the failure of the Brazilian venture, the French King Charles IX (1550–74) attempted to colonize the region discovered by Verrazano. Admiral Gaspard de Coligny chose Jean Ribault (ca. 1520–1565) of Dieppe, an excellent navigator, to head an exploration of Florida. Second in command was another competent sailor, René de Goulaine de Laudonnière (fl. 1562–1582) of Poitou. They sailed from France to Florida in 1562. Aboard the ship they sang daily the psalms, in the translation of Clément Marot and to the melodies of Claude Goudimel (ca. 1505–1572), just as they had in their home towns. While

Plate 2. This engraving by Jacques Le Moyne depicts Jean Ribault and Florida Indians, and a stone marker at the mouth of the St. Johns River which was erected by the French Calvinists in 1562 (Courtesy Library of Congress).

the religious aspect of the exploration continued to be present, Gallic candor caused some members of the company to allege that the king supported the venture in order to increase his possessions on earth.

They arrived at the mouth of the St. Johns River on the first of May, disembarked long enough to erect a stone marker (see Plate 2), then chose a northward course along the Atlantic coast. They sailed to present-day Parris Island, South Carolina, where they built Charlesfort and left thirty men to guard it. Ribault and his crew returned to France. Believing themselves abandoned, the thirty settlers built a ship and also set out for France. The venture was about to end in disaster when they were rescued and placed aboard an English ship.

A second attempt to establish a French settlement in Florida was made by René de Laudonnière in 1564. In June he reached Florida with approximately three hundred men and a small number of women. Concerning the events of the following morning, he wrote:

> At daybreak I ordered a trumpet to sound so that we could as-
> semble and give thanks to God and prayed that it would please Him
> of His holy grace to continue His accustomed goodness toward us,
> His poor servants, and to give us aid in all our enterprises so that all
> might redound to His great glory and to the advancement of our king.
> The prayers being ended, everyone began to take courage
> (Laudonnière 1975:70; also see Bennett 1964:19 and 55).

They sang a psalm of thanksgiving and settled themselves in a fort they built near the mouth of the St. Johns River which they named Fort Caroline. Thus the psalms were sung on the shores of Florida long before they were to be heard in Virginia and New England. The Florida landscape was described by René de Laudonnière:

> We found a spacious countryside with high pine trees growing
> close together, and under these we noticed a large number of deer
> gamboling across the open spaces through which we passed. We
> found a hillside on the edge of a great green valley, and in its open
> spaces there were the most beautiful prairies in the world. . . It was
> surrounded by little fresh water streams and by a tall forest which
> made the valley very beautiful to see (Laudonnière 1853:81–83).

This scene he described was so pleasant that those who were melancholy could not help but change to a more pleasant dispostion. Captain Giles de Pysiere, another French maritime officer, provided the following provocative description of the new settlement:

Among all the books giving spiritual and honest pleasure, none gives me more pleasurable entertainment than those dealing with stories about new lands and the conquest of distant and strange lands, among which is the Island of Florida which has been the latest discovery in the world. Without a doubt it is to be admired over any other place as to singularity and riches because it is full of unknown lands and seas, of strange people, animals and plants; and the spirit is enriched there by the voluptuous delight of novelty, public opinion is formed and instructed with new knowledge, and the uncertainty of things imagined becomes an assurance by beholding with the eye things as marvelous as prodigious land and sea monsters long ago seen and known in that land of Florida (1565; quoted in Bennett 1964:74).

MUSIC OF THE RELIGION

While the French Kings Henry II and Francis I were Catholic, out of their recreation with the psalms grew one of the distinguishing practices of Calvinism, the singing of metrical psalms. The colonists at Fort Caroline were called to worship every afternoon. This custom was familiar to all European Huguenots of the time. An Italian writer, who visited Geneva in 1557, described the practice:

On week-days as the first sound of the bell is heard, all shops are closed and from all sides the people hasten to the nearest meeting-place. There each one draws from his pocket a small book which contains the psalms with notes, and out of full hearts, in the native speech, the congregation sings before and after the sermon. Everyone testifies to me how great consolation and edification is derived from this custom (Dickinson 1902:361).

For their daily services the music comprised the metrical psalms set in the vernacular to popular tunes of the day and sung in unison. The early editions were those published in Strasbourg (1539) and the one by Clément Marot (1542). French settlers of Florida probably sang from the most important of all metrical versions of the psalms, published in Paris, in 1562, just two years before Laudonnière's second voyage. No record has been left of the music they sang for recreation, but if they followed the lead of their European counterparts, they sang at home the contrapuntal settings by Louis Bourgeois (ca. 1523–1570/1600) and Claude Goudimel[2] of the poetry of Clément Marot and his successor

[2]An example of the practice is Claude Goudimel's setting of *Psalm 65* in an edition prepared by Carleton Sprague Smith (1938).

Théodore Bèze (1519–1605). These polyphonic settings made free use of the first lines of secular *chansons* as motto lines, just as Palestrina, at about the same time, was using quotations from plainchant and other sources for his head motives. Plainsong was also used in this manner among the Huguenot composers.

There was no clergyman on the first French voyage of 1562, but one did accompany the 1564 voyage. The singing of church music by the French as well as the Indians was documented by members of the settlement. Nicolas Le Challeux, a sixty-year old carpenter among the colonists, noted that the Indians sang Psalm 130 "Du fons de ma pensée," and 137, "Estans assis aux rives aquatiques" (1579:96). Gabriel Gravier, editor of the earliest account of Jean Ribault's first visit, wrote that the settlers sang psalm translations of Marot and melodies of Goudimel. Le Challeux reported the incident of Captain Ribault singing, after his capture by the Spaniards and just before his death, the psalm "Domine, memento mei." The old man's memory may have failed to reproduce the first line exactly, but he must have understood how appropriate it was for his captain to sing Psalm 132, "Memento Domine, David," with its triumphant last lines: "His enemies will I clothe with shame: but upon himself shall his crown flourish."   When Ribault finished singing his Huguenot valedictory, he quoted Genesis 3:19, reminding all that they came from the earth and to earth they must return, that a few years were of little account. "Then," Le Challeux wrote, "in a din of drums, flutes, and trumpets, the Spaniards spent their courage wildly upon the poor Frenchmen. . . still bound" (1946:116).

The French forces at Fort Caroline were not prepared for the attack by Pedro Menéndez de Avilès (1519–1574). Lord de la Vigne was in charge of the squad of sentinels at the time. Observing the incessant rain, he took pity on his men and allowed them to leave their posts and he himself retired to his quarters. Laudonnière credits his trumpeter with alerting the Frenchmen by sounding the alarm. Few survived the brutal attack. Ribault and his officer Ottigny were taken in another encounter since they were far away from the Fort. Their hands were bound and they were brutally stabbed and beaten to death. At the Fort, Laudonnière lacked sufficient military force to defend his position. Not more than ten men could bear arms. Others were a cook, four dog trainers, a beermaker, a crossbow maker, two shoemakers, a spinet player, laborers, women, and children. Most of them were slaughtered by the Spanish; the Fort was taken and given the name San Mateo. There is disagreement among both the French and Spanish as to the

number of survivors. All agree, however, that the musicians were spared
and taken to St. Augustine to play for Menéndez and his settlers. Known
to be musicians in the colony were a spinet player whose name is not
given; Masslin, listed as a violinist and trumpeter; Lieutenant Jean
Mennin, who played the horn (*cor*); four trumpet players, three from
Normandy and Jacques Dulac from Bordeaux; three drummers, two
from Rouen and one named Dronet from Dieppe. One fifer was also
from Dieppe.[3] It is possible that other fifers were present to complement
the number of known drums.

In 1567, when Dominique de Gourgues (c. 1530–1593) led an
expedition across the Atlantic to avenge the French defeat at Fort
Caroline, he ordered his men to sing psalms in praise of God. When they
arrived, the Indians greeted them with a noisy marching band, celebrating the event by leaping and dancing. They sang for the French psalms
that were taught to them by the early French settlers. Among them were
Psalm 43, "Revenge moy, prens la querelle," Psalm 50, "Le Dieu, le fort,
l'eternel parlera," and Psalm 91, "Qui en la garde du hat Dieu" (de
Gourgues 1958:243). Charles E. Bennett, a twentieth-century historian
of Fort Caroline, wrote that the Indians also sang another hymn for de
Gourgues which they learned from the French, entitled, "Happy is one
to be a volunteer for God" (Pidoux 1962:I, 116). This is clearly a
reference to Clément Marot's version of Psalm 128, "Bien heureux est
Quiconques, sert a Dieu volontiers."

Dominique had disembarked to the sound of martial music. When
the dancing and whooping had subsided, he distributed gifts among the
Indians, who responded by ordering their women to dance, thereby
showing respect to the visitors. Saturiba and his Indians were willing
partners to the French in the raid of San Mateo. With their help, the
Fort was stormed and Spaniards were shot or hanged. Thus, the Fort
Caroline tragedy of 1564 was avenged. The Indians, jubilant in victory,
celebrated in their usual manner with singing and dancing. Dominique
de Gourgues and his men returned to France, but for political reasons
were denied the gratitude or honor of their countrymen. Later, when
the Spaniards returned and rebuilt San Mateo, France was not willing
or able to continue the battle for so dubious a prize as Florida.

[3]From the "Deposition of Jean Menin" in Gaffarel (1875:145 and 445) and
Laudonnière (1853:196), regarding "un joueur d'éspinette."

SECULAR MUSIC

One of the fifers, who became a prisoner when the Spanish took Fort Caroline, played a leading role in an incident almost twenty years later. With his English Fleet, Sir Francis Drake (1540–1596) sailed into St. Augustine harbor on 6 June 1586 and the following morning ordered several pinnaces to take depth soundings. They were met with Spanish artillery fire and retreated. Later that day the British landed their own artillery and, to the sound of music, displayed six red flags and then moved to the edge of the Matanzas River. On the following night Nicholas Bourguignon, the French fifer, discovered a small skiff and rowed silently across the river. As he came within sight of English sentries he played on his fife, with all his might, the march tune "William of Nassau," the well-known song of the Prince of Orange. The melody, popular among French Huguenots in the 1560's, was called "The Tune of Chartres." "Wihelmus von Nassouwe" is one of the oldest national anthems. Playing it certified Bourguignon a Frenchman rather than a Spaniard. He assured Captain Christopher Carleill and other English officers that the three hundred Spanish residents had been intimidated by Drake's show of force and had abandoned St. Augustine. Drake burned the city to the ground, and Bourguignon sailed back across the Atlantic aboard an English ship, saved from death or imprisonment because he knew an appropriate tune and could play it on his fife.

The Frenchmen who settled in Fort Caroline possessed a particularly rich musical heritage. Apart from the Calvinist poets were such illustrious new lyric poets as Pierre de Ronsard (1525–1585). The courtly restraint of Claude de Sermisy's (ca. 1490–1562) homophonic settings of the poems of Clément Marot were matched by the free *chanson* of Clément Janequin (c. 1490–1562) and Pierre Certon (c. 1510–1572). Published in the numerous collections of Pierre Attaignant and Jacques Moderne, these tunes, with lively rhythms, sectional construction, and frequent repetition, were popular throughout Europe in both vocal and instrumental versions. The French at Fort Caroline had the instruments and musicians to play this music on their violin, spinet, horn, trumpets, and fifes. To sing this music and the *chansons* of their homeland required no more skill than to sing a psalm tune. As Jean-Jacques Rousseau (1712–1778) defined the *chanson* a few generations later, it seemed appropriate to comfort homesick young noblemen, who were seeking their fortunes abroad, or artisans, who had memories of youthful romances but little hope for anything more. To him the *chanson* was:

> a short lyric poem, generally upon some pleasant subject, to which an air is added, so that it can be sung on intimate occasions, at a table with one's friends, with one's sweetheart, or even when one is alone, in order for a few moments to drive away boredom if one is rich, or to help bear misery and labor if one is poor (Scholes 1950:156).

What music could be better suited to a young Frenchman so far from Paris?

The Fort Caroline settlement was composed of gentlemen, artisans, and servants, as were the French settlements in Brazil and Canada. Their musical preferences were undoubtedly as varied as their social classes. There were instruments available to play the *pavanes*, *basse* dances, *branles*, *gaillardes*, and *tourdions*, and there were both French and Indian women for dancing partners.

The titles of their secular songs were not recorded, but a few are candidates for the honor. In their leisure hours the young gentlemen officers may have sung the courtly fifteenth- century "L'amour de moy," as they joined the soldiers and sailors in lively marches, drinking songs or familiar rounds. Jean Memyn, a young lieutenant from La Rochelle probably knew the *chanson de marin*, "Ce sont les filles de la Rochelle," popular long before the Huguenots and Richelieu battled in his home town in 1628, or the fifteenth-century variant, "En revenant de la joli Rochelle." The sailing men of Brittany and Normandy probably knew "La Fille a la fontaine" (Brittany) and "Ah! Qui me passera la hois" (Normandy). At Christmastide they may have sung the familiar "Il est né le divin enfant." Numerous French renaissance love songs were sentimental or cerebral laments of the disappointed or deceived lover. Others sang of the delights of physical love with Marie, or Madeleine, or Marguerite, *mon fils, jeune fils*, or *trois jeunes filles*. Transplanting a Frenchman to a new land did not make him forget his homeland, his religion, his lovers, nor his songs.

More than twenty years before the birth of Virginia Dare, in the Roanoke colony, eight or more children were born in the French settlement at Fort Caroline (Ribault 1964:Part II, X, 132). Excepting children of the ill-fated 1559 Tristan de Luna settlement in Pensacola, they were the first children of European parents born within the present limits of the United States or Canada (see Bothwell 1965:foreword). Among the earliest European lullabies sung in Florida, at that time, were French—both words and music. Again, speculation must substitute for documentation of the titles sung. Possibly, along the Florida coast, French mothers crooned "Ah! Vous dirai-je, maman?," "Sur le pont d'Avignon," "Au clair de la lune," or perhaps "Frère Jacques."

The instrument upon which the "joueur d'épinette" played is not described but it undoubtedly was the earliest spinet in the Western world, since it was constructed before 1565. Frank Hubbard, harpsichord maker and historian, cites as the earliest known: Hans Rucker's instrument, "a fine double virginal made in 1581 which was found in Peru where it apparently was taken in the sixteenth century" (1965:51). He reports that the French used "épinette" as a general term, just as the English used "virginal." Burgundian and Italian instruments antedate those of France, but Jean Potin, "faiseur d'épinette du Roy ('harpsichord maker to the king')," is mentioned as early as 1561 (Lesure 1954: quoted in Hubbard 1965:86). Among other French spinet makers of the sixteenth century were Merry Lorillat, Anton Potin, Pierre Lorillart, and members of the Dugue family. Spinets were included in the inventories of three harpsichord makers: Yves Mesnage (d. 1556), Claude Denis (d. 1587), and Robert Denis the Younger (d. 1589). Any of these men could have created this first instrument heard on the Florida east coast, or it could have been the work of a maker from Antwerp or Venice.

Those who heard the French spinet player perform in Florida did not record the titles of his pieces. It can only be speculated that he played from the published collections of his period, among which were two collections published in Lyon in tablature, three of the 1531 Pierre Attaignant collections, and a 1551 Venice publication by Antonio Gardane [Gardano]. Neither the French nor Italian publishers name the arrangers of these dance collections.

MUSIC OF THE INDIANS

The music and dance of the aborigines were described by the early French explorers, and their ceremonies became the subjects of drawings by the cartographer of the second expedition. René Laudonnière gave one of the first descriptions of the Timucuan Indian warfare custom of scalping male enemies. On returning from victory, the Indians joined in a singing-and-dancing celebration that lasted three days and three nights. The old women danced while holding scalps in their hands. All sang songs worshiping the sun and honoring the victory. Their deities, according to Laudonnière (1975:11–15), were the sun and moon. The celebration was, in fact, a religious rite.

One of the most important religious ceremonies was observed soon after the French arrived. During his first exploration, Ribault captured two Indians from the west arm of the Liborne River to take back to the Queen of France. Upon learning that they were not to return to their tribe, they attempted to buy their freedom by returning gifts that the French had given them. The French would not accept them, but guarded the men closely. According to Laudonnière, the melancholy Indian warriors then "joined each other in singing softly and sweetly in a way that made us think they were lamenting the absence of their friends. They continued singing all night long without stopping" (1975:28). They also persisted in asking to be returned to their tribe, promising Laudonnière the privilege of seeing their secret ceremonies called "Toya," if he would comply with their request. Later, they escaped and it was left to another Indian cacique, Andusta, to invite the Frenchmen to the secret feast.

Toya was an outdoor religious banquet ceremony observed by Andusta and his tribe. It was rendered with great solemnity by the Indians, but, among the French, it was thought to be a primitive joke. Their laughter so provoked the chief that he banned them from witnessing the ritual and ordered them inside the house. Only by chance did one man observe it from a discrete distance. The ceremony was directed by a shaman and his assistants. They were thought to have the ability to heal diseases with herbs and could order sacrificial rituals. Indian women cleared a circular plane which the celebrants called the place of Toya. On the morning of the celebration they met at the chief's house, painted and plumed in a variety of colors. Three Indians, painted in distinctive colors, led the others in an orderly procession to the place of Toya. Each Indian carried a small drum in his hand. They entered the center of the circle dancing and "singing in doleful tones." One group sang and was followed by others which answered them. After singing, dancing, and turning three times, they ran swiftly into the woods. The women then began singing and crying in lamentation. They grabbed the arms of the young girls and cut them with sharp clam shells until the blood flowed, then they leaped about crying, "He, Toya," three times. Two days later the men, who had run into the forest, returned and began to dance. Their enthusiasm and gaiety cheered the elder Indian fathers who were too old or feeble to participate in the festival.

When the dancing was over, the Indians sent for the Frenchmen and asked them to join in a great banquet. The French observed that the Indians ate ravenously, for they had neither food nor drink during their two days of absence. One Frenchman inquired what the Indians did while they were in the woods. He was told that the shaman prayed to Toya, then by magic made Toya appear. Thereupon the men spoke to him, demanding strange things of him—so strange that for fear of the shaman one dared not recount (Laudonnière 1975:41–42).

Chief Saturiba's marching band of musicians and warriors greeted the second wave of French voyagers to Florida in 1564. Saturiba ruled the large territory between the St. John's River and Savannah. He had twenty musician who, according to Jacques Le Moyne, blew hideous discords with their reed pipes. An advance- company of twenty warriors came armed with darts, bows and arrows, and clubs. They wore multicolored feathers, shell necklaces, fish teeth bracelets, "belts of silver-colored balls, round and oblong, and pearl anklets. Many of the men wore round, flat plates of gold, silver or brass, which hung upon their legs, tinkling like little bells" (Le Moyne 1946:38). Two hours later Chief Saturiba appeared escorted by seven or eight hundred strong, swift, and handsome warriors. At the head of the army were fifty youths with javelins and spears. Behind them, next to the chief "came twenty pipers making the wildest kind of noise, without any harmony or rhythm, each blowing with all his might as if to see who could blow the loudest" (*Ibid.*:38). If there was singing, it was not mentioned by Jacques le Moyne. A Theodore de Bry engraving of a Le Moyne drawing depicts two men playing large-size reed pipes hung with oval-shaped metal balls, which run the entire length of the instrument (*Ibid.*:109)(see Plate 3).

Primitive music accompanied many ceremonial events of the Indians. Eyewitness accounts and skillful drawings have preserved remarkably clear details of the celebrations. The narratives and drawings of Jacques Le Moyne are the richest sources.[4] When they returned from war, the Indians gathered at a ceremonial site and erected tall poles, upon which they solemnly placed the scalps, legs, and arms of

[4]Jacques Le Moyne de Morgues wrote his *Brevis Narratio* in London about twenty years after he left Florida. This narrative was first published in Latin, then the German translation and engravings were published by Theodore de Bry in Frankfurt in 1591. An English translation from the Latin, including the de Bry engravings, was published in Boston in 1875 by James R. Osgood and Company. A modern printing of the narrative and the engravings can be found in Le Moyne (1946:33–87) and Le Challeux (1946:88–119). The most extensive recent studies are those of Bennett (1964, 1968, and 1976). Accounts here are based on those of Le Moyne.

Plate 3. Small metal bells were attached to wind instruments played by Timucuan musicians. In this engraving by Jacques Le Moyne, they are shown escorting a bride-elect to an Indian chieftan (Courtesy of the Photo Division of the Florida State Archives, Tallahassee, Florida).

their defeated adversaries. Then both the men and women sat in a circle facing the poles. The sorcerer, holding a small image, rose and began to dance about, cursing the enemy and muttering a thousand imprecations in a low voice. Three kneeling musicians enhanced the ceremony. One beat a large flat stone with a large club, marking time to the spells cast by the shaman. On either side were the other two, holding in each hand a dried gourd or pumpkin filled with small stones or seeds. They rattled these instruments and accompanied the sorcerer's imprecations with a song. This was their ceremony after every victory.

Another ceremony was particularly gruesome. It was a rite in which a first born child was sacrificed to honor the chief. Relatives accompanied the mother and child to a place where the chief was seated on a bench. Nearby was a tree stump, measuring about two feet high and two feet thick, before which the mother squatted on her heels and with her hands covered her face in deep distress. The child was taken by a female relative and ceremoniously offered to the chief. The women then danced about joyfully in a circle while one of them held the child aloft in the center of the ring. As they danced, they sang songs in praise of the chief. Six Indian men observed the ceremony. A seventh, magnificently dressed, stepped forward, placed the child on a stump, and killed it with his club. All witnessed the death of the child in honor of the chief.

Just before springtime emerged, Chief Outina and his subjects gathered at a flat, open space. They brought with them the skin of the largest stag killed during the year. It was stuffed with the finest roots of the harvest, then the horns, neck, and body were decorated with wreaths of flowers or garlands of fruit. Music and song signalled the beginning of the religious procession and continued as the stag was borne to a high tree and there suspended with its head and breast facing the sun. The chief and his sorcerer offered prayers to the sun that his bounty would continue. At a distance, members of the tribe made their responses. Kneeling, they saluted the sun, then departed, leaving the stag in place until the following year.

Two of the most elaborate Indian ceremonies occurred when the Timucuan chief decided to take a wife. He made his choice among tallest and most beautiful daughters of his highest ranking men. A procession was formed to escort her to the king. At the head of entourage were the musicians, trumpeters blowing bark horns. The instruments were large at one end and small at the other. They were hung with small oval balls of gold, silver, and brass. Their tinkling enriched the variety of instrumental color. The bride-elect was borne on a rare fur skin litter canopied with leafy branches. Her bearers were four strong men who carried the litter on their shoulders. Each of them also carried a forked stick to support the litter frame when the company halted. Two men walked alongside with large elaborately decorated fans which shielded her from the sun. Following the bride-elect were the most beautiful girls that could be found. Their bodies were draped with Spanish moss. Around their necks, arms, and midsections they wore strings of pearls and each of them carried a basket of fruit. At the end of the procession came the bodyguards, carrying their bows and wearing their plumed headdresses.

The French fascination with exotic settings, populated by red Indians, did not end with the destruction of Fort Caroline and the death of its martyrs. One example of its continuance is the *ballet heroique*, "Les Indes Galantes ('Love in the Indies')," by Jean Phillipe Rameau (1683–1764). This large-scale work comprises four *entrées*, which are set in a Turkish pasha's garden, a Peruvian Inca's volcano, a grand Persian park, and the last of which is set among the noble savages of Florida who dance a chaconne in the final scene. The work was first produced at the Paris Opera in 1735 and its fourth *entrée* was added a year later.

It is from the narratives and drawings of eye and ear witnesses and confirmations by later historians from which conclusions about the music of the Indians and French colonists may be drawn. The explicit designation of nine metrical psalms sung in the new world has been documented. Seven of them were sung in Florida (43, 50, 91, 128, 130, 132, and 137) and two in Brazil (5 and 104). References to daily services in both locations suggests the likelihood that other psalms were sung as well. To make their identification even more precise, Marot's versification and Claude Goudimel's musical settings were mentioned by those who were present. This music was taught to the Indians as a phase of the commitment to their religious education. It was taught so well that, when Captain Dominique de Gourgues led an expedition to Florida in 1567 to avenge the destruction of Fort Caroline, the Indians greeted him with the singing of Psalms in French.

To play secular music, the French settlers brought a string instrument (violin), a keyboard instrument (spinet) and wind instruments (horn, trumpet, and fife). None of the colonists recorded the titles of secular music they played, sang, or heard, but it is known that collections of books arrived from time to time. It is unlikely that, having brought musical instruments, colonists lacked the foresight to bring music as well. The monumental collections of Pierre Attaignant, published throughout the sixteenth century, contained both music for singing and for dancing. The sixteenth century was one of the most distinguished and productive in music history throughout Europe. The lyric poetry of Pierre de Ronsard and the simple beauty of the free *chanson* were unique. It was the music that was known among the young French noblemen. To the artisans of the company, the many folk songs of their home provinces retained their appeal not only in their century but in our's as well.

From the French have come some of the earliest descriptions of aboriginal music of North America. The singing and dancing of the Timucuans were described. Music in religious rites were reported. The strong role of music in preparing warriors for battle and in celebrating victory was repeated by observers. The music of large marching bands of Indians was heard and reported by European noblemen. None of this music was notated nor given a title. The context, the occasion, however, was related to the music. These verbal descriptions were buttressed by the remarkable drawings of Jacques Le Moyne, cartographer of the mission who observed and drew for posterity, and in fine detail, the ceremonies of the Florida Indians and the musical consorts which accompanied them.

REFERENCES CITED

Baird, Charles W.

    1885   *History of the Huguenot Emigration.* Vol. 1. New York: Dodd, Mead and Co.

Bennett, Charles E.

    1964   *Laudonnière and Fort Caroline.* Gainesville: University of Florida Press.

    1968   *The Settlement of Florida.* Gainesville: University of Florida Press.

    1976   *Fort Caroline and Its Leader.* Gainesville: University Presses of Florida.

Benzoni, Girolamo

    1579   *Histoire nouvelle du Nouveau Monde.* Geneva: Eustace Vignon. (ESAIE XXVI)

Bothwell, Jean

    1965   *Lady of Roanoke.* New York: Holt, Reinhardt and Winston.

de Gourgues, Dominique

1958   "Histoire memorable de la Reprise de l'Isle de la Floride [1568]," in Susanne Lussagnet, ed., *Les Franais en Amerique pendant la deuxième moitié du XVIe siècle* (Paris: Presses Universitaires de France), pp. 241–49.

Dickinson, Edward

1902   *Music in the History of the Western Church*. New York: Charles Scribner's Sons.

Gaffarel, Paul

1875   *Histoire de la Floride Française*. Paris: Librairie de Firmin-Didot.

García Arias, Luis

1954–56   "Una frase famosa en las relaciones marítimas hispano-franceses del siglo XVI," *Cuadernos de Historia Diplomática*, 3:131–62 (Madrid).

Hubbard, Frank

1965   *Three Centuries of Harpischord Making*. Cambridge: Harvard University Press.

Laudonnière, René Goulaine de

1853   *L'Histoire notable de la Floride située es Indes Occidentales, contenant les trois voyages faits en icelle par certains capitanes et pilotes françois, descrits par le capitaine Laudonnière que y a commandé l'espace d'un an trois moys: à laquelle a esté adiousté un quatriesme voyage fait par le capitaine Gourgues*. Edited by Martin M. Basanier. Paris: P. Jannet.

1975   *Three Voyages*. Edited and translated by Charles E. Bennett. Gainesville: University Presses of Florida.

Le Challeux, Nicolas

1579   "Bref discours et histoire d'un voyage de quelques Franois en la Floride," bound with Girolamo Benzoni, *Histoire nouvelle du Nouveau Monde* (Geneva: Eustace Vignon), pp. 9–104.

1946   "The Narrative of Nicholas Le Challeaux [1579]," in Stefan Lorant, ed., *The New World* (New York: Duell, Sloane and Pearce), pp. 88–119.

Le Moyne de Morgues, Jacques

1946 "The Narrative of Jacques le Moyne de Morgues [*Brevis Narratio Eorum Quae in Florida Americae Provincia Gallis Acciderunt* (1591)]," in Stefan Lorant, ed., *The New World* (New York: Duell, Sloan and Pearce), Vol. 1, pp. 33–87.

Lescarbot, Marc

1907 *History of New France.* Vol. 1. Toronto: The Champlain Society.

Lesure, François

1954 "La Facture instrumentale à Paris au seizième siècle," *Galpin Society Journal,* 7:11–52 (London).

Lyon, Eugene

1971 "Captives of Florida," *Florida Historical Quarterly,* 50:1–24.

Pidoux, Pierre, ed.

1962 *Le Psautier Huguenot du XVIe siècle. Mélodies et documents.* Basel: Bärenreiter. 2 vols.

Pysiere, Giles de.

1565 *Discours de l'enterprise et saccagement que les Forsaires de l'Isle Florideavoient conclud de faire à leurs capitaines et gouverneurs, estans sauvages unis en liberté.* Avec la description des bestes tant marines que terrestres, qui ont estez trouvés dans le circuit de la Floride. . . Paris: Pierre de Langre. [A translation of this can be found in Bennett (1964:74–75).]

Ribault, Jean

1964 *The Whole and True Discoverye of Terra Florida* [London: Rowland Hall for Thomas Hacket, 1563]. Reprint edition, Gainesville: University Presses of Florida. [Facsimile reprint for Florida Historical Society, De Land, Florida, 1927.]

Scholes, Percy A., ed.

1950 *Oxford Companion to Music.* London: Oxford University Press.

Smith, Carleton Sprague, ed.

1938 *The Ainsworth Psalter. Psalm 65, with Settings by Claude Goudimel.* New York: The New York Public Library (Early Psalmody in American Series, 1).

Eleanor Lawry

SOME OBSERVATIONS ON GOUDIMEL'S PSALM SETTINGS

Among Renaissance composers whose works include settings of the metrical French texts and melodies of the Genevan Psalter, none was more prolific than Claude Goudimel (ca. 1505–1572). In fact, ten of the fourteen volumes of his collected works are devoted to these settings, which occupied him throughout his entire period of creativity. To be sure, they were published concurrently with his motets, magnificats, and masses, all with Latin texts; and his numerous *chansons*, some twenty of which appeared in anthologies prior to his first volume of psalm motets published in 1551 by Nicholas du Chemin. All nine motets of this volume have texts by Clément Marot (1496?–1544). Unfortunately only the Superius and Tenor parts of the 1551 edition have survived, but they are sufficient to give some insight as to how this edition was "Nouuellement par luy mesme reveu, corrigé & augmenté du Psalme, Quand Israel" in the publication by Le Roy & Ballard in 1557, reprinted in 1558 and 1565. These revisions, numbering approximately one hundred, range from slight changes to extensive reworking and have to do with rhythmic alterations, resetting of entire sections, and more effective text underlaying (Cf. Critical Notes, Claude Goudimel *Oeuvres Complètes*, Vol. I).

Eleanor Lawry, Ph.D, pianist and musicologist, transcribed, analyzed, and edited Volumes II, IV, VI, and VIII of the Oeuvres Complètes *of Claude Goudimel.*

The second volume of psalm motets, also using Marot's texts, exists only in the "Nouuellement reveu & corrigé par ledit Auteur" edition of 1559. However, since half of the motets were included in an anthology published by Guillaume Simon Dubosc & Guillaume Guéroult in 1555, there is some basis for comparison with the 1559 edition. Here the revisions seem to be of a similar nature as in Volume I, though not nearly as extensive.

For Volume III, the edition of 1557, again with texts by Marot, is the earliest printing known. Though not indicated as a revised edition, that of 1561 contains a few variants. No copy of the 1566 edition is extant. The complete 1560 edition of Volume IV underwent extensive modification in a 1565 publication of which only the Contratenor and Bassus survive. Extensive portions of Psalms II and LXXII have been newly composed, variants in rhythm and text underlaying occur, and in eleven instances Marot's original texts have been supplanted by those of the Genevan Psalter of 1562.

Of Volume V only the Bassus of a 1562 edition and the Contratenor and Bassus of a 1556 edition have survived. These are sufficient to show a most interesting development, which is his first use of texts by Théodore de Bèze (1519–1605) and melodies by Louis Bourgeois (ca. 1510–ca. 1561). Comparison of the two bass parts shows extensive alteration of the second part of Psalm XC as well as variants in the use of accidentals. Only one edition each is known for Volumes VI (1565), VII (1566), and VIII (1566), all with texts by Bèze, except for Psalm CIV in Volume VI, Psalms III and XVIII in Volume VII, and Psalms VI, XIX, and XXXII in Volume VIII, with texts by Marot.

Judging from Volume I, Goudimel, as a disciple of the Pléiade devoted to the furtherance of masterpieces in the French language, was attracted at first to Marot's metrical translations regardless of any melodies associated with them. Here the only exact use of a pre-existant melody occurs in the Tenor of the opening line of Psalm CXXVIII. A few fleeting melodic resemblances, which involve scale passages, may be due to coincidence rather than intent. Free imitative polyphony prevails throughout these ten motets. An increase in the use of borrowed melodies is evident in Volume II, especially in the first strophe of Psalm CXIII and also in Psalm LXXXVI. In fact, about half of the psalms in this volume exhibit occasional and free use of their given melodies. By the third Volume, Goudimel seems to have felt the affinity of melody and text to such an extent that he gave Psalm I a complete *cantus firmus* setting. Here the *cantus*, with imitations, moves back and forth between Tenor and Superius and is even taken over by the Contratenor in the fifth line of the third strophe. Psalter melodies also appear prominently in the first strophes of Psalms V and XXXIII and occasionally elsewhere throughout these motets. The Lyon Psalters of 1547, 1548, and 1549 were frequent melodic sources for Volume IV. Noteworthy here are the settings of Psalms XXV and LXXII in which the psalter melody permeates the entire structure.

The only extant part books of Volume V, those of the Contratenor and Bassus, prove to be amazingly revealing. Though usually the parts least used for the *cantus,* here the melodies by Bourgeois, set to texts by Bèze, appear intact throughout all ten motets. They fluctuate between Contratenor and Bassus with frequent imitative support. Psalms XXXV and XL contain the most free treatment, which might serve as counterpoint to a *cantus* setting in Superius or Tenor. To what extent the missing parts use the *cantus* continues to remain a mystery.

Extensive use of psalter melodies is characteristic of five of the eight motets of Volume VI. Psalm LXXXV is a tenor *cantus firmus* composition. In Psalms XXXIX, LVI, XCII, and CXVII, the *cantus* predominates; but in the two longest motets, Psalms CII and CIV, free material is more prevalent. This is true also of Psalm LXXXVII, in which the *cantus* is drawn upon for only the first and third lines of the first strophe.

Throughout Volume VII the exact or modified psalter melodies are prevalent. Their use seems to diminish in proportion to the length of the psalms to which they are related. Two free settings, those for Psalms XLVIII and CXLII, occur in Volume VIII. Their melodies had not been included in psalters before 1562. However, since Psalm CXLII shares the same melody as Psalm CXXXI, Goudimel had already set it in the first of the four strophes of his motet on that psalm in Volume VII. The psalter melodies prevalent in the other six motets are all contained in psalters dated 1551 and 1554. Also, the Bourgeois Psalter of 1547 contains three of the six melodies, those for Psalms VI, XIX, and XXXVII. In the latter, slight variants occur between the two editions. It is interesting to observe that Goudimel chose the 1547 version. Could this imply that there might have been an earlier edition of the only extant publication of Volume VIII dated 1566?

In his sixty-six motets, Goudimel set the psalm texts in their entirety, from the single strophe of Psalm CXVII to the twenty-eight strophes of Psalm CXVIII. Structurally a motet was divided into *parties,* each containing two or more strophes, thus giving the opportunity to vary the texture. Though *parties* range from two- to eight-part settings, a typical sequence for the number of voices in each *partie* is four, three, four, with an additional voice part for each successive *partie*. In his only seven-part setting, the seventh *partie* of Psalm XVIII, the two bass parts alternate, coming together cadentially at four-line intervals. Its *partie* for eight voices, with two voice parts in each range, frequently has sections for four voices (one voice part in each range) in alternation. However, antiphonal performance is not intended as the groupings change in the course of the *partie*.

In several psalms in Volumes I and II an eight-line text is divided into two sections of four lines each, and a ten-line text into two sections of four and six lines, respectively. It is not only the syllabic patterns of the sections that differ, such as 10, 11, 11, 10, followed by 10, 11, 10, 11 in Psalm LI; and 11, 11, 11, 11, followed by 6, 6, 7, 6, 6, 7, in Psalm LXXIX, but their treatment from one *partie* to the next. A first section concludes a four-voice *partie* and the second section begins the next three-voice *partie*. The reverse treatment also occurs. Both psalms conclude with first sections.

Throughout his psalm motets Goudimel's ingenuity in the use of *cantus firmus* settings with imitation, free imitative polyphony, occasional chordal passages, sections in ternary rhythm, balance of voice parts within a *partie*, melismatic flow in seminimims, as well as syllabic settings of them, is highly admirable. Here is portrayed the work of a skilled composer at the height of his creativity.

The enthusiasm of composers over the completed Genevan Psalter, with its 150 texts and 125 melodies, resulted in various settings of the work in its entirety. Goudimel's first publication of a complete setting, dated 1564 and reprinted in 1565, which included, in addition to the psalms, the Ten Commandments, Song of Simeon, and Graces before and after meals, is frequently described as a note against note setting. Actually a sixth of the settings are polyphonic. Since twenty-five Genevan Psalm texts lacked melodies of their own and were assigned melodies already used for other psalms, Goudimel chose to set the duplicating melodies polyphonically. Although these settings show infinite variety, it is possible to make a few generalities, including their exceptions. Note against note settings are used for the first line of all of those psalms except Psalm LXV, which begins by setting all voice parts polyphonically; and Psalm CXXXIX, in which only Superius and Contratenor are set initially for the opening line, though Tenor and Bassus follow with a similar version of that line. In Psalms LXII, XCV, and CXI (all set to the melody of Psalm XXIV), the Bassus enters a semibreve after the other parts. The settings of the first lines of Psalms XCV and CXI are identical, except for their Contratenors. The first line note against note settings in the polyphonic pieces are entirely different from their counterparts, which are set note against note throughout. There is one exception. The first line of polyphonic Psalm C is the same as that of chordal Psalm CXXXI. In Psalm CXLII, based on the same melody, the voices enter simultaneously but proceed rhythmically independent of one another.

In three of the melodies having two settings each, the Genevan melody is given to the Superius, an innovation attributed to Goudimel. Particularly noteworthy is the setting of Psalm CXXXIX, wherein the Tenor follows the *cantus firmus* of the Superius canonically throughout. Then, too, there are several instances where the imitative Superius precedes the Tenor *cantus* as in Psalms LXIII, LXVI, and C. In Psalm CXVI the same plan is coupled with imitation between Contratenor and Bassus using free material. In addition to similar imitation between Superius and Tenor in Psalm LXVIII, its Tenor *cantus* for the seventh line, which is repeated for the eighth, is followed by an imitative Superius, first at the octave for the seventh line, then at the 5th for the eighth.

Imitation, to a greater or lesser degree, occurs throughout these polyphonic settings, the least instance of which is confined to the first setting of a repeated text in the bass of the final line of Psalm CXLII. Only the Contratenor and Bassus of Psalm XCVIII are imitative.

Rarely is the contrapuntal texture thinned, as by the omission of bass parts in the fourth line of Psalm CXI, the sixth line of Psalm LXIII, and half of the initial line and all of the fifth line (which is crowded out by a setting of text repetition of the preceding line) of Psalm XCVIII.

The setting of Psalm LXVII is interesting structurally. The *cantus*, with its setting of the first and second lines, is repeated for the third and fourth. However, the first and third lines are set chordally and the second and fourth, polyphonically. The chordal settings differ from chordal Psalm XXXIII, which shares the same *cantus*. The eighth line, having the same *cantus* as the seventh, is given the same setting in Psalm XXXIII, but this is not true of Psalm LXVII (see Ex. 1).

Example 1. A comparison of the structural plans of Psalms LXVII (Goudimel 1967–: X, 135–36) and XXXIII (Goudimel 1967–:IX, 28).

Psalm LXVII.

Psalm XXXIII

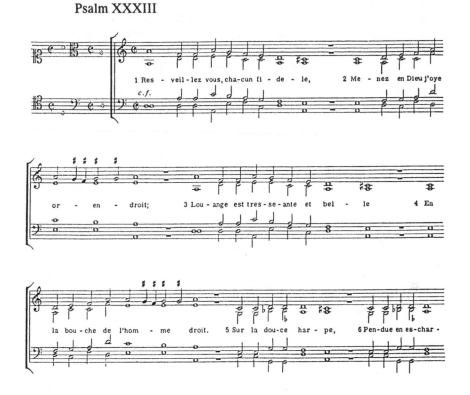

1 Res - veil - lez vous, cha-cun fi - de - le, 2 Me - nez en Dieu J'oye

or - en - droit; 3 Lou - ange est tres - se - ante et bel - le 4 En

la bou - che de l'hom - me droit. 5 Sur la dou - ce har - pe, 6 Pen-due en es-char -

In chordal Psalm LXXXVI and polyphonic Psalm LXXVII, the *cantus* and setting of the first line equals the second; the fourth equals the eighth; the fifth equals the sixth; but only the *cantus* of the third line equals that of the seventh in both psalms.

Goudimel's other complete setting of the psalter is a polyphonic one which survives only in the posthumous edition of 1580 (he died in 1572) and is identical with an extant Superius part book of 1568. Why the 1568/1580 edition did not follow the Biblical order of the psalms or what prompted the sequence used remains an enigma. Pierre Pidoux suggests a modal arrangement (cf. the Preface to Vol. X of the *Oeuvres Complètes*).

To compose polyphonic settings for such an extensive collection is a somewhat formidable task and it is fascinating to observe with what skill Goudimel made use of the contrapuntal technique of his era to accomplish this. Here the Genevan melody is in the Superius, except for eighteen of the polyphonic settings taken over from the 1564/1565 editions, wherein it is in the Tenor. Also, chordal initial lines are used for some fifteen of the new settings. Otherwise, free polyphony, coupled with imitation of the *cantus* to a greater or lesser extent, is used ingeniously throughout these settings. Only six (Psalms XII, XVI, XXXVII, LVII, XLVIII, and LXXXI) are without a vestige of *cantus* imitation.

There are instances where a single line of the *cantus* is chosen for imitative treatment, sometimes involving only one voice part toward the end, as in the Bassus of Psalm III. At other times all voice parts participate in imitation of a single line. More frequently imitation of whole or half lines, exact or modified, occurs throughout a setting. As would be expected, the prevailing intervals of imitation are the octave, 5th, 4th, and unison. However, there are several instances of imitation at the 2nd (Psalm LV)(Ex. 2a) 6th (Psalms VI, XXXVI, and LI), the 7th (Psalms XXXVI, LV, and CXLVII [Ex. 2b]), the 9th changed to 10th (Psalm XLVI)(Ex. 2c).

Example 2: Examples of less common imitations:

a) Imitation at the 2nd (Psalm LV, mm. 12–13; between Superius and Contratenor) (Goudimel 1967–:X, 182)

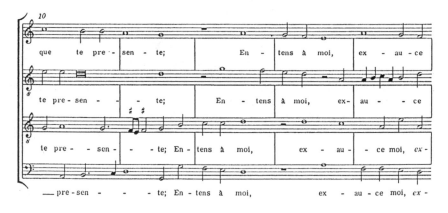

b) Imitation at the 7th (Psalm CXLVII, mm. 24–26; between Superius and Tenor) (Goudimel 1967:X, 206)

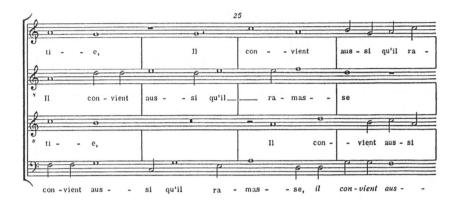

c) Imitation moving from 9ths to 10ths (Psalm XLVI, mm. 10–13; between Bassus and Superius) (Goudimel 1967–:X, 213)

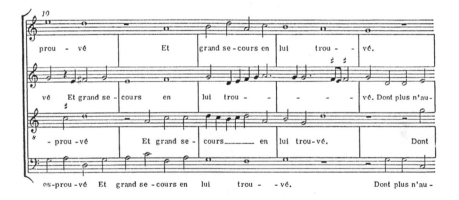

Repeated melodies with different texts are treated in a variety of ways. For Psalm XL, the fifth line is set with exact imitation at the octave in the Tenor, and with modified imitation at the 4th in the Bassus; but the melody repeated for the sixth line has a free setting. Also the eighth line, with exact imitation at the 5th for the Contratenor's text repetition, is followed by a free setting of the same melody in the ninth line.

In Psalm CIII, the melody for the third line is preceded by the Contratenor's imitative entry at the 5th, while the Tenor supports the *cantus* briefly with preceding syncopated 6ths. Its counterpart in the sixth line is a free setting.

The first and second lines of Psalm LXXXIX share the same *cantus*, with an imitative Tenor entry in the first and an imitative Bassus entry in the second, but with different surrounding polyphony.

In Psalm XXXVI the entire free setting of the first three lines, of course, with different texts, is repeated; the seventh line is melismatic, and in line eight, the same melody is supported in 6ths by the Contratenor.

In Psalm L, the third and fourth lines share the same melody but have different settings. The only reference to the *cantus* occurs in the Bassus. Balance of voice parts gives contrast to the free settings of duplicate melodies in Psalm XLVIII. The opening melody, set with only Superius and Contratenor, is repeated with a four-voice setting. Lines three and four, also with duplicated melodies, are set for three-voice parts, line three lacking Contratenor, line four lacking Bassus. Three melodic pairs in Psalm XXXIII have individual settings with imitation in the Contratenor and Tenor, except for line two, which has a free setting.

The three melodic pairs of Psalm XIX have a different plan. The imitative Tenor of line one changes midway from 5th to octave, but in line four it precedes the duplicate *cantus* at the octave throughout. Lines five and six are repetitions of two and three except for an imitative Contratenor introducing line five.

Identical free settings of the first and third lines occur in Psalm XCI. Lines two and four have only their melodies in common. Line two has an imitative tenor with a melismatic ending; line four has free polyphony.

These one-stanza settings, which include the polyphonic pieces in the preceding edition, are truly masterworks in miniature! But it was the note against note settings, in conformity with the austere tenets of the Reformation, that attained the most wide spread popularity. They were reprinted in France well into the nineteenth century. Also the 1580 edition was reprinted by Henry Expert in vols. II (1895), IV (1897a), and VI (1897b) of the series *Maîtres Musiciens de la Renaissance Française*. But the complete motet settings, the greatest expression of Goudimel's creativity, were not published until 1967–73.

In conclusion, it is of particular significance to note that it was the microfilm of some of Goudimel's Psalm Motets, procured by Carleton Sprague Smith from the Bibliothèque Nationale in Paris, that proved to

be the initial spark of the edition of the *Oeuvres complètes* of Claude
Goudimel (1967–).

REFERENCES CITED

Expert, Henry, ed.

1895　　*Claude Goudimel. 150 Psaumes de David (1580).* Book I.
Paris: Alphonse Leduc (Vol. II of *Maîtres Musiciens de la
Renaissance Française*)

1897a　　Claude Goudimel. *150 Psaumes de David (1580).* Book II.
Paris: Alphonse Leduc (Vol. IV of *Maîtres Musiciens de la
Renaissance Française*).

1897b　　Claude Goudimel. *150 Psaumes de David (1580).* Book III.
Paris: Alphonse Leduc (Vol. IV of *Maîtres Musiciens de la
Renaissance Française*).

Goudimel, Claude

1967–　　*Oevures Complètes.* Edited by Henri Gagnebin, Rudolf
Häusler, and Eleanor Lawry., under the direction of Luther
Dittmer and Pierre Pidoux. New York: The Institute of
Mediaeval Music, Ltd./Basel: Société Suisse de Musicologie.

[Vols. I (1967); II (1967); III (1969); IV (1970); V (1972); VI
(1972); VII (1973); VIII (1973); IX (1967); and X (1969).]

Jean R. Longland, Translator

THREE BRAZILIAN POEMS[1]

No Meio do Caminho[2]   *In the Middle of the Road*

by Carlos Drummond de Andrade

No meio do caminho tinha uma pedra
tinha uma pedra no meio do caminho
tinha uma pedra
no meio do caminho tinha uma pedra.

Nunca me esquecerei dêsse aconteci-
mento
na vida de minhas retinas tão fatigadas.

Nunca me esquecerei que no meio do
caminho
tinha uma pedra
tinha uma pedra no meio do caminho
no meio do caminho tinha uma pedra.

In the middle of the road there was a stone
there was a stone in the middle of the road
there was a stone
in the middle of the road there was a stone.

Never shall I forget that event

in the life of my weary retinas.

Never shall I forget that in the middle of the
road
there was a stone
there was a stone in the middle of the road
in the middle of the road there was a stone.

[1]These translations are offered to Carleton Sprague Smith as a tribute to his interest in Brazil. Long years ago I took his course in Brazilian history at New York University.

[2]Carlos Drummond de Andrade (1902–1987) ranks as one of the most admired poets of Brazil. "No Meio do Caminho," from his *Obra Completa* (Rio de Janeiro: Companhia Aguilar Editora, 1964), pp. 61–62, has been translated into many languages and there is even a whole book about it.

Jean R. Longland is retired as Curator of the Library at The Hispanic Society of America. She has published many translations of Portuguese and Brazilian poetry, including an anthology, Selections from Contemporary Portuguese Poetry *(Irvington-on-Hudson, 1966).*

O Lutador[3]   *The Wrestler*
                    by Carlos Drummond de Andrade

Lutar com palavras	To wrestle words is surely
é a luta mais vã.	wrestling in vain.
Entanto lutamos	However, we start wrestling
mal rompe a manhã.	as soon as day is plain.
São muitas, eu pouco.	They're many, I am few.
Algumas, tão fortes	Some are quite as strong
como o javali.	as wild boars in attack.
Não me julgo louco.	I do not think I'm mad.
Se o fôsse, teria	If so, I would not lack
poder de encantá-las.	the power to bewitch them.
Mas lúcido e frio,	But lucidly and coldly
apareço e tento	I come out, and try
apanhar algumas	to gather a supply
para meu sustento	to serve as nourishment
num dia de vida.	through one more day of life.
Deixam-se enlaçar,	They let themselves be snared,
tontas à carícia	dizzy with my caress,
e súbito fogem	and suddenly run away
e não há ameaça	and neither threatening
e nem há sevícia	nor even churlishness
que as traga de nôvo	can bring them back again
ao centro da praça.	to the center of the ring.
Insisto, solerte.	Craftily I persist,
Busco persuadí-las.	attempting to persuade.
Ser-lhes-ei escravo	I will be their slave
de rara humildade.	in rare humility.
Guardarei sigilo	I will guard the secret
de nosso comércio.	that we engage in trade.
Na voz, nenhum travo	In my voice no acid
de zanga ou desgôsto.	of anger or disgust.
Sem me ouvir deslizam,	Unheedingly they glide,
perpassam levíssimas	weightlessly they slide,
e viram-me o rosto.	and turn their heads away.
Lutar com palavras	To wrestle words would seem
parece sem fruto.	to be a fruitless game.
Não têm carne e sangue...	They are not flesh and blood...
Entretanto, luto.	I wrestle, all the same.

[3]"O Lutador" is of special interest to me because translators spend their lives wrestling with words. From his *Seleta em Prosa e Verso* (Rio de Janeiro: Livraria José Olympio, 1971), pp. 174–76.

Palavra, palavra
(digo exasperado)
se me desafias,
aceito o combate.
Quisera possuir-te
neste descampado,
sem roteiro de unha
ou marca de dente
nessa pele clara.
Preferes o amor
de uma posse impura
e que venha o gôzo
da maior tortura.

Luto corpo a corpo,
luto todo o tempo,
sem maior proveito
que o da caça ao vento.
Não encontro vestes,
não seguro formas,
é fluido inimigo
que me dobra os músculos
e ri-se das normas
da boa peleja.

Iludo-me às vêzes,
pressinto que a entrega
se consumará.
Já vejo palavras
em côro submisso,
esta me ofertando
seu velho calor,
aquela sua glória
feita de mistério,
outra seu desdém,
outra seu ciúme,
e um sapiente amor
me ensina a fruir
de cada palavra
a essência captada,
o sutil queixume.
Mas ai! é o instante
de entreabrir os olhos;
entre beijo e bôca,
tudo se evapora.

O ciclo do dia
ora se conclui
e o inútil duelo
jamais se resolve.

Oh word, oh word, oh word
(angrily I shout)
if you challenge me,
then I accept the bout.
I would like to possess you
here inside the ropes,
without a sign of toothmarks
or path of fingernails
on your transparent flesh.
You prefer love forced
by unnatural possession
where pleasure is derived
from the maximum of torture.

I wrestle hand to hand,
I wrestle all the time,
with no more benefit
than if I chased the breeze.
I cannot touch their clothing,
I cannot grasp their forms,
because an enemy fluid
knots my muscles up
and laughs at all the norms
of scientific combat.

Sometimes I am deluded,
I foresee that the surrender
will certainly be made.
Already I envision
words in submissive chorus,
this one offering me
her antiquarian warmth,
another giving her glory
made of mystery,
another her disdain,
another jealousy,
and love sagaciously
teaching me to enjoy
of every single word
the subjugated essence,
the subtle lamentation.
Alas! in just an instant,
the blinking of an eye:
between the kiss and mouth
nothing but a vapor.

The cycle of the day
is now a perfect ring
and yet the futile duel
never can be won.

O teu rosto belo,
ó palavra, esplende
na curva da noite
que tôda me envolve
Tamanha paixão
e nenhum pecúlio.
Cerradas as portas,
a luta prossegue
nas ruas do sono.

Your lovely countenance,
oh word, is shimmering
in the curving of the night
that wraps me all around.
Passion so immense
with no reward to keep.
After the doors are closed,
the wrestling continues
along the streets of sleep.

Washington Square[4]
by Cassiano Nunes

De madrugada,
atravesso o parque
deserto.

Ficou
de minha propriedade
particular.

Até a névoa
me pertence.

A estrela
fui eu que inventei.

Early in the morning
I walk across the
deserted park.

It has become
my private
property.

Even the mist
belongs to me.

The star
is my own invention.

[4]The contemporary poet Cassiano Nunes also taught at New York University and "Washington Square" reflects that experience. From his *Jornada; Poemas* (São Paulo: Clube de Poesia, 1972), p. 13.

Kate Van Winkle Keller

JAMES ALEXANDER'S COLLECTION OF COUNTRY DANCES, NEW YORK, 1730

James and Mary Alexander, a headstrong, talented, and canny Scotsman and a shrewd, dynamic, and loving Dutchwoman, lived in New York City during the first half of the eighteenth century.[1] Born of privileged families, he in Scotland, she in New York, they were among the city's most prominent citizens. Soon after his arrival in 1715, James was appointed Surveyor-General of both New York and New Jersey.[2] Later he was to become Attorney-General for New York, member of governing assemblies and councils in both colonies, large landholder, amateur

[1] The chief sources of biographical information for this article have been H. N. Mac-Cracken (1964), L. Rutherford (1894), and the Alexander papers at the New York Historical Society.

[2] James Alexander was born in Menstrie, Scotland on May 27, 1691, second son of David Alexander. After service on H. M. S. *Arundel* (1712–13), he moved to London, where he read law and was admitted to the bar in February of 1714/15. In August of that same year he arrived in New York. Following his death on April 2, 1756, *The New York Mercury* (April 5) carried the following tribute:

> A Gentleman in his Disposition, generous, courteous and humane, steadfast in Friendship, delicate in his sense of Honour, of Strict Probity, temperate in his Diet and in business indefatigable. The relations of Husband, Father and Master he sustained with highest Reputation. In these parts of the World few men surpass him either in the Natural sagacity and Strength of his Intellectual powers or in his Literary Acquirements. . .(Rutherford 1894:44).

Kate Van Winkle Keller is Executive Director of The Sonneck Society for American Music and co-director of "American Performing Arts in the 18th Century: The Newspaper Sources," an NEH-funded project based at the State University at New Paltz.

astronomer, and most of all, outspoken defender of the rights and liberties of citizens. In his arguments during the trial of publisher John Peter Zenger, an affair precipitated through his own actions, James helped set legal precedents still cited today.

Mary was the young widow of a wealthy Dutch merchant when she married James, and she continued to maintain their importing business with her new spouse's enthusiastic support.[3] Although the first documents of their marriage imply a carefully considered business arrangement, the warmth and ebullience of the combined households soon made the legal protections unnecessary. Mary's two children and the seven new Alexanders melded into a boisterous family, whose complaints were only that their father was so vigorously employed in business that they hardly saw him at home. Late in their life, James observed that his wife "for two months past has been in a bad state of health, and continues so; but if she is able to crawl she will be in the shop. By which means she often gets fresh colds, being very tender."[4]

Both James and Mary preserved their business papers. James's were mostly legal briefs, notes, and a vast collection of business letters. Mary's refer chiefly to her business. Although there must have been personal correspondence, none remains.

However, two documents now at the New York Historical Society give us an unequalled opportunity to view social life in early New York. Among Mary Alexander's papers are several large cards with samples of the fabric and tapes she imported.[5] Today they still glow with the bright colors and textures of the contemporary personal and domestic clothing.[6]

Among his voluminous papers, James also left an unusual treasure: a tattered pocket notebook comprising five sheets of thin paper, not much larger than modern index cards folded lengthwise and secured in the fold by a large straight pin. In it, James made a number of handwritten entries, including the dates of May 14, November 11 and 13, 1730.[7]

---

[3]Mary (or Maria) was born on April 17, 1694 in New York. She was the daughter of John Spratt and Maria DePeyster. She married Samuel Provôst on October 15, 1711. Soon widowed, she married James Alexander on January 5, 1721 and shared a long and happy life, surviving him by only four years. She died on April 18, 1760.

[4]Alexander to Colden (February 2, 1753) (quoted in MacCracken 1964:140, n. 18).

[5]Alexander Collection. Box 68: "Samples of Tapes and Cloth handled by Mary Alexander at her store in New York City in the 1730's."

[6]For a discussion of the significance and color photographs of these swatch books, see F. M. Montgomery (1983:384–85 and plates D8–11).

[7]James Alexander. Misc. Mss. Alexander, Box 10, no. 2: "List of Dances in N. Y. 1730."

Along with his inscribed surveying measurements, he referred briefly to a catalog of books in Governor Montgomery's library,[8] and maintained several "tickler" pages with reminders to check into the collection of debts and the value of properties. His experiences as a surveyor must have made the remedy for rattlesnake bite worth entering as well. Most startling among these random business notes are verbal instructions for the figures of twenty-seven country dances (see Figs. 1, 2 and 3).[9]

In 1730, James would have been thirty-nine years old, and Mary thirty-six. Her most recent child was born in 1727, and another was to arrive on 1 July 1731. They were mature, busy adults living in a bustling seaport that whirled with political intrigue and mercantile activity.

It is certainly possible that James's collection of dances was assembled for his children's dancing lessons. John and David Provoost would then have been sixteen and eleven, respectively, and Mary and William Alexander, nine and seven.[10] However, as they were written into a personal pocket notebook, it seems more likely that the instructions were written as *aides-memoires* for the children's parents.

James appears to have marked down hastily all the dances and, at the same time. It is probable that he copied them from another source. Nothing seems to have been added at a later date, since there are no erasures, crossings out, or insertions. The pen nib progresses from newly sharpened to a bit dull over the period of the transcription.

He did not copy them from a known commercial publication, yet they can be traced to several, quite different contemporary sources, but none exactly. His descriptions are cryptic; some are quite detailed, while others give only the simplest clues—usually from the active man's perspective. While some of his abbreviations can be found in printed

[8]Montgomery's library was sold in New York in 1732 (*The New York Gazette*, May 1–8, 1732).

[9]Before the discovery of the Alexander manuscript, the earliest known American dance source was Aaron Thompson's collection of five country dances among one hundred fife tunes made between 1777 and 1782. (See K. Van Winkle Keller 1986:90–111.)

[10]In 1729, *The New York Gazette* announced the sale of the "house commonly called the Dancing School," quoted by Norman Benson (1963:289). In the same paper, dated June 7–June 14, 1731, George Brownell announced that he would teach "Reading, Writing, Cyphering. . . Dancing,. . . and various Sorts of works. Any Persons may be taught as private as they please." Brownell managed boarding and day schools in several cities between 1703 to after 1750. From about 1721 to 1734 he was teaching in New York City and may well have taught the Alexander children. (See Hoover 1985:738–41 and Lambert 1985:954–69.)

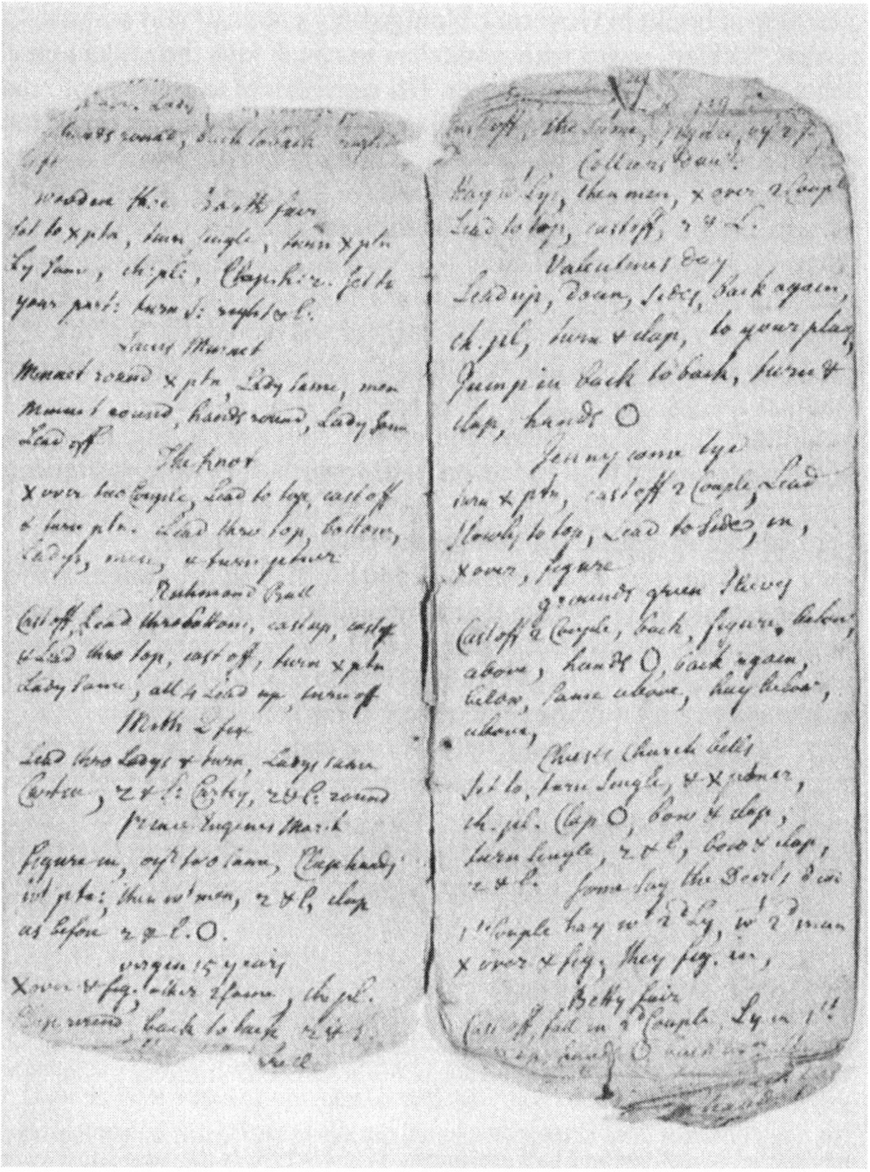

Figure 1. Leaves 2^v and 3^r. James Alexander. "List of Dances in N. Y.

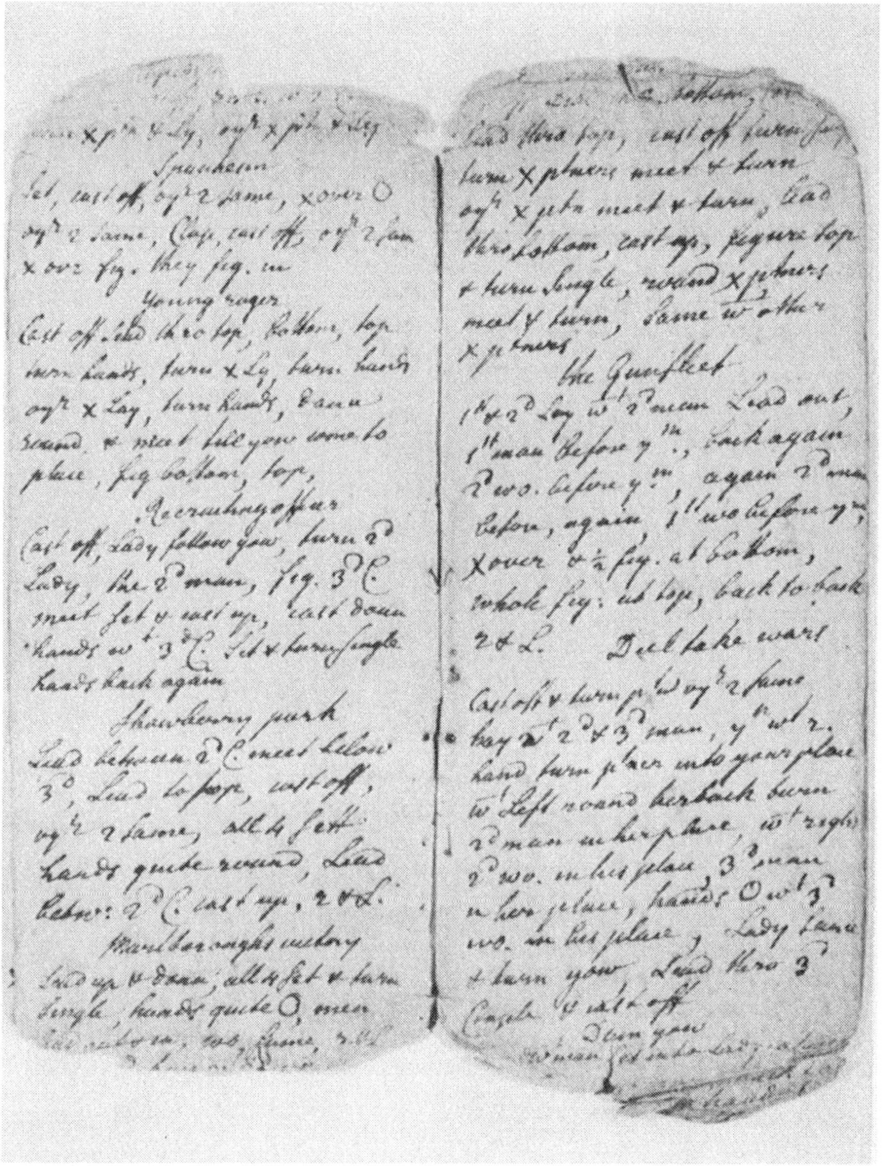

Figure 2. Leaves 3^{v} and 4^{r}. *Ibid.*

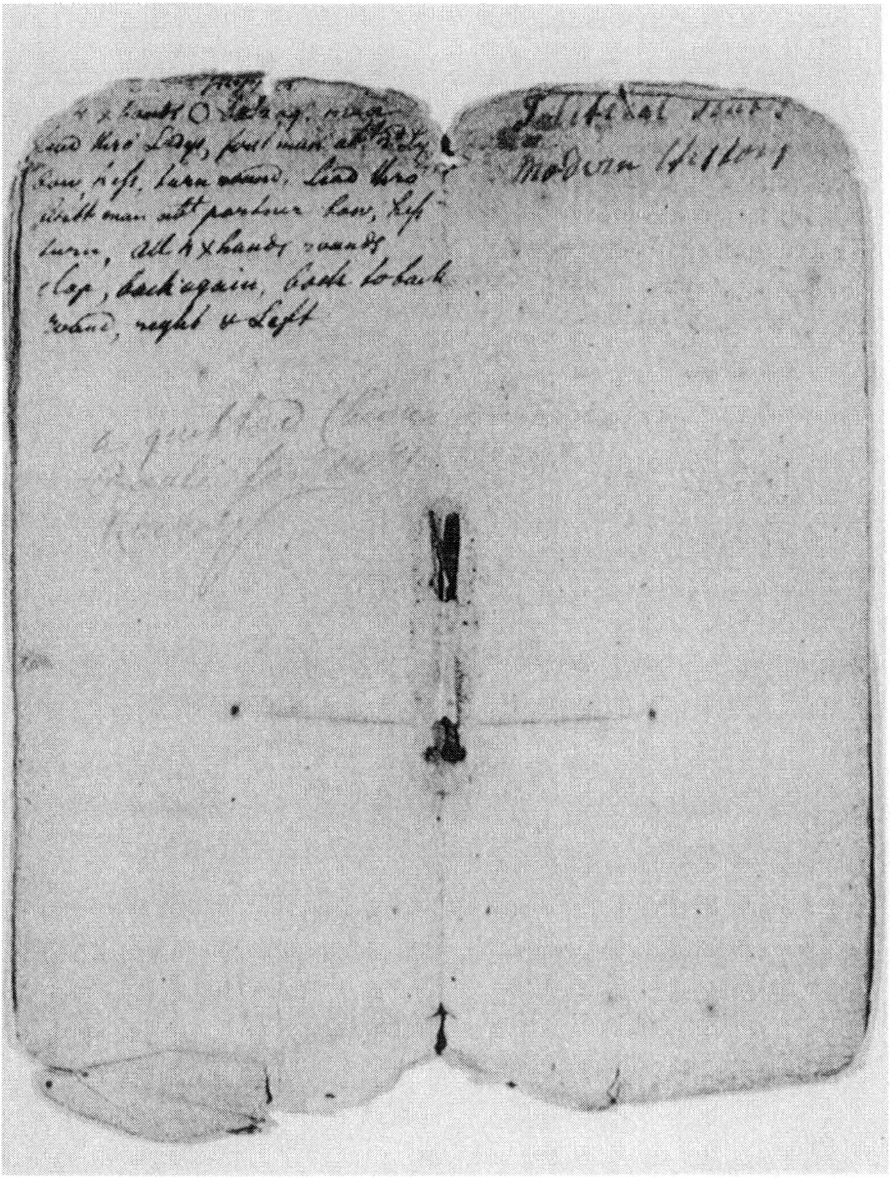

Figure 3. Leaves 4^v and 5^r. *Ibid*.

dance literature, most are simply personal shorthand.[11] In some cases, his choice of words is exactly the same as those in printed sources. Often, even if the words vary, the distinctive figures can be identified in sequence and indicate a concordance. In some, a detailed performance reconstruction will be necessary to determine whether the figures described in such varied terms are indeed the same. Yet, overall, it is clear that the dances had an integrity of title, figures, and music which did not change except incidentally through the process of oral transmission. Alexander wrote down the important parts of most of the dances—key figures, sequences, or specific wording—which provided the clues he needed to identify and remember specific dances.

He chose fairly-recently composed dances, most of them having been first published within the past two decades. Seven were published in 1713 while he was in London. Five did not appear in print until after he had left England. The Alexanders probably learned the new dances from books, dancing masters, or friends.

The selection was made chiefly from among dances then popular in London society. Most had been reprinted often in the successive editions of *The Dancing Master* series, in the competing compilations of John Walsh, and several appeared in William Neal's Dublin collection of 1726.[12]

Dancing parties for people of James and Mary Alexander's social position would have varied from informal house-parties to formal court

---

[11]Some of these are obvious, some less so: x = corner; Ly = lady; ch. pl. = change places; w = with; y = th; oyr = other; and o = hands-round or circle.

[12]The dance publications printed before 1730 in which concordances can be found are:

   a. *A Choice Collection of Country Dances*. Dublin: Iohn and William Neal, [1726].

   b. *The Compleat [and "Second Book of the Compleat"] Country Dancing-Master*. London: John Walsh and John Hare, 1718 [and 1719].

   c. *The Dancing Master*. Volume I. 2nd-7th editions. London: John Playford, 1652–1686.

   d. *The Dancing Master*. Volume I. 8th–12th editions. London: Henry Playford, 1690–1703.

   e. *The Dancing Master*. Volume I. 13th–17th editions London: John Young, 1706–1721.

   f. *The Dancing Master*. Volume I. 18th edition. London: Edward Midwinter and John Young, ca. 1728.

   g. *The Dancing Master*. Volume II. 1st edition. London: John Cullen, John Young [et al.], ca. 1713.

   h. *The Dancing Master*. Volume II. 2nd-4th editions. London: John Young, 1718–1728.

   i. *The Dancing Master*. Volume III. 2nd [only surviving] edition. London: John Young, [1726].

or state balls in large rooms at taverns or other public buildings. Like today, the deportment of the participants and the degree of display and exhibition depended on the reason for the gathering.

A public or ceremonial ball consisted chiefly of presentational dances such as minuets and gavottes, which were performed as duets for two dancers with choreographed foot, hand, and arm movements and decorative tracks. When, towards the end of the evening, the country dances were announced, the company relaxed, because these dances were focused on partners, rather than on the audience, and everyone could join in the dance at the same time. However, formalities would not be abandoned entirely; the environment was still one of exhibition and display (see Plates 1 and 2).

Wright's Compleat Collection of Celebrated Country Dances both Old and New, that are in Vouge, with the Newest and best Directions to each Dance y' whole Carefully corrected Voll.1.st Price 3. 6d

Printed for I: Iohnfon Mufical Inftrument Maker, at y' Harp & Crown in Cheapside London.

Plate 1. A public dancing party, with a full orchestra on one side and a booth offering pastries and drink on the other. A considerable number of spectators watch the country dance in progress. This is the title page of a book, published in London about 1740 and owned by a Salem, Massachusetts resident by 1749.[13] (Courtesy of the English Country Dance and Song Society.)

[13]See B. Lambert (1980:xvii), J. Van Cleef and K. Van Winkle Keller (1980:10), and C. A. Hoover (1985:741–43).

Plate 2: A Country Dance at a public Assembly in 1744. The company is dancing with considerable spirit and a large audience watches from the side of the room. (Courtesy of the Trustees of the Bodleian Library, Oxford University.)

At a party at home on the other hand, while proud parents might call on the children to show-off their dancing school minuets, the adults would spend most of the time dancing country dances (see Plates 3 and 4). Improvised reels for three or four, and the solo step dances, jigs and hornpipes, were also popular vehicles for energetic dancers.

The dances in James Alexander's collection are all performed in longways formation, partners facing each other, the gentlemen in one line and their ladies opposite. They are progressive dances in which the top couple, after performing a series of movements with the two below, finish the dance in the second place, and then repeat it with the next two below. After three repetitions, the couple then at the top could also dance the figures, because by then there would be two couples below them, the leading couple having progressed to the fourth place.

Each dance had between six and twelve figures, ranging from a simple hand turn with partner to complex weaving figures for three or four, clapping sequences, and large circles. The last dance Alexander wrote down involves a good bit of bowing and kissing!

Plate 3: Woodcut frontispiece to *Twenty Four New Country-Dances For the Year 1713* (London: John Walsh and J. Hare, [1713]) depicting an elegant house-party dance from the period that Alexander lived in London. (Courtesy of the British Library.)

Plate 4: A dancing party in a private home between 1728 and 1732. This is the title page of the last edition of volume one of *The Dancing Master*. Many of James Alexander's dances are printed in this book and its earlier editions. (Courtesy of the Library of Congress.)

There is no indication of footwork at all, except, as would be expected, in "Lanes Minuet." In the printed instructions of "Lane's Trumpet Minuet," which is a longways dance like the rest, there is the specific note: "This must be done with the Minuet Step."

We know from other sources that cultivated dancers knew and often used elaborate steps, and certainly the Alexanders and their friends would have been trained in these skills. Their position among the political, business, and social leaders of the colony meant that they probably were occasionally called on to open Assemblies with a minuet or other choreographed dance. Depending on the occasion and the dancers, country dances could be performed with or without steps, some of these being the minuet, the *pas de gavotte, pas de bourrée, contretemps*, and *rigadoon*. More informally the dancers might move with a simple dance-walk, skip, or *chassée*.

The music to which these dances were set is British. There are no obvious French or Dutch influences. Of the music that we can identify, fifteen of the tunes are instrumental pieces and eight are songs. Fifteen are in duple time and six in 6/8 or in 6/4 (=6/8). "Young Roger," which is based on the classic slip jig "Roger of Coverly," is in 9/4 and the minuet is, of course, in 3. Eighteen of the tunes are in the Major mode, and five are in the Minor. Fourteen appear to be carefully composed pieces, while only six are from the repertory of simple, folk-like melodies, a typical mix for the period.

Here then, thanks to James and Mary Alexander, is a collection of popular country dances and a spectrum of lovely brocades, broadcloths, and decorative tapes to choose from. We can reconstruct the window dressings and the slip-covers, the ladies' dresses, the men's suits, the children's garb and the servants liveries.[14] The picture can then come to life in music and in dance, as it did 250 years ago.

THE DANCES IN THE MANUSCRIPT

1. The top of this page has been worn off, and much of the dance lost. A hands-round, back-to-back and a right-and-left can be discerned as the final figures.

---

[14] Alexander's negro servant, Yaff, ran away in June of 1729. The advertisement requesting his return describes his clothes in detail (*The New York Gazette*, June 23–30, 1729).

2. "Wooden Shoe Barth Fair"

The first part of this dance is from "Wooden Shooes" (DMI.12:339 [1703],[15] music in duple time, written by Jeremiah Clark as "Autumn Dance by a French Clown and Country Woman in Wooden Shoes" for *The Island Princess*, 1699). The second part is closer to "Bartholomew Fair or The Whim" (DMI.9:170 [1695], "The Whim," music in 6/4 [=6/8] time). Alexander's title implies a combination or confusion, for although his dance is not identical to either, the second half of both dances includes change-places, back-to-back, and right-and-left figures.

3. "Lanes Minuet"

Alexander's abbreviated directions are modeled on "Mr. Lane's Trumpet Minuet" (DMI.9II:2 [1698]) rather than on Lane's Minuet," which has the same opening figure (DMI.9:174 [1695]).

4. "The Knot"

In Alexander's dance of "The Knot," the active couple traces extended figures across and up and down the dance. This pictorial element is present in all of the printed versions (DMI.7:206 [1686]). Neal's version (p. 15 [1726]) is closes to these abbreviated instructions (see Fig. 4).

Figure 4: "The Knott" from *A Choice Collection of Country Dances.* Dublin: Iohn & William Neal, [1726], p. 8. (Courtesy of the National Library of Ireland.)

[15]Citation is to the earliest known printing of the dance figures and the melody with this title.

5. "Richmond Ball"
Known in several sources as "Richmond Ball or Mr. Lane's Maggot" or simply "Lane's Maggot," this dance features casts, leads, hand-turns, and a four-abreast lead-up (DMI.9:194 [1695]). Again, Neal's "Richmond Ball" (p. 2 [1726]) is the closest concordance.

6. "Moth Q Loge"
Initially this title appeared to be abbreviated from "Mother Quoth Hodge," but the dance proved to be modeled on "O Mother Roger" instead (DMI.9:166 [1695]).

7. "Prince Eugene's March"
The model for this dance might have been that in DMII.I:87 (1713), although the points of concordance are few. The music was written by Jeremiah Clark.

8. "Virgin 15 Years"
Alexander's dance derives from the second of two with the title "Wou'd you have a young Virgin; or, poor Robin's Maggot" (DMII.1:148 [1713]). The opening *poussettes* in Neal's "A Young Virgin of 15 Years" (p. 14 [1726]) may be the "back-to-back" figure which is not in the DM dance.

9. At the top of the page are fragments of a dance once titled: . . . Jig." Although the remnants are too brief to make a reconstruction, they feature a cast, figure, and possibly a right-and-left. These figures comprise the end of "Spanish Jigg" (Neal p. 22 [1726]), which is printed on the same page as Alexander's next entry, "Collier's Dau r."

10. "Collier's Dau r"
Although here the dance begins with a hay, the remainder is an abbreviated version of "The Collier's Daughter, or, Duke of Rutland's Delight" (DMII.3:209 [1718]).

11. "Valentines Day"
This popular dance has a distinctive clap and back-ring figure (DMI.6:172 [1679]). Alexander probably knew it well, and while the printed versions spell out the figures in great detail, he needed only a few cues to remember the sequence.

12. "Jenny come Tye"

Alexander's version of "Jenny, come tye my Cravat" appears to be developed from the dance as it appears in DMI.8:199 (1690). The figures are simply in a different order.

13. "Grounds Green Sleeves"

This dance is closest to "Green Sleeves" in Neal (p. 12 [1726]), which is an extended version of "Green Sleeves" and Yellow Lace" (DMI.17.113 [1721]; see Fig. 5). The figures are different from the more widely-published dance to the same tune, called "Greens Sleeves and Pudding Pies" (DMI.7:186 [1686]).

[113]

Green Sleeves and Yellow Lace.   *Longways for as many as will*

Note : *Each Strain is to be play'd twice, and the Tune twice through.*

The 1. cu. fett and caft off then fett and caft off 2. cu. Then the fame to their places again. The 1.Man wholefigure with the 3. cu. and the Wo. with the 2.cu. Then the 1. Man whole Figure with the 2. cu.and the Wo. with the 3. cu.

Then the 1. Man hands half round with the 3. cu. and the 1. Wo. hands half round with the 2. cu. Then the 1. Wo. hands round with the 3. cu. and the Man hands round with the 2 cu. The firft Man hay with the 3. cu. and the 1. Wo. hays with the 2. cu. Then the 1. Wo. hays with the 3. cu. and the Man hays with the 2. cu.

Figure 5: "Green Sleeves and Yellow Lace" from *The Dancing Master*, volume one, 17th edition (London: John Young, 1721), p. 113. (Courtesy of The English Folk Dance and Song Society.)

14. "Christs Church Bells"

The version of "Christ Church Bells in Oxon," found in DMI.17:104 [1721], is the dance recorded here. It is a variant of the dance of the same title in which the clap/circle figure is altered and the right-and-left omitted (DMI.6:177 [1679], "Christchurch Bells").

15. "Some Say the Devils Dead"

Neal's "Aberdeene, or ye Deel's Dead" is closest to Alexander's version of this dance (p. 35 [1726]). The hays, crossings, and figure-eight movements are all present, although Alexander does not describe the dramatic four-abreast leads, and his opening hays are for active couple and one corner, rather than the three men or the three women. A variant dance to this same melody occurs with a number of different titles: "Devonshire Lass," "Scotch Ayre," "Scotch Moggy," and "The Devil's Dead" (DMI.12:353 [1703]).

16. "Betty Fair"
With directions to the active man, this fragment is the opening of "Bury Fair" (DMI.9II:15 [1698]).

17. Fragments of a dance are visible at the top of this page.

18. "Spanheim"
"The Spanheim" appears in DMII.1:812 (1713). It may not be a coincidence that this entire page consists of dances first published in 1713, when Alexander was working in London.

19. "Young Roger"
Elements of Alexander's dance appear in "Young Roger" (DMII.1:190 [1713]). The study of the dances set to variants of the circular slip-jig tune "Roger of Coverly" from the seventeenth to the nineteenth century promises to be interesting.

20. "Recruiting officer"
This dance appears in DMII.1:175 [1713] (see Fig. 6.).

21. "Shawberry Park"
Here Alexander carefully describes "Shawbury Park" with its distinctive leading figures as it appears in DMII.1:15 [1713] (see Fig. 6).

22. "Marlboroughs Victory"
Despite text loss, this dance can be identified as "Marlborough's Victory" (DMII.1:167 [1713]).

23. Although this dance too has lost text, the elaborate sequence of corner turns identify it as a possible concordance to "The Dusty Miller" in Neal (p. 15 [1726]).

(193)

Note, Each Strain is to be play'd twice over.

The 1ft Man caft off and turn the 2d Wo. quite round, the 1ft Wo. at the fame Time follows him below the 2d Man, and turns him quite round... Then Figure thro' the 3d Cu. and caft up to the Top... The 1ft Cu. caft off and take with the 3d Cu. and go half round... All fet and turn fingle, then Hands back again, which brings the 1ft Cu. into the 2d Cu. Place proper...

Figure 6. "Recruiting Officer" from *The Second Book of the Compleat Country Dancing-Master* (London: J. Walsh and J. Hare, 1719), p. 193. (Courtesy of the Library of Congress.)

24. "The Gunfleet"

Alexander's directions for this dance with its odd chasing movements are very specific and are modeled on "The Gun Fleet" in DMI.17:13 [1721].

25. "Diel take wars"

Again, a long and careful description, possibly to distinguish this dance, which appears in DMI.17:219 [1721], from the more frequently printed version (DMI.9IIA1:3 [1698]). The song to which the dance is set was written by Jeremiah Clark.

26. "Durn you"

The scraps of words and curious title point to a concordance with the opening figure of "Damme" (DMI.9IIA1:42 [1698]), retitled "Dampier" in CCDMI:111 [1718]).

27. "Happy. . ."

Of all the "Happy. . ." dances in contemporary literature, none include the specific "bow, kiss, turn" of this last dance, "Happy Meeting" (DMI.9II:14 [1698]) is the closest concordance to the figures.

REFERENCES CITED

Alexander, James

n. d.   *Misc. Mss. Alexander.* New York: New-York Historical
             Society.

Benson, Norman

1963   *The Itinerant Dancing and Music Masters of Eighteenth-Cen-
            tury America.* Unpublished Ph.D. diss. Minneapolis: Univer-
            sity of Minnesota.

Hoover, Cynthia Adams

1985   "Epilogue to Secular Music in Early Massachusetts," in Bar-
            bara Lambert, ed. *Music in Colonial Massachusetts 1630–
            1820* (Boston: Colonial Society of Massachusetts), Vol. 2, pp.
            715–867.

Lambert, Barbara, ed.

1980   "Introduction," in Barbara Lambert, ed., *Music in Colonial
            Massachusetts 1630–1820* (Boston: Colonial Society of Mas-
            sachusetts), Vol. I, pp. ix–xv.

1985   "Appendix C: Music Masters in Colonial Boston," *Ibid.,* Vol.
            2, pp. 935–1157.

MacCracken, Henry Noble

1964   *Prologue to Independence: The Trials of James Alexander,
            American 1715–1756.* New York: James H. Heineman.

Montgomery, Florence M.

1983   *Textiles in America 1650–1870.* New York: W. W. Norton.

Rutherford, Livingston

1894   *Family Records and Events.* New York: DeVinne Press.

Van Cleef, Joy, and Kate Van Winkle Keller

1980   "Selected American Country Dances and Their English
            Sources," in Barbara Lambert, ed., *Music in Colonial Mas-
            sachussetts 1630–1820* (Boston: The Colonial Society of
            Massachussetts), Vol. 1, pp. 3–73.

Van Winkle Keller, Kate

1986   "John Griffiths, Eighteenth-Century Itinerant Dancing
            Master," in Peter Benes, ed., Itinerancy New England and
            New York (Boston: Boston University), pp. 90–111.

Charles Wagley

TAPIRAPÉ INDIAN MUSIC IN CENTRAL BRAZIL

A Memoir

In 1939–40, I spent more than a year doing social anthropological research among the Tapirapé Indians of central Brazil. Since then I have made three additional brief visits. The Tapirapé live on the river that bears their name and is a western tributary of the Araguaia River. In 1939, the Tapirapé village was about 450 to 500 miles from the nearest motor road on the Araguaia River and at least 150 miles from the nearest settlement of non-Indian backwoodsmen. The Tapirapé had already suffered decimation from Old World diseases (i.e., common cold, smallpox, measles, etc.) contracted second hand from other Indian tribes. In 1939–40, they had seen few Brazilians and were still isolated in their own territory.

I have written articles on the Tapirapé for scientific journals and one book (1977), describing their way of life in detail. However, I mentioned their music—actually their songs—only briefly, taking care to state in my book that "the reader must be warned about my description of the music... [for which] I have no technical training whatsoever" (*Ibid.*: 215). Furthermore, my visits took place before the availability of battery-operated tape recorders.[1] Yet, I dare to write about Tapirapé

---

[1]A few rolls of old fashioned dictaphone recordings are on file (Pre'54-055-F) at the University of Indiana Archives of Traditional Music (Indiana 1975:6).

Charles Wagley is Graduate Research Professor Emeritus at the University of Florida in Gainesville. He taught anthropology for many years at Columbia University, where he was also Director of Latin American Studies. He has written widely on Brazil.

music, because song is a central focus of their recreational and ceremonial life and, moreover, to share my account with my friend of many years, Carleton Sprague Smith.

To understand the social role of song, one should know something about the social life of the Tapirapé. Traditionally, they live in villages of about 200 people. There are six or seven dwellings arranged in a circle. Each dwelling is a multi-family longhouse made of palm leaves— somewhat like a bowl turned upside down. In the center of the village circle there is a much larger edifice built in the same manner. This is the men's club house, the *takana*, which, prohibited to women, is essential to the organization of song and ceremony. All men belong to one of the two men's societies—the White Birds or the Parrots. Each of these are further divided into a Boys, Youths, and Adult Mens sub-group (e.g., Parakeet, Talking Parrot, and the Large Macaw). A boy belongs to the men's society of his father. It is the men's societies that do most of the singing and take the lead in the ceremonials. Each of these societies has a "singing leader," a man of exceptional voice who knows most of the traditional songs for different occasions. The *takana* serves as the clubhouse of both men's societies wherein men lounge through the day and maintain the accouterments of their ceremonials.

Tapirapé music is vocal. Their instruments comprise only rattles made of gourds or hollow bamboo stems filled with beans. Sometimes they may bind the hoofs of wild pigs around their ankles to mark the rhythm of their songs. They dance while they sing, except for one type of solo singing; but their dance is simple and is secondary to their songs. Never did I hear a comment as to how well an individual danced, although I heard many comments on the quality of a person's voice or their extensive repertoire of songs.

Tapirapé music follows distinct styles during the different seasons of the year, much like we do for the Christmas season. During the rainy season (December through April), when their gardens have been planted and are now growing, they sing in a style which they call *káo* ('large garden'). In the dry season (May through November), they mainly sing *kawí* songs, which are sung by masked dancers who represent animal spirits believed by the women to visit the *takana*. In addition, there are special songs which are sung any time during the year and which comprise long monotonous sagas relating to distant ancestral heroes.

In April of 1939, when I arrived for the first time in the Tapirapé village called *Tampiitawa* ('the village of the Tapirs'), I encountered a colorful festival in progress. People had decorated their nude bodies with red (*urucu*) and black (*genipa*) dye. They wore *rosettes* made of bird down and parrot feathers as earrings. They danced and sang throughout the night. In fact, most Tapirapé ceremonies take place at night. This occasion was *kawió*, the beginning of both the dry season and the harvest of their gardens. The dancing was simple. There were two lines of dancers—one of males and the other of females, each of whom was situated directly behind a male dancer. The dancers provided the rhythm for the songs, simply by stomping their right foot. The songs were sung chorally, in a style and with melodies that were pleasant to my Western ear. The men introduced the verses and, after an interval, the women joined in singing the choral refrain. The singing continued throughout the night for two nights. *Kawió* is not a religious observance, but rather a recreational occasion.

Following *kawió*, during my residence among them in 1939–40, the Tapirapé celebrated the arrival of supernatural spirits at the men's *takana*. According to the Tapirapé, many animals and fish have *anchunga* ('souls'), such as the *jacu* ('forest fowl'), wild pigs, *tucanaré* fish, the savanna deer, and others. In each dry season, pairs of animal *anchunga* come to lodge in the *takana*. Costumes which cover the entire body, including the face, are made for the male masked dancers from buriti palm fiber. The costume is then decorated with macaw feathers. The women, who are supposed to believe that the masked dancers are dangerous supernatural spirits, are afraid.[2]

Several times a day, mainly in the late afternoon, pairs of dancers emerge from the *takana* singing the special songs of the spirit which their costumes represent. Each of the dancers comes from one of the men's societies. They dance and sing their way to dwellings at each end of the village, where a woman offers them *kawí* ('a soup made of the juice from the tuber of the manioc plant'). This was explained to me as the women's obligation to feed the spirits. Generally the dancers were surrounded by young women as they returned to the *takana*. In 1939, only two pairs of *anchunga* occupied the *takana*—"because they did not have enough feathers to make more masks."

The dancer-singers, representing animal *anchunga*, appeared each day or so during the dry season. Their songs and masks were almost

---

[2]The Tapirape are relaxed in the custom of keeping the secret from the women. The neighboring Carajá Indians, who share this custom with the Tapirapé, subject women, who admit to know, to mass rape.

identical to those of the Carajá Indians, with whom the Tapirapé had been closely associated in the past. The style of singing was quite different from the choral songs I had heard during the earlier *kawió* ceremony. It seems to me that this music must have been borrowed from the Carajá.

In December, with the approach of the rains, the style of dancing and singing among the Tapirapé changed markedly. The *anchunga* masks were dismantled. The men congregate in their *takana*. In the evening they would begin singing, in choral style, with the boys singing in a higher range than the adult males. After a while one group would emerge singing from one club house door. Soon after, another group emerges from another door. My Tapirapé teachers explained that each men's society "owns" a door. Each group represented one of the two men's societies mentioned earlier. They danced facing one other and slowly their wives gathered behind them. One group introduced a song, then the other joined the refrain. The women sang along a phrase behind the men. Then the other group introduced a different song. Such song fests continued throughout the night; sometimes as many as fifteen couples were singing and dancing, sometimes only two or three. They did not sing every night—perhaps twice a week, when, if by chance, it was not raining. This is the style called *káo*, which ends with the approach of the dry season and the celebration of the *kawió* harvest festival.

In 1940, during a four- or five-day exhibition in the month of January, *káo* singing was interrupted by the medicine men "to fight against Thunder." Again, songs played an important role in this ceremony. Thunder is believed to be a supernatural being living in the sky. He controls other dangerous beings called *topu*. These supernatural spirits are depicted as small doll-like figures riding in miniature canoes. Lightning are *topu*'s arrows, sent down to destroy the ripening corn. The shamans must fight Thunder in order to protect the new corn crop. Side doors are opened in the family dwellings and paths are swept between the houses. The shamans and their apprentices gather in one of the dwellings, where they smoke raw tobacco in a tubular pipe and sing songs challenging Thunder. As they sing they gesture aggressively toward the sky. They inhale and swallow the smoke deep inside their lungs until it often causes them to vomit. The rhythmical cadence of the song is marked by a bamboo rattle as they move from one house to another in the village. Suddenly a shaman or an apprentice would quiver for a few moments and then his body would become rigid. He had fallen into a trance, intoxicated both by the tobacco and his song. As the Tapirapé explain it, "he had lost the battle with Thunder." He has been shot down by a *topu*. Instantaneously the young men lifted the defeated shaman to their shoulders and carried him through the remaining dwellings to complete the circle. A more powerful shaman massages the fallen shaman's body, blows more tobacco smoke over it, and sings "to bring him back to life." This exhibition of power by the shamans continued for four days. Only two of the medicine men were said to confront Thunder successfully. An aspirant to the status of medicine man, if successful in the fight against Thunder, gains fame. If he knows the appropriate songs, he will then be called often to treat the sick. Thus music plays an important role in protecting the Tapirapé against the dangerous supernatural spirits.

On occasion a few men, who are known for their voices and knowledge, choose to sing long, rather monotonous songs, in solo, interrupted now and again by a low male chorus. These songs, which may last for four hours or more, relate the story of a mythological ancestor. In 1940 I heard Maeuma, a man of about forty years old, sing the story of Chawanamu. Maeuma was said to be the only person who knew that particular song, which did not follow a story of the ancestor hero's travels or exploits in any detail. In fact, after long hours of trying to obtain the exact words in phonetic transcription, I was forced to the conclusion that the song did not tell the story, but only referred to incidents. Only after Maeuma had explained to me the story in Tapirapé prose, did I begin to understand the incidents to which the song referred: how Chawanamu travelled, met dangerous animals, was captured by an enemy tribe, escaped, was recaptured by cannibals, and finally eaten by his captors. This reference of songs to myth seems to extend to most Tapirapé music. One well-known song, often sung as part of the *káo* festival during the rainy season, had the following simple words:

> The little birds sang. *Hé Hé*
> The large birds sang. *Hé Hé*
> All the birds sang. *Hé Hé* (chorus)

It was explained that it referred to the singing of birds which the great ancestor, called Petura, witnessed, and to the origin of the men's bird societies.

Vocal music is a focal point of Tapirapé culture and in keeping with that interest they are remarkably receptive to the music of others. They learn foreign songs easily. This led to one of the most mystifying experiences of my field work. One evening, shortly after my arrival, a young Tapirapé man sat next to my hammock and sang, in recognizable English with a heavy Scotch burn, "Loch Lomond" and the hymn "The Roll is Called up Yonder." Only much later, when I became better acquainted with their language did I unravel this mystery. Two or three years earlier a Scotch Protestant missionary, Frederick Kepel, had spent several weeks with them. He liked to sing, and every evening he would render his hymns and Scotch songs in the village plaza. A few Tapirapé learned to sing along with him. His songs came to be known as *Federico monika* ('Frederick's songs'), which they added to their repertoire. Even to my inexpert ear the Tapirapé sang songs which they had borrowed from the Carajá Indians of the Araguaia River. Years later when I paid a visit to Kayapo village far to the north of the Tapirapé, I heard them sing songs which I had heard in the Tapirapé village. This confirmed my suspicion that the two tribes had close relations in the past. One evening the youths entertained us by singing songs in Portuguese (learned from Brazilian backwoodsmen), English (the hymns of Frederick Kepel), and French ("Frère Jacques" from the French missionary Sisters who now live among them).

In 1965, when I again revisited the Tapirapé village, now established and more accessible on the Araguaia River, about forty kilometers from an airport, I found them still singing their traditional songs in the *kawí*, *káo*, and *anchunga* styles. Now surrounded by Brazilian farmers and adjacent to a Carajá Indian village, they have continued to borrow foreign music. As was to be expected, the Tapirapé had also adopted much peasant music. They sang many *modinhas* ('simple songs' of Portuguese origin) and a few modern carnival tunes. In imitation of the surrounding Brazilians, they organized Saturday night *festinhas* ('little parties'), which were dancing parties in Western style, during which the men and women danced in pairs to the music of a *cavaquinho* ('a small stringed instrument similar to a ukulele'), a flute, and a tambourine. Several Tapirapé men had learned to play these instruments. Both men and women had learned to dance at least adequately in Brazilian style, and, besides, they had learned to sing along to carnival music.

However, The Little Sisters of Jesus, the missionary nuns who have lived among the Tapirapé since 1953, were opposed to these parties. They urged the Tapirapé to sing their own traditional songs and to continue their traditional ceremonies. They discouraged the *festinhas*, because Brazilian backwoodsmen often attended and brought with them *cachaça* ('raw sugar cane rum'), which led to brawls. The Indians had not acquired the taste nor the habit of alcohol. An Indian often misunderstood the situation and tried to seduce a drunken Brazilian's wife, or a Brazilian misunderstood the Indian women, when, in the heat of the dance, would strip down their upper garments. Yet the *festinhas* continued despite the missionary efforts to prohibit them. Foreign music and traditional Tapirapé music continued side by side during the 1960's and 1970's, according to occasional letters from the Little Sisters of Jesus.

Music is the central focus of Tapirapé ceremony, religion, and recreation. For me it became a barrier to efficient field research. I had no musical skills. I could not notate the music I heard, for I can hardly carry a tune. My Tapirapé friends were obviously disappointed with me—yet polite—allowing me to dance to their songs. My companion and employee, Valentine Gomes, who was my guide and cook, saved the situation. Valentine, a converted Seventh Day Adventist, had a good voice. On Saturdays, he sang hymns and prayed. The Tapirapé would sing along with him. Furthermore, on other days, he played his *violão* ('guitar') and sang, in a good voice, popular *modinhas*. Thus, another song style emerged, called *Valentine monika* which was added to the Tapirapé song repertoire.

Tapirapé music made my residence in their village more pleasant. I remember with great pleasure long evenings resting in my hammock listening to them sing their *káo* songs. I also remember wakening at dawn to the increased volume of their singing as added voices joined in the all night song fest. I even began to recognize specific traditional songs and to learn something about their contents. The Tapirapé are altogether a charming people and one important factor in that charm is their love for music.

REFERENCES CITED

Indiana University. Archives of Traditional Music

    1975   *A Catalog of Phonorecordings of Music and Oral Data Held by the Archives of Traditional Music.* New York: G.K. Hall & Co.

Wagley, Charles

    1977   *Welcome of Tears: The Tapirapé Indians of Brazil.* New York: Oxford University Press.

John M. Ward

"EXCUSE ME": A DANCE TO A TUNE OF JOHN DOWLAND'S MAKING

Country-dance tunes—of which there are literally hundreds—were most of them composed by nobody and written down or published by somebody else, to paraphrase an old saw. Before the days of copyright vested in the composer, there was no economic spur to claiming authorship of a three-strain, twenty-bar air, like the tune that is the theme of this essay, and nothing to keep a business man like John Playford from helping himself to what, at the time he published "Excuse me," was music in the public domain. Those who bought the book or heard the tune or danced to it doubtless knew little if anything about the identity of its inventor.

Certainly Playford provides little help in identifying the composers of the tunes he published, no doubt because he was as ignorant of who most of them were, as we are. For example, of the 104 tunes in the first edition of *The Dancing Master* (1651), most have what appear to be invented titles, like "Trenchmore," "Halfe Hannikin," and "Skellamesago," some of them quite old; a few have titles with specific associations, like "Graies Inne Maske" (an occasion), "Newcastle" (a place), "My Lady Cullen" (a dedicatee), "Kemps Jigg" (an actor), and "Confesse" (a dancing master}. Only "Adsons Saraband" bears the name of a composer, and not because he invented the tune, which is likely,

John M. Ward, William Powell Mason Professor of Music Emeritus, Harvard University, is the author of studies on Spanish and English instrumental music of the 16th century, broadside ballad tunes, dance music, and folksong.

but because it was one way to distinguish Adson's from all the other sarabands, of which there were a great many.[1]

Thus it is the music itself and the hint provided by the title that make it possible to identify "Excuse me" as a tune based on John Dowland's song, "Can she excuse my wrongs with vertues cloake," one of the composer's most widely printed, copied, and arranged pieces, as much court as chamber, street, and theater music, well known at home and abroad, and still performed in one of its many guises well into the eighteenth century, a "pop" tune in every sense of the word.[2]

Whoever it was who cobbled "Excuse me" out of "Can she excuse" first changed the time from the 3/2 of a galliard to the 6/4 of the country dance, then proceeded to reorganize the three strains, each of which offered a different problem. The interstices of the first strain's singing part he filled-in with repeated and passing tones, producing a jigging rhythm ♩ ♩ ♩ ♩ . The unpromising second strain he halved, replacing with a one-bar twice-stated figure the six repeated *a*'s, with which the vocal part begins, then skipped to a slightly elaborated form of the strain's last two bars. The third strain required the most tinkering. The vocal part consists almost entirely of repeated notes—eight *a*'s, followed by nine *b*'s, followed by eight more *a*'s—plus a two-bar cadence; the accompaniment has the tune, or, rather, a bit of the old popular song, "Will you go walk the woods so wild?" The arranger took the accompanimental one-bar figure, repeated it in sequence twice, then switched back to the singing part for a slightly elaborated form of the cadence. A fine example of scissors-and-past composition! (See Ex. 1.)

"Excuse me" may already have been danced to in 1609; however, the earliest known mention of this use of the tune is in James Shirley's play, *Hyde Park* (1632), Act II, Scene ii, wherein a character, forced to dance against his will, asks, "Will you excuse me yet?" At which his tormentor commands the musicians, "Play *excuse me*," and says to the

---

[1]See the facs. of *Playford's English Dancing Master, 1651*, ed. Margaret Dean-Smith, London, 1957.

[2]"Can she excuse" is No. 5 of Dowland's *The First Book of Songes or Ayres* (London, 1597; repr. 1600, 1603, 1606, 1613; facs. of the 1597 and 1613 eds. in *English Lute Songs*, ed. F. W. Sternfeld, Vol. 4, 1970). The arrangement for instrumental ensemble, entitled "The Earle of Essex Galliard," is No. 12 in Dowland's *Lachrimae* (London, [1604]; facs. ed. Warwick Edwards, Leeds, [1974]). Arrangements for solo lute are ascribed to Dowland in a number of manuscripts; two of them are printed in *The Collected Lute Music of John Dowland*, ed. Diana Poulton & Basil Lam (London, 1974), Nos. 42, 89.

Example 1:

Transposed

a. John Dowland, 'Can she excuse my wrongs,' 1597 (Singing part).

b. Thomas Robinson, 'Excuse me,' 1609 (for cittern only).

c. A Choice Collection of Country Dances, 'Excuse me,' c. 1726.

(Voice)

(Lute)

dancer, "yes, anything you'll call for." Ten years later the dance appears to have been *vieux jeu*, for a character in Thomas Jordan's play, *The Walks of Islington and Hogsdon* (licensed 1641, printed 1654), Act II, Scene i, exclaims, "You shall not dance excuse me then, that Country trip is old, we'll have some novelty."

The dance may have been considered "old hat" by the smart set, but not by the purchasers of *The Dancing Master*. Playford first published "Excuse me," along with "several new Dances, and Tunes of Dances, never before printed"—these included "Green Sleeves" and "Joan Sanderson," both "oldies"—in the seventh edition (1686), and it continued to appear in country-dance books until at least 1740. The dance was to have been performed at the end of the still-born ballad opera, *The Disappointment; or, The Force of Credulity*, in New York in 1767.[3]

It appears unlikely that Dowland was responsible for "Excuse me," and far more likely the cobbler was Thomas Robinson, for the country-dance form of the music first appears in his *New Citharen Lessons* (1609), a volume containing other pieces by Dowland presumably arranged by Robinson, including the "Essex Galliard" version of "Can she excuse my wrongs,"[4] and "The Frogge" (that is, the song, "Now O now I needs must part," also known as "Frog Galliard"). Robinson was certainly responsible for setting "Excuse me" for the cittern; Dowland is not known to have written for the instrument.

Of the nineteen sources of "Excuse me" known to the writer, all but five are like the one in *The Dancing Master*; the others, mostly pre-Playford in date, differ, viz.:

> *Version 1.*
>
> Thomas Robinson, *New Citharen Lessons* (London: Barley, 1609), No. 21.
>
> *Version 2.*
>
> Vilnius, Lithuanian Academic Library, MS F15/285 MLF–LXXIX (*olim* Königsberg, Staatsarchiv, MS A 116 fol.), f. 58ᵛ, for lute. Facs. in the *Königsberg Manuscript*, ed. Arthur Ness and J. Ward (Columbus, 1989).

---

[3]The Playford tune is supplied for the dance in J. C. Graue's edition of the play, Madison, 1976, p. 55.

[4]This arrangement is different from the one for cittern ascribed to "Tho. Robinson" in Cambridge University Library MS Dd. 4.23, f. 4ᵛ.

Version 3.

> Paris, Bibliothèque nationale, MS Rés. 1186 (ca. 1630s), f. 117ᵛ = New York Public Library, MS Drexel 5609, pp. 90–91 (an eighteenth-century copy), for keyboard. Printed in *English Pastime Music, 1630–1660,* ed. Martha Maas (Madison, 1974), p. 68.

> Jacob van Eyk, *Den Fluyten Lust-Hof,* Tweede Deel (Amsterdam, 1654), ff. 30–31, "Excusemoy," Printed in Gerrit Vellekoop's ed. of van Eyk's work, Vol. III (Amsterdam: Matthysz, 1957), pp. 14–25.

> *Oude en Nieuwe Hollantse Boeren Lietjes en Contredansen,* Tiende Deel (Amsterdam: Roger, n.d.), p. 9, No. 733. Facs. ed. Marie Veldhuyzen, n.p., 1972.

Fourteen versions are either identical with the one published by Playford in 1686 or differ but slightly from it; viz.,

Version 4.

> *The Dancing Master,* 7th ed., 1686, p. 188, "Excuse me. Longways for as many as will." Repr. in the 8th ed. (1690), p. 174, and the 9th through 18th ed. (1690–post 1728), p. 115. Pr. Michael Barraclough, "'Excuse me' or An Old Country Trip," *Folk Music Journal,* III (1978), 345 (after the 16th ed.).

> Paris, Bibliothèque nationale, MS fr. 1687 (André Lorin's "Livre de contredance presente au Roy," ca. 1685), ff. 20ᵛ–21, "Contredance pour Madame De Maintenon."[5] Pr. Barraclough 1978, pp. 350–51.

> Raoul Feuillet, *Recüeil de contredances mises en chorégraphie* (Paris: Chez l'Auteur, 1706), pp. 25–32. Pr. Barraclough 1978, pp. 346–49, again on pp. 352–57, both times with the wrong clef sign; all pitches are a 3rd too low.

> *A Hundred & Twenty Country Dances for the Flute* (London: Pippard, 1711), No. 83 (transposed up a 4th).

---

[5]On the dating of Lorin's MS, see Lillian and Julian Pilling "The Rehabilitation of André Lorin," *Historical Dance,* IX (1979), 21.

The Compleat Country Dancing-Master (London: Walsh, 1718), p. 128; also in the editions of 1731 and 1735, No. 251.

A Choice Collection of Country Dances (Dublin: Neal, ca. 1726), p. 21.

A Choice Collection of 200 Country Dances, Vol. I (London: Johnson, ca. 1740), No. 193.

British Library, Add. MS 29371, f. 46.

National Library of Scotland, MS 2085 (Walter McFarlan's violin MS, ca. 1740), p. 201.

The Playford version of the tune is also found in the following ballad operas:

A. *With the music.*

John Gay, *Polly* (1729), Air XLIII. Facs. in *The Ballad Opera*, ed. Walter H. Rubsamen (New York, 1974), I, C.

William Chetwood, *The Lover's Opera* (1729), Air V, the tune wrongly identified as "Buff=Coat." Facs. in Rubsamen 1974, XII, B.

Edward Ward, *The Prisoners Opera* (1730), [Air] IV, no title. Facs. in Rubsamen 1974, IX, C.

Edward Phillips, *The Mock Lawyer* (1733), Air VII (text), Air 3 (music, end of the volume). Facs. in Rubsamen 1974, IV, C.

B. *The tune named, the music not printed.*

Anon., *The Footman* (1732), Air LXIV. Facs, in Rubsamen 1974, XII, C.

Robert Drury, *The Mad Captain* (1733), Air XXX (recte 27). Facs. Rubsamen 1974, XII, C.

James Worsdale, *A Cure for a Scold* (1735), Air XIV. Facs. in Rubsamen 1974, IV, D.

Seven of the sources include a description of the steps of the dance, two of them in the pictographic notation associated with the name of Raoul Feuillet.

A. *With the music.*

The Dancing=Master, 7th through 18th edition, Pr. Barraclough 1978, p. 345.

The Compleat Country Dancing-Master (Walsh, 1718), p. 128; repr. in 1731 and 1735, No. 251.

A Choice Collection (Neal, ca. 1726), p. 21.

A Choice Collection (Johnson, ca. 1740), No. 193.

In Feuillet notation.

Lorin's "Libre de contredance," ff.20ᵛ–21.Diplomatic copy in Barraclough 1978, pp. 350–51.

Feuillet, *Recüeil de contredances*, pp. 25–32. Diplomatic copy in Barraclough 1978, pp. 346–49.

B. *Without the music.*

A New Academy of Compliments; or, The Lover's Secretary, 4th ed. (London: Bates & Beetesworth, 1715), two versions. Pr. Barraclough 1978, p. 344. The dances are included in the Worcester, Mass. reprint of the work in 1795, pp. 141, 142.[6]

Cambridge, Mass., the writer's library, William Woolball's MS of country dances (dated 1719), No. 39. Pr. Barraclough 1978, p. 344, with a few orthographic changes.

The verbal and diagrammatic descriptions of the dance are in substantial agreement. When the sources differ, it is sometimes in the choice of words to describe a movement ("take hands, turn round" in Playford, "ring hands round" in one of the *New Academy* versions); sometimes in the choreography ("go whole figure" in Playford, "half figure with 2ᵈ. cu:" in Neal; "cast off" in Lorin and Playford, "cross over" in the other sources). How such differences came about is easily surmised. "Excuse me" was transmitted without benefit of print for more than half a century before Playford published a version acquired from an unidentified source, no doubt edited for him by an unidentified "knowing Friend," like the one who assisted the publisher in compiling the first edition of *The Dancing Master*. Playford's version was reprinted

---

[6]I have been informed the dances do not appear in the English editions of 1669, 1671, and 1681. The section of dances in the American edition is headed "The Modish Dancing Master. Or Brief and Plain Instructions for Dancing Country Dances." I am indebted to Kate Van Winkle Keller for a copy of this source.

by him and other publishers at least fifteen times between 1686 and 1740.

From the same half century four slightly different versions of the dance survive (three of them in printed sources, one in manuscript), acquired in ways we can only guess at—foot-to-eye; from a dancing master; copied out by a "knowing Friend;" a deliberate variation of Playford's version; accidental change? What I find striking is the degree to which separately derived versions transmit what is essentially the same tune. The shape of the music probably restrained change in the dance, just as the dance probably kept the tune from substantial change.

As could be expected, at least one ballad, Thomas D'Urfey's "The Crafty Mistris's Resolution," was written to the tune and printed in the second volume of *Wit and Mirth: or, Pills to Purge Melancholy* (London: Playford, 1700; repr. 1707, 1712). A copy of what appears to have been a broadsheet printing, headed "A New Song, made to a pretty Country Dance att Court, call'd Excuse me," is the first item in a manuscript commonplace-book of ca. 1700. Set to the tune in *Pills* (Ex. 2), it reads as follows:[7]

Example 2: "A New Song. . . call'd Excuse me"

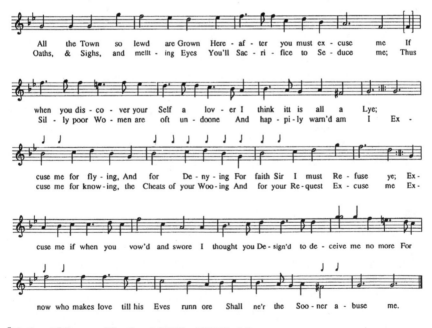

[7]National Library of Scotland, MS La.III.489, f. 2.

All the Town So lewd are Grown
    Hereafter you must excuse me
If when you discover your Self a lover
    I think itt is all a Lye;
Oaths, & Sighs, and mellting Eyes
    you'll Sacrifice to Seduce me;
Thus Silly poor Women are oft undoone
    And happily warn'd am I.
Excuse me for flying, And for Denying
    For faith Sir I must Refuse ye;
Excuse me for Knowing, the Cheats of your Wooing
    And for your Request Excuse me
Excuse me if when you Vow'd and Swore
    I Thought you Design'd to deceive me no more
For now Who makes love till his Eyes ruun ore
    Shall never the Sooner abuse me.

Youth & Witt, did once Invade
    My heart, e'r I scarce was Twenty
And I silly creature, through mere good Nature
    Believ'd him what er'e he Swore
Young, unpractis'd in the Trade
    of Favours I was not Scanty
But, he who my Innocent Love betray'd
    Shall never Deceive me more
For now Though he flatter; & Ogle & Chatter,
    And Still in the Dance does Choose mee
Nay argue the case too: And look like an Ass too
    He after all this Shall loose me
For now I will Feamale=cunning Use
    and all our Stock of Revenge Produce
One Rebell to honour has broke the Truce
    And all Mankind shall Excuse me.

As noted earlier, we have no reason to believe Dowland was responsible for "Excuse me." His recastings of the song, "Can she excuse my wrongs," involved no dismembering of the vocal part for the sake of a country-dance tune, but were reworkings of the whole structure, once for solo lute, and once for instrumental ensemble, both times in the guise of a galliard. Many musicians, continental and English and mostly anonymous, made arrangements of the galliard—for lute, cittern, lyra viol, keyboard, mixed ensemble, etc.—, some with more taste and skill than others. The list is long; to the one in Diana Poulton's study of the composer can be added more than a dozen versions, and these do not include those based on the song but on the galliard.[8]

That song was written "at a time when the activities of composer, performer, arranger, editor, and teacher were closely allied and little or no attempt was made in the written sources to identify the contributions of different musicians; at a time when the technique of variation permeated both composition and performance, and the altering of a composer's music—by himself as well as by others—was common practice, especially among instrumentalists; a time when the *ad hoc* nature of the occasions on which music was performed required accommodating the notes to the number and ability of the players involved."[9]

Dowland was responsible for only three of the sixty-odd ways in which "Can she excuse my wrongs" *alias* "Essex Galliard" comes down to us, and even his versions come to us multiform; the rest are mostly by nobodies. What they did with Dowland's music is essentially of antiquarian interest in the context of this paper; he provided the theme for other men's transcriptions, variations, and borrowings. "Excuse me" is to the song from which it was extracted as Walter Murphy's "A Fifth of Beethoven" is to the piece it parodies.[10] In other words, "Can she excuse" was both a song and a means for making music, different kinds of music, from a "pop" tune for ballad singing and country dancing to a sophisticated set of variations for lute. Context and performance determined the difference between the two, not *das Ding an sich*.

---

[8]To the list of versions in Poulton's *John Dowland: His Life and Works* (Berkeley, 1972), pp. 483–84, can be added "Galliarda 2. à 5" in Valentin Haussmann's *Neue Intrade*, Nürnberg, 1604.

[9]John Ward, "A Dowland Miscellany." *Journal of the Lute Society of America*, X (1977), p. 36.

[10]The piece, published by RFT Music, BMI, is included in the soundtrack of *Saturday Night Fever*, RSO Records (1977), RS-2-4001, side 2, band 1.

Richard J. Wolfe

JOHN GOODMAN (1778-1848) OF FRANKFORT, KENTUCKY

Musician, Music Teacher, Musical Instrument Maker, Engraver, and First Publisher of Sheet Music West of the Allegheny Mountains

While preparing final copy for my bibliography of early nineteenth-century American sheet music, *Secular Music in America* (1964),[1] nearly a quarter of a century ago, I was faced with making arbitrary decisions concerning a small number of publications that were to be included in this compilation. Although the vast majority of the ten thousand odd entries presented little difficulty with regard to identification and dating, falling into categories that were reasonably orderly or at least manageable, a few handfuls did not. Those items which presented great problems were mainly the products of small, irregular publishers, who worked away from the main stream of American sheet music publishing. Usually, there was no information available on the individuals who had produced them. Thus, it was especially difficult to date such publications and, in one or two cases, even to assign probable places of origin to them.

---

[1]The inception of this somewhat ambitious, six-year project was owing in large part to the backing and prestige of Carleton Sprague Smith.

Richard J. Wolfe is both Curator of Rare Books and Manuscripts in The Francis A. Countway Library of Medicine of Harvard University and Joseph Garland Librarian of the Boston Medical Library. He has published on early American music, medical history and several aspects of the book arts.

390 RICHARD J. WOLFE

One such problem was presented by an edition of "Sandy and Jenny," a popular song of the English composer James Sanderson (1769–1841) which had all of the appearances of an early American music sheet. Its imprint merely specified that it had been published by one John Goodman in a place identified as "Frankfort." This was the only music publication I had encountered in a search of nearly forty public and private music collections, over a period of more than four years, that bore the names of that publisher and place; what's more, at that time it existed in but a single known copy.[2]

The Kentucky town came first to mind as the probable place where this oddity originated, for contemporary gazetteers listed no other American locality spelled exactly that way. However, after searching through available local histories and other printed sources, and after directing inquiries to contacts in Kentucky with negative results, I reasoned how unlikely it was that a single edition of a popular song would have emanated from that far off place on the American frontier which had no known association with sheet music publishing in that early period.

After giving the matter much thought, I attributed its probable place of issue to Frankford, Pennsylvania, a village that now forms part of the city of Philadelphia. This locality seemed a far more likely possibility, for Philadelphia was the music and music publishing capitol of America during the first forty years of the United States. One reasonably might conclude that the otherwise unidentified Goodman was a local musician of the Philadelphia area who had some unknown connection with sheet music publishing there. Such a conclusion was supported by the fact that George E. Blake, Philadelphia's most active early publisher of sheet music, issued arrangements of music by a John Goodman in the period around 1815 (Wolfe 1964:nos. 3169–170). The differences between the spelling of "Frankfort" and the Pennsylvania village could be explained by variations in orthography which were prevalent at that time.

Then, taking into consideration engraving style, paper, and other physical and musicological evidence, I concluded that this odd edition had been published during the first decade of the nineteenth century and assigned the date "180–" to it, for like most sheet music published in early America (an in contemporary Europe), it lacked a date or year

[2]A second copy has since been located at the University of Chicago Library and is discussed later on.

of issue on its imprint. Finally, because of its early appearance, I added a note that this edition had been issued probably circa 1805.

It is an idiosyncrasy of American music publishing during this early period, that infrequently an edition, or a small number of editions of sheet music, appeared in geographical locations in the East, far removed from the major metropolitan centers of Philadelphia, New York, Boston, and Baltimore, where almost all sheet music publishing occurred at that time. These "irregular" editions bore the names of publishers who otherwise had no known or continuing associations with music publishing. For example, we find that occasional editions of sheet music were published in the early decades of the nineteenth century in Washington, D.C., by Frederick A. and Charles K. Wagler, in Albany, New York, by John C. Goldberg, and in Hartford, Connecticut, by A. Willoughby, all of whom can be identified as local musicians or music teachers. And in 1826 another music master, John Saxton, issued about a dozen pieces in, of all places, Cooperstown, New York.[3] Sometimes research revealed that some of the irregular publishers had their music engraved and printed by "regular" music engravers or publishers in the major metropolitan centers. But in a few cases, including apparently the above examples, they had not.

How these irregular publishers acquired the necessary music punches and engraving tools in their isolated locations, and how they gained the necessary knowledge and experience to use them properly could not be explained. On close examination, they usually proved to be local musicians or music teachers, who, for some personal or professional reason, found it expedient or desirable to publish this material. Seemingly, however, it would not repay a musician his time, expense, and effort to procure a set of the necessary punches and other tools, if, indeed, these were readily available on the market, and to employ them only once or for a few times and never again (assuming, again, that they actually knew how to do so). Yet, in several instances this very thing appears to have happened, with one case in point centering around the aforementioned John Goodman. How he could have obtained and learned to utilize these specialized tools on the Kentucky frontier, at a time when no known musical publishing had taken place beyond the East, was another argument against the likelihood of music publishing in Frankfort, Kentucky in this early period.

---

[3] While Saxton's publications are undated, their year of issue is proved by entries for them in extant copyright registers, which, fortunately, are preserved in The Library of Congress.

The subject of music engraving and music punching tools present a thorny problem to anyone attempting to understand and interpret our early music publishing trade. These implements formed the most important part of the process of publishing sheet music. Yet, hardly any information about them exists today, particularly as regards their places of origin and makers. The question of where such tools originated and, specifically, how these irregular publishers could have procured them and learned to use them correctly in their isolated locations remained unanswerable questions when, some years after the publication of *Secular Music in America*, I compiled a history of our early music engraving, music printing, and music publishing trade (Wolfe 1980).

One possibility, a purely conjectural one, would suppose that by the early nineteenth century enough sets of these chisel-like implements with musical notations and other signs on their tips had increased to the point that there was a surplus of them and that such tools could readily be procured from individuals or agencies that had accumulated a large number of them.[4] Although the music engraving trade was a specialized one, there was much activity in this early period. It does not seem unreasonable to conclude that, during this time, the number of sets of tools produced far exceeded the number of workmen at a given period who could utilize them all. I have encountered several present-day engravers of music who had amassed a great many sets of these tools, a number far in excess of their ability of ever using them all, simply by acquiring through gift, purchase, or abandonment of the tools of retired or deceased engravers.

Like bookbinder's punches, which they resemble in shape and form (and which present us with similar problems in regard to the nature of their origin and manufacture), music punches are practically indestructible under use. As was the case in the bookbinding trade, it was a common practice for one generation of workmen to turn their tools over to a succeeding one. This transfer sometimes occurred several times in the life of a given set of punches. It is also possible that some of our irregular publishers were immigrant musicians, who had learned to engrave in their prior locations and had brought with them a kit of tools on their journeys westward. Finally, the less likely possibility exists that these off-beat publishers could have fabricated their own tools or had a local metal engraver make them.

---

[4]Music punches of nineteenth-century American manufacturers are pictured in Illustrations 15 and 16 of Wolfe (1980).

In any event, the question of John Goodman's place and period of activity no longer remains a moot one, for the recent and fortuitous discovery of one of his music books puts an end to speculation about him once and for all. And, indeed, it does prove that, at this early time, he was engraving and publishing sheet music on the Kentucky frontier. Goodman's book, which contains sheet music produced by some of our early major publishers in the East, as well as by himself in Kentucky, and, additionally, some of his own music in manuscript, was brought to my attention a few years ago by a fellow librarian who was aware of my interest and prior work in early American music publishing.[5] It had been quoted to him by an antiquarian bookseller in the Boston area. In order to set the record straight on Goodman, I purchased it, and I have recently presented it to the Houghton Library of Harvard University, where other interested parties can examine and utilize it.

Goodman's book resembles the "usual" bound-up collection of American sheet music of this early period. It is rectangular in shape and small folio in format, measuring approximately twelve and three quarters inches in height and nine in width. Its binding consists of quarter, contemporary suede leather and pasteboards, with an engraved map serving as cover material on the latter. The volume contains seventeen printed music publications—originally eighteen, but one has been removed—and eighteen pages of music in manuscript at the back. On the front free endpaper appears "A List of the Music Scholars at the Domestic Academy, Home at Last, Ky., 1811," written in a large, fancy hand; and the last page of music at the back of the volume is followed by two pages containing the manuscript text of a preceding song in manuscript, "Mary's Dream."

Throughout the collection, Goodman's name is written several times in different manuscript hands. After one such entry appear additional ones that read "Frankfort, Kentucky" and "Mrs. John Goodman, Scott City.," and on the blank side of one of the pieces is penned "Musician Georgetown Seminary, six shillings." The list of the music scholars on the front flyleaf reads: C. S. Tarleton, E. C. Anderson, H. Castleman, L. Nance, M. M. Reed, E. J. Buckner, E. R. Weisiger, E. C. Jonstone, E. Fant, M. W. Anderson, L. P. Greenup, L. B. Morton, H. Croghn, C. J. Barr, E. C. Croghn, and S. Worthington.

---

[5] I extend my thanks to Roger E. Stoddard of the Houghton Library of Harvard University for bringing this important piece of musical Americana to my attention.

Plate 1: First page of Goodman's five-page collection of printed music.

Most of the printed music in Goodman's volume was published by two of the earliest music publishers of Philadelphia, Benjamin Carr and George Willig. It comprises many of the popular titles they issued between 1795 and 1805 or 1806.[6] Among the last pieces printed is a five-page collection of instrumental music issued by Goodman himself at Frankfort. This commences with his own composition, "Gen. Russel's March" (see Plate 1). Finally, the remaining three published sheets are foreign. Two were issued in Dublin and the third in London. The imprints of the music in this volume possibly reflect Goodman's trip westward from Germany, which was his native land, through the British Isles to Philadelphia, and ultimately to Kentucky, where, it appears, he was "home at last." As was noted earlier, the printed music is followed by nine leaves or eighteen pages of music in manuscript, concluding the volume.

While a few of the publications and the pieces in manuscript can be identified as Goodman's own compositions, others cannot. His printed five-page collection, which begins with "Gen. Russel's March," has the combined subtitle and imprint "Frankfort, Composed, Printed and Sold.by I. Goodman." A two-hand piano arrangement of "Gen. Russel's March" extends over sixty percent of the initial page, followed by its arrangement for two violins or flutes. The suceeding page (the verso) contains "Washington's March," also in a two-hand piano arrangement, with an additional arrangement for the German flute following. Other pieces in the collections are: "Ecosoise" [p. 3], containing a reel and "March in Bassorer," the first arranged for piano two hands and the second for both piano and flute; "A German March" [p. 4], arranged for both piano and German flute or two violins; and, finally, "Gen. Posey's March" [p. 5], arranged for piano four hands. The final page of the collection is blank. The last named piece commemorates Thomas Posey, who fought Indians under General Anthony Wayne, served in the Kentucky legislature, and organized and equipped the Kentucky forces in 1809, when war was threatening between France and England.

---

[6]Willig's publications bound herein are "Think Not My Love," by the immigrant Philadelphia composer Henry Capron; "The Blue Bell of Scotland;" "When the Lads Began to Teize" and "The Caledonian Laddy" by James Hook; "The Soldier's Return;" two sets of "Easy Lessons;" and "Sonata I" by Nicolai. Benjamin Carr's publications include "Then Say My Sweet Girl Can You Love Me" and "Lucy or Selim's Complaint" by Hook, and "Henry's Cottage Maid" by Pleyel.

Plate 2: The first page of, assumedly, Goodman's autograph of "Miss Sally Ann Overton's Favorite Waltz" and "Waltz by Mr. Goodman."

The music in manuscript contains the following titles: "Buonapartes Grand March," "Miss Sally Ann Overton's Favorite Waltz" (see Plate 2), "Waltz, by Mr. Goodman," "Miss Hall's Waltz," "Mary's Dream," "The Gardener's Duett," "Paul and Mary," and "Nature's Holliday-Belville." How much of the above music Goodman actually composed is unknown. However, it is likely that he was responsible for arranging some of it, and all of the music in the printed collection as well. His "Gen. Russel's March" undoubtedly honors William Russel, a hero of the Revolutionary War who later left his native Virginia to settle in Kentucky, where he became a well known Indian fighter. Russel was an annual delegate to the Kentucky legislature until 1808, when President Madison appointed him Colonel of the 7th U. S. Infantry. In 1811, he succeeded William Henry Harrison in command of the frontier of Indiana, Illinois, and Missouri, and in 1812, he planned and commanded the expedition that was sent against Peoria. Because Goodman might have composed this march to celebrate one of the latter events, the publication of his small collection could have occurred as late as 1811, though it was probably issued much earlier, as we shall later see, perhaps even within the earliest years of the new century. With regard to the printed titles in Goodman's music book, one gets the impression from the scattered signatures on pieces therein, that, before binding took place, the loose music was lent or rented or otherwise circulated to pupils and others.

If the discovery of Goodman's music collection was a fortuitous event, attempts to track him at this later time and to uncover facts about his place and period of activity proved to be even more eventful. Success followed this time, because the bound volume of music provided tangible clues and a clear focus for investigation. A letter of inquiry to the Kentucky Historical Society in Frankfort brought a reply that was loaded with information on the hitherto unknown John Goodman (at least beyond very local precincts). Goodman's activities obviously had provoked the curiosity of others at an earlier time, and one of these individuals, who collected information on him, left notes and correspondence in public institutions for others to use. Thanks to this foresightedness, we can now sketch a reasonably accurate picture of John Goodman and obtain some insights into his musical and music publishing activities.

It was not his music, however, but the map—the one, we mentioned before, that served as cover paper on the bound volume—that lead to these earliest researches on John Goodman (see Plates 3 and 4). This is evident from the photocopied notes and correspondence that

Plate 3: Front cover of John Gooman's music book.

Plate 4: Back cover of John Goodman's music book.

were received, first from the Kentucky Historical Society and later from the Filson Club in Louisville. While the notes from the Historical Society give no clues to the identity of the person who made them, the materials obtained from the Filson Club, which are more numerous, identify this individual as Rogers Clark Ballard Thruston, an Americanist, a Kentucky local historian, and a past president of the Filson Club.[7] While there is a slight overlapping of information in both sets of material, they do not really duplicate, but rather seem to compliment one another. One could conclude that the small pack of notes from the Historical Society were removed from the other set, perhaps to be utilized later for some specific project or purpose.

Thruston's notes or memoranda from the Kentucky Historical Society clearly indicate that he first became interested in John Goodman in 1910, when he was gathering data to determine the exact location of Fort on Shore, an early military installation near Louisville. At that time Col. R. T. Durrett of Louisville had given Thruston a photograph of what was commonly called "Brooks' Map of Louisville." This rather crude or simple map, depicting the rapids of the Ohio River at Louisville and the adjacent areas of Jeffersonville and Clarksville, was signed "Engraved & Printed by John Goodman, Frankfort, Kentucky, 1806." It also bore an inscription dedicating it to Christopher Greenup, Governor of Kentucky, by its maker Jared Brooks. Reference to Thruston's initial interest in this map appears in a five-page memorandum he made about 28 June 1922, or shortly thereafter.[8] The memorandum, which is

---

[7]Rogers Clark Ballard Thruston (1858–1946)—actually, he was born a Ballard, but at his mother's request, in 1884, added her family name—received his undergraduate degree from the Sheffield Scientific School of Yale University in 1880. After working five years as a metallurgist and assistant geologist with the Kentucky Geological Survey, he resigned in 1887 to devote himself to private enterprises, thereafter applying himself mainly to scientific, historical, and patriotic work. He was an enthusiastic local historian and served as Vice-President of the Filson Club before 1923 and as President thereafter. He wrote or compiled more than half a dozen books, several of which dealt with his ancestor George Rogers Clark.

[8]R. C. B. Thruston, "John Goodman, 1778–1848," a five-page manuscript memorandum containing the final date of 28 June 1922. The initial part of the "Memorandum," occupying its first three pages, contains information gathered from various sources about the life and work of Goodman. The fourth page, entitled "Brooks Map of Louisville, Ky., 1806," contains Thruston's notes or memoranda of the events that followed the quotation of a copy of the map sent to him in 1922 by the Cadmus Book Shop of New York. And the fifth and final page contains a sketch of the location of the "John Goodman House" in Frankfort, Kentucky. This memorandum, and a separate, single-page memorandum by another person, headed "John Goodman's Music Book," which will be referred to later, comprise the whole file (docketed under "Goodman")

now in the Kentucky Historical Society in Frankfort, is unsigned. However, as noted earlier, the Filson Club's file of Thruston's letters clearly indicates that it was written by him.

Our story now jumps to 1922, for it appears that Thruston did little or nothing more about this matter after 1910, being satisfied with the photograph of the map, which he framed and hung in his office. However, late in May of 1922, as the documentation clearly indicates, Thruston was quoted a set of the *Magazine of American History*, which apparently he had been seeking, by the Cadmus Book Shop of New York City. In that same letter Cadmus also offered for sale an original copy of the Brooks' map at the enormous price of $1,500.00, describing it as "a new bibliographical discovery." While Thruston's memorandum indicates that he declined to purchase the map,[9] his interest in the map, nonetheless, had been reawakened and he showed both Durrett's photograph (of the map) and Cadmus' correspondence to members attending a meeting of the Filson Club on 5 June 1922. As a result, Thruston recorded in his memorandum: "Judge Seymour [a fellow member] suggested that Dr. Henry Miller Goodman of this city, a grandson of John Goodman, could give me information."

Thruston's memorandum indicates that he subsequently interviewed Dr. Goodman and his wife. Speaking from memory, Goodman related that his grandfather had been born in Holland, had run away from home at the age of fourteen, and had come to America in 1800, settling probably first in Philadelphia and later in Frankfort, Kentucky. Here, late in life, he married Jane Winter, had one child, and died in 1845, at the age of 85. The grandson also told Thruston that John Goodman had been an engineer and musician and had manufactured musical instruments. However, as Thruston later ascertained, Dr. Goodman was mistaken about some of his facts and dates.

With the help of several contacts, Thruston subsequently succeeded in locating the house in Frankfort where John Goodman lived.

---

in the Kentucky Historical Society. I would like to acknowledge the help and cooperation of Anne McDonnell, Librarian of the Society, who sent photocopies of the file to me in June of 1984. All other letters and documents referred to hereafter are included in the file of Thruston's materials in the Filson Club's in collection that relate to Brooks' map of Louisville.

[9]The original letter of the Cadmus Book Shop to R. C. Ballard Thruston of 23 May, 1922, and Thruston's reply on 25 May 1922 are in the Filson Club file.

Indeed, the final page of his memorandum exhibits a sketch of the site. Then, on 8 June 1822, according to the memorandum, he and Mrs. Jouett Taylor Cannon, Secretary of the Kentucky Historical Society, visited the farm of Mr. C. T. Freeman, then eighty-five years old, on the Leestown Pike, some nine miles from Frankfort. Here Freeman showed them the old burial ground, whence, some twenty-five years earlier, the remains of John Goodman and his wife and Joel Scott and his second wife, who was Mrs. Goodman's sister, had been transferred to the cemetery in Frankfort. The Scott monument had also been removed at that time, but not the Goodman's, which, in the interim, had fallen to pieces and was still lying in the old graveyard at the time of Thruston's and Mrs. Cannon's visit. Thruston recorded that he "Kodacked this fragment and portion of the graveyard showing scattered condition of the fragment." According to his notes, the inscription on the monument related that:

> The remains of
> JOHN GOODMAN
> Rest here
> Hew was Born &
> raised in Germany
> has lived in Frankf[or]t
> near forty y[ears]
> long a member [of the]
> Presbyterian [Church]
> He was uprig[ht in]
> all his dealings &
> Died on the 4th of
> June 1848
>
> Aged 70 years

Thruston also learned, from a variety of sources, that Goodman was a musician and teacher of music at one of the schools in Frankfort. Among his pupils was Mrs. Cannon's mother. He also manufactured musical instruments, which he made at his house on Main Street near St. Clair. One of these was a spinet, made for Governor Gerard. It was said to be the first instrument of its kind in the Governor's mansion, and Thruston's memorandum added that it "is said to be still owned by one of the Governor's descendants." Thruston was informed that, at the time of his death, John Goodman had been building an organ which he hoped would reproduce the human voice. This instrument, Thruston recorded, "disintegrated after his death and Mrs. Lewis told me that reeds seem to be infinite in number & ranged from a couple of inches in length to three feet, and every child in the neighborhood seemed to have one of these reeds and was blowing on it at the same time."

Thruston's memorandum contains a few other facts about John Goodman. It notes that while no one knew of Goodman as an engineer or an engraver, it was well known that he was a musician and an artisan of ability. Furthermore, Goodman and his wife had two children: a daughter, who died in infancy, and a son, also named John, who was born in 1837.[10] Goodman had married Jane Winter on 13 January 1825, when he was about forty-seven years old (and Jane's sister, Deborah Winter Gano, had married Joel Scott four years earlier). Finally, the Franklin County tax list of 1822 had designated Goodman as part owner of a lot in Frankfort valued at $7,500.00, and of another lot valued at $500.00; the tax lists of 1839 indicated that John Goodman then owned four town lots valued at $5,700.00, two slaves valued at $1,000, one horse valued at $100.00, and other property that totaled over $10,700.00.

It appears obvious from the details engraved on John Goodman's original tombstone and from other sources that his grandson's memory was faulty with regard to many of the facts of the elder John Goodman's life. More likely he had been born in Germany and not in Holland, and the years of his birth and death were actually 1778 and 1848, indicating a life span of seventy years. There is no actual information regarding his background in engineering, and it seems reasonable to guess that in the course of time he might have been confused with Jared Brooks, the engineer who made the map that Goodman subsequently engraved and printed.

While Thruston's notes and correspondence contain no other references to Goodman's life or his musical activities, several important allusions to him appear in an address which John Mason Brown

---

[10]The younger John Goodman attended B. B. Sayre's school in Frankfort and afterwards matriculated at Tulane University, from which he received the medical degree and thereafter practiced in Louisville. It was from his oldest child, Dr. Henry Miller Goodman (b. 1861) that Thruston obtained information concerning John Goodman Sr.

delivered on the occasion of the centennial celebration of the town of Frankfort in October of 1886.[11] Brown at that time reported that:

> The advent of Mr. John Goodman was for Frankfort the importation of the art of music, and the first appearance of engraving in the State. His skill supplied that which was unattainable by transportation from abroad. Until his day there was not in the Commonwealth a musical instrument less portable than the wicked violin or the pocket flute. And we may well believe how crude was the music produced by performers wholly uninstructed in the art. It was a notable undertaking when Mr. Goodman, in 1801, constructed out and out, in his house on Main Street, next but one to the southeast corner of Washington, a complete piano forte. It was made for the daughter of Governor Gerard, and its first exhibition was an event in the town.

Brown relates how the piano made its debut at a Christmas dinner in 1801, quoting the details from a letter written by a Frankfort lady in January 1802 to her absent husband:

> Mrs. Garrard's piano forte, made here by Mr. Goodman, is now at home, and is a pretty a piece of furniture as I ever saw. I think it will be well toned when it is better seasoned. The tones are now sweet but weak. It cost two hundred dollars.

In addition to providing many important facts about John Goodman, including information about his person and mannerisms, Brown established a time-reference for his arrival in Frankfort, placing him there in 1801, when he was about twenty-three years old. Thus, he was one of the town's earlier citizens, for Frankfort had been founded and chartered by an act of the Virginia legislature in 1786, and on the admission of Kentucky to the Union as a state in 1792, had become its capitol. Brown tells us (1886:18) that in 1797, about four years before Goodman's arrival in Frankfort, the town's total population numbered no more than 441 souls. Of these, ninety were white males, 112 were negro slaves, and the remaining 239 were women and children. One

[11]Brown 1886:24–25. A copy of this slender volume is listed in the card catalog of The New York Public Library. Unfortunately, as my descriptive notes on the card for the Goodman edition of "Sandy and Jenny" indicate, this could not be located in the stacks of the Genealogy and Local History Division of the Library during the year that I was doing final editing on the bibliography. Otherwise, it is likely that Goodman's location would have been ascertained and some of the material presented here would not now be needed.

notable event occurred during the earliest years of Goodman's residence there. In 1805, and for a year or so afterward, Frankfort was the scene of Gen. James Wilkinson's activities in connection with the Aaron Burr conspiracy against the United States; and, as Brown relates, Burr, that petrel of political storm, resided there (*Ibid.*:25–31).

With but one exception, the remaining correspondence and notes in the Kentucky Historical Society's and Filson Club's files relate to the Brooks' map. That exception is a single typescript leaf among the Historical Society's materials. This indicates that as of 30 October 1953, Goodman's music book was in the possession of Mrs. S. I. M. Major (presumably of Frankfort). Also included on the typescript were the names of the musical scholars at the domestic academy, "Home at Last," Kentucky, in 1811, and the titles of all of the music contained therein. How and when this list came into the Society's possession is unknown. Nor is it known how Goodman's music book migrated from Kentucky to Cambridge, Massachusetts, where I purchased it in 1984. However, it is not unreasonable to suppose that Thruston's memoranda concerning John Goodman might have come into the Society's files in connection with Mrs. Major's attempts to identify the original owner of the book.

Because it was a key factor leading to the earlier collection of information on John Goodman, because it indeed is a rare piece of Americana, and because it helps round out our picture of Goodman and his engraving activities, the Brooks' map and Thruston's interest in it deserve more of our attention. In his recent book, Thomas D. Clark devotes about a page and a half to this document, referring to it as the first map printed in Kentucky (1979:77–78).[12] Clark recounts that Jared Brooks was a Louisville surveyor who laid out that part of the city located on the escheated tract of the famous Tory land speculator, Dr. John Connolly. Brooks made this survey at the request of the newly-chartered Ohio Canal Company. Clark suggests that Brooks may have been instructed to make the survey by the United State War Department, for a map drawn by him in 1805 was transmitted to Congress in 1807. In the meantime, Brooks had prepared the version of the map in a somewhat more picturesque design than was engraved and printed by John Goodman in 1806. A portfolio of facsimiles accompanying Clark's text includes a reproduction of the Brooks' map made from an original

---

[12]There is an accompanying volume of facsimile plates.

engraved copy in the Lilly Library of Indiana University. In response to an inquiry I made in 1984, James A. Flatness of the Geography and Map Division of The Library of Congress reported that another original copy of the Brooks' map had been located in the collections of the Kentucky Historical Society. However, an inquiry to the Society has determined that it possesses only a photocopy of the Brooks' map of 1806, not the original, as well as a photocopy of the map that Jared Brooks sent to the War Department in 1807, which is now in the National Archives.[13]

Judging from the file of letters he accumulated on this subject, it is obvious that in 1922, in the aftermath of the Cadmus quotation, R. C. Ballard Thruston had become intensely interested in Brooks' map of Louisville and he very much wanted to obtain a copy of it for the Filson Club, where his pertinent letters are preserved. His first move in that direction was to talk with the grandson of the engraver, who informed him that his father had owned one of the maps and that Col. Durrett had another. Knowing that Durrett's library had been sold to the University of Chicago library, Thruston immediately had his secretary direct an inquiry to that institution.[14] However, subsequent correspondence indicates that the map could not be found there. In late June, in a letter he sent Dr. Goodman containing a copy of the notes he had made of their earlier conversation, Thruston asked the doctor if he would object to his attempt in obtaining from his father's widow the copy of the map which his father owned.[15] A few days later the doctor consented; however, he told Thruston that his father had given all of his possessions to his second wife and widow, and that the books, with the map enfolded in one of them, may have been sold by her or by another person occupying her house.[16]

[13]James A. Flatness (Senior Reference Library, Geography and Map Division, The Library of Congress) to Richard J. Wolfe, 16 July 1984, in the authors possession. Mr. Flatness states that the attribution of this other copy to the Kentucky Historical Society was made in a book by James W. Sames (1973). However, Mary Winters, who is the Society's specialist on maps, when reporting only the presence of a photocopy of the Brooks' map there in a telephone conversation with the author on 18 May 1986, stated that the Sames index is very unreliable and must be used with great caution.

[14]From the unnamed secretary of R. C. Ballard Thruston to Edward A. Henry (of the University of Chicago Libraries), 7 June 1922. She opens her letter by relating that Thruston had gone to Frankfort for the meeting of the Kentucky Historical Society, but before leaving he had directed her to write regarding the Brooks' map. Later in this letter she states that Thruston had talked with Dr. Goodman about his grandfather's map. The letter is in the Filson Club's file on the Brooks' map.

[15]R. C. Ballard Thruston to Dr. H. M. Goodman, 29 June 1922. Filson Club file.

[16]Dr. H. M. Goodman to R. C. Ballard Thruston 1 July 1922. Filson Club file.

Thruston had actually written to the widow earlier, on 6 June 1922, asking if she would donate to the Filson Club the copy of the map that her husband had owned.[17] He addressed his letter to her residence in Louisville, but because she had since moved to Michigan, it took some time for the letter to be forwarded and for her to reply. In mid-July she answered Thruston,[18] informing him that the map, which had been in the possession of the engraver's son, had been loaned to Col. Durrett. She related that "Col. Durrett borrowed it one day from Dr. Goodman and kept it a while, then returned a copy. The original map was never returned."

Two days after Thruston received Mrs. Goodman's letter, Professor Edward A. Henry of the University of Chicago libraries wrote and informed him that through a more careful and extended search the Brooks' map was found.[19] It had been folded into some modern maps of Louisville, along with a photographic copy of it. While, as later correspondence indicates, the Filson Club authorities thought that the Durrett copy by rights should be theirs, they could do little about claiming it, and the delicate matter was dropped. Additional correspondence indicates that in December of 1929 the Cadmus Book Shop quoted its copy of the Brooks' map, still unsold, to the Kentucky Geological Survey in Frankfort.[20] We might conjecture that because of the recent stock market crash, Cadmus was trying to sell assets and raise cash. However, the deepening depression put an end to any such possibility, and it was not until 1953 that Cadmus again quoted the map to the Filson authorities, once more to be turned down.[21]

---

[17]R. C. Ballard Thruston to Mrs. John Goodman, 6 June 1922. Filson Club file.

[18]Mrs. John Goodman to R. C. Ballard Thruston, undated (but stamped "received Jul 17, 1922"). Filson Club file. Mrs. Goodman's address then was "Mountain Ash," Fern Avenue, Bay View, Michigan.

[19]Edward A. Henry to R. C. Ballard Thruston, 19 July 1922, Filson Club file.

[20]The Cadmus letter is not preserved in the Filson Club file, but a letter from W. R. Jillison of the Kentucky Geological Survey to Miss L. J. Kinkead of the Filson Club, dated 21 December 1929, provides all of the details, including a description of the map, which was still priced at $1,500.00. On December 24, Miss Kinkead wrote to Jillison, giving him a resume of everything that had transpired since 1922. On 3 January 1930, Jillison sent to Thruston the photostatic copy of the map that Cadmus assumedly had sent to him.

[21]The Cadmus Book Shop to Miss Mary Verhoeff (Chairlady of the Library Committee of the Filson Club), 3 August 1953; Mary Verhoeff to Cadmus Book Shop, 6 August 1953, Filson Club file.

The Brooks' map of Louisville finally was sold in 1956, not by the Cadmus Book Shop, but by the New York bookselling firm of Henry Stevens, Son & Stiles, which in the interim had acquired the piece from Cadmus.[22] The purchaser was David A. Randall, formerly an antiquarian bookseller in New York City (Scribner's Book Store) and recently appointed Librarian of the Lilly Library of Indiana University.[23] And with that sale ends our story of the Brooks' map, which, like John Goodman, can be described as having come "home at last." Its saga extended over four decades, or more, and ended in defeat for R. C. Ballad Thruston (though by 1956 he had been dead for a decade) and the Filson Club of Louisville to acquire a copy of this early Kentucky rarity. As of this date, I have been able to establish the existence of only two copies of the Brooks' map: the Lilly copy, which Randall purchased in 1956 and which Clark reproduced in facsimile in 1979, and the composite copy serving as cover paper on John Goodman's music book.[24] The aforementioned original copy that Col. Durrett held, and

[22]This is established by a letter written by Martin F. Schmidt of Louisville, a member of the Board of Directors of the Filson Club, to Roland Tree of the Stevens firm, dated 17 October 1955, and a reply from Tree to Schmidt dated November 29 following, both of which are in the Filson Club's file. Schmidt's letter, responding to an earlier inquiry of Tree's, provided details on Brooks, Goodman, and the making of the map. The information apparently was obtained from Thruston's files.

[23]We may assume that, on the advice of Mr. Tree, David Randall wrote to Schimdt, seeking details on the map, perhaps because he had been told about its clouded history, for the Filson Club's file contains a two-page letter from Schmidt to Randall giving details of the whole affair. Schmidt's letter, a copy of which is also preserved in Randall's files at the Lilly Library, is dated 1 September 1956 and is unsigned, but it contains the typescript initials "MFS." In 1954, Schmidt had published, in the *Filson Club History Quarterly*, a checklist of existing copies of the 1784 Filson map of Kentucky, supplementing research on this subject that R. C. Ballard Thruston had published in the same magazine in 1934. Schmidt told Randall that, during Col. Durrett's lifetime, the Filson Club met in his home and many of its possessions were kept there. Unfortunately, they had not been identified and separated from his personal belongings; as a result, there had always been the feeling in Louisville that a good many things actually belonging to the Club had been sold to the University of Chicago, and Schmidt noted that the Chicago people appeared somewhat touchy about this point. Schmidt also reported that the Filson Club had some years before sent a request to Chicago for another photostat of the map, but at that time the University authorities claimed that they could not locate the Brooks' map, a situation which seems to persist to the present day.

[24]The original Brooks' map measures just under 13 inches in height and just under 16 inches in width. As Goodman's music book measure about 13 x 9 inches, the entire printed part of the map appears to be glued on its cover, though in two halves. A comparison of the map on the music book with the facsimile in Clark's portfolio shows that just about all of the text is there, including legends. Thus, another full copy of the map is preserved, though without outer blank margins and in a soiled, darkened, and somewhat rubbed condition.

which was located at the University of Chicago in 1922, cannot now be found, for the authorities there recently reported that the University's collections contained only a photocopy.[25]

We can now turn our attention to John Goodman once more and recapitulate some of the facts that we have learned from his music book and from other evidence introduced here concerning his life and work, though admittedly there are still many blank spots and many areas open to speculation. First of all, since the evidence indicates that he was born in Germany in 1778 and left home at the age of fourteen, it was about the year 1792 that he began his independent life and possibly his migration westward, settling finally in Frankfort in 1801, or perhaps a year earlier. Thus, we have an eight or nine year period of his life, and undoubtedly a critical one, during which absolutely nothing is known about him. These obviously were formative years, during which he learned (or continued to learn) music, musical instrument making, and perhaps music engraving. Part of this time was spent in Philadelphia, by his grandson's account, but once more details are lacking, particularly regarding the length of his stay and the nature of his occupation there. He passed the remainder of his life in Kentucky, arriving there about the age of twenty-three and dying there in his seventieth or seventy-first year.

During his residence in Kentucky of nearly half a century (and not the "nearly forty years" inscribed on his tombstone) he taught music and made musical instruments. In addition, he engraved and published some music and produced the first map to be printed in that state. It seems a likely guess that he began his musical education at an early age, perhaps before leaving Germany. However, no information is available concerning his early life and it would be pointless to speculate about it or about when and where he learned to make musical instruments and to engrave music. Whether he acquired knowledge of these fields before arriving in Kentucky or whether he learned them there through self-application and self-teaching are aspects of his life that remain unknown. It would not be incorrect to presume that he probably made a trip back to Philadelphia, around 1815, where he negotiated with George E. Blake to issue editions of his aforementioned musical arrangements, and this

---

[25]Personal telephone conversation between the author and Ms. Margaret Fusco of the Department of Special Collections of the University of Chicago Libraries, 23 May 1986.

matter tends to indicate that he had abandoned music engraving and publishing by that time.

Goodman's involvement in producing the Brooks' map in 1806 was not really an extraordinary occurrence in American frontier publishing. In my *Early American Music Engraving and Printing* (1980), I pointed out how general engravers and other artisans of ability sometimes were recruited to produce specific music publications that were required or desired, and Goodman's participation in the publication of Jared Brooks' map was merely an extension of his capability in another direction. However, his foray into map engraving strongly indicates that he had obtained some previous experience with engraving, possibly through music engraving. Elsewise, why would he be recruited and pressed into action to produce this historic piece, the first map to be printed in Kentucky?

Once again the map was a focal point that enabled us to learn a little more about John Goodman and his music publishing activities. While making final inquiries to insure that a copy of the Brooks' map could no longer be located at the University of Chicago, I was informed that in Col. Durrett's library, which the University had purchased earlier in this century, was a small packet or group of music sheets—four titles, actually—that had been identified as music published by John Goodman in Kentucky.[26] These pieces originally had been stitched together, but over the years they had become separated, and to this packet Durrett had prefixed a blank sheet of paper, upon which he had written "Music Published by J. Goodman, Frankfort, Ky., 1800–1806." The pieces forming this group are "Sandy and Jenny," the one that precipitated this study, and three others bearing caption titles, but without imprints or other important identifications: "A Rosy Cheek," "Oh Lady Fair," and "Love Sounds the Trumpet of Joy." The University of Chicago library authorities kindly sent these on in photocopied form, and close examination proves that "Sandy and Jenny" alone was published by John Goodman. The ballad "Oh Lady Fair," by Thomas Moore (1779–1852), actually can be identified as a separate issue from *The Ladies Collection of Glees. Rounds & Chorusses*, issued in Philadelphia by Carr & Schetky in the 1804–1805 period (Wolfe 1980:no. 7355A). "A Rosy Cheek" can be identified as a song by the American composer Charles Gilfert of New York and Charleston which appeared on the first two pages of his

---

[26]Personal telephone communication from Ms. Fusco to the author, 5 June 1986, followed by her transmittal of photocopies of the music titles.

collection entitled *Four Songs* (New York, 1813).[27] And, "Love Sounds the Trumpet of Joy," by the English composer William Reeve, proves to be a separate issue, without imprint, of the edition published by Carr & Schetky at Philadelphia in 1806 (Wolfe 1964: 7355A).

Thus, only "Sandy and Jenny," which we now know exists in two copies, and Goodman's five-page collection, which commences with "Gen. Russel's March" and ends with "Gen. Posey's March," and which exists in but a single known copy in the composer's music book, can be identified as music publications of John Goodman. Where Col. Durrett obtained his information on Goodman's music publications and period of activity, which we now know to be partially incorrect, cannot be determined, though a likely guess would be from the engraver's son, from whom Durrett also obtained a copy of the Louisville map. Nor are we any more knowledgeable of the origin of John Goodman's music punches. He could have brought them to Kentucky, possibly having obtained them in London, for the images they left on his two legitimate music publications suggest the appearance of an English music sheet, or he could have obtained them from a contact in the East. Finally, the allusion made to his implements in John Mason Brown's centennial address raises the additional possibility that he himself might have fabricated them, or at least some of them. However, there is insufficient evidence to follow up any of these possibilities at the present time.

Although he was a homeless and faceless person twenty-five years ago—not even a blur, actually—when I was concluding *Secular Music in America*, John Goodman now stands out in reasonably clear profile. Equally important, we are now certain of the location and time period of his activities. Thanks to the evidence provided by his music book and to other proofs which it and the Brooks' map enabled us to find, we now have a fairly good picture of one of the "irregulars" who trod the early American music publishing scene. While the view is less than perfect, it is, nonetheless, clear enough to give us a better perception of those individuals who carried the art of music westward or to isolated communities in pioneer America, coloring it and enriching it with sound in the process.

As Carleton Sprague Smith has aptly observed in his intuitive introduction to *Secular Music in America*, our early musicians, com-

---

[27]The photocopies do not allow us to know if printing existed on the reverse sides. However, this appears to be a separate issue of the piece in Gilfert's *Four Songs*, an issue that I did not encounter earlier when compiling *Secular Music in America*.

posers, and publishers—like Goodman, they sometimes combined all of these things—helped early America sing and dance and mourn and express its religious, martial, sentimental, humorous, and patriotic feelings, and celebrate both its national and local events and personalities in sound. Despite their homespun qualities, we are all the richer for their efforts. And now, at last, we have some good insights into John Goodman's individual participation in this overall expression and, in this sense, can also consider ourselves "home at last."

REFERENCES CITED

Brown, John Mason
   1886   *An Address Delivered on the Occasion of the Centennial Commemoration of the Town of Frankfurt, Kentucky, 6th October 1886.* Louisville: Kentucky Lithograph and Printing Co.

Clark, Thomas D.
   1979   *Historic Maps of Kentucky.* Lexington: The University Press of Kentucky.

Wolfe, Richard J.
   1964   *Secular Music in America, 1801–1825: A Bibliography.* Introduction by Carleton Sprague Smith. New York: The New York Public Library. 2 vols.

   1980   *Early American Music Engraving and Printing: A History of Music Publishing in America from 1787 to 1825, with Commentary of Earlier and Later Practices.* Urbana: University of Illinois Press.

APPENDICES

Letter sent from Romain Rolland to C. S. Smith prior to the International Congress of the American Musicological Society held in New York (Sept. 11–16, 1939)*

Mr. President:

I send my cordial greetings to the American Musicological Society. I greatly regret that my age and my health do not allow me to attend the meetings of the International Music Congress, which it has called.

The veterans of musicology, like myself, have every reason to rejoice over the importance given to such a Congress, which reaffirms the place in the front rank that the aesthetics and history of music have today conquered among the branches of learning. What strides musicology has made in the last forty years! If it has always held its place in education in Germany, it was completely absent from that of most other countries, notably of the Latin countries. The history of art ignored music. Through our efforts, music is now being included on an equal footing with the other arts. And all combined, all the arts form an integral part of general history. How could the latter have passed them by so long? They are the flower and the fruit of civilizations. And often enough they bear the seed for the coming age. The great artists are the precursors. The great works, in many instances, are the swallows that herald the return of a new springtime.

*From *The Musical Quarterly*, XXV, No. 4 (Oct., 1939), 510–12. The original letter, in French, appeared in *Papers Read at the International Congress of Musicology* (Richmond, Virginia, 1944), pp. 7–9. A slightly revised translation.

It is not only to history that musicology is and should be an indispensable aid. It offers resources still untapped for the study of human psychology. Music is—and I have tried to show this in my Beethoven analyses—a most precise langauge, and the most exact, of the subconscious. The secret life, the deep inner life, is written there; and one may watch it and thus observe among the masters, the mysterious travail of creation.

On the other hand, historical and ethnographic research have tremendously enlarged the domain of music. We have, in the last half-century, disinterred the wonderful riches of misjudged ages, such as the centuries of the mediaeval period in the West, and we have made the discovery that music was then the peer of architecture—whether during the epoch of the Romanesque basilicas and Gregorian Chant or the epoch of the Gothic cathedrals and the choir-school of Notre-Dame de Paris, of Maître Perotin, of Guillaume de Machault, and of the *Ars Nova*.

There has been the same spread in space as in time. We collect the songs of all races, of all peoples, of all the earth.

These discoveries do not remain shut up within the dead halls of libraries and museums. The radio broadcasts them to vast audiences. In them creative artists find a source of nourishment. And thus living art becomes rejuvenated. I have myself witnessed the deep impression, felt by Claude Debussy and by an *élite* of the Schola Cantorum of Paris, while listening for the first time to the divine art of Monteverdi or to the orchestras and the dances of the Far East. The seeds of this ancient and exotic music (modes, rhythms, and orchestral colors) have blossomed again on French soil. You doubtless have had similar experiences in America.

Let us congratulate ourselves that we have come into an age so fruitful for musicology! And let us exert ourselves to organize our labors along international lines.

I express the wish that, before anything else, a catalogue be prepared, in every country, of the musical archives preserved in the libraries and collections, public and private.

There was a time when musicological publications maintained a jealously national character: like the fine collections of the *Denkmäler der Tonkunst*, the *Maîtres musiciens de la renaissance française*, etc. Why not seek to continue such projects on a truly world-wide basis? In the past two decades, international concerts have successfully been given in Salzburg, Lucerne, Florence, etc. Could one not envisage the internationalization of the societies devoted to musical history and science, with journals written in the four languages of the great musical nations (German, Italian, French, and English) and with documental publications issued under the aegis of those societies? The troubled condition, from which certain European nations suffer, paralyzes their means of publication. Here it is twenty years since Walther Nohl began the important publication of Beethoven's conversation note-books, and the undertaking remains unfinished for financial reasons. Does not such a responsibility devolve upon all nations? Does not Beethoven belong to all? We must create an all-embracing collection of the great musicological publications of every nation. We must create the Musical Archives of the World.

In the field of art, there is not—nor should there be—any rivalry among nations. The only combat worthy of us is that which is waged, in every country, and at every hour, between culture and ignorance, between light and chaos. Let us save all of the light that can be saved! There is none more refulgent than music. It is the sun of the inner universe.

Vézelay, August 20, 1939

C. S. Smith: A Chronology

1905: Born in New York, August 8th.

1917: Began his musical studies at David Mannes's Institute of Musical Arts. Studied flute with a student of Georges Barrère

1920–22: Attended Hackley School for Boys, Tarrytown, New York.

1922–23: Studied French at École Yersin, in Paris, and continued flute studies with Louis François Fleury.

1927: B.A. (cum laude), Harvard University.

1927–28: Music critic, *Boston Transcript.*

1928: M.A., Harvard University; John Harvard Fellow.

1929: Woodbury Lowery Fellow.

1930: Ph.D., University of Vienna; Vice-Chairman of the Committee on Inter-American Relations in the field of music (U.S. Department of State).

1931–59: Chief the Music Division (The New York Public Library):
   a. Established a Music Americana Department with John Tasker Howard as Curator.
   b. Directed the WPA Copying Project.
   c. Chairman and Moderator, "Composers Forum Concerts" (1935–39).
   d. Actively promoted the formation of the musical libraries at Columbia and New York Universities.
   e. In 1932, drew up the initial concept of "A Library-Museum of the Performing Arts" to include the circulating and reference collections of all the performing arts, and a research center with major holdings in

theatre, dance, film, and audio-visual equipment. The long-awaited project became a reality in 1957, and was inaugurated in November of 1965 at Lincoln Center.

   f. With the encouragement of Curt Sachs, launched plans for a Dance Division at The New York Public Library.

1931: Founder of the Music Library Association. He proposed the idea at a meeting of the American Library Association, Yale University (June).

1931–35: Instructor, Columbia University (taught Iberian and European history).

1933–39: Instructor and later Adjunct Professor of Music, New York University.

1934: Married Elisabeth Cowles Sperry (Geneva, Switzerland, June 30).
   Member, first Executive Board, American Musicological Society.

1936: Delegate at the International Congress for Music Education (Prague).
   Delegate at the International Musicological Congress (Barcelona), where he presented Brenda Putnam's bust of Pablo Casals from the cellists of America to the capital city of Catalonia.

1936–38: President of the Music Library Association.

1937: Encouraged the appointment of Curt Sachs as Performing Arts Consultant at The New York Public Library (1937–1959)

1938: Lectured at Stanford University, where he delivered the first comprehensive course on Music in America.

1939–40: President, American Musicological Society. Extremely active in planning the First International Musicological Congress to be held in the United States (1939).

1939–42: Instructor, New York University (gave courses in music history).

1940: First tour of Latin America. Undertook a survey of performing arts in South America (with an emphasis on music) for the American Council of Learned Societies and the U.S. Department of State (June to October). He wrote a report entitled *The Performing Arts Past and Present in Ibero-America.*

1941–42: Commentator for Music of the Americas, Columbia School of the Air radio program, presented over CBS network.

1943: Chairman, Performing Arts activities in office of Nelson A. Rockefeller, who was Coordinator of Inter-American Affairs. Among the projects carried out were Aaron Copland's lecture tour and Lincoln Kirstein's Ballet Caravan performances in Latin America.

1943: Second tour of Latin America under joint sponsorship of the Carnegie Foundation and the Office of the Coordinator of Inter-American Affairs; Lectured in Brazil. The talks were in Portuguese and dealt with International Relations. One series was delivered in French at the Institute Français.

1944–46: Served as U.S. Foreign Service Officer, Cultural Attaché, São Paulo, Brazil; Lecturer in Brazil at the University of São Paulo, the Escola Livre de Sociologia e Política and the Sedes Sapientiae (1945–46).

1947: Delegate to the International Musicological Congress (Prague).

1947–58: Adjunct Professor, Institute of Public Affairs and Regional Studies, New York University (lectured on Latin American Civilization).

1947–59: Chairman of the Composer's Forum Concerts, when it was reactivated after the War by Ashley Pettis (1947).

1948: Delegate to the UNESCO Conference in Paris.

1949: Delivered the Patton Lectures at Indiana University (Bloomington) on "Music and Politics."

1950: Attended Luso-Brazilian Colloquia in Washington.
Director of the Aspen Institute for Humanistic Studies (Aspen, Colorado) (summer).

1950–51: Lectured at University of Southern California (summers).

1951–52: Member of the Mission for the American Council on Education in Germany. Prepared a study of Multi-Cultural Centers, which were set up through NATO for the purpose of coordinating the "New Europe." Took part in the Congrés pour la Liberté de la Culture (Paris).

1954: Attended Luso-Brazilian Colloquia in São Paulo.

1957: Attended Luso-Brazilian Colloquia in Lisbon.
Presented final draft of *Library-Museum of the Performing Arts,* NYPL concept.

1959: Co-founder, with Ernesto Da Cal, of the Brazilian Institute, New York University.

1959–61: Director of New York University's Brazilian Institute; Shortly before appointment, he resigned (Feb. 28, 1959) his post at the NYPL, remaining associated with it as music consultant to the Chief of the Reference Department.

1960: Accompanied Adlai Stevenson and former Senator William Benton as adviser and interpreter on a three-month tour of Latin America.

1961: Member, Advisory Commission of the National Cultural Center (today the John F. Kennedy Center), appointed by President Kennedy, November 14, 1961. Prepared a report for the Board of the National Culture Center: "What Goes into the National Culture Center?"

1962: Testified before a special Subcommittee of the Senate on Labor and Public Welfare regarding "Government and the Arts," 87th Congress, second session on s. 1250: A bill to establish the United States Art Foundation.
    Attended Conference on Tensions in Development in the Western Hemisphere, University of Bahia, Brazil.

1962–66: Chairman of the Academic Committee of the Brazilian Institute.

1963: Discussion Leader, Asian-American Symposium on "Cultural Affairs and International Understanding," Kuala Lumpur, Malaya.

1963–66: Panel member, U.S. Department of State, Office of Cultural Presentations.

1965: Delegate, Council on World Tensions Meeting, Manquerere University, Kampala, Uganda.

1965–80: Visiting Professor, Douglass College, Rutgers University; annual offering of "Music in America."

1967–82: Director, The Spanish Institute.

1984– Senior Research Associate, Yale School of Music

* * *

As a professional flutist, he performed with the Berkshire, Carmirelli, Juilliard, Lener, Musical Art, New Music, Roth, Salzburg, and Stradivarius String Quartets. He also performed with Yehudi Menuhin at the Gstaad Summer Festival (1964), with the Pasquier Trio (1965), and at the Adirondack Music Festival (1964–70).

Affiliations and Memberships (past and present): Academy of Political Science; American Historical Society; American Musicological Society (Pres. 1939–40); American-Portuguese Cultural Society; Associated Musicians of America; Association for Latin American Studies; Colonial Society of Massachusetts; Composer's Forum Concerts (former Chairman); Council on Foreign Relations; Hispanic Society of America (Corresponding Member); Hymn Society of America; Instituto Geográfico e Histórico da Bahia (Brazil); International Music Fund;

Interamerican Music Center; International Society of Contemporary Music; MacDowell Association; Music Library Association (Founder and Pres. 1936–38); New York State Historical Society; Society for Ethnomusicology; and the Sonneck Society (Honorary Member).

Board Memberships (past and present): Aspen Institute; Brandeis University Creative Arts Awards; International Society of Contemporary Music; Metropolitan Opera Association; MacDowell Association; Museum of Modern Art; National Council on the Arts and the Government; New York Philharmonic Symphony Society; Paderewski Foundation (Trustee); UNESCO; and Yale Summer School of Music and Art (Trustee).

Honors (chronological):
Ruy Barbosa Commemorative Medal (1949)
National Association for American Composers and Conductors (Award of Merit, 1951)
Doctor (*Honoris Causa*), University of Brazil (Rio de Janeiro, 1958)
Doctor (*Honoris Causa*), University of Bahia (Salvador, Brazil, 1959)
Anchieta Medal (Brazil, 1959)
Dalcroze School of Music (Citation awarded in 1966)
Doctor of Music, Hamilton College (Clinton, New York, 1976)
George Peabody Medal, Peabody Conservatory of Johns Hopkins University for his "outstanding contributions to music in America" (1981)
Doctor of Humane Letters, *Honoris causa*, Syracuse University, 1987

> *Carleton Sprague Smith,* you took a deep love of music and fashioned a life complete. Your vision of the performing arts has provided the structure for librarianship and scholarship for over 50 years.
>
> Because of your work and encouragement of others, our musical heritage is being preserved. And as you travel the globe using the universal language of music, you serve as a catalyst for international understanding.
>
> Your contributions to musicology and the performing arts, to librarianship, diplomacy, and education are unprecedented."

Encomienda de número, Orden de Isabel la Católica (Awarded by the Spanish Government, 1988)

Membership in Clubs: Harvard; Grolier; and Century

C. S. Smith: A Topical Bibliography of His Collected Writings

Reports

The Lincoln Center Library-Museum of the Performing Arts: Preliminary Report (New York, Dec., 1957). 19 pp. [The culmination, beginning in 1931, of a dozen drafts pertaining to the importance and practicality of the Library-Museum concept.]

What Goes into the National Cultural Center? Report prepared for the Board of the National Culture Center (Washington, D.C., 1961). 67 pp.

A Survey of Multi-National Cooperation Made in Europe from June 24 to September 2 [1961] for the Bureau of Educational and Cultural Affairs, The United States Department of State (New York, Feb., 1962). 54 pp.

American Music

"Music Teachers and Music Scholars," *Papers Read at the Annual Meeting of the American Musicological Society* (Washington, D.C.), No. 3 (Washington, D.C., 1938), 1–7.[Musicological activity in the United States from Colonial times to the present.]

Editor: *Early Psalmody in America*. Series 1–3. New York: The New York Public Library, 1938–39. [1. *The Ainsworth Psalter* (6 settings) and *Psalm 65, with Settings by Claude Goudimel* (1938); 2. *The Bay Psalm Book, 1640 and 1651* (27 settings) (1939); 3. *The Dathenus Psalter, 1566, 1567, etc.* (3 settings) (1939).]

"Folk Songs of Old New York," *Musical America*, LIX (Sept., 1939), 7, 40.

"Music of the *Ainsworth Psalter* and *Bay Psalm Book*," *Bulletin of the American Musicological Society*, No. 5 (Aug., 1941), No. 5. [Abstract of paper.].

Review: "John Tasker Howard, *Our American Music*, 3rd ed. (New York, 1946)," *MLA Notes*, IV/1 (Dec., 1946), 68–70.

Review: "Harry Dichter, comp., *Handbook of American Sheet Music* (Philadelphia, 1947)," *Ibid.*, V/1 (Dec., 1947), 100–1.

"The 1774 Psalm Book of the Reformed Protestant Dutch Church of New York City," *The Musical Quarterly*, XXXIV/1 (Jan., 1948), 84–96.

"Foreword" to *The First Book of Consort Lessons Collected by Thomas Morley 1599 & 1611*. Reconstructed and edited with an Introduction and Critical Notes by Sydney Beck. (New York: Published for The New York Public Library by C.F. Peters Corporation, 1959), xi–xiv.

"Introduction" to Richard J. Wolfe, *Secular Music in America 1801–1825: A Bibliography* (New York: The New York Public Library, 1964), Vol. I, pp. ix–xviii. [Published separately as "America in 1801–1825. The Musicians and the Music," *Bulletin of The New York Public Library*, LXVIII (Oct., 1964), 483–92.]

Review: "Claude M. Simpson, *The British Broadside Ballad and Its Music* (New Brunswick, N.J., 1966)," *MLA Notes*, XXIII/4 (June, 1967), 739–40.

"Broadsides and Their Music in Colonial America," in Barbara Lambert, ed., *Music in Colonial Massachusetts 1630–1820. I. Music in Public Places* (Boston: The Colonial Society of Massachusetts, 1980), Vol. I, pp. 157–367 (the first study to recognize the existence of Border Ballads with texts and tunes pertaining to French and Indian Wars). With appendix A: "Commentary on the Tunes," by Israel J. Katz, pp. 369–75.

Review: "Richard Crawford, *A Historian's Introduction to Early American Music* (Worcester, 1980)," *American Music*, I/3 (Fall, 1983), 93–94.

Review: "Charles Hamm, *Music in the New World* (New York, 1983)," *MLA Notes*, XLI/1 (Sept., 1984), 43–45.

"A Tune for Benjamin Franklin's Drinking Song *Fair Venus Calls*," *Inter-American Music Review*, X/2 (Los Angeles, 1989), 147–55 (in an issue [Part I] honoring Robert M. Stevenson).

Spain

"Documentos referentes al *Cancionero* de Claudio de la Sablonara," *Revista de Filología Española*, XVI (Madrid, Apr., 1929), 168–73.

Review: "Robert Stevenson, *Spanish Cathedral Music in the Golden Age* (Berkeley/Los Angeles, 1961)," *Journal of Research in Music Education,* XI/1 (Spring, 1963), 83–85.

Luso-Brazilian Studies

"William James in Brazil," in *Four Papers Presented in the Institute for Brazilian Studies* (Nashville: Vanderbilt University Press, 1951), 95–138.

"Os tradutores brasileiros em Lisboa e a América do Norte há um século e meio," *III Colóquio Internacional de Estudos Luso-Brasileiros (Coimbra, 1957), Actas* (Lisbon, 1960), Vol. II, pp. 95–402.

"Recollections of Five Luso-Brazilian Colloquia." Paper presented before the Sixth International Colloquium on Luso-Brazilian Studies (Harvard University, Cambridge, September, 1966); two copies of the paper were deposited at Harvard University Library.

"William Jarvis e o comércio em Portugal no fim do século XVIII," *V Colóquio Internacional de Estudos Luso-Brasileiros (Coimbra, 1963) Actas* (Coimbra: Gráfica de Coimbra, 1965), Vol. II, pp. 519–26.

"Two Copies of the First Book published in Brazil at The New York Public Library," in Hellmut Lehman-Haupt, ed., *Homage to a Bookman: Essays on Manuscripts, Books and Printing Written for Hans P. Kraus on his 60th Birthday-October 12, 1967* (Berlin: Mann, 1967), 187–94.

Latin America

Musical Tour through South America, June – October, 1940 Manuscript. New York: The New York Public Library, 1940. xxxiv, 290 [+33] pp.

"What Not to Expect of South America," *Musical America,* LXI/3 (New York, Feb. 10, 1941), 217, 220.

"The Song Makers," *Survey Graphic,* XXX/3 (New York, Mar., 1941), 179–83. ["To understand Latin America, learn to know its arts—its music, murals, billboards, its radio wits, journalists, dancers, actors, and poets."]

"The Music of Latin America," *Progressive Education,* XVIII/6 (New York, Oct., 1941), 307–9. [Mainly bibliographical.]

"The Composers of Chile," *Modern Music,* XIX/1 (New York, Nov.–Dec., 1941), 26–31.[Divides the modern Chilean school into 3 groups: 1) Enrique Sors; 2) Humberto Allende, and 3) Domingo Santa Cruz and Alfonso Leng.]

"Relações musicais entre o Brasil e os Estados Unidos de Norte America," *Boletín Latino-americana de Música*, IV, Primera parte (Rio de Janeiro, Apr., 1946), 141–48.

"Music Publications in Brazil," *Notes*, IV/4 (Sept., 1947), 425–30. [Paper read at the Music Library Association Meeting, New York Public Library on 11 Jan. 1947.]

"Brazil's Big Four (Heitor Villa Lobos, Comargo Guarnieri, Oscar Lorenzo Fernândez and Francisco Mignone)," *The Musical Digest*, XXIX (New York, Nov. 1947), 22–25.

"Brasilien Moderne," *Stimmen*, I/5 (Berlin, 1948), 142–44.

"Brazil in Songs," *Brazil*, XXIII/3 (New York, Mar., 1949), 3–6, 17–18. [Discusses the song characteristics of the various regions: The Amazon, Northeast, Baíanos, the Carioca composers, Mineiros, and Paulistas.]

"Carlos Chavez," *The Pan American*, X/5 (New York, Oct., 1949), 3–6.

"Music of the New World," *Music Today* [Journal of the International Society for Contemporary Music], I (London, 1949), 46–54 (with French summary, 54–56).

"Song of Brazil," *Américas*, II/10 (Pan American Union) (Washington, D.C., Oct., 1950), 14–16, 43–44. [Concerns Heitor Villa-Lobos.]

"Montparnesse of the Hemisphere," *United Nations World*, IV/10 (Oct., 1950), 52–53.

"Villa-Lobos, músico rebelde," *Américas,* II/11 (Nov., 1950), 14–16, 43, 47.

"Contemporary Music in Chile," *Conference on Latin-American Fine Arts, June 14 – 17, 1951.* Proceedings (Austin University of Texas Press, 1952), pp. 115–23. (Latin-American Studies, XIII.)

"Musical Settings of Caribbean Poetry," in A[lva] Curtis Wilgus, ed., *The Caribbean: Its Ecomony* (Gainesville: University of Florida Press, 1954), pp. 240–58 (School of Inter-American Studies Series 1, IV.).

"Factors of Intercultural Influences," in Angel del Río, ed., *Responsible Freedom in the Americas* (Garden City, New York: Doubleday, 1955), pp. 480–93. (Columbia University Bicentennial Conference Series.)

Editor: *Perspectives of Brazil.* New York: Intercultural Publications, 1956 (an *Atlantic Monthly* supplement, CXCVII/2 [Feb., 1956], pp. 97–168).

"Editor's Introduction," *Perspectives of Brazil* (an *Atlantic Monthly* supplement, CXCVII/2 (New York, Feb., 1956), 100.

"Heitor Villa Lobos (1889–1959)," *Compositores de América. Datos biográficos y catálogos de sus obras*, III. Washington, D.C.: Pan American Union, Music Section, 1957, pp. 1–9. Bilingual Spanish and English columns. [Reprinted in *Inter-American Music Bulletin*, No. 15 (Washington, D.C.: Pan America Union, Jan., 1960), 1–4, "as a tribute to this great Brazilian musician who died in Rio de Janeiro on 17 November 1959." Also in *Boletín Interamericano de Música*, No. 15 (Washington, D.C.: División de Publicaciones, Unión Panamericana, January, 1960), 3–6.

Review: "Peppercorn, Lisa M., *Heitor Villa-Lobos. Leben und Werk des brasilianischen Komponisten* (Zurich, 1972)," *Yearbook of Inter-American Music Research*, VIII (1972), 174–76.

The Flute

"Haydn's Chamber Music and the Flute: Parts I and II," *The Musical Quarterly*, XIX/2 (New York, July, 1933), 341–50; XIX/3 (Oct.), 434–55.

"Bibliography of Music for the Flute," *Woodwind Magazine*, I, No. 5 (New York, Mar., 1949), 7; No. 6 (Apr.), 7; No. 7 (May), 7; No. 8 (June), 7; [Contains fifty-odd titles, mainly concertos. Reprinted in Rudo S. Globus, ed., *Woodwind Anthology* (New York: Woodwind Magazine, 1952), pp. 42–45.]

"Albert Ginastera's *Duo for Flute and Oboe*," *Latin American Music Review*, VI/1 (Spring–Summer, 1985), 85–93.

Review: "Flute Music," *MLA Notes*, VI/1 (1943), 178. [Guarneri Comargo, *Sonatina for Flute and Piano* (New York, 1943); Gardner Read, *Threnody*, Op. 66, for Flute and Piano (New York, 1948); and Howard Hanson, *Serenade for Flute and Piano* (New York, 1948)]

Review: "Herbert Kölbel, *Von der Flöte, Brevier für Flötenspeiler* (Cologne, 1951); Hans Peter Schmitz, *Querflöte und Querflötenspiel*," *Ibid.*, XI/1 (Dec., 1953), 115–16.

Editor: Serge Prokofieff. *Sonata in D Major for Flute and Piano*, Opus 94. New York: International Music Company, 1945. [Although he never discussed the matter with Prokofieff, CSS did so with Dmitri Shostakovich in Prague and later in New York. Shostakovich considered the flute version more interesting than the violin version (Op. 94a) made by Prokofieff in collaboration with David Oistrakh.]

Guitar and Guitarists

"Impressions of Manuel Ponce," *The Guitar Review*, No. 7 (New York, 1948), 10.

"Aristocratic Patronage and the Spanish Guitar in the Seventeenth Century (I)," *Guitar Review*, No. 49 (Fall, 1981), 2–3, 6–10; (II), No. 50 (Spring, 1982), 12–23.

"About the Cover [Nicolas Larmessin's engraving, *A Musician's Dress*]," *Ibid.*, No. 52 (Fall, 1982), ii.

"Recollections of an Old Friend [Andrés Segovia]," *Ibid.*, No. 52 (1983), 18–19.

Review: "Richard T. Pinnell, *Francesco Corbetta and the Baroque Guitar, with a Transcription of his Works* (Ann Arbor, 1980), 2 vols.," *MLA Notes*, XXXVIII/1 (Sept. 1981), 67–68.

Conference Activities

"The I. S. C. M. Meets at Barcelona," *Modern Music*, XIII (May–June, 1936), 30–34. [Concerns musical events at the 14th Festival of the International Society for Contemporary Music held during the end of April, 1936.]

"Welcoming Remarks," *Papers Read at the International Congress of Musicology* (Held at New York, September 11th to 16th, 1939), [No. 4] (Richmond, Virginia, 1944), 2–5. [Delivered, as President of the AMS, to the International Congress of Musicology during the luncheon on Monday, Sept. 11th.]

"Presidential Address," *Papers of the American Musicological Society* (Annual Meeting, 1940, Cleveland, Ohio), [No. 5] (Richmond, Virginia, 1946), 1–4. [Delivered on Monday Morning, Dec. 30).]

Music Librarianship

"The Service of the Library to Musicology," *Music Teachers National Association. Proceedings*, XXXI (Chicago, Dec. 29, 1936), pp. 239–45. [Reprinted in *Papers Read at the Annual Meeting of the American Musicological Society* (Chicago, Dec. 29, 1936), No. 1 (Washington, D.C., 1936), 35–41.]

"Some Methods and Costs of Reproducing Music," *Notes*, 1st series, No. 5 (Nov., 1937), 16–18. [A somewhat condensed version.]

"Libraries of Music," in *The International Cyclopedia of Music and Musicians*, 1st through 9th eds. (New York: Dodd, Mead, 1938–1964). [1st through 4th eds. (1938, 1943, 1944, 1946) edited by Oscar Thompson, pp. 1003–9; 5th through 8th eds. (1949, 1952, 1956, 1958), edited by Nicolas Slonimsky, pp. 1003–9; 9th ed. (1964) edited by Robert Sabin, pp. 1198–1204.]

"Music on Microfilm," *Journal of Documentary Reproduction*, II (Chicago: American Library Association, Dec., 1939), 249–53.

"Music Libraries in South America," *MLA Notes*, 1st series, No. 11 (New Haven, Aug., 1941), 19–31. [Caracas (Venezuela); Recife, Bahia, Rio de Janeiro, and São Paulo (Brazil); Montivedeo (Uruguay); Buenos Aires (Argentina); Santiago(Chile); Lima (Peru); Quito (Ecuador); and Bogotá (Colombia).]

"Notes for *Notes*: Union Lists," *Ibid.*, III/4 (Sept., 1946), 390–91. [An appeal to get the Union List on music (from 1500 to 1800) at The New York Public Library "caught up once more."]

"Musicology and the Library," *Music Journal*, IV/6 (New York, Nov.–Dec., 1946), 13, 44–46.

"Do You Know About: Your Music Libraries?," *Allegro*, XXII/10 (New York, August, 1948), 8, 31. [About the music resources at The New York Public Library.]

"Music and Dance in The New York Public Library," in Sigmund Spaeth, Wiliam J. Perlman, and Joseph A. Bollew, eds., *Music and Dance in New York State*. 1952 edition (New York: Bureau of Musical Research, [1951]), pp. 55–60.

"Communication to Editor [Susan T. Sommer]," *MLA Notes*, XXXIX/2 (Dec., 1982), 490–91.

"Introduction" to Alfred Mann, ed., *Modern Music Librarianship: Essays in Honor of Ruth Watanabe* (New York: Pendragon Press, 1989), pp. xi–xiv. (Festschrift Series, No. 8)

Musical Manuscripts

"Preface" to Paul Nettl, *The Book of Music Documents* (New York: Philosophical Library, 1948), vii–x.

"Introduction" to Otto E. Albrecht, *A Census of Autograph Music Manuscripts of European Composers in American Libraries* (Philadelphia: University of Pennsylvania Press, 1953), pp. xi–xvii.

Musicology and Music Education

"Etats-Unis d'Amérique," *L'Education musicale trait d'Union entre les Peuples. Rapports et discours sur l'education musicale dans les divers pays* (Prague: Société d'Education Musicale; Published by *Orbis* Société Anonyme d'Impression, d'Edition et de Publicité, 1937), pp. 55–60. [Report read during the First International Congress on Music Education, organized by Leo Kestenberg, in Prague, 1936].

"Musicology as a Means of Inter-Cultural Understanding," *Music Teachers National Association, Proceedings*, XXXV (Hartford, Conn., 1941), pp. 54–57.

"The Study of Music as an Academic Subject," *Music Educators' Journal*, XLIX/1 (Chicago, Sept.–Oct., 1962), 31–34. [Reprinted in a slightly abridged version in *The Education Digest*, XXVIII (Ann Arbor, Jan., 1963), 49–51.]

Religious Music

Ten Sacred Songs for Soprano, Strings and Organ. By J. Dencke, J.F. Peter, J. Herbst, G.G. Muller, and J. Antes. Edited by Hans T. David. English text adapted by Carleton Sprague Smith. New York: The New York Public Library and Peters, 1947. (Peters Edition 6084) (Music of the Moravians in America from the Archive of the Moravian Church at Bethlehem, Pennsylvania, No. 1)

"Religious Music and the Lute," *The Guitar Review*, No. 9 (New York, 1949), 31–37.

"Table Blessings Set to Music," in Gustave Reese and Rose Brandel, eds., *The Commonwealth of Music: Writings on Music in History, Art, and Culture in Honor of Curt Sachs* (New York: The Free Press of Glencoe, 1965), pp. 236–82.

Editor:*American Hymns Old and New*. New York: Columbia University Press, 1980. 2 vols. (with Albert Christ-Janer and Charles William Hughes.) [Concept of the anthology was primarily the work of C.S.S. and the musical editing and biographies were done by Charles Hughes. Albert Christ-Janer obtained cooperation from contemporary composers and was active in raising funds which made the publication possible.]

Musicologists in our Time

"Otto Kinkeldey," *MLA Notes*, VI/1 (Washington, D.C., Dec., 1948), 27–37 (includes three photographs).

"Harold Spivacke Remembered (1904–1977)," *The Musical Quarterly*, LXIII/3 (July, 1977), 425–27.

"Curt Sachs,"*Acta Musicologica*, XXXI/2 (Apr.–June, 1959), 45–46.

"Curt Sachs and the Library-Museum of the Performing Arts," *Musica Judaica*, IV (New York, 1981/82), 9–19.

Miscellaneous Topics and Reviews

Ein Vetternzwist im Hause Habsburg: Die Beziehungen zwischen Spanien und Österreich am Anfang des 17. Jahrhundert (Ph.D. diss., University of Vienna, 1930).

"Why Music is the Greatest of the Arts," *The American Music Lover*, IV (New York, May, 1938), 2–4.

"Recent Work on Music in the Renaissance," *Modern Philology*, XLII/1 (Chicago, Aug., 1944), 41–58 (with William Dinneen).

"Preface" to Helen Duprey Bullock, *My Head and My Heart: A Little History of Thomas Jefferson and Maria Cosway* (New York: B.P. Putnam's Sons, 1945), vii–x.

"Introduction" to Kathleen O. Hoover, *Makers of Opera* (New York: H. Bittner and Company, 1948), vii–xii.

"New Music Frontiers," *Music Journal*, V/6 (Nov.–Dec., 1947), 14, 55.

"If You Like It. It's Music," *The Musical Digest*, I/1 (New York, Winter, 1947), 23–24.

"Discs and Cultural Exchange," *Music Journal*, VI/1 (New York, Jan., 1948), 7, 43–45.

Review: "Peter Gradenwitz, *The Music of Israel, Its Rise and Growth through 5000 Years* (New York, 1959)," *MLA Notes*, VI/3 (June, 1949), 469–70.

"The First Half Century," *Music Clubs Magazine*, XXIX/3 (New York, Feb., 1950), 5–6, 34 (with Peggy Glanville Hicks).

"Commencement Address," *Juilliard Review*, V/3 (Fall, 1958), 16–18. [Condensation of a full speech.]

Review: "Norman S. Grabo, *Edward Taylor* (New York, 1961) and Norman S. Grabo, ed., *Edward Taylor's Christographia* (New Haven, 1962)," *The New England Quarterly*, XXXVI/4 (Dec., 1963), 559–64.

"Remembrances of My Mother," in Carleton Sprague Smith, *et al.*, eds., *Remembrances of Catharine Cook Smith* (Wilton, Connecticut, 1977), pp. 111–50.

In Progress

A Selected Annotated Bibliography of Spain, 1898–1975. Metuchen, New Jersey: Scarecrow Press (over 5,000 titles, in preparation).

Six Centuries of Table Blessings. Atlanta, Georgia: John Knox Press (in preparation).

Associated with the following publications:

1) Hans Theodore David's edition of *Ten Sacred Songs for Soprano, Strings and Organ* (New York: NYPL, 1947), for which he adapted the English text.

2) Encouraged Sydney Beck's edition of Thomas Morley's *First Book of Consort Lessons* (New York: C.F. Peters, 1959).

Editor and annotater: *Music in America*. New York: New Records, Inc. 1940's.

Manuscripts (Unpublished):

"A Worthy Music Center for New York City: The Library" *Music and Politics in Western Civilization* (The Patten Foundation Lectures, 1948):

1. The Voice of the People—Folksong and City Song; 2) The Pulse of Society—Military Marches, Ballet, and Popular Dances; 3) Music and the State—Religious and Dramatic Compositions in the Service of the Government and the Church; 4) The Revolt of the Individual Musician— Opera, Oratorio, and Symphony in the Romantic Era; 5) The Mechanical Age—Mass Production and the Musical Market; and 6) The Future of Music—Propaganda and Censorship in a Democratic World. [Prepared for the University of Indiana Press.]

"The John F. Kennedy Memorial" (written at Amherst College, 1963) [Recommendation "that a Museum of the Performing Arts. . . be planned and designed as an integral part of the John F. Kennedy Memorial within the Kennedy Center."

Manuscripts in Progress:

A Comparison between North and South America in the Seventeenth Century.

A History of Graces (preliminary study appeared in 1965)

Birthday Music

Cutbert Pudsey and the Dutch in Brazil

Dom Pedro I [1798–1834] and the Marquesa dos Santos (Unpublished letters in the Hispanic Society of America)

Early Translations from English to Portuguese (First part was published in *Actas do III Coloquio Internacional de Estudos Luso-Brasileiros* [Lisbon, 1960–1967].)

Music for New Years Day

Music in North America (with Raymond Kendall)

Prefaces for American Hymn Book (to be published by the University of Chicago Press)

Thomas Jefferson and the Arts

William Jarvis, American Charge and Consul in Portugal, 1802–1810)

William Tudor in Brazil

Willoughby Bertie, Lord Abingdon and His Role as a Music Patron

Women and Music

Biographical Listings:

Baker's Biographical Dictionary of Musicians. Eighth edition. Edited by Nicolas Slonimsky. New York: Schirmers Books, 1991.

Bradley, Carol June. *The Genesis of American Music Librarianship, 1902 – 1942*. Unpublished Ph.D. diss. (Library Science) Tallahassee: Florida State University, 1978.

_____. "The Music Library Association: The Founding Generation and Its Work," *MLA Notes*, XXXVII, No. 4 (June, 1981), 763–822. [Contains a photograph of Carleton (ca. 1950), 767.] In his "Communication to Editor [Susan T. Sommer]," *MLA Notes*, XXXIX/2 (Dec., 1982), 490–91, C.S.S. clarifies Carol Bradley's assumptions about the founding of the Music Library Association.

"Carleton Sprague Smith," *Visão* (São Paulo, April 17, 1959), 20–21.

Current Biography, XXI, No. 11 (December, 1960), 29–31.

Grove's Dictionary of Music and Musicians. Fifth edition. Edited by Eric Blom. London: Macmillan, 1954.

Miller, Philip L., and Campbell, Frank C. "How the Music Division of The New York Public Library Grew," *Notes*, XXXV, No. 3 (Mar., 1979), 537–55.

Musik in Geschichte und Gegenwart. Edited by Friedrich Blume. Basel: Bärenreiter, 1959–68.

New Grove Dictionary of American Music. Edited by Wiley H. Hitchcock and Stanley Sadie. London: Macmillan, 1986.

New Grove Dictionary of Music and Musicians. Edited by Stanley Sadie. London: Macmillan, 1980.

Stevenson, Robert M. "Carleton Sprague Smith on his 75th Birthday," *Inter-American Music Review*, III, No. 1 (1980), 1–2.

The International Cyclopedia of Music and Musicians. Eleventh edition. Edited by Bruce Bohle. New York: Dodd, Mead, 1985.

Musical Compositions Dedicated to or Involved in Some Manner with C. S. Smith

George Antheil (1900–1959). *Sonata for Flute and Piano.* New York: Weintraub Music Company, 1965. [The autograph copy bears the dedication.]
   Three movements: Allegro; Adagio; and Presto.

Robert Russel Bennet (1936–). *Piece for Solo Flute.* Unpublished ms.

Vanraj Bhatia (1927–): *Music for Unaccompanied Flute.* New York: Oxford University Press, 1966.
   Four movements: Night Music; Song; Dance (7+10); and Night Music.

Julián Carrillo (1875–1965): *Triple Concerto for Flute, Violin, Cello and Orchestra* (1941). Unpublished ms. Dedicated to Jenö Léner, C.S.S., and Imre Hartmann.

Arthur Farwell (1872–1952): *Suite for Flute and Piano.* Op. 114 [Ms with dedication can be seen in Brice Farwell, ed., *A Guide to the Music of Arthur Farwell and to the Microfilm Collection of his Works.* Briarcliff Manor, New York, 1972.]
   Two movements: Woodland Colloquy and Nocturn.

Oscar Lorenzo Fernândez (1897–1948): *Duas Invencões Seresteiras* for flute, clarinet, and bassoon. New York: Southern Music Publishing Co., 1944.

Roberto Gerhard (1896–1970): *Capriccio for Solo Flute* (1949). Melville, New York: Belwin-Mills Music Publishers, 1964.
   Three sections.

Alberto Ginastera (1916–1983): *Duo for Flute and Oboe,* Op. 13. New York: Music Press, 1947. On the autographed copy, Ginastera wrote:

> Escribí el *Duo, Opus 13,* para flauta y oboe en 1945 para mi amigo el musicólogo y flautista Carleton Sprague Smith, quien lo estrenó en New York en un concierto de la League of Composers con la oboista Lois Wann el 23 de febrero de 1947. En ese momento yo he encontraba en esa ciudad en associo becado de la Guggenheim Foundation.

> El *Duo* es una obra lineal que consta de tres movimientos: Preludio, Patorales y Fuga. En el segundo movimiento aparece un tema basado en escalas amerindias que yo ya había empleado en obras anteriores a ésta y que aún empleo hoy, en obras reciente, aunque bajo otro tratamiento estilístico.

Mozart Camargo Guarnieri (1907–): *Sonatina for Flute and Piano.* New York: Music Press, 1947.
Three movements: Allegro; Melancólico; and Saltitante.

_____. *Desafio.* Poesía de Manuel Bandeira (São Paulo, 1943). Unpublished ms. (Para Elisabeth Sprague Smith).

Everett Helm (1913–): *Sonata for Flute and Piano.* Unpublished ms. 1951?

Elliot Levine: *The Unicorn.* Set to music for flute and voice. Text by Catharine Cook Smith (1879–1961). Unpublished ms. (New York, 1984) (For Elisabeth and Carleton).

Quincy Porter (1897–1966): *Introspections on the Banks o'Doon for Flute, Voice and Piano* (Dedicated to Helen Boatwright and C.S.S.).

Andrés Sas (1900–1967): *Amanecer. Canción para canto y flauta.* Versos de Enrique Bustamente y Ballivián. From *Cuatro melodías* in the *Album Canciones Indias.* Montevideo: Editorial Cooperativa Interamericana de Compositores, 1930 (Para la Señora Elisabeth Sprague Smith).

Randall Thompson (1899–1984): *A Hymn for Scholars and Pupils.* SSA and chamber orchestra. Text by George Wither (1588–1667). Boston: E. C. Schirmer, 1975 (Dedicated to Elisabeth and C.S.S.).

Douglas Townsend (1921–). *Sonatina for Flute and Piano.* Unpublished ms. Three movements.

Heitor Villa-Lobos (1887–1959): *Assobio a Játo* (*'The Jet Whistle'*) for Flute and Violoncello. New York: Southern Music Publishing Co., Inc., 1953 (Dedicated to Elisabeth and C.S.S.).
Three movements: Allegro ma non troppo; Adagio; and Vivo—Poco meno—Prestissimo.

N.B. C.S.S. chose the text for Villa-Lobos's six-part a cappella choral work, *Bedita sabedoria*. Dedicated to New York University, where the composer received a doctorate (*honoris causa*) in 1943.

In the 1950s Carleton wrote Igor Stravinsky soliciting a short twentieth-century chamber music work for flute, strings, and piano. The composer's clearly-stated reply was that he would gladly do so for a fee, calculated per measure, which came to a sum of nearly $3,000! On another occasion Carleton received an unsolicited letter from Leopold Stokowski, who was present at a private chamber music concert where Carleton and four other musicians participated. Stokowski took the trouble to write a most favorable and detailed critique of their performance. Unfortunately all these letters have not been located to date.

INDEX